Between the Sea
& the Lagoon

Western African Studies

Between the Sea
& the Lagoon

An Eco-social History
of the Anlo of Southeastern Ghana
c. 1850 to Recent Times

EMMANUEL KWAKU AKYEAMPONG

Professor of History
Harvard University

Ohio University Press
ATHENS

James Currey
OXFORD

James Currey
an imprint of Boydell and Brewer Ltd,
PO Box 9, Woodbridge, Suffolk IP12 3DF, UK
and 668 Mount Hope Avenue, Rochester NY 14620-2731, USA
www.jamescurrey.com
www.boydell and brewer.com

Ohio University Press
19 Circle Drive, The Ridges
Athens, Ohio, 45701-2979 ,USA

A catalogue record is available from the British Library

ISBN 978–0–85255–776–8 (James Currey paper)
ISBN 978–0–85255–777–1 (James Currey cloth)

Library of Congress Catalog Card Number 2001051018

ISBN 978–0–8214–1409–5 (Ohio University Press paper)
ISBN 978–0–8214–1408–8 (Ohio University Press cloth)

Typeset in 10.5/12 pt Monotype Ehrhardt
by Long House Publishing Services, Cumbria, UK

For Ruth,
Kojo Nyamekye
& Leroy

A Note on Sources

Apart from the published literature, I consulted several unpublished theses at the University of Ghana and elsewhere on Anlo environment, society, economy and religion. These are cited in the relevant chapters. Research was conducted in the National Archives of Ghana (Accra and Ho) between July 1996 and August 1997. A two-month interlude was spent in Europe in May–July 1997. In England I consulted the colonial records at the Public Records Office in London, the private papers of colonial officials and British merchants housed at Rhodes House Library (Oxford University) and the newspaper library at Colindale. I spent part of June 1997 consulting the mission records of the North German Missionary Society at Bremen, Germany. Fieldwork was done mostly between August 1996 and April 1997, as I alternated residence between Accra and the Keta district. Photography was an important source and research tool, as early photos taken by Bremen missionaries in the Keta area from the 1890s and those I took in 1994, 1996 and 1997 aided in reconstructing the changing environment of the lower Volta basin. Together with charts drawn by the Geological Survey Department indicating the high-water marks in Keta from 1907, the photographs provide a vivid sense of a rapidly changing environment during the period under study.

Contents

7

Coastal Erosion, Political Ecology
& the Discourse of Environmental Citizenship
in Twentieth-century Anlo

8

Living with the Sea

Society & Culture in Contemporary Anlo

Maps, Figures & Photographs

Acknowledgements

This project was made possible by research grants from the Clark Fund at Harvard University and the National Endowment of the Humanities (January–September 1997). I am indebted to a long list of friends and colleagues, who aided the collection of data and the editing of this manuscript. In Anlo, numerous interviews with Togbuivi Kumassah, Togbui James Ocloo IV, Togbui Honi II, Emmanuel Keteku and Obed Nutsugah were indispensable to the development of this project. Togbuivi Kumassah, a geography teacher at Keta Secondary School and a subchief at Dzelukope, became my unpaid assistant and brought rich insights to my fieldwork. I owe him an inestimable debt. Steven Selormey, the then District Coordinating Director for Keta, provided me with valuable economic reports on the district. David Atta-Peters gave me lectures on geological processes, and A.K. Armah provided scientific grounding, as an oceanographer, for my interviews on Anlo local knowledge on fishing. Thomas Spear, Richard Rathbone and G.K. Nukunya read the entire manuscript in draft and provided invaluable comments and suggestions. Albert Adu Boahen, Nissio Fiagbedzi, Sandra Greene, Paul Nugent and Leroy Vail read parts of the draft manuscript and gave important commentaries. I am indebted to Zayde Antrim and Caroline Elkins for superb editorial assistance. I would also like to acknowledge my gratitude to James Currey and Douglas Johnson for the interest they have shown in my career and scholarship, and their support in various ways. Finally, I am deeply grateful to my wife, Ruth, for her material and moral support during the research and writing period. The year of writing was eventful: I lost my friend and colleague Leroy Vail, but gained a son, Kojo Nyamekye. I am sad that Leroy did not live to see this book finished. I dedicate this book to Ruth, Kojo Nyamekye and Leroy.

Abbreviations

AEC	All Ewe Conference
AESC	Architectural and Engineering Services Corporation
AFRC	Armed Forces Revolutionary Council
AME	African Methodist Episcopal Zion Church
BIFAN	Bulletin de l'Institut Fondamental d'Afrique Noire
CEP	Commissioner for the Eastern Province
CPP	Convention People's Party
CUT	Comité d'Unité Togolaise
DC	District Commissioner
EPC	Evangelical Presbyterian Church
FESLIM	Fetish Slaves Liberation Movement
GBC	Ghana Broadcasting Company
GNAFF	Ghana National Association of Farmers and Fishermen
KMAC	King's Medal for African Chiefs
MAST	*Maritime Anthropological Studies*
NAL	National Alliance of Liberals
NCP	National Convention Party
NDC	National Democratic Congress
NIP	National Independence Party
NLC	National Liberation Council
NPP	New Patriotic Party
NRC	National Redemption Council
PCP	People's Convention Party
PFP	Popular Front Party
PHP	People's Heritage Party
PNC	People's National Convention
PNDC	Provisional National Defence Council
PNP	People's National Party
PP	Progress Party
SMC	Supreme Military Council
SSNIT	Social Security and National Insurance Trust
TC	Togoland Congress
TU	Togoland Union
UAC	United African Company
UGCC	United Gold Coast Convention
UNC	United National Convention
UP	United Party
VALCO	Volta Aluminum Company

Glossary

Unless otherwise stated, all the words below are in Ewe.

abirempon (Twi): big men
abɔbi: anchovy; 'Keta schoolboys'
adotri: centre
adruku: herring
adzaduvi: fingerling of the Spanish mackerel
adze: witchcraft
afafa: horse-mackerel; *yevudor* net with a larger mesh size
agble: farm
agbodedefu: 'sending a ram into the sea'; Yewe sea rituals for bumper fishing seasons
agbonufia: sentinel god
agbosi: women attached to shrines in perpetuity
agbotadua: 'one who sits behind a chief'
agli (Ga, *ali*): purse net, surface drift net
agô: fan palm
agôwu: canoe made from the trunk of a fan palm
ahosi: widow
ahotsilele: ceremonial washing of the widow
ahoyo: sacred name for the sea during Anlo rituals
akatamanso (Twi): umbrella; NDC party emblem
akpeteshie (Ga): local gin
alaga: Yewe devotee 'gone wild' (possessed) because of a demeaning insult
alagadzedze: rite in which an insulted Yewe devotee gone wild (*alaga*) is restored to normalcy at a heavy cost to the culprit
Anlo akuaku: Anlo proper
asafohene (Twi): war chiefs

asafohenega: commander of a military wing
atsiafu: sea
atsi zotsi: walking stick with which an infirm person walks
avadada: war mother (commander-in-chief)
avadezi: stools of valour
awoame: Anlo paramount chieftaincy; 'place of seclusion'
awoamefia: Anlo paramount chief
bisi: black calico cloth
bo: shallot bed
bodada: renting of shallot bed
dame: system of 'farm renting' or share-cropping
dedexo: period of seclusion for a wife (four to eight months, depending on the bride-groom's wealth) after the payment of the bride price
dipo (Adangme): Krobo puberty rite
dodede: the ritual cleansing and expurgation of disease
dogbledi: similar to the *agli*, but left in the sea overnight
dufia: town chief
dulegbawo: public shrines
dzefi: the place of salt
dzenkple: maize flour mixed with palm oil and cooked as porridge
dzɔkpleanyi trɔwo: autochthonous gods
ekpo: walking sticks as repositories of spiritual power
eto: reddish powder
fame: system of 'farm renting' or share-cropping
fia: chief of a town
fiabo: gifts
fiasidi: young servant woman assigned in perpetuity to the *Nyigbla* shrine

Glossary

foasi: ceremony to recruit *zizidzelawo*

Fofie: nineteenth-century slave religious cult in Anlo

fu: sea

gbe: the spoken word

gbekle: grass from the lagoon side

gbekoke: shallot beds

hanua: headman of a village

hanududu: communal meal

Hevieso: god of thunder and patron deity of the Yewe cult

hlo: clan

hlobiabia: vengeance; 'asking the clan'

hogbetsotso: annual celebration and commemoration of the flight of Anlo's ancestors from the tyrannical rule of King Agokoli of Notsie (Togo)

hozikpui: stool of wealth or fortune for rich traders

kakorviwo: 'those who carry the rope'; women employees of the fishing companies

kalezi: stools of valour

kele: common Anlo term for local gin

kome: lagoon islands

kpôtomenui: former word for local gin; 'something hidden in a coconut matting fence'

kpotiwo: stakes

kyidom (Twi): rearguard

lashibi: left wing

lemu: a stable canoe

mamanyigba: land traced to a woman; 'grandmother's land'

Mawu: Supreme Being

nekpeli: *yevudor* with a half-inch mesh

nkuvuvu: 'eye opening'; civilization

nugbidodo: Anlo ritual of renewal reconciling aggrieved parties

nunya: knowledge or wisdom

nusê: power

nuto: self; ownership (of property)

nyi: corrode, wear

Nyigbla: national war god; Anlo's chief deity; the name of Anlo's most prestigious religious cult

'*Nyɔnuwo (gbolowo) la amevunolawoe*': 'Women (harlots) are bloodsuckers'

panyarring: the seizure of person(s), not necessarily related to a debtor (e.g. people from the same village as the debtor) to apply local pressure on the debtor to repay the debt

sabala: shallot

shime: marshland

srô da: to respect

sronu: Anlo marriage payment

ta: spiritual knowledge

tekali: the practice of drawing a long rope across the surface of the lagoon to catch fish

tengiraf: bottom drift net

togbagba: the rite of powdering a bride with *eto*

tôgbenôliwo: ancestral spirits

torgome: flood plains of the lagoon

trɔkosi: female religious bondage; vestal virgin

trôsi (male, *trônua*): priest

trôwo: gods

tsi de ame: 'water has married a person'; sea erosion

tsiefe: land of the dead

tsikpe: rain-stone; name of the *awoame* stool

tsikuviwo: 'those who fetch water'; women employees of the fishing companies

tumi: the ability to produce change; power

vetsimu: herring

vevetô: 'smelly one'; Anlo nickname for *akpeteshie*

voku: sack

watsa: purse-seine, cast net

wego: deeper areas of the Keta Lagoon

weme: marshy or freshwater depressions

woba: to pledge

woe: right military wing

yevudor: beach-seine net; 'European net'

yewesi: female Yewe devotee

zizidzelawo: voluntary female initiates in the cult of *Nyigbla*

Zongo: strangers' quarters or the Muslim section of a town

zumeyiyi: test during *ahotsilele* to see whether or not the widow has been seduced since the death of her husband

Introduction

I was drawn to study the ecological and social history of the Anlo-Ewe homeland in south-eastern Ghana for several reasons. The Anlo are a part of the Ewe-speaking peoples, who occupy the West African coast between the Volta and Mono Rivers (sections of Ghana and Togo). Keta, the major entrepôt in the Anlo Traditional State for most of this century, has been the site of acute coastal erosion since about 1907. Growing up in Ghana as a child, stories of Keta's battle against the sea abounded. The Volta River has created an east–west geographical divide in Ghana, and Keta seemed so far away. Safe in Kumasi, in the heartland of Ghana and west of the Volta, we pondered over the refusal of Keta's residents to relocate away from the advancing sea. As coastal erosion has persisted over decades, I wondered if the government could do nothing to protect what remained of Keta. I have been fascinated for years by what sounded like an unequal battle between humans and nature.

My knowledge of Asante history has deepened my awareness of the influence of environment (in this particular case, the rain forest) on Asante culture and history.[1] Asante perceptions of the individual, family, community, state, kingship, citizenship, success, wealth and power were permeated by images of the forest and Asante's assiduous toil against nature. I welcomed the opportunity to examine the relationship between a contrasting environment and culture, economy and society. The hydrology of the coast east of the Volta River was immensely appealing: the Atlantic Ocean to the south, the Volta as the western boundary and a lagoon system that stretched from east of the Volta estuary all the way to the Lagos Channel, some 200 miles away. Rivers, streams, ponds and creeks criss-crossed the physical landscape of Anlo, creating an environment unique in Ghana – excluding the Ada area of the Volta estuary – but very similar to the coastlands of Togo, Benin, and Nigeria. The

---

[1] For revealing insights, see T.C. McCaskie, 'People and animals: constru(ct)ing the Asante experience', *Africa*, 62, 2 (1992): 221–44; Norman A. Klein, 'Toward a new understanding of Akan origins', *Africa* 66, 2 (1996): 248–73; and Emmanuel Akyeampong and Pashington Obeng, 'Spirituality, gender, and power in Asante history', *International Journal of African Historical Studies* 28, 3 (1995): 481–508.

1

coastal stretch, labelled as the 'Slave Coast' by early European traders to West Africa, also coincided with the 'Benin Gap', the natural break in the West African forest belt and the extension of savannah grassland to the coast. The openness of the land facilitated communications, commerce and political integration within this region. As I plumbed the secondary literature on the Anlo – and the Slave Coast of which it formed a part – I discovered a dynamic environment in a constant state of change: coastal accretion and attrition, sand spits being created and eroded, waterways being formed and erased. History often emphasizes how humans shape their environment; on the Anlo coast humans were involved in a dynamic relationship with their environment, changing and being changed by it.

The eco-social history of the Anlo chronicled in this book underscores a nuanced Anlo understanding of their environment: its opportunities and constraints. Migrants to the aquatic ecosystem of south-east Ghana, the Anlo became acquainted with their environment through daily use, followed by a complex cultural mapping of their novel environment. Environmental adaptation had an internal dynamic, as oral traditions and contemporary European accounts described the area of the upper Slave Coast as sparsely populated, and the autochthonous peoples left little physical or cultural trace in Anlo outside the cluster of deities believed to have been associated with these early settlers. Increasing familiarity with the environment, outside technological and ritual knowledge and a constantly changing environment (from both natural and human causes) forged a series of complex equilibria between the Anlo and their environment. Anlo history exhibits a mutualism between persons and environment, though this did not necessarily idealize a 'harmonious' relationship between culture and nature. The Anlo sometimes ascribed a capricious agency to the environment, manifested at times in drought and floods.[2] But the Anlo were also aware that large-scale 'development' projects, such as harbours and dams, could alter the intricate hydrology of their landscape and endanger their existence and subsistence. The Anlo relationship with their environment is thus one of constant change and adjustment. Tim Ingold has observed that the work of shaping the environment requires several hands and is never complete.[3] Ute Luig and Achim von Oppen comment in their introduction to a special issue on landscape in Africa, that humans shape landscape and landscape shapes humans; it is a 'historical process rather than a finished result'.[4]

It is necessary to situate my work within the burgeoning studies on environment and ecology. This is, perhaps, best achieved by defining both terms and what I mean by 'eco-social' history. A theoretical framework that provides a conceptual grid for this book is provided later in this introductory chapter. Environmentalism in Africa has often been manifested in the conservation of wildlife, soil, water and forests and

---

[2] On the mutualism of nature and culture based on African and Asian examples see Elisabeth Croll and David Parkin, eds, *Bush Base: Forest Farm – Culture, Environment and Development* (London and New York, 1992).

[3] Tim Ingold, 'Culture and the perception of the environment', in Croll and Parkin, eds, *Bush Base: Forest Farm*, 50.

[4] Ute Luig and Achim von Oppen, 'Landscape in Africa: process and vision – an introductory essay', *Paideuma* 43 (1997): 16.

Introduction

the concept of sustainable development or a utilitarian use of the environment.[5] Though conservation was not alien to African cultures, these have not received the studies that have been accorded to Amerindians, for example, and African environmental history is often framed in the discourse that European colonialism has bequeathed.[6] In this environmental discourse, African subsistence activities were often portrayed as predatory and environmental policies were aimed at restraining the onslaught of humans on a defenceless nature. In this approach the natural environment was itself the focus of analysis with human agency important often as an explanatory factor in environmental degradation. Richard Grove has demonstrated recently that environmental destruction often characterized European activities in the tropics rather than those of the indigenes.[7] This book does not fit the genre of works on environmental history, as the focus is not on 'conservation'. Indeed, the limits of conservation are revealed in this particular study with the onset of coastal erosion in Anlo, for colonial environmental policy in the Gold Coast did not encompass environmental degradation that was not land-based and was not linked to human agency. This omission in colonial environmental policy is examined further in the conceptual framework.

Ingold provides a succinct definition of ecology as 'the study of the interactions between organisms and their environments'.[8] As William H. McNeill demonstrated

[5] See, for example, David Anderson and Richard Grove, eds, *Conservation in Africa: People, Policies and Practice* (Cambridge, 1987). Environmental history transcends conservation, and it is the broad study 'of human engagement over time with the physical environment, of the environment as context, agent, and influence in human history'. David Arnold and Ramachandra Guha, 'Introduction: themes and issues in the environmental history of South Asia', in David Arnold and Ramachandra Guha, eds, *Nature, Culture, Imperialism: Essays on the Environmental History of South Asia* (Delhi, 1996), 3. On environmental history, see Donald Worster, 'Appendix: doing environmental history', in Donald Worster, ed., *The Ends of the Earth: Perspectives on Modern Environmental History* (Cambridge, 1988), 289–307. The narrower focus on conservation here is a reflection of the historiography. For some works on Africa that capture the environment as context, agent and influence on human history, see Sharon Nicholson, 'The methodology of historical climate reconstruction and its application to Africa', *Journal of African History* 20, 1 (1979): 31–49; George Brooks, 'A historical schema for Western Africa based on seven climate periods', *Cahiers d'Etudes Africaines* 26 (1986): 43–62; and idem, *Landlords and Strangers: Ecology, Society, and Trade in Western Africa, 1000–1630* (Boulder, 1993).

[6] See, for examples, Johannes Wilbert, *Mindful of Famine: Religious Climatology of the Warao Indians* (Cambridge, MA, 1996), which examines the complex environmental management and religious ecology of the Warao of Venezuela; and William Cronon, *Changes in the Land: Indians, Colonists, and the Ecology of New England* (New York, 1983). James Fairhead and Melissa Leach pay similar attention to the environmental management of West African forest–savannah peoples in *Misreading the African Landscape: Society and Ecology in a Forest–Savanna Mosaic* (Cambridge, 1996); and idem, 'Deforestation in question: dialogue and dissonance in ecological, social and historical knowledge of West Africa – cases from Liberia and Sierra Leone', *Paideuma* 43 (1997): 193–225.

[7] Richard Grove, *Green Imperialism: Colonial Expansion, Tropical Island Edens and the Origins of Environmentalism, 1600–1800* (Cambridge, 1995); and idem, *Ecology, Climate and Empire: Colonialism and Global Environmental History, 1400–1940* (Cambridge, 1997). In an earlier article, Leroy Vail examined the destructive impact on African economies and societies of ill-conceived European conservation policies in colonial Zambia. Leroy Vail, 'Ecology and history: the example of eastern Zambia', *Journal of Southern African Studies* 3, 2 (1977): 129–55.

[8] Ingold, 'Culture and the perception of the environment', 39. Ingold draws on Worster, 'Doing environmental

3

in *Plagues and Peoples* (New York, 1977), humans like other organisms are enmeshed in webs of environmental relations.[9] I use 'eco-social' in this book to emphasize the dynamic and symbiotic relationship between people and their environment, and how this mutualism is the focus of analysis. I emphasize 'ecology' as 'context' and not as 'method,' as a sustained work on ecology requires a familiarity with the natural sciences. The findings of such natural scientists are incorporated where relevant (see Chapters 5 and 6), though the book's methodology is not premised on a tight fusion of history and ecological science. But human ecology also has a distinctly social component, and this book is interested in the cultural tools, the social structures and relations that humans forge in their interaction with the environment. Ingold emphasizes the social dimension of ecology: 'But the environment of any animal normally includes individuals of the *same* species, so that its relations with its environment must include interactions with conspecifics of the kind usually called "social".'[10]

An eco-social history of the Anlo thus examines the dynamic relations between the Anlo and their environment and how this is reflected through social structures and processes: economy and livelihood, accumulation and social differentiation, marriage and family, knowledge, belief and power, modernity and social change, and the sustainability of 'development'. This approach fits more into the older genre of 'landscape history' – landscape describing both physical land surface ('territory') and the 'social construction' of it – before the field bifurcated into the separate pursuits of environmental and ecological histories.[11] As David William Cohen and E.S. Atieno Odhiambo opine: '"Landscape" means "existence"', and this encompasses 'the physical land, the people on it, and the culture through which people work out the possibilities of the land'.[12] Working within the paradigm of landscape history, the eco-social history of the Anlo presented here draws on the insights of ecological anthropology, and is enriched by the vividness that social history brings to the description and analysis of everyday life.

Historical context and chapter outline

The history of Anlo presents the development of a maritime tradition by a previously non-maritime people. By the 1960s, researchers hailed the Anlo-Ewe as the quintessential sea fishermen of the West African coast.[13] Their presence extended along the Guinea coast from Sierra Leone to Cameroon. As recently as January 1997, A.K. Armah, a Ghanaian oceanographer, visited a fishing community in coastal

[8 (cont.)] history', 294, in this definition of ecology. Ecological history strives for a closer alliance between history and ecological science.

[9] See also Alfred W. Crosby, *Germs, Seeds, and Animals: Studies in Ecological History* (London, 1994).

[10] Ingold, 'Culture and the perception of the environment', 54.

[11] Luig and von Oppen, 'Landscape in Africa'.

[12] David W. Cohen and E.S. Atieno Odhiambo, *Siaya: The Historical Anthropology of an African Landscape* (London and Athens, OH, 1989), 9.

[13] See, for example, Polly Hill, 'Pan-African fisherman', *West Africa*, 28 December 1963 and 4 January 1964.

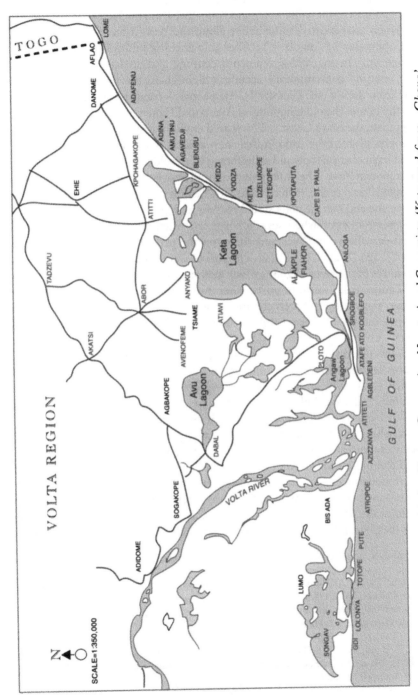

Map 1.1 A physical map of Anlo (*Source: Cooperativa Muratori and Cementiste, 'Keta sea defence – Ghana'* (*June 1987*), *11*).

Introduction

Cameroon. About 200 Ghanaian fishermen resided in this community, mostly Adangme from west of the Volta River and Anlo–Ewe from the Keta area.[14] Currently, Anlo fishermen are reported to be active along the West African coast from Cape Verde to Lobito Bay in Angola.[15] Yet the Anlo ancestors migrated from Notsie in central Togo only in the mid-seventeenth century, and, as late as the end of the eighteenth century, contemporary accounts highlighted the oddity that the Anlo shied away from the sea (see Chapter 1). Aja peoples – comprising the Ewe of Ghana and Togo, the Fon of the old kingdoms of Allada and Dahomey and the Gun of Porto-Novo – populate the Slave Coast.[16] The shared environment, language and culture of the Aja peoples enabled the Anlo in their new aquatic eco-zone to borrow and adapt cultural and technological tools and skills forged by the older Aja kingdoms on the coast or by the lagoon system. The Anlo plugged into the existing lagoon trade east of the Volta; adopted new canoe, fishing and salt-making technologies; and borrowed relevant riverine and marine gods suited to their new environment.

Anlo's ancestors established several small settlements along the 42-mile coastal stretch between the Volta River and Aflao, on the present-day boundary with the Republic of Togo (Map 1.1). These settlements were mostly on the southern and northern shores of the Keta Lagoon, which currently measures 20 miles from west to east and 12 miles from south to north when full. Several of these settlements were independent, though they shared common migration traditions and sometimes co-operated in a loosely organized military alliance. This military alliance, an 'Anlo confederacy', existed by the 1680s.[17] Strictly speaking, 'Anlo proper' (*Anlo akuaku*) in the mid-seventeenth century was restricted to the south-western margins of the Keta Lagoon. It stretched from the Volta at Anyanui east to Tegbi, extended to lagoon islands, such as Alakple and Fiahor, and included major towns like Anloga (the capital), Whuti and Woe. Anlo's economy was based mainly on agriculture. Keta, to the east of Anloga, was independent and, with its villages of Agudza and Kpoduwa, focused on fishing and salt making. Further east lay Klikor and Aflao, and north of the lagoon were settlements such as Anyako, Avenor, Tsiame, Dzodze and Wheta.

Though Robin Law views Keta as an integral part of the traditional Anlo state in the late seventeenth century, Sandra Greene effectively argues for a very loose and opportunistic cooperation.[18] Indeed, Keta was often involved in conflict with Anlo and sometimes allied with Anlo's enemies. D.E.K. Amenumey has pointed out the disadvantages these small Ewe polities faced in their endeavour to remain independent.[19]

[14] Interview with A.K. Armah (Department of Oceanography and Fisheries), University of Ghana, Accra, 14 August 1997.

[15] G.K. Nukunya, 'The land and the people', in Francis Agbodeka, ed., *A Handbook of Eweland*, Vol. I: *The Ewes of Southeastern Ghana* (Accra, 1997), 11.

[16] A.I. Asiwaju and Robin Law, 'From the Volta to the Niger, *c.* 1600–1800', in J.F.A. Ajayi and Michael Crowder, eds, *History of West Africa*, Vol. 1 (Harlow, Essex, 1985), 412–64.

[17] Ibid., 431.

[18] Robin Law, *The Slave Coast of West Africa 1550–1750: The Impact of the Atlantic Slave Trade on African Society* (Oxford, 1991), 250; and Sandra E. Greene, *Gender, Ethnicity, and Social Change on the Upper Slave Coast: A History of Anlo-Ewe* (Portsmouth and Oxford, 1996), 82–3.

[19] D.E.K. Amenumey, *The Ewe in Pre-colonial Times* (Accra, 1986).

6

Introduction

Conquerors invaded the Volta basin from the west and east. In 1702 the Akan state of Akwamu annexed both Anlo and Keta. Akwamu over-rule collapsed with the defeat of Akwamu in 1730 by an Akyem–Akwapim–Ga alliance. But Anlo and Keta quickly lost their independence again in 1741, this time to Anexo (Little Popo) from the east. Anlo single-handedly overthrew Anexo's rule in 1750 and embarked upon territorial expansion north of the Keta Lagoon. Keta remained under Anexo influence until the 1770s, when it moved towards a closer union with Anlo. Conflict between Anlo and Keta led to war in 1792, and Keta was razed to the ground. Keta's denizens migrated east, and founded the state of Some on land granted to them by Klikor and Aflao. This war strained the Anlo confederacy, which remained in a disunited state for the rest of the precolonial period.

British colonial rule was imposed on the Anlo coast in 1874, but resistance to colonial rule persisted north of the lagoons into the 1880s. British colonial rule would significantly expand the boundaries of the Anlo Traditional State in 1912, when a commission of inquiry defined the jurisdiction of Anlo to coincide with the boundaries of the former Anlo confederacy. Keta was made the administrative headquarters of the 'Keta District' in 1906, and the district included the coastal area east of the Volta to Aflao and the settlements north of the Keta Lagoon – that is, Anlo as currently defined. The Anlo traditional capital, Anloga, was thus subsumed administratively under Keta. The local government system was reorganized in 1951, when the Convention People's Party formed the first African government in late colonial Gold Coast. The Anlo District Council was thus established in 1951. The Gold Coast attained independence in 1957 under the name Ghana, and the country was divided into administrative regions, with the Anlo in the Volta Region. Today, the Anlo are divided into three administrative districts: Anlo, Ketu (Denu) and Akatsi (Avenor).

I chose 1850 as the starting date for this book because it marks the beginning of British influence east of the Volta and a convenient baseline for examining a continuous tradition of official environmental policy – or the lack thereof – under colonial and postcolonial governments. This period also coincides roughly with the arrival of missionaries from the North German Missionary Society in the Keta area in 1853 and the compilation of relevant ethnographic material crucial to reconstructing Anlo history in the nineteenth century. Lastly, urbanization and urbanism in Keta and other Anlo towns are major themes in this book and, as the geographer K.B. Dickson rightly points out, it is difficult to present a coherent account of urbanization in Ghana before 1850.[20] Exceptions should be made for old towns such as Accra, Elmina, Cape Coast and Kumasi. But most mining, railway and port towns emerged within the nexus of the colonial economy.

The historical context for this book, however, necessarily predates the British presence. The migration and settlement of Anlo's ancestors east of the Volta, the physical setting and adjustment to an aquatic environment and the early institutions that emerged are examined in Chapter 1. The chapter also explores the relationship between the Keta Lagoon and the sea. These two bodies of water were not only

[20] Kwamina B. Dickson, *A Historical Geography of Ghana* (Cambridge, 1969), xi.

connected hydrologically through a riverine network, but the lagoon also appears to have served as the site for experimentation in canoe and fishing technology, which was later transferred to the sea. The lagoon's calmer waters constituted a maritime nursery. This is not to obliterate the significant differences between lagoon and maritime navigation, as the currents and heavy surf of the Slave Coast required a distinctive type of canoe. But the lagoon promoted an increasing familiarity with the water world, and the Anlo became strong sea swimmers even before they acquired marine navigational skills (see Chapter 2). The Keta Lagoon's economic importance runs through Anlo's history: lagoon fishing and salt making supplemented other economic occupations, and experience and capital garnered in lagoon exploits could later be invested in sea fishing. The reverse also happened, and impoverished sea fishermen sometimes reverted to the less capital-intensive lagoon fishing. Open to women and children, lagoon fishing was a more egalitarian economic base than the more specialized sea fishing. As the sea eroded Keta's coastline in the twentieth century, the search for space would be towards the lagoon.

The economy of the south-eastern Gold Coast remained a local one through most of the seventeenth century. Trade flowed in two directions: an east–west orientation along the coast, and a south–north one between the littoral towns and farming communities on the northern shore of the Keta Lagoon. The rise of the forest Akan state of Asante in the early eighteenth century and the determination of other southern and coastal Akan states to prevent Asante access to European firearms, coastal salt and other trade goods benefited the coast east of the Volta. Asante traders became active in Atorkor, Keta and other coastal towns east of the Volta. The Anlo effectively entered international trade in the early eighteenth century as slave traders, and their ports constituted the western fringe of the Slave Coast. The slave trade on this western fringe of the Slave Coast did not compare favourably with eastern centres like Allada, Whydah and Dahomey. The area fell under Danish influence largely by default, as the more powerful European nations – Dutch, English and French – were not strongly interested in the Anlo coast. Danish influence rested lightly, and the communities along the Anlo coast essentially traded freely with passing European ships. Danish and British abolition of the slave-trade at the beginning of the nineteenth century and British naval efforts to suppress the trade shifted the focus of the slave-trade in the Gold Coast east of the Volta to the less-patrolled Anlo coast. The Anlo would persist in the slave-trade until the 1860s, smuggling slaves in through the lagoons and creeks, and on to Portuguese and Brazilian ships when the patrolling British naval squadron left Anlo seas. The slave-trade and slavery became important forces in eighteenth- and nineteenth-century Anlo. The introduction of beach-seine nets into Anlo eased the transition from slave-trading to commercial marine fishing in the second half of the nineteenth century (see Chapter 2). A 'maritime tradition' was in the making, and the Anlo would emerge as experts in beach-seine fishing along the West African coast.

The Anlo resented the extension of British influence east of the Volta, when the British purchased Danish forts and lodges in 1850. British control threatened Anlo economic prosperity based on free trade – and the slave-trade. It took two military campaigns in 1874 and 1889 for the British to forcefully incorporate Anlo into the colonial Gold Coast. The Anlo discovered that colonial rule did not necessarily preclude African prosperity. The British designated Keta as the first port east of the Volta and, as the redistribution point in an extensive commercial network, Keta prospered. The second port at Denu presented weak competition to Keta's premier position, and suffered under the strict British restrictions to prevent smuggling to and from adjacent Lome. The colonial government closed the Denu port in 1916. Chapter 3 examines urbanization and urbanism in early colonial Keta with a detailed analysis of Keta's engagement with 'modernity' between about 1885 and 1910. Urbanization in Keta was unique, as it encouraged free trade and a cosmopolitan milieu but not large permanent settlement. Land was extremely scarce in Anlo, and the distance between the sea and the Keta Lagoon seldom exceeded 3 miles all along the littoral. On market-days held in Keta every four days, traders came from as far as Accra, the Republic of Benin and Nigeria. German, French, British and other European merchants were based in Keta. Kru men from the Liberian coast worked as stevedores in Keta's surf port. The colonial military presence was evident in the stationed Hausa Constabulary. The ethnic and racial mix was staggering, and on market-days Keta's mobile population exploded. Keta's social life was unique, and underneath lay nascent class, ethnic, gender and racial tensions, which are examined in this chapter.

Keta's growth and economic prosperity came under sudden threat in less than three decades. The old pattern of coastal attrition and accretion – resulting in equilibrium – took a new turn. From about 1907 coastal erosion became chronic along the Anlo coast, particularly around Atiteti and between Dzelukope and Kedzi. The Anlo confidently expected that the colonial government would intervene because of Keta's privileged position within the colonial economy. Indeed, Anlo recruits had played a major role in the military expedition that secured the surrender of German Togoland in 1914. The Anlo were thus devastated by the Coode Report of 1929, which ruled out the feasibility of permanent sea defence in the Keta area. Especially galling was the report's conclusion that it would take in excess of 1,000,000 pounds sterling to save Keta, and the value of real estate in Keta did not merit this expenditure. The report undermined Anlo's sense of self-worth and trivialized Anlo's contribution to the colonial economy. It marked the onset of a new vulnerability, an Anlo sense of marginality within the political economy of the Gold Coast. The Anlo turned to their belief system and to their knowledge of the environment in an endeavour to understand the sea's unrelenting assault and to repair what they perceived as a breach in their 'moral ecology'.[21] They also turned to other Ewe groups for solidarity in an age of growing pan-Ewe consciousness (see Chapter 4).

Chapter 5 examines sea erosion and the search for space between 1930 and 1957. Keta's rise had been predicated on its strategic location east of the Volta, where it served as a point of redistribution in the regional economy. Keta's economic role was

[21] The concept of moral ecology is examined in detail in the conceptual framework presented later in this Introduction and in Chapter 4.

not based on any productive capacity. And, as Dickson has argued in the case of Ghana, the 'importance of a port was affected not so much by advantages of site, which were incidental in the choice of a port, as by a complex of political and other factors'.[22] The onset of coastal erosion and the colonial government's definitive refusal to construct a permanent sea defence wall triggered a search for a new redistribution centre by expatriate and African commercial concerns in Keta. In the Keta District, coastal erosion affected beach-seine fishing, land availability, land values and household structure. The importance of land and the family home as the basis for social organization among the Anlo meant that the erosion of land and buildings deprived families and lineages of an operating base in their own homeland. Then the Cape St Paul's wilt disease attacked coconut trees in Anlo in the 1930s and wiped out the previously lucrative copra industry. The Anlo embarked on a search for physical space and alternative economic ventures. Land was reclaimed from the lagoon at great expense. Anlo fishermen followed the migration of fish along the West African coast, and searched for beach land suitable for beach-seine fishing. Intensive shallot and vegetable cultivation, aided by heavy fertilization, developed around Anloga and Woe, and illicit liquor distillation provided an important avenue for sugar-cane farmers.

Independence, the endeavour to industrialize and modernize the Ghanaian economy and the siting or distribution of development projects would inform Anlo interpretations of their relative underdevelopment. Under colonial rule, the Anlo criticized the British for the inadequate number of schools established in the Volta region and the paucity of other socio-economic infrastructure. In the colonial and postcolonial era, the Anlo especially criticized the siting of deep-water harbours west of the Volta. They vied for benefits in the decision to construct a hydroelectric dam on the Volta in the early years of independence and argued that the associated harbour should be located close to the mouth of the Volta River. The government chose Tema, close to the capital of Accra, as the site of the new harbour and an aluminium smelter, and the Anlo and other northern Ewe groups were naturally disappointed. As the aquatic environment and the economy east of the Volta deteriorated, the Anlo explicitly connected these reverses with national development projects – especially harbours and dams – which altered the coastal hydrology. Chapter 6 examines the impact of harbours and dams on hydrology, fishing seasons and the disease environment of the lower Volta basin.

Chapter 7 examines the impact of coastal erosion and political ecology on Anlo-Ewe perceptions of political inclusion and exclusion in independent Ghana. Political ecology sheds light on the ways that larger imperatives of political economy (regional, national and international) affect human–landscape relations in locales.[23] An intriguing aspect of the Anlo interpretation of political ecology was the evaluation of

---

[22] Dickson, *Historical Geography of Ghana*, 117.

[23] On political ecology, see Paul Richards, 'Ecological change and the politics of African land-use', *African Studies Review*, 26, 2 (1983): 50–6; James L. Giblin, *The Politics of Environmental Control in Northeastern Tanzania, 1840–1940* (Philadelphia, 1992); and R.L. Bryant, 'Political ecology: an emerging research agenda in Third World studies', *Political Geography* 11, 1 (1992): 12–36.

each government of Ghana on the basis of its response to Anlo's coastal erosion and environmental degradation. The lack of official responsiveness to coastal erosion in Anlo was partly due to the fact that independent governments inherited colonial environmental policies that did not address this issue. Frequent changes in government in the independent era meant a lack of continuity in environmental policy, and new governments in ignorance reattempted old experiments that had failed to halt coastal erosion.[24] But the Anlo drew a different lesson in their critique of political ecology and concluded that the only governments sensitive to Anlo's environmental crisis were those that included sons of Anlo.

Landscape and ethnicity have interacted in important ways to inform Anlo-Ewe political identity in the twentieth century. In the colonial period, Anlo politicians exploited the geographical contiguity of Ewe-speaking peoples east of the Volta River as a factor for Ewe unification. Anlo politicians have also pointed to the socio-economic neglect of the region east of the Volta. These grievances, especially coastal erosion and environmental deterioration in Anlo, would come to the fore in party politics. In contemporary Ghana, newspapers highlight what they perceive as 'Ewe tribalism', labelling the Ewe as a close-knit group that refuses to identify with the rest of Ghana. This chapter analyses the importance of environment to the definition of polity. It examines the centrality of a 'shared environment and culture' to the Ewe unification movement in the colonial period, and the continuing relevance of environmental issues to Anlo perceptions of 'citizenship' in independent Ghana.

The concluding chapter of the book examines continuity and change in society and culture in Anlo's changing environment. It examines life in Anlo today, drawing on the journal I kept during my fieldwork between August 1996 and May 1997. The period coincided with the national and international uproar over *trɔkosi*[25] – female religious bondage – among the Anlo-Ewe, Tongu-Ewe, and Adangme. The chapter offers some thoughts on how this anachronistic institution has survived, largely unnoticed by the wider nation, for so long. The interplay of environment and culture in shaping and preserving this institution is analysed. The chapter probes the ambivalence of power within Anlo, contrasting the avariciousness of power in internal Anlo relations with the sense of powerlessness the Anlo feel when they seek to effect policy changes at the national level. The case of David Amekudzi in April 1997 provides an important illustration. This secondary school student was killed near the Keta Lagoon by lightning, the exclusive instrument of Yewe retribution, for alleged insolence to a member of the Yewe cult. The cult had dictated that no one should go near the corpse. The cult had the sole right to bury the body after due monetary pacification of 1,000,000 Ghanaian cedis. The goal in this concluding chapter is to convey a vivid sense of what it means to live between the sea and the lagoon in present-day Anlo.

Today the Keta District stands at the dawn of a new phase in its history. The current National Democratic Congress government of Ghana has committed itself

---

[24] Grove, *Ecology, Climate and Empire*, 3, comments on how postcolonial governments have inherited colonial environmental policies, with their biases and mistakes.

[25] Unless otherwise indicated, all vernacular words are in Ewe.

to the construction of a permanent sea defence wall and the rejuvenation of the economy of the Volta basin. The history of the Anlo has been one of environmental and cultural adaptation, economic prosperity, urbanization, environmental crisis and relative decline. The people, however, display an indomitable spirit, even in the face of severe environmental deterioration. It is a microhistory of continuity and change from the precolonial era to the present, of a people with close cultural and kinship ties to other peoples divided and confined within arbitrary colonial boundaries. It is a history of the forging of local and broader identities – Keta, Anlo, Gold Coast/ Ghana and pan-Ewe identities. It is a history of geopolitical isolation and then integration into the Gold Coast colony and Ghana. It is, to some extent, a portrait of two remarkable worlds east and west of the Volta River.

The conceptual framework

Even a casual visitor to the Anlo littoral would be struck by the impressive and inescapable presence of the Atlantic Ocean and the inland lagoons (Keta, Angaw and Avu) in the Anlo landscape. At various sections in Keta, Vodza, and Kedzi, the sea and the Keta Lagoon are within 50–100 feet of each other, separated by a thin sand spit. The importance of these bodies of water to fishing dictated a scholarly engagement with hydrology, fisheries and inland and marine fishing. A major limitation in the literature on African environmental history is the focus on land – as a factor of production and historical space – to the neglect of water resources.[26] Maritime history and anthropology remedy this deficiency by supplying tools for exploring the evolution of a maritime tradition in Anlo. Maritime history reviews the development of canoe and sailing technology, the acquisition of sea navigational skills, the systematic exploitation of marine resources and the sea as an avenue of trade and conquest.[27] Maritime anthropology, especially the anthropology of fishing, examines how humans adapt to a marine environment, the evolution of fishing methods, life in fishing communities and the requisite rituals that characterize sea fishing.[28] The sea thus exerts an important influence in the shaping of social identity.[29]

That the myriad themes tackled in this book – migration histories, adjustment to

[26] Important exceptions include Robert W. Harms, *River of Wealth, River of Sorrow: The Central Zaire Basin in the Era of the Slave and Ivory Trade, 1500–1891* (New Haven and London, 1981); and idem, *Games against Nature: An Eco-cultural History of the Nunu of Equatorial Africa* (Cambridge, 1987).

[27] See, for examples, Robert Smith, 'The canoe in West African history', *Journal of African History* 11, 4 (1970): 513–33; George Brooks, *The Kru Mariner in the Nineteenth Century: An Historical Compendium* (Newark, 1972); Jerry C. Stone, ed., *Africa and the Sea* (Aberdeen, 1985); W. Jeffrey Bolster, *Black Jacks: African American Seamen in the Age of Sail* (Cambridge, MA, 1997), ch. 2. Relevant information on maritime history is also scattered in the numerous European travel accounts of the Africa coast, and these are cited in subsequent chapters.

[28] A classic in this vein is Bronislaw Malinowski, *Argonauts of the Western Pacific* (London, 1922). For a useful review of the literature, see James M. Acheson, 'Anthropology of fishing', *Annual Review of Anthropology* 10 (1981): 275–316. Relevant works on Africa include A.H.J. Prins, *Sailing from Lamu: A Study of Maritime Culture in Islamic East Africa* (Assen, 1965); Emile Vercruijsse, *The Penetration of Capitalism: A West African Case Study* (London, 1984).

[29] Rita Astuti, *People of the Sea: Identity and Descent among the Vezo of Madagascar* (Cambridge, 1995).

an aquatic environment, overlapping trade networks, the advent of sea fishing, modernity and socio-environmental change, intensive agricultural techniques, harbours, dams – fit into a coherent narrative owes more to the fact that my Anlo informants viewed these as connected. I frequently shuttled between fieldwork in Anlo, the archives in Accra and Ho, the Department of Oceanography and Fisheries, and the Department of Geology at the University of Ghana as I endeavoured to unravel and also substantiate the links posited by my Anlo informants. Finding a cohesive theoretical framework for this study proved elusive, and so I wrote the chapters first to be true to the historical record, and then reflected on how I could conceptualize the study and provide readers with an accessible framework.

Culture and nature: in search of a mode of production

Anlo views on the relationship between nature and culture present an important starting point. The Anlo view their relations with nature as a symbiotic one that is constantly changing. Insights from ecological anthropology highlight the fact that, for African societies, the dichotomy or opposition between culture and nature is often inapplicable. Indeed, humans perceive themselves as living in nature and the cooperation between humans and nature is necessary to the reproduction of culture and nature.[30] Culture provides people with the tools to map their environment and render even harsh environments familiar and accessible. For the Warao of Venzuela, religion plays a significant role in 'converting a climatologically adverse region into a habitat viable for human occupation'.[31] But this invests ecology with a moral component. Thus, among the Warao a harmonious balance between climatology, botany and human behaviour averts regional and local famines.[32] J.M. Schoffeleers notes for some Central African societies that:

> Apparently, we are dealing with a kind of symbiotic language in which incest, murder, and forms of general moral laxity stand for irregularities in the ecological order. Translated into everyday language the message would read: serious abuses in a community lead to ecological disaster, which in turn threatens the life of a community.[33]

Anlo oral traditions on the early phase of settlement in the present homeland highlight the bounty of nature and how subsistence was easily earned in their new

[30] See, for examples, Edward B. Tengan, 'The Sisala universe: its composition and structure (an essay in cosmology)', *Journal of Religion in Africa* 20, 1 (1990): 2–19; Jon Abbink, 'Ritual and environment: the *Mosit* ceremony of the Ethiopian Me'en people', *Journal of Religion in Africa* 25, 2 (1995): 163–90; and Terrence Ranger, 'Making Zimbabwean landscapes: painters, projectors and priests', *Paideuma* 43 (1997): 59–73. As Harms demonstrates in *Games against Nature*, symbiosis between nature and culture in African societies does not necessarily imply conservation. The socially competive atmosphere of Nunu culture encouraged a zero-sum-game exploitative attitude towards the fisheries of the Ubangi–Zaire Rivers, typical of the tragedy of the commons. Though not unaware of conservation, the Nunu in the quest for accumulation opted to believe – incorrectly, as Harms shows over the course of the twentieth century – that the annual floods of the rivers would always bring fish.
[31] Wilbert, *Mindful of Famine*, xxi.
[32] Ibid., 93.
[33] J.M. Schoffeleers, 'Introduction', in J. M. Schoffeleers, ed., *Guardians of the Land: Essays on Central African Territorial Cults* (Gwelo, 1979), 5.

Introduction

environment. Yet historical geography documents that the Anlo moved into a harsh environment with infertile soil, irregular rainfall and frequent droughts (Chapter 1). How to reconcile these views proved difficult, and yet to dismiss the oral traditions would deprivilege the Anlo historical perspective. As the Anlo became more familiar with their environment, they developed and adopted technologies that facilitated the intensive exploitation of their environment. Incidentally, this new phase coincided with the onset of persistent sea erosion. Anlo was threatened on two fronts: by floods on the lagoon side and by coastal erosion on the sea side. Many thoughtful Anlo wondered if their intrusive inscriptions on the natural world had resulted in this ecological imbalance.

Karl Marx's distinction between land as a subject of labour and land as an instrument of labour provided the first important insight as to how I could conceptualize the Anlo's early experience of their environment. Marx, significantly, defined land to include water, hence enabling the incorporation of Anlo's intricate hydrology.[34] The French Marxist anthropologist, Claude Meillassoux, has pushed Marx's distinction further in his elaboration of the 'modes of production' model and its application to Africa.[35]

> Land is a subject of labour when it is exploited directly, no human energy being invested previously in it. The productive activity consists of taking from the soil products which it has produced on its own, with no further alteration of environment by man.[36]

Hunting and gathering and fishing represent this mode of land use. 'Compared with agriculture, which requires an investment of labour in the land, and a delayed return on investment, the extraction economy gives instant returns.'[37]

Anlo's agrarian ancestors, faced with the novel aquatic ecosystem of south-east Ghana, initially used land as a 'subject of labour'. In this unfamiliar environment, they 'harvested nature': gathering salt when the lagoon dried, catching fish in the shallow parts of pools and the lagoons, and hunting. The soil in Anlo was sandy and infertile, and it took generations for the Anlo to develop intensive organic manuring and the mixing of sand from the seaside with the heavy clay soil from the lagoon-side that permitted decent yields in land-scarce Anlo, where opportunities for shifting cultivation were limited. Anlo subsistence at the time of settlement took the form of a 'natural economy', marked by very little accumulation.[38]

[34] Karl Marx, *Capital*, I (London, 1970), 178–80.

[35] See Claude Meillassoux, 'From reproduction to production: a Marxist approach to economic anthropology', *Economy and Society* 1 (1972): 93–108; idem, 'The social organization of the peasantry: the economic basis of kinship', *Journal of Peasant Studies* 1, 1 (1973): 81–90; and idem, *Maidens, Meal and Money: Capitalism and the Domestic Community* (Cambridge, 1981). On the use of modes of production analyses in African historiography, see also Donald Crummey and C.C. Stewart, eds, *Modes of Production in Africa: The Precolonial Era* (Beverly Hills, 1981); Wim van Binsbergen and Peter Geschiere, eds, *Old Modes of Production and Capitalist Encroachment: Anthropological Explorations in Africa* (London, 1985); and the special issue of *Canadian Journal of African Studies* 19, 1 (1985). On the application of modes of production theory to the Gold Coast's history, see Ray A. Kea, *Settlements, Trade, and Polities in the Seventeenth-century Gold Coast* (Baltimore, 1982).

[36] Meillassoux, *Maidens, Meal and Money*, 14.

[37] Ibid.

[38] Ibid., 15; and Meillassoux, 'Reproduction to production', 98.

Introduction

Though Anlo's ancestors – according to oral traditions – lived in a particular ward in the walled town of Notsie and migrated in kinship groups, the environment of south-east Ghana and the different material base imposed a dispersed settlement system on early migrants.[39] Modes of production theorists argue that the material base determines the relations of production or the social organization of the community or polity. Thus, a foraging economy would support a small, loosely organized, mobile society. In the Anlo case there was an important paradox: the Anlo migrated from Notsie with a relatively developed social organization – including a priest-kingship – and could not be described as a hunting and gathering society. Yet, in their early years in south-eastern Ghana, the Anlo foraged on nature and lived in small settlements. From living in a walled town in Notsie, the Anlo in south-eastern Ghana were compelled to adopt a dispersed settlement system. This was the product of an unfamiliar material base.[40] Hence Anlo oral traditions are filled with stories of *wanderlust* at this early phase: stories of hunting and of hamlet settlements on lagoon islands and along the littoral. This marked a phase when agriculture and fishing were not intensive enough to support concentrated settlement. It was the import of foodstuffs as early trade networks were forged across different ecological niches and the fears of land alienation caused by the influx of war refugees into Anlo from the 1670s that facilitated the recongregation of Anlo migrants in littoral towns (Chapter 1). These refugees brought new technologies of salt making and canoe manufacture, which aided Anlo subsistence in the new material base.

Culturally mapping the Anlo environment

The early settlers gradually became familiar with their new environment through daily use. Tim Ingold and Jon Abbink have argued that people use their environment before they come to conceptualize it.[41] Though ecological anthropology emphasizes the importance of culturally mapping the environment to give meaning to physical space and to facilitate human mediation, this is often a sequel to the practical, everyday use of the environment. To quote Ingold:

> *Culture* is a framework not for *perceiving* the world, but for *interpreting it*, to oneself and others. We do not have to interpret things in order to perceive them; and much of what we perceive, we fail to interpret, i.e. our knowledge of them remains tacit.[42]

The cultural mapping of the environment is not so much 'a *prelude* to practical action

---

[39] By the sixteenth and seventeenth centuries, Notsie had emerged as an important political and religious centre located about 100 kilometres north of the coast of Togo and surrounded by a wall which enclosed a town of 14 square kilometres. Sandra E. Greene, 'Religion, history and the supreme gods of Africa: a contribution to the debate', *Journal of Religion in Africa* 26, 2 (1996): 122–38.

[40] Harms, *Games against Nature*, chs 3–4, refers to a similar dynamic among Nunu migrants, aspirant 'big men', who moved away from the social competition of the core homeland in the Zaïre–Ubangi peninsula in search of less-contested, rich fishing grounds. These migrants sometimes settled in microenvironments different from the original homeland, which required new tactics and strategies of survival and accumulation. But Nunu migrations were often within the water world – albeit between different microenvironments – as distinct from the Anlo migration from an inland agrarian setting to a coastal aquatic environment.

[41] Ingold, 'Culture and the perception of the environment'; and Abbink, 'Ritual and environment'.

[42] Ingold, 'Culture and the perception of the environment', 53.

as an (optional) *epilogue*'.[43] The cultural construction of the environment, however, is crucial to the social reproduction of the community as it facilitates the transmission of knowledge about the environment from generation to generation.

The Anlo cultural mapping of their new environment indicated their growing familiarity with the landscape and the development of survival strategies. Mobility or flexibility enabled the early Anlo migrants to subsist in their homeland in spite of irregular rainfall, periodic flooding on the lagoon side and the seasonal character of fishing, salt extraction and farming. The Anlo developed 'extensive seasonal and circulatory migrations between water and land'.[44] Early Anlo settlements were limited to the narrow sand spit between the Atlantic Ocean and the Keta Lagoon, to lagoon settlements, such as Alakple and Kodzi and to the northern fringes of the Keta Lagoon. This area encompassed different microenvironmental zones. There were six distinct microenvironmental zones, and the Anlo named each zone to 'reflect particular environmental features and types of economic activities'.[45]

These microenvironmental zones can be pictured as concentric circles, radiating outward from the narrow sand spit with its marshy or freshwater depressions (*weme*) to the deeper areas of the Keta Lagoon (*wego*). From the coastal depressions (*weme*), one encountered in an outward projection the relatively fertile flood-plains of the lagoon (*torgome*). Then came the salt front or *dzefi* (literally, 'the place of salt'), where salt was mined in the dry season. The next zone from *dzefi* was the lagoon islands (*kome*), which were rich fishing grounds. Marshland or *shime* constituted the next zone, and mangrove grew here. The sixth zone comprised the deeper areas of the lagoon (*wego*).[46] In particular dry seasons, when farming and fishing along the littoral failed, the Anlo moved towards *wego* (the deeper end of the lagoon) or even toward the River Volta and the forest districts of the northern Ewe.

> In wet seasons when the optimum water level existed for farming and fishing, the people returned to cultivate the depressions of the sandbar (*weme*) and the flood plains of the lagoon. Salt-extraction, a domain of women, occurred in very dry season when the men emigrated. These movements were circulatory to begin with, but when conditions for reproducing themselves and their families were established the people settled away from the coastal strip.[47]

Conducive conditions for 'reproducing themselves and their families' were linked to the growing knowledge of the environment and the inflow of new technologies, which facilitated that Anlo manipulation of their environment.

The total land area of early Anlo was about 94 square miles, with only 20 square

[43] Ibid., 52.

[44] Christian Yao Ocloo, *The Anlo Shallot Revolution, 1930s–1992: A Study of the Local Agricultural History of Anloga in the Volta Region of Ghana* (Trondheim, 1996), 25.

[45] Ibid., 26.

[46] Ibid., 25–7. David Lee Schoenbrun, *A Green Place, A Good Place: Agrarian Change, Gender, and Social Identity in the Great Lakes Region to the 15th Century* (Portsmouth and Oxford, 1998), 7, highlights the creative choices a community makes in naming new forms of knowledge, and how 'words and meanings reveal both social relations and historical processes'. On the need to order physical space – to give it social meaning – in order to make it livable, see also Elizabeth Colson, 'Places of power and shrines of the land', *Paideuma* 43 (1997): 47–57.

[47] Ocloo, *Anlo Shallot Revolution*, 27.

miles being suitable for cultivation.[48] With scarce land, the Anlo political aristocracy was never able to appropriate land and turn itself into a landed aristocracy. Clans owned land corporately and even land acquired by individuals became 'clan land'. To accumulate the necessary wealth to affirm and strengthen incipient social differentiation, Anlo's political classes turned to banditry, war and trade as routes to accumulation. The first two modes of accumulation provided the necessary capital for participating in trade. In the precolonial era, war as a means of accumulation occupied a central place in the Anlo political economy. These processes privileged Anlo chiefs. And, in the precolonial and early colonial eras, Anlo chiefs were almost invariably traders. War and banditry procured slaves for the slave-trade and led to the expansion of internal slavery, which underpinned other forms of trade through an increased supply of labour (Chapter 2). It was colonial rule that halted these modes of accumulation by outlawing warfare, the slave-trade and slavery. Until the colonial economy became well established in Anlo to provide avenues of wage labour and new markets within the imposed colonial boundaries, smuggling provided the Anlo with an important transitional device. Historically, accumulation in Anlo society had often been externally derived because of a limited material base. As fishing resources were more extensive – the ocean – the Anlo with colonial imposition shifted to exploit the economic resources of the sea. This development was made possible by the introduction of the beach-seine net into Anlo between 1850 and 1860. Anlo migration in the colonial era included new patterns (migrating to the cocoa-producing areas in southern Gold Coast, migrant fishing in the Ivory Coast, civil service jobs within the colony) but continued the older tradition of seeking economic resources outside Anlo to invest within Anlo (Chapters 5 and 6). Increasingly, migration would take on a permanent nature as acute coastal erosion further reduced land in land-scarce Anlo and made social life tenuous.[49] This in turn would affect Anlo social relations and household structure.

An important consequence of the different microenvironmental zones within Anlo was the coexistence of parallel and overlapping modes of production: salt making, fishing, agriculture. Commerce would transform the material base of Keta, Anlo's leading town in the nineteeth and twentieth centuries, a trend reinforced by Keta's selection as a colonial port and an administrative centre for the Keta-Ada District. Economy and society in late nineteenth-century Anlo would encompass the salt grounds of Anyako and Afiadenyigba; the sea-fishing centres of Vodza and Kedzi; palm oil-rich Dzodze, the bread basket of Anlo; coconut plantations along the littoral; the commercial and educational centre of Keta; and the relatively intensive horticulture of Anloga. Subtle differences in social formation accompanied these different economic systems, underpinning diversity and friction in Anlo. The most important rivalry would involve the traditional capital of Anloga – with its relatively unsophisticated economy before the Second World War – and Keta, the commercial jewel of Anlo.

[48] Greene, *History of Anlo-Ewe*, 26.
[49] An important recent work on African migration emphasizes the continuities between the more 'traditional' forms of migration in the precolonial era, and those of the colonial and postcolonial periods to African cities and European metropoles. François Manchuelle, *Willing Migrants: Soninke Labor Diasporas* (Oxford, 1997).

Introduction

That coastal erosion should commence in the early twentieth century and be most pernicious along the Keta coast was, perhaps, not surprising to many Anlo outside Keta. Keta had engaged 'modernity' at the most intense level, transformed its social life the most, and represented the site for the concentrated accumulation of wealth and the growth of a new individualism.[50] Arjun Appadurai makes the perceptive observation that the production of locality is always historically grounded and thus contextual, and that this context is at once an ecological, social and cosmological terrain.[51] As highlighted above, the management of the environment in several African cultures included a moral component. This insight addresses the concept of moral ecology and sheds important light on our understanding of the context of coastal erosion in twentieth-century Anlo. The timing of sea erosion was uncanny, just after Keta's commercial transformation, and the sea seemed to have selected the Keta area for special attention. Why this sudden and inexplicable onslaught?

For humans the marine world constitutes alien territory, strange and unpredictable. Sea fishing can be unpredictable in catch and dangerous in relationship to life. Not surprisingly, sea-fishing communities, from East Africa to New England, are noted for their 'rituals' to propitiate the sea, to safeguard life and to maximize catch.[52] The sea being a separate realm, fishermen have rituals of entry and exit.[53] Anlo ambivalence towards the sea even at the end of the eighteenth century has been mentioned. Perhaps this ambivalence was made even stronger for the Anlo with their non-maritime traditions. Anlo perception of the sea was framed from an agrarian perspective, and a maritime tradition was a late development. The interface of an agrarian world-view with a marine world made the sea a highly charged symbol in Anlo cosmology. Again, Meillassoux's insights on human relations to land/water are perceptive.

> For a peasant nothing comes from the land unless something else is given in exchange for it: he invests his labor and seed and draws his subsistence food in return. In this respect, activities which are predatory or merely extractive disturb him: they must be compensated by 'sacrifice' which re-establishes equilibrium since extracting resources from nature infringes the principle of advances and returns which dominate the domestic agricultural economy.[54]

For the Anlo, sea fishing represented harvesting where one had not sown. An important feature of sea fishing in Anlo is the performance of the *agbodedefu* ('sending a ram into the sea') ritual, annually observed to promote bountiful fishing.

---

[50] Indeed, as late as 1987, adherents of Nyigbla (the Anlo national god of war) in Anloga destroyed two Pentecostal chapels in Anloga because their members contravened a temporary ban on drumming imposed by the Nyigbla priest. Anloga's history emphasized the exclusion of external influences. Sandra E. Greene, 'Sacred terrain: religion, politics and place in the history of Anloga (Ghana)', *International Journal of African Historical Studies* 30, 1 (1997): 1–22.

[51] Arjun Appadurai, *Modernity at Large: Cultural Dimensions of Globalization* (Minneapolis, 1996), 182–3.

[52] See, for examples, Acheson, 'Anthropology of fishing', 287–8; Malinowski, *Argonauts*; idem, *Magic, Science and Religion* (New York, 1948), 30–1; Prins, *Sailing from Lamu*, 254; and John J. Poggie, Jr. and Carl Gersuny, 'Risk and ritual: An interpretation of fishermen's folklore in a New England community', *Journal of American Folklore* 85 (1972): 66–72.

[53] Acheson, 'Anthropology of fishing', 288.

[54] Meillassoux, *Maidens, Meal and Money*, 66.

Introduction

For the Anlo, the sea is a natural and supernatural realm populated by fish and deities. The sea yields its largesse when a proper and harmonious relationship is struck with it. The assault of the sea on the Anlo shoreline, after a previous century of coastal accretion, seemed to signal some irreparable damage in the human relationship with the supernatural (Chapter 4). The Anlo plumbed their history and belief system for explanations and solutions, and examined contemporary morality for clues as to this breach in relations with the sea. Coastal erosion became an important context for the review of the Anlo past and present, and the contemplation of the future.

Environmental policy in colonial Gold Coast

The Anlo turned to their colonial benefactors for help in redressing coastal erosion. The coastline of the Gold Coast has been extremely dynamic, with numerous points of erosion identified in the twentieth century (Chapter 7). But coastline stability and fisheries seemed to have received low priority in colonial environmental policy. Enviromental policy focused on conservation with a priority on the forests of southern Gold Coast and the regulation of timber felling and mineral extraction. Anlo, situated in the Benin Gap, had no forests and also lacked exploitable mineral wealth. Early West African foresters drew on theories and assumptions prevalent in European and Indian forestry circles in the late nineteenth century, which tied deforestation to climate desiccation.[55] Forests and the spectre of deforestation in West Africa have consequently received undue emphasis in forestry and social science analysis, sometimes based on very faulty assumptions.[56] The first forestry department was established in the Gold Coast in 1909, following the 1908 effort of H.N. Thompson, a trained forester in the Nigerian Forestry Department, to detail the Gold Coast's forests.[57] Thompson, then Chief Conservator of Southern Nigeria, had previously served in the Indian Forest Service and the Indian experience was influential in the early history of the Gold Coast Forestry Department.[58] Richard Grove has highlighted the singular failure of conservation in the Gold Coast, compared with other tropical colonies, as the colonial government was unable to wrest control of forests, minerals and 'wastelands' from the chiefs and peoples of the Gold Coast. Successive forestry laws and land bills were defeated between 1894 and 1916. The Forestry Department was actually closed down in 1917, partly as a result of the rise of the peasant cocoa industry, which thrived in forest regions, and an official acknowledgement of the primacy of cocoa in colonial revenues.[59]

In contrast, it was not until 1945 that we had the first detailed study of coastal

---

[55] Fairhead and Leach, 'Deforestation in question', 196.

[56] Ibid. and idem, *Misreading the African Landscape*, provide an important corrective to the assumption of deforestation that has dominated studies of the West African environment. See also, H.B.S. Kandeh and Paul Richards, 'Rural people as conservationists: querying neo-Malthusian assumptions about biodiversity in Sierra Leone', *Africa* 66, 1 (1996): 90–103.

[57] Fairhead and Leach, 'Deforestation in question', 196.

[58] Ibid.; and Grove, *Ecology, Climate and Empire*, 173.

[59] Ibid., 147–78.

geology and hydrology.[60] Previous studies of coastal hydrology were specific, often directed at finding a suitable site for a harbour.[61] Colonial endeavours to promote the fishing industry in British West Africa date from 1930.[62] The Gold Coast colonial government commissioned its first study of a local fishing industry in 1936.[63] And the first comprehensive study of the fishes and fisheries of the Gold Coast – still the authoritative account – came out in 1947.[64] It is only recently that the protection of coastal wetlands and the promotion of 'sustainable development' in coastal ecozones in West Africa have received national and international attention.[65]

Ironically, the dearth of institutional expertise on coastline stability and coastal fisheries privileged local environmental knowledge – or at least lent it audience – as colonial and postcolonial governments struggled to deal with Anlo's coastal erosion. Insights from the sociology of science on the relationship between 'citizen science' and 'expert institutions' in Europe have some relevance to the Anlo case.[66] The work of James Fairhead and Melissa Leach underscores the fact that rural West Africans, though affected in their daily lives by official environmental policy, seldom engage in the official discourse on conservation or seek to revise it as a package.[67] Anlo residents, particularly those of Keta, differ significantly in their engagement in environmental discourse and its politics, drawing on expert local knowledge (Chapters 4 to 7). The long tradition of education in Keta significantly broadened the Anlo social horizon and sharpened their articulation of environmental issues. Alan Irwin highlights the relevance of '"contextual knowledges" which are generated outside of formal scientific institutions'.[68] Anlo's problem was that it lacked funds to initiate a permanent sea defence, though it experimented with temporary measures aimed at slowing down the pace of erosion. This meant that the Anlo had to lobby government for financial assistance, and the larger the constituency, the more effective the lobby. Anlo joined ranks with its Ewe-speaking neighbours. And, being aware of the lack of institutional expertise on coastal erosion, the Anlo concluded that only governments with significant Anlo representation could understand their enviromental plight and

---

[60] N.R. Juner and D.A. Bates, *Reports on the Geology and Hydrology of the Coastal Area East of the Akwapim Range* (Accra, 1945). Also National Archives of Ghana (NAG), Accra, ADM 5/4/49.

[61] Public Records Office (PRO), London, CO 554/465.

[62] PRO, CO 554/84/11.

[63] PRO, CO 96/729/12. A. P. Brown, 'Survey of the fishing industry at Labadi' (1936).

[64] F.R. Irvine, *Fishes and Fisheries of the Gold Coast* (London, 1947).

[65] D.S. Clark and R. Foster-Smith, *A Management Information System for the Coastal Ecosystem of Ghana: Its Application to Planning and Developing Multiple Resource Use Strategies*, 2 vols (Overseas Development Administration, 1996); and S.M. Evans, C.J. Vanderpuye and A.K. Armah, eds, *The Coastal Zone of West Africa: Problems and Management* (Cleadon, 1997).

[66] A. Irwin, *Citizen Science: A Study of People, Expertise and Sustainable Development* (London, 1995).

[67] Fairhead and Leach, *Misreading the African Landscape*; idem, 'Deforestation in question'; and idem 'Silence from the forest: exploring the ramifications of international environmental analysis in West Africa' (Paper presented at the African Studies Association UK, London, September 1998).

[68] Irwin, *Citizen Science*, xi. See also Jane Guyer and Paul Richards, 'The invention of biodiversity: social perspectives on the management of biological variety in Africa', *Africa* 66, 1 (1996): 4–5; and especially Fairhead and Leach, *Misreading the African Landscape*, which underscores the saliency of local, experience-grounded, agroecological knowledge.

provide the needed funds for a permanent sea defence. Thus, Anlo's experience of environmental disaster came to inform Anlo perceptions of and discourse about political inclusion and exclusion; the environment had come to frame Anlo understandings of citizenship in what Irwin has labelled 'environmental citizenship' (Chapter 7).[69]

[69] Irwin, *Citizen Science*, ch. 7.

Vodza beach, 23 July 1994

1

Migration, Topography & Early Settlements in the Keta Lagoon Basin

Introduction

The Ewe ancestors who founded the settlements that fringed the Keta Lagoon basin in what is now Anlo in south-eastern Ghana migrated from Notsie in central Togoland around the mid-seventeenth century. Political dissension and, most probably, land pressure were key motives in this migration. The Ewe migrants moved into the aquatic and marine environment east of the Volta River's estuary. This was a landscape littered with bodies of water. The river Volta served as the western boundary; the Atlantic Ocean bordered the south; and the large inland Angaw, Avu and Keta Lagoons,[1] fed by the Volta and Todzie Rivers through a system of channels and smaller lagoons, dominated the Anlo interior. The hydrology of the area was dynamic and the sea, rivers and lagoons were interconnected through a complex network. Although Notsie was located between the Haho and Shio Rivers,[2] nothing in the experience of the Ewe migrants seemed to have prepared them adequately for the aquatic ecosystem in south-eastern Ghana. Nevertheless, J.M. Grove has commented on how the Ewe migrants 'adapted themselves to their new, and apparently rather unfavourable environment' with remarkable skill and completeness'.[3] This chapter examines Anlo-Ewe oral traditions about migration, the impact of topography on settlement patterns, early efforts to explore and exploit the novel environment and the gradual extension of an early economy based on the safe and calm waters of the

[1] A.K. Armah and D.S. Amlalo, 'Coastal zone profile of Ghana' (National Workshop on Integrated Coastal Area Management, Accra, July 1997), 3, gives the surface area of these three lagoons as 702 square kilometres or approximately 271 square miles. This is a third of the total Anlo land space of 883 square miles. The dynamic nature of the coastal ecosystem, the relative dryness of the twentieth century and the damming of the Volta River in the mid-1960s may have shrunk the surface area previously covered by these three lagoons.

[2] Charles M.K. Mamattah, *The Ewes of West Africa* (Accra, 1979), 46; R.S. Rattray, 'History of the Ewe people', *Etudes Togolaises* 11, 1 (1967): 92.

[3] J.M. Grove, 'Some aspects of the economy of the Volta delta (Ghana)', *Bulletin de l'Institute Fondamnental d'Afrique Noire* 28, 1–2 (1966): 381–432.

lagoon system to maritime trade. The chapter highlights the intimate relationship between lagoon and sea, and how this has influenced the history of the Anlo area, the cultural and technological mechanics of transition to the aquatic environment and the social institutions that emerged or were forged in this new area. Anlo oral traditions on migration provide a charter for kingship and the alternating succession between the Adzovia and Bate clans. These traditions also shed light on the religious nature of kinghip and the importance of the *awoamefia* (the Anlo paramount chief) as priest-king in the domestication of nature. From an initial foraging of nature in an unfamiliar environment, Anlo's economy and society developed a more systematized structure based on agriculture, fishing, salt making and trade. The chapter provides the relevant historical context for the rest of the book by tracing the evolution of the Anlo polity from the fragmented independent settlements established by related groups of migrants into the more cohesive 'Anlo State' that existed by the early nineteenth century.

Anlo-Ewe traditions of migration

Though several versions of the Anlo-Ewe migration tradition exist, they seem to agree in substance on the centrality of Ketu, Tado and Notsie as important points in migration and on the political insecurity caused by wars and oppressive over-rule as the major factor in this constant movement. However, there are still problems of inter-pretation in assessing the exact nature of the Anlo-Ewe links to Tado and Ketu in particular, the scale of migration into south-eastern Ghana and the dating of this last movement.

The Anlo-Ewe oral traditions cite Ketu, an ancient Yoruba town now in the Republic of Benin, as the original home of the Ewe.[4] In a recent collection of essays by Ewe scholars on the Ewe past and present, the historian D.E.K. Amenumey recounts this tradition of migration from Ketu.

> It was the expansion of the Yorubas that pushed the Ewe and related peoples westwards. On leaving Ketu the people split into two big divisions. One of these went south and in turn divided into two. One of these sub-divisions went to found a settlement near river Mono and called it Tado. The second sub-division also founded a settlement between the rivers Haho and Mono and called it Notsie.
>
> The second big group went to the Adele region in the present-day Togo. To this group belonged the people who came to be known as Anlo, Be and Fon. They later joined their relations at Notsie. There they were known collectively as *Dogboawo*. Their leaders were Amega Wenya and his nephew Sri who was the son of the king of Tado. Sri had fled from Tado with his father's stool following a succession dispute with his half-brothers after his father's death.[5]

[4] See D.E.K. Amenumey, *The Ewe in Pre-colonial Times* (Accra, 1986), 2–7; Madeline Manoukian, *The Ewe-Speaking People of Togoland and the Gold Coast* (London, 1952), 12. This tradition is mentioned in Geoffrey Parrinder's history of Ketu, although he does not substantiate the tradition. E.G. Parrinder, *The Story of Ketu: An Ancient Yoruba Kingdom* (Ibadan, 1956), 16. Indeed, Mamattah, *Ewes of West Africa*, ch. 1, cites Egypt as the original cradle of the Ewe before their migration to Yorubaland.

[5] D.E.K. Amenumey, 'A brief history', in Agbodeka, *Handbook of Eweland*, Vol. I: *The Ewes of Southeastern Ghana* (Accra, 1989), 15. The historian Francis Agbodeka affirms this tradition of migration in the 'Introduction' to the book.

The Keta Lagoon Basin

In this series of migrations, the component that became the Anlo was led successively by Togbui Gbe, his son Gemedra and his grandson Wenya. Wenya's sister married the chief of Tado, Adza Ashimadi, and the marriage produced Kpone, later installed as Sri I.[6] Wenya notified King Agokoli of Notsie of the arrival of his nephew with Ashimadi's stool. The ageing Wenya appointed Kpone leader of the Dogbo, and Agokoli installed Kpone as chief of the Dogbo under the name Sri (from the Ewe word *srô da*, 'to respect').[7]

Tensions emerged between the Dogbo and their Notsie hosts. Charles Mamattah informs us that this was because Sri believed that Agokoli had unduly delayed his installation as chief after his nomination by Wenya.[8] A dispute erupted between the Notsie and the Dogbo during a drumming session in the Dogbo quarter of Notsie.

> During the resultant fracas, a native of Notsie and a close relative of King Agokoli brutally hit a Dogbo elder by name Aga with a piece of sharp instrument on the forehead. When King Agokoli was informed, he personally offered his good offices to take the wounded man Aga into his royal house and nurse him himself. Sri I prevailed on the Dogbo to reject the kind gesture. Shortly after this incident, a Dogbo elder died and the other Dogbo elders sent word to King Agokoli that the deceased was Aga the injured man.[9]

The Ewe law of vengeance demanded that Agokoli hand over his relative for execution in compensation for the Dogbo loss.[10] This was accordingly carried out, but Agokoli later discovered the Dogbo ruse: the Dogbo deceased was not the injured Aga.

A new phase opened in Notsie–Dogbo relations, marked by the harsh rule of Agokoli. Anlo traditions vividly recount this experience.

> When we were staying at Notsie, Togbui Agokoli was very wicked to the Anlos. At times he would put broken pots [thorns and thistles in other traditions] into clay and ask the Anlo to knead it and build with it. The Anlo decided to flee. One day the Anlo celebrated in their quarter of town. They drummed and danced right into the night. Agokoli thought they were enjoying [themselves]. All of Notsie was surrounded by a thick [clay] wall. The Anlo were continuously pouring water on a section of the wall to soften it. They made an opening in the wall with a sword. They fled from Notsie.[11]

In Anlo today, this flight is commemorated in the annual festival of *hogbetsotso*.[12] Anlo traditions recount that a small group of famous Dogbo hunters at Notsie – Tsatsu Adeladza, Amesimeku Atogolo, Akplomada, Sri, Etse Tsadia Tsali – had often gone hunting west of Notsie and had discovered the region of south-eastern

[6] Interview with Togbui Honi II, head of the Agorti family, Dzelukope, 4 September 1996.

[7] Ibid.

[8] Mamattah, *Ewes of West Africa*, 83.

[9] Ibid.

[10] Corporate responsibility and the law of clan retaliation are central to Ewe custom and have proved pivotal to Anlo history at several junctures. *Hlobiabia* (vengeance), literally means 'asking the clan'. G.K. Nukunya, 'Social and political organization', in Agbodeka, ed., *Handbook of Eweland*, 48. The destruction of Keta in 1792 and the founding of the State of Some were linked to a dispute between residents of Keta and Danish officers in the local Fort Prindsensten over the principle of clan retaliation.

[11] Interview with Esther Kwawukume, daughter of Sri II, Keta, 25 January 1997.

[12] For a description of the festival and its importance in Anlo history, see J.G. Kodzo-Vordoagu, *Anlo Hogbetsotso Festival* (Accra, *c.* 1994).

Ghana.[13] They had informed Wenya of this sparsely populated and yet attractive region.[14] The distance between Notsie and Anlo makes it unlikely that hunters from Notsie ranged that far. The emphasis here is on the fact that these named hunters played a pivotal role in the successful establishment of settlements in early Anlo. As hunters they were comfortable both in nature and culture and served as frontiersmen. The Dogbo who fled Notsie split into three groups. One group went north–west and founded settlements such as Hohoe, Peki, Awudome and Alavanyo in the northern Volta Region of present-day Ghana. The second group fled west and founded Ho, Klevi, Abutia, Adaklu and other polities in the central section of the Volta Region. The third group, led by Wenya and Sri, headed south–west to the coast and set up settlements such as Keta, Tegbi, Woe, Anloga and Kodzi, which formed the core of *Anlo akuaku* (Anlo proper).[15]

Various scholars and this author's work confirm this general outline of Anlo's migration history.[16] The traditions contain rich information on the sojourn at Notsie and current customs, such as the sending of a delegation to the king of Notsie to receive sandals for every new *awoamefia* (paramount chief) of Anlo and the celebration of *hogbetsotso*, keep these ties alive.[17] The links with Tado and Ketu are less substantiated, though present in most traditions. Historians Francis Agbodeka and Amenumey cite the Ewe practice of walling towns and fencing property as a Yoruba trait from the Ketu sojourn.[18] Robin Law has cautioned against a literal interpretation of these purported links to Tado and Ketu to imply actual claims of kinship. He suggests, instead, cultural and political influences from these alleged cradles of migration.[19] K.B. Dickson, the historical geographer, has also questioned the implication in Anlo oral traditions of a massive emigration from Notsie to Ghana at a single point in time. The material evidence supports 'a slow process extending over many years and referring to small family or kindred groups coming in at different times to join those that had arrived before them'.[20] But Dickson could be describing the dispersed settlement system and the small communities established by Anlo's ancestors in the new aquatic environment. The settlement pattern in early Anlo does not necessarily imply that the ancestors migrated in smaller groups.

Dating the Anlo migration into south-eastern Ghana remains problematic. Amenumey has advocated for the late sixteenth century or early seventeenth

[13] Mamattah, *Ewes of West Africa*, 85.

[14] E.Y. Aduamah, *Ewe Traditions*, no. 1 (Institute of African Studies, University of Ghana, 1965), 20.

[15] Amenumey, 'Brief history', 15–16.

[16] Ibid.; Mamattah, *Ewes of West Africa*, ch. 1; Sandra Greene, 'The past and present of an Anlo-Ewe oral tradition', *History in Africa* 12 (1985): 73–87; Aduamah, *Ewe Traditions*. See also interview with Togbui Honi II, Dzelukope, 4 September 1996; interview with L.C.M. Seshie, Dzelukope, 16 October 1996.

[17] Interview with Togbui Honi II and Togbuivi Kumassah (*agbotadua* of Dzelukope), Woe, 24 January 1997.

[18] Agbodeka, 'Introduction', 5; Amenumey, 'Brief history', 15.

[19] Robin Law, *The Slave Coast of West Africa 1550–1750: The Impact of the Atlantic Slave Trade in African Society* (Oxford, 1991), 27–8. Hans Debrunner has expressed a similar caution in the extension of the Notsie tie to all Ewe speakers, for he saw this legend being accepted 'wherever the Ewe language has gained ascendancy; even in the areas where Ewe is not spoken, the myth has begun to make its way'. Hans Debrunner, *A Church between Colonial Powers: A Study of the Church in Togo* (London, 1965), 5.

[20] Dickson, *Historical Geography of Ghana*, 28.

century.[21] J.M. Grove and A.M. Johansen recorded local traditions that emphasized the seventeenth century as the time the Anlo-Ewe penetrated the Keta sand bar and gave *c.* 1678 as the date for the founding of Keta.[22] H.S. Newlands, District Commissioner (DC) in Keta in 1922, accepted *c.* 1670 as the date for the migration from Notsie in his compilation of 'Some dates in the history of the Awunas'.[23] It is noteworthy that the Dutch trader, Pieter de Marees, in 1602 reported that there were no towns or villages of consequence east of the River Volta in the area that became the Anlo coast.[24] The Dutch factor, Willem Bosman, visited Keta in 1698. He described the kingdom of Coto (Keta) as 'inconsiderable in strength' though warlike.[25] The situation had changed again by the early eighteenth century, and the Dutch Bookkeeper-General, Eytzen, who travelled over land from Whydah via Keta and Anlo to Elmina in December 1717, was quite favourably impressed by these fairly large villages, rich in cattle.[26] Sandra Greene convincingly argues for the mid-seventeenth century as the period of Anlo settlement in south-eastern Ghana. It is significant that the Anlo were quite settled enough by the 1660s to assist Ga-Adangme refugees who fled across the Volta in the wake of Akwamu wars on Accra and Ladoku in the 1670s and 1680s.[27] Law considers the Anlo migration date of the mid-seventeenth century much too late, though he produces no new evidence to change the mid-seventeenth-century date.[28] The following sections of this chapter attempt to reconstruct the settlement history of the Anlo from the mid-seventeenth century and the society and economy that had come into existence by the early nineteenth century. What has been established from the preceding historical examination of Anlo-Ewe migration traditions is that the Anlo ancestors were inland dwellers with no maritime traditions.[29] Their earlier peregrinations had been inland. The transition to the aquatic ecosystem of the south-eastern coast of Ghana would involve intense cultural and technological innovation.

---

[21] Amenumey, 'Brief history', 16.

[22] Grove and Johansen, 'Historical geography of the Volta delta', 1377.

[23] National Archives of Ghana (NAG), Accra, ADM 41/5/8. Keta District Record Book, 1900–27.

[24] Pieter de Marees, *Description and Historical Account of the Gold Kingdom of Guinea*, trans. and ed. Albert van Dantzig and Adam Jones (Oxford, 1987), 87.

[25] Willem Bosman, *A New and Accurate Description of the Coast of Guinea, Divided into the Gold, the Slave, and the Ivory Coasts* (London, 1721), 306. 'Coto' in early European sources was sometimes used to refer also to the politically separate kingdoms of Anlo, Keta and Aflao. Sandra E. Greene, 'Land, lineage and clan in early Anlo', *Africa* 51, 1 (1981): 456.

[26] Albert van Dantzig, *The Dutch and the Guinea Coast 1674–1742: A Collection of Documents from the General State Archive at The Hague* (Accra, 1978), 199–201. Doc. 228. WIC: Minutes of Council Meeting, Elmina, 17 February 1718.

[27] Sandra Greene, *Gender, Ethnicity and Social Change on the Upper Slave Coast: A History of the Anlo-Ewe* (Portsmouth, 1996); C.C. Reindorf, *History of the Gold Coast and Asante* (Basle, 1895), 25; and Grove and Johansen, 'Historical geography of the Volta delta', 1378.

[28] Law, *Slave Coast of West Africa*, 31.

[29] A.K. Amuzu, 'The economic resources and activities of the Keta Lagoon and their contribution to the life of the people of south Anlo' (BA Thesis, University of Ghana, 1961), 51, highlights the agrarian tradition at Notsie.

27

Environment and early settlement
in the Keta Lagoon basin

The Dogbo migrants to south-eastern Ghana moved in two parties headed by Wenya and Sri and founded the early Anlo settlements through a series of stops and splits from the main parties. Oral traditions have it that the aged Wenya was carried by two famous hunters, Atsu Etso and Etse Gbadze (twins), as they headed south-west from Notsie. They hit the northern shore of the Keta Lagoon at Ewetoko (present-day Atititi near Afife), and the group proceeded through a narrow creek to Kedzi on the coast.[30] After negotiating the vast watery expanse of the Keta Lagoon, a relieved Wenya is reported to have exclaimed: 'Mie do eke dzi azo' ('We have at last arrived on sand'). The place was named 'Kedzi' from Wenya's exclamation.[31] The group now moved west along the narrow sand bar sandwiched between the Keta Lagoon and the Atlantic Ocean. The migrants were impressed by the unique physical features of the landscape. Further west of Kedzi, Wenya reached another spot and was struck by the shape of the coastline. He remarked: 'Mekpo ke fe ta' ('I have at last seen the head of the sand'), and the name 'Keta' was given to this location.[32] Keta literally means 'on top of the sand'. Wenya's party continued westwards, founding Tegbi, Woe and Anloga. At Anloga, the tired Wenya protested: 'Menlo!' ('I can go no further'; 'I have coiled'). Anlo oral traditions see 'Anlo' as derived from Wenya's 'Menlo', and 'Anloga' ('big' or 'great' Anlo) became the political capital of Anlo.[33] Sri's party moved south-west along the northern shore of the Keta Lagoon, and members from this group hived off to establish settlements such as Wheta, Dzodze and Afife. Sri and his followers founded Kodzi and later settled on the lagoon island of Fiahor (literally, 'chief's hut'). Wenya sent for his nephew to join him at Anloga.[34] Through the process of naming, the new Anlo landscape was made recognizable and invested with meaning. Settlements and their names constituted signposts in the Anlo historical experience.

Bodies of water dominated the land the Anlo ancestors moved into, and the surface area of Anloland offered little arable or solid land for settlement. This explains the concentration of settlements along the narrow coastal strip and the northern shore of the Keta Lagoon. The geographical features of Anloland from south to north are: a narrow coastal sand bar from the Volta River east to Aflao; the Keta, Avu and Angaw Lagoons, with their associated islands, creeks and marshland; and plains extending north of the Keta Lagoon to the southern border of Togo.[35] A series of depressions marked the coastal strip between Whuti and Tegbi, perceived as the former basins of

[30] Mamattah, *Ewes of West Africa*, 129.

[31] Evans Klutse, 'A social history of Keta – an Anlo community' (BA Thesis, History Department, University of Ghana, 1976), 11.

[32] Ibid., 12.

[33] Sophia Amable, 'The 1953 riot in Anloga and its aftermath' (BA thesis, History Department, University of Ghana, 1977), 5.

[34] Amenumey, 'Brief history', 15–16; Aduamah, *Ewe Traditions*, no. 1, 20–1.

[35] D.A. Chapman, *The Anlo Constitution* (Accra, 1944), 3; idem, *Our Homeland A Regional Geography*, Book 1: *South-east Gold Coast* (Accra, 1943), 1–3.

dried-up lagoons.[36] Anlo soil is sandy and infertile, and these depressions constituted an important part of the scarce arable land. Anloland is situated in the Benin (Dahomey) Gap, the natural extension of savannah land that interrupts the West African forest belt and extends to the coast between the Volta River and the Lagos Channel. This open land facilitated commercial and cultural exchanges among the Ewe-speaking peoples and sustained the political ambitions of Aja states such as Allada, Whydah and Dahomey.[37]

The area of south-eastern Ghana exhibited a complex drainage system. A hydrographic study of the area, commissioned by the colonial government in 1945, underscores this intricate hydrology:

> There are only two perennial rivers, the Volta and the Todje. The Volta is subject to tidal influence up to Sopwe, and below that point the water becomes brackish or salty in the dry season when the flow of fresh water is not strong. The lagoons and deserted river channels north and west of Kaja lagoon hold permanent fresh water, including the upper part of the Angaw lagoon. Kaja and Duse lagoons and the part of Angaw channel below them become brackish in the dry season. Kunye lagoon, which is a depression with no discharge, holds fresh water throughout the year. East of the River Volta the network of lagoons and channels is fed with fresh water from the Todje River. The river discharges into Avu lagoon, from which the water finds its way to the sea by a network of channels; these lead via Eka lagoon to the River Volta, via Nugui, Kpenigago and Lugui lagoons to Keta lagoon, and via Hurontololi lagoon and a series of smaller lagoons and channels to Agblatuhu channel and the mouth of the River Volta.[38]

This quote emphasizes the impressive interconnections between these numerous bodies of water in south-eastern Ghana. The Atlantic Ocean, the Volta and Todzie Rivers, and the large Keta, Avu and Angaw Lagoons were all linked in a unique hydrological regime. The Volta flows into the Atlantic Ocean, but its estuary is often sand-blocked and is characterized by islands. In the low tides or dry season, the river lacks the force to break through to the sea and meanders in both directions of the estuary in a parallel course to the coast, creating lagoons in the process. These lagoons thus remain connected to the Volta and the sea.[39] The presence of brackish water in the lower Volta and the connected lagoons created an aquatic culture favourable to both freshwater and marine fish. The degree of brackishness also determined possible sites of salt manufacture on the lagoons. Rainfall also contributed to the volume of water in the rivers and lagoons. Rainfall is unpredictable in this area, and between 25 and 30 inches of rain fall in the main rainy season between March and June. The variability of rainfall makes drought and flooding frequent occurrences, as the slow-moving lagoons do not drain easily.[40] The connected hydrology of the lower Volta highlights the transformative potential of a Volta River dam for the environment of

---

[36] Greene, 'Land, lineage and clan', 453.

[37] See Law, *Slave Coast of West Africa*. On the Aja people in the precolonial era, see A.I. Asiwaju and Robin Law, 'From the Volta to the Niger, c. 1600–1800', in J.F.A. Ajayi and Michael Crowder, eds, *History of West Africa*, Vol. 1 (Essex, 1985), 412–64; and I. A. Akinjogbin, *Dahomey and its Neighbours 1708–1778* (Cambridge, 1967).

[38] N.R. Juner and D.A. Bates, *Reports on the Geology and Hydrology of the Coastal Area East of the Akwapian Range* (Accra, 1945), 18.

[39] F.R. Irvine, *Fishes and Fisheries of the Gold Coast* (London, 1947), 8.

[40] Greene, 'Land, lineage and clan', 452.

the Volta delta.[41] These physical features reveal the environmental challenge faced by the Anlo migrants.

Lacking maritime skills, early Anlo migrants shunned exploiting the sea. Geographical factors along the coast east of the Volta were not conducive to seafaring. For West Africa as a whole, John Hargreaves has pointed to 'the geomorphology of the coastline, the pattern of prevailing winds, the lack of relatively sheltered seas which could, like the Baltic or Mediterranean, serve as navigational nurseries'.[42] Maritime communities along the West African coast were few and far between, the Kru of Liberia and the Ga and Fanti of the Gold Coast being notable exceptions.[43] The coast east of the Volta experiences heavy surf and is marked by a sand bar, which rendered embarkation and landing dangerous. This is worsened by the open beach and the absence of sheltered landing places comparable to the rocky headlands west of the Volta.[44] Law has argued that before the eighteenth century the Anlo of south-east Ghana seldom ventured out on to the open sea.[45] In the 1780s, P.E. Isert, a Danish physician who visited the Anlo region, recorded that Anlo towns faced the lagoon with their backs to the sea.[46] The Volta River served as an interesting divide in maritime skills. Early European accounts lauded the navigational skills of the Fanti and the Ga, and ships travelling to the Slave Coast took aboard Fanti canoemen and their canoes to facilitate the offloading of goods east of the Volta. Jean Barbot, writing in 1688, praised the Mina (Elmina) as 'the fittest and most experienced men to manage and paddle the canoes over the bars and breakings'.[47] People east of the Volta explored the calmer waters of the lagoon system that extended east of the Volta estuary to Lagos.[48] According to A.B. Ellis, this lagoon highway had silted up between Elmina Chica and Bagida and at Godomey by the late nineteenth century.[49] But Law

[41] See Chapter 6.

[42] J.D. Hargreaves, 'The Atlantic Ocean in West African history', in Jerry Stone, ed., *Africa and the Sea* (Aberdeen, 1985), 5.

[43] See, for examples, George Brooks, *The Kru Mariner in the Nineteenth Century: A Historical Compendium* (Newark, 1972); James B. Christensen, 'Motor power and woman power: technological and economic change among the Fanti fishermen of Ghana', in M.E. Smith, ed., *Those who Live from the Sea: A Study in Maritime Anthropology* (St Paul, NY, 1977), 71–95; and Peter C. W. Gutkind, 'Trade and labor in early precolonial African history: the canoemen of southern Ghana', in Catherine Coquery-Vidrovitch and Paul E. Lovejoy, eds, *The Workers of African Trade* (Beverly Hills, 1985), 25–49.

[44] J.D. Fage, 'A commentary on Duarte Pacheco Pereira's account of the lower Guinea coastlands in his *Esmeraldo de Situ Orbis*, and on some other early accounts', *History in Africa* 7 (1980): 64. Pacheco Pereira wrote between 1505 and 1508.

[45] Law, *Slave Coast of West Africa*, 42.

[46] Paul Erdmann Isert, *Letters on West Africa and the Slave Trade (1788)*, trans. and ed. Selena A. Winsnes (Oxford, 1992), 42; Grove, 'Economy of the Volta delta', 383. Isert became the first commandant of the Danish Fort Kongensten, built on the Ada mainland in the early 1780s. Isert's book was originally published in German as *Journey to Guinea and the Caribbean Islands in Columbia* (Copenhagen, 1788). The pagination used here is that of the Winsnes edition, though Isert's original pagination is indicated in Winsnes's translation.

[47] Cited in Robert Smith, 'The canoe in West African history', *Journal of African History* 11, 4 (1970): 516–17. On the role of Fante canoemen in early Euro-African trade on the Gold Coast, see, especially, Gutkind, 'The canoemen of southern Ghana'.

[48] See, for example, Robin Law, 'Between the sea and the lagoon: the interaction of maritime and inland navigation on the precolonial Slave Coast', *Cahiers d'Etudes Africaines* 114, xxix-2 (1989): 209–37.

[49] A.B. Ellis, *The Ewe Speaking Peoples of the Slave Coast of West Africa* (London, 1890), ix.

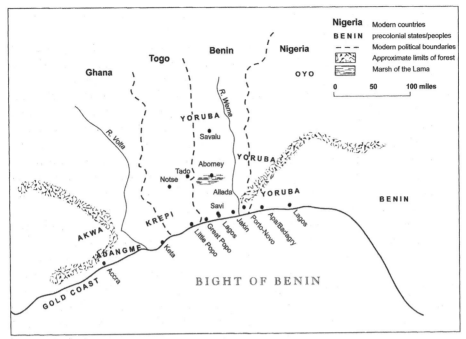

Map 1.2 Slave Coast of West Africa   (Source: Robin Law, *The Slave Coast of West Africa 1550–1750* (Oxford, 1991), 18).

points out that seventeenth-century European accounts noted that the lagoon tended to disappear in the dry season around Jakin (Godomey).[50] Indeed, Jakin's economic prosperity was based on that very accident of geography for it served as the overland connection between Glehue (modern Ouidah or Whydah) and Lake Nokwe (Map 1.2).[51]

The aquatic environment shaped the economies and societies that emerged in south-eastern Ghana from the mid-seventeenth century. The dearth of land that characterized this region created a fierce attachment to land among the Anlo, and the influx of war refugees from west of the Volta in the late seventeenth century precipitated the formation of clans to control access to land.[52] This is in sharp contrast to studies of maritime societies, which underscore the lack of attachment to land.[53] The land-bound heritage of the Anlo migrants may partly account for this difference, and land pressure may have influenced the constant migration of Anlo's ancestors. The little land available in Anlo was far from arable. Willem Bosman, a Dutch trader, visited Keta in 1698 and described it thus:

[50] Law, 'Between the sea and the lagoon', 214.

[51] Ibid., 210. Manning, 'Coastal society in the Republic of Benin: reproduction of a regional system', *Cahiers d'Etudes Africaines* 114, xxix–2 (1989): 239–57, provides a description of the lagoon system and trade in the Republic of Benin from the fifteenth century to the present.

[52] Greene, *History of the Anlo-Ewe*.

[53] See, for examples, A.H.J. Prins, *Sailing from Lamu: A Study of Maritime Culture in Islamic East Africa* (Assen, 1965); and Rita Astuti, *People of the Sea: Identity and Descent among the Vezo of Madagascar* (Cambridge, 1995).

31

The land of Coto [Keta] is of a direct contrary sort of nature to that of the Gold Coast; for as the latter is full of hills, so the former hath not one; but the soil is flat, sandy, dry, barren, and void of all trees except the palm or wild coco; of which it produceth a great number.[54]

Exploiting the aquatic environment was imperative to Anlo survival. Areas around Keta and further east focused on lagoon fishing and salt making, as that part of the Keta Lagoon was more saline. Brackish water enhanced the species of available fish, and evaporation in the dry season facilitated the natural formation of salt crystals on the lagoon bed. Further west around Anloga, a more extensive sand bar, the deeper waters of the lagoon (especially around Woe) and the entry of fresh water from the Todzie through the adjacent Avu Lagoon eliminated salt making and encouraged agriculture.[55] The Keta Lagoon – and its shores and islands – was perhaps the most important economic resource base in early Anlo.[56] Considering that the entire Anlo coastline from the Volta estuary to Aflao measures 42 miles and Anlo seldom exceeds 35 miles from south to north, the lagoon occupied the larger part of the Anlo landscape.

In addition to dealing with a novel environment, Anlo settlement in south-eastern Ghana coincided with a period of severe droughts, further testing the mettle of the migrants. Sharon Nicholson and George Brooks have established through climate studies that the period from c.1630 to 1860 coincided with a dry phase in West Africa.[57] In the area of south-east Ghana, severe droughts occurred in 1661, 1680 and 1683.[58] Religion and the intercession of autochthonous deities were crucial to Anlo survival in this early transition. The migrants discovered on their arrival in Anlo that the stool Sri I had been installed upon had been left in their haste in Notsie. The stool was named *tsikpe* ('rain-stone') and was credited with rain-making powers.[59] The Anlo connected its absence to the period of drought and infertility. Retrieving the stool was urgent for Anlo's survival, and yet Sri's son, Fui Agbeve, refused the dangerous undertaking.[60] Greene provides an account of what transpired, whereby, according to Anlo oral traditions:

A meeting was called and they decided to go to Notsie to bring the stool. The sent a delegation of Adeladza [founder of the Bate clan, a nephew of Sri] and Amesimeku Atogolo [founder of the Like clan and also a nephew to Sri] to convince Togbui Agokoli to give up the stool … When they went there, Togbui Agokoli refused to give it to them unless they brought the head of Togbui Sri I. The nephews … conferred and left quietly. When they returned [to Anlo] they reported the message … There was no alternative … Having looked around, they saw that Amega Le I [founder of the Wifeme clan] had a follower whose arm was spotted by yaws [as was the arm of Sri][61] … They had a council with Le and he agreed to allow his servant, Foli, to carry their

[54] Bosman, *New and Accurate Description*, 307.
[55] Grove and Johansen, 'Historical geography of the Volta delta', 1386.
[56] The lagoon currently measures 12 miles from south to north and 20 miles from west to east when full.
[57] Sharon Nicholson, 'The methodology of historical climate reconstruction and its application to Africa', *Journal of African History* 20, 1 (1979): 47; George Brooks, 'A historical schema for Western Africa based on seven climate periods', *Cahiers d'Etudes Africaines* 26 (1986): 44–5.
[58] Greene, *History of Anlo-Ewe*, 53.
[59] NAG, Accra, ADM 41/5/8; Greene, *History of Anlo-Ewe*, 53–4.
[60] Aduamah, *Ewe Traditions*, no. 1: 5.
[61] It is unclear to the author whether Sri I had yaws or a peculiar skin pigmentation on his hand (birthmark). Intriguingly, Sri II (1907–56) had the same odd skin pigmentation on his hand. Though not mentioned in the

baggage and accompany them to Notsie without revealing to Foli [their agreement to kill the servant and deliver his arm to Agokoli in lieu of Sri's head]. Foli ignorantly went on the errand ... When near Notsie, Foli was killed by Amesimeku who with the arm wrapped in leaves, went with it to Togbui Agokoli ... They told him 'Togbui Sri is old and feeble; it was useless to kill him and bring the head so we cut his arm.'[62]

Agokoli relented and released the stool to Adeladza and Amesimeku.

Adeladza and Amesimeku, two of the hunters cited by Anlo traditions for discovering the site of Anlo in hunting expeditions from Notsie, thus played a significant role in establishing the viability of the Anlo polity. On their return, a delighted Sri proclaimed that Adeladza be made *awoamefia* after him, and that the *awoame* stool should henceforth alternate between the Adzovia and Bate clans. Though the traditions laud Amesimeku's role in the retrieval of the stool, he and his Like clan were rendered ineligible for kingship, since he performed the actual deed of killing Foli. The return of the stool occasioned abundant rainfall and general fertility.[63] The environment was being made cognitively accessible, and the fertility of nature and culture symbolized a symbiotic relationship or the successful occupancy of the land. The *awoamefia* became a secluded priest-king, mediating Anlo's relations with nature from hidden groves (*awoame*). Oral traditions indicate that the Anlo evaluated the reigns of the early *awoamefia* by their ability or inability to control natural disasters such as plagues of locusts, droughts and famines.[64]

Adeladza is also credited with the courtship of Mama Bate, an autochthonous goddess who is perceived as instrumental to the accretion of the beach along the Anlo coastline, which made possible the development of the littoral. Greene comments:

> She [Mama Bate] and other *dzokpleanyi trowo* [autochthonous gods] that lived in the area are said to have created the very land on which the Anlo established their new homes. They reportedly did so by commanding the sea to retreat from the littoral, thereby creating the extensive set of depressions ... in which the Anlo found the only soils suitable for agricultural activity.[65]

The clan Adeladza founded was named Bate in honour of this association with Mama Bate, and the clan gained a reputation for its spiritual power. Oral traditions claim that the coastline was closer at the time of migration than it is today.[66] It is certain that as late as the end of the nineteenth century, and maybe even at the turn of the twentieth

[61 (cont.)] historical records, this may have strengthened his nomination as *awoamefia* in 1906. Instructively, he took as his stool name Sri. The author breached the norms of decorum, when he noticed the same birthmark on the hand of Esther Kwawukume, daughter of Sri II. He politely enquired about this physical anomaly, and was informed that it was a birthmark. Thus, the trait appears to be genetic. Interview with Esther Kwawukume, Keta, 25 January 1997. Winsnes comments that the congenital condition of Africans with white hands and feet that Isert encountered on his visit to Whydah in 1784–5 could be vitiligo, 'a condition characterised by local lack of pigmentation'. Isert, *Letters on West Africa*, 108, fn. 49. Considering the Anlo requirement that the *awoamefia* must be free from physical deformities, the king-makers apparently did not consider Sri II's 'bleached hand' as a deformity. See Nukunya, 'Social and political organization', 63.

[62] Greene, 'Anlo-Ewe oral tradition', 75.

[63] Interview with Togbui James Ocloo IV, *dufia* (chief) of Keta, 24 January 1997; and Aduamah, *Ewe Traditions*, no. 1: 6.

[64] NAG, Accra, ADM 41/5/8.

[65] Greene, *History of the Anlo-Ewe*, 54.

[66] Interview with Togbui Honi II and Togbuivi Kumassah, Woe, 24 January 1997.

century, the area around Keta was gaining beach land through the process of attrition and accretion caused by longshore movements of the ocean. It is uncertain, however, exactly when this land gain commenced. A.B. Ellis, the DC of Keta in 1878, observed that 'it is evident that the continent is at this part gaining upon the sea'.[67] He further remarked that:

> In 1878 a sand-bank began to appear above water at Quittah [Keta], parallel with and about two hundred yards from the existing beach, and, as far as I could then ascertain, it was caused solely by the action of the current.[68]

Anlo oral traditions record that this accretion of shoreline was a later development after the Anlo settlement.[69] It appeared that local gods had endorsed the Anlo settlement in their new habitat. Gods, especially autochthonous ones, are central to settlement in foreign lands by migrant groups in precolonial Africa. The co-optation of such local gods facilitated the cognitive grasp of new landscapes.[70]

Between the lagoon and the sea

The dynamics of a natural economy

The Anlo migrants initially lacked technological sophistication in the aquatic environment, and hunting and gathering dominated the early economy. This was especially so during the phase of migration or constant movement. As they settled, traditions have it that the migrants grew beans and guinea-corn.[71] Greene has argued that for the late seventeenth and early eighteenth centuries, cultivation of food crops was the primary occupation in Anloland.[72] Farming was the major strength in the technological repertoire of the agrarian Anlo. In this early period, only the coastal depressions were brought under cultivation, for the barren and highly saline soil of the lagoon side was then uncultivable under the limited agrarian techniques. Greene reports on the use of fish and vegetable manure in this early period, and a system of shifting cultivation. Crops were harvested once a year.[73] The dispersed nature of settlement in early Anlo, in spite of the coherent kinship networks of the migrants, suggests that agricultural production was inadequate to support concentrated settlements. It was imperative that the early migrants tap into the resources of their aquatic habitat. In this initial endeavour they harvested nature, using land as a subject of labour.

---

[67] Ellis, *Ewe-Speaking Peoples*, 2.

[68] Ibid., 3.

[69] Interview with Togbi Honi II and Togbuivi Kumassah, Woe, 24 January 1997.

[70] See Jack Goody, *Technology, Tradition, and the State in Africa* (London, 1971), ch. 4; Igor Kopytoff, 'The internal African frontier: the making of African political culture', in idem, ed., *The African Frontier: The Reproduction of Traditional African Societies* (Bloomington, 1987), 3–84; Carola Lentz, 'Agricultural expansion in changing contexts: settlement histories in southwestern Burkina Faso' (paper presented at Harvard University, October 1998).

[71] Aduamah, *Ewe Traditions*, no. 1: 21.

[72] Sandra E. Greene, 'Social change in eighteenth-century Anlo: the role of technology, markets and military conflict', *Africa* 58, 1 (1988): 73.

[73] Greene, 'Land, lineage and clan', 454.

The Keta Lagoon Basin

Through daily contact and use, Anlo knowledge of their new environment grew.

It is striking how even the sparse vegetation that grew in the highly infertile soils along the lagoon and seashore found multiple uses. On this imaginative use of nature's scarce resources, Nukunya notes that:

The land immediately bordering the seashore is very sandy and its vegetation is greatly limited. However, where the soil is coarse and underlain by a thicker layer, thorny creepers with large burns are found. But midway between the sea and the lagoons, the soil is darker and richer and here we find a species of thatch (*Imperatus cylindrica*) locally known as *be*. Also found here are groves of a stunted tree with a very hard stem, tangled branches and stiff leaves called *fotigba* (*Chrysobalamus orbicularis*). Mangoes and palm trees are also found in fairly large numbers. Another common tree is a species of fig (*Ficus polita*), locally known as *agbafloti* which is planted solely to provide shade and firewood because its fruit is not edible. Other common trees are *avia* (*Newbouldia locuis*) and *kpokplo* (*Ficus umbellata*) both of which are used to support fences of palm branches around houses ...

The lagoon shores, marked by wetter and heavier soils, produce a luxuriant growth of grass which is softer and shorter than grasses of the sea-board. Where the soil is more compact and less moist, a typical lagoon tree (*Avicennia germinanus*) locally known as *amuti*, which is also associated with the Volta River is found ... A related tree is the mangrove which is also found at the mouth of the Volta and is locally known as *atra* or *atrati*.[74]

Nature's resources were utilized to the optimum. According to traditions, the reeds that grew around the fringes of the lagoon provided the base for a mat-weaving industry. These reeds also provided thatch roofs for houses.[75] The fruit of the coconut tree along the seashore was edible, and its shell served as wood fuel. The oil-palm grew wild in the region and contributed to the Anlo diet. Its fibre provided the earliest textiles on the Slave Coast.[76] Women also used the palm fronds to weave baskets, while men used the fronds to weave mats, which served as fences for houses.[77] The easy accommodation with nature, the non-invasive ways in which a livelihood could be secured, prompted Tetteh Asimetsi, founder of the much later town of Afiadenyigba, to comment that: 'there is no place on earth where the land itself works for the man settling on it and provides him with the requisite food'.

The migrants' early experience with lagoon resources followed the pattern of serendipitous encounters:

A discovery brought by the alternate drying and rising of the lagoons was fishing. For when the lagoons dried many fishes are naturally left in the hollows. When people saw fish for the first time they collected these by baling out the water by hand, so that the fishes could be caught. In this way game was supplemented with fish. Arrows and spears were used in course of time to kill the fishes.[78]

Anlo traditions affirm that unfamiliarity with boats compelled the early migrants to restrict their fishing activities to the shallower parts of the Keta Lagoon.[79] Early

[74] G.K. Nukunya, 'The land and the people', in Francis Agbodeka, ed., *A Handbook of Eweland*, Vol. I: *The Ewes of Southeastern Ghana* (Accra, 1997), 10.

[75] Interview with Togbuivi Kumassah, Woe, 3 September 1996.

[76] Law, *Slave Coast of West Africa*, 44.

[77] Interview with Togbuivi Kumassah, Woe, 3 September 1996.

[78] Aduamah, *Ewe Traditions*, no. 1: 22.

[79] Greene, 'Social change in eighteenth-century Anlo', 70.

experimentation with canoe technology was not very successful. The first canoe was hollowed out of the trunk of the local fan palm or *agô* (*Borassus aethiopium*) and was called *agôwu*, but it capsized easily.[80] Likewise, Anlo oral traditions state that the migrants lacked the technology for systematic extraction of salt from the saline waters of the Keta Lagoon, apart from the salt crystals yielded naturally when the lagoon dried up. Indeed, salt extracted from vegetable material remained important in this early phase.[81]

New technologies and the exploitation of environmental resources

The way for a more systematic exploitation of aquatic resources, 'land' as an instrument of labour, was paved by the entry of war refugees from west of the Volta from the 1670s. These strangers brought technological skills that improved boat making and salt extraction. Oral traditions collected by Greene indicate that Aduadui, a refugee from the Adangme State of Ladoku and founder of the Dzevi clan, introduced the technique of producing salt from the saline waters of the Keta Lagoon. This technique, which involved evaporation of saline water, resulted in crystal-white salt in abundant quantity. Aduadui probably arrived in Anloga in 1679, when Akwamu launched its first military expedition against Ladoku.[82] A later campaign by Akwamu against Ladoku in 1702 forced another wave of refugees into Anlo. Included in this influx were Amega Le and his followers. Amega Le, Anlo traditions claim, was part of the Dogbo migrants from Notsie, whose wanderings took him to Accra and Ladoku before rejoining his kinsfolk at Anloga. He made canoes for his followers to cross the Volta River to Anlo and subsequently introduced canoes on the lagoon in Anlo.[83] Le introduced a more stable canoe, the *lemu*, still in use in Anlo. Greene raises the strong possibility that Amega Le was not Anlo, but a refugee from Ladoku.[84] There is an interesting contradiction here, for Greene, in the tradition cited earlier in this chapter about the retrieval of the stool from Notsie puts Foli, Amega Le's servant, in the company of Adeladza and Amesimeku. Indeed, it was Foli's discoloured arm that prompted Agokoli to release the stool. If this incident occurred shortly after Anlo settlement and Amega Le supposedly arrived in Anlo around 1702, it is difficult to reconcile these two accounts. This does not rule out the possible engineering of tradition to insert Amega Le, a valuable latecomer, in the founding traditions of Anlo.[85]

These refugees brought new tensions into Anlo, for they put severe pressure on scarce land resources, precipitating the process of clan (*hlo*) formation to restrict access to land to 'insiders'.[86] The Anlo themselves prefer to see the development of

[80] Aduamah, *Ewe Traditions*, no. 1: 22; Greene, 'Social change in eighteenth-century Anlo', 70.

[81] Greene, 'Social change in eighteenth-century Anlo', 71.

[82] Ibid. On the cultural and linguistic legacy of Adangme migrants in Eweland, see R.G.S. Sprigge, 'Eweland's Adangbe', *Transactions of the Historical Society of Ghana* 10 (1969): 87–128.

[83] Mamattah, *Ewes of West Africa*, 136–9; interview with Togbui Honi II and Togbuivi Kumassah, Woe, 24 January 1997.

[84] Greene, 'Social change in eighteenth-century Anlo', 70.

[85] G.K. Nukunya drew the author's attention to this contradiction. Personal correspondence, 28 September 1999.

[86] Greene, *History of the Anlo-Ewe*.

clans as a response to administrative needs in the growing polity.[87] The emergence of a complex polity also reflected the growth of technological sophistication, a more secure material base and the expansion or condensation of settlements. Each clan was associated with specific functions or skills. Today, there are fifteen clans in Anlo, and the Anlo openly acknowledge three – Dzevi, Vifeme and Blu – as founded by foreigners.[88] The induction of outsiders as insiders over the Anlo past may have drastically revised the public transcript, for outsiders who brought powerful gods, acquired great wealth and rendered important services to the Anlo polity were redefined as insiders and provided with the appropriate genealogy and traditions.[89]

These strangers brought new technology, and the process of technological infiltration may have begun even before 1679. It has been pointed out that European trading ships often took on Fanti canoemen and their canoes from Elmina to facilitate the off-loading of goods on the Slave Coast. A group of Fanti canoemen from Elmina had settled permanently at Anexo by the mid-seventeenth century.[90] The Fanti were noted for their maritime skills and were adept at canoe navigation and sea fishing. Wilhelm Johann Muller, a German chaplain at the Danish Fort Frederiksborg, in the vicinity of Cape Coast, provided illuminating information on Fanti seafaring skills in the 1660s:

> Every day except Tuesday (which, as mentioned, they celebrate in honour of their sea-gods), they go in large numbers 2 or 3 miles out into the open sea to fish in *cano* [canoe], a small fishing boat called *ehenne* by the Blacks. Their principal fishing tackle consists of a net, hooks and barbed spears for throwing or stabbing with, generally harpoons.
> They make their fishing nets out of a tree-bark, by beating long leaves, such as those of *benninas* or palm tree,[91] with a club, plaiting twine from the veins of the leaves, winding it on to a spindle and then preparing nets with large and small mesh, after the manner of European fishermen.[92]

Boat-making and net technology may have spread more easily from Anexo to the Anlo because of the open nature of the savannah.

One of the earliest descriptions of net manufacture in the Volta delta area underscores the similarity in methods. In 1774 the Danish Governor Aarestrup sent a report to the home company on agriculture and local trade in the Danish sphere of influence in the Guinea. On fishing in the Volta delta area, he commented:

> The negroes make a kind of thread, both for sewing and for making fishing nets. They take the largest pineapple leaves they can find, soak them in water for twelve hours, and then beat them on an even piece of wood or stone, with a very straight or even wooden hammer until the green part

[87] Interview with Togbui Honi II and Togbuivi Kumassah, Woe, 24 January 1997.

[88] Nukunya, 'Social and political organization', 48.

[89] Greene, *History of the Anlo-Ewe*, chs 2–3.

[90] Reindorf, *Gold Coast and Asante*, 37; Law, *Slave Coast of West Africa*, 24–5.

[91] The translator and editor of Muller's document, Adam Jones, notes that *benninas* could mean either pineapple or plantain.

[92] 'Wilhelm Johann Muller's description of the Fetu country, 1662–9', in Adam Jones, *German Sources for West African History 1599–1669* (Wiesbaden, 1983), 231–2. See also Bosman, *New and Accurate Description*, 38, 48. In Anlo Wednesday is generally observed as the fishermen's day of rest and a day for fishing rituals, but some Anlo fishing communities prefer Tuesday. This flexibility may indicate that there is no rigid religious reason for the selection of a day of rest.

of the leaves disappears and they become quite mouldy. After that they pull the leaves through a wooden knife on the piece of wood until nothing but the strings of the leaves are left. These they wash in fresh water until they become quite white. When dry, they twist them on their right thigh till they become as thick as they want them.[93]

However, the origin of this technology is unclear, though the technique could have spread from the Fanti canoemen in Anexo. The coastal Hula had a pre-European tradition of lagoon fishing and salt making.[94] A further concentration of skilled fishermen and seafarers occurred with the Akwamu defeat of Accra between 1677 and 1681 and the relocation of Ga refugees east of the Volta to found the state of Little Popo on the coast of Togo in the 1680s. The Gen (Ge) state, or Little Popo as known by Europeans, absorbed the Fanti community at Anexo.[95] Notwithstanding the introduction of technologies that promoted a more systematic exploitation of the aquatic – and, indeed, the marine – world, the absence of markets held these innovations in check until the 1720s, and sea fishing had to wait until the nineteenth century. But, by strengthening occupational pursuits and the generation of surplus, these new technologies promoted the internal consolidation of Anlo economy and society.

Economy and society in the Keta Lagoon basin

The Ewe of south-eastern Ghana appear to have organized their communities quickly after settlement, for they were able to militarily assist Accra refugees in the 1680s against the Be-Ewe of the Togo coast. Indeed, Anlo in 1682 successfully repulsed a punitive force sent against her by Great Popo, the overlord of the Be.[96] Again, in 1694, Anlo allied with Whydah in another military confrontation with Great Popo.[97] The scarcity of land, the influx of refugees, the expansionist aspirations of states west and east of the Volta, and the growing awareness of trade systems along the coast and into the interior galvanized the rapid social organization of the Anlo and their neighbours. The results were an elaboration of the clan system and a more defined Anlo identity, the establishment of early trade networks that facilitated the exchange of basic agricultural commodities produced in different environmental niches, Anlo expansionism in a search for more land and increasing Anlo incorporation into the Atlantic trade.

The exchange of local food produce dominated the economy of south-eastern Ghana in the late seventeenth and eighteenth centuries. Throughout this period, societies of the Slave Coast in general remained basically agricultural, and local trade was more central to the early Anlo economy than international trade.[98] Polities north

---

[93] Grove and Johansen, 'Historical geography of the Volta delta', 1388.

[94] Law, *Slave Coast of West Africa*, 42–3.

[95] Bosman, *New and Accurate Description*, 61–2; Reindorf, *Gold Coast and Asante*, 25; Law, *Slave Coast of West Africa*, 25. For Anexo oral traditions tracing the Elmina and Accra antecedents, see Nicoue L. Gayibor, ed., *Sources orales de la région d'Aneho* (Niamey, 1980). The traditions emphasize the role of the Ajigo (Elmina) ancestors at Anexo as boatmen and fishermen from the seventeenth century.

[96] Grove and Johansen, 'Historical geography of the Volta delta', 1378.

[97] Law, *Slave Coast of West Africa*, 60–1.

[98] Ibid., 33–5; Grove and Johansen, 'Historical geography of the Volta delta', 1387.

of the lagoon had more arable land, and trade developed across the lagoon linking north and south, and in an east–west direction via the coastal lagoon system.

[Thus] ... much of the north–south and east–west trade conducted by the Anlo during this period was primarily a use-value exchange involving the sale of locally produced surplus fish for those commodities not produced in Anlo society, such as yams and the red ochre used in religious ceremonies.[99]

The Danish Governor Aarestrup, in a 1774 report to his home company on agriculture and local trade in the Danish sphere of influence, commented on the exchange of millet, rice, palm oil, beans, yams, dried fish and salt.[100]

Salt was a valuable item in the east–west coasting trade, but the Anlo had little salt. Anlo thus specialized in fishing and agriculture, and Isert in 1784 found many farms with plantains, bananas, yams and sugar-cane on the seaward side.[101] Keta and its fishing and salt-making villages of Agudza and Kpoduwa (Pottebra) were better endowed in their aquatic resources. Isert left a vivid, later description of the salt and fishing industries in this eastern section of the Keta Lagoon, where the sand spit separating sea and lagoon was also narrower:

The Augnas and Pottebras live mainly by extracting salt from sea water, and by fishing. Enormous quantities of salt were found in store. Next to every house there are one or two great haystack-shaped huts made of thick, very tightly woven grass huts, with very strong roofs of the same material. These huts are filled with clean salt that they produce ... The method of preparing the salt is as simple as it is easy. When the sea is very high it floods over the beach and leaves a pool of water on the smooth, loamy, sandy ground. The excessively hot rays of the sun in this land cause the moisture to evaporate very quickly and the salt solidifies with the mud. The Blacks gather this crust into a pile, throw it into a hole which they have dug in a clean, dry sand and pour sea water over it. They allow the salt to dissolve and then solidify in the sunshine again. By this process the impurities settle at the bottom of the hole. The crystal-white salt is then removed and stored for use.[102]

Isert opined that Keta had the most favourable location in the Danish sphere of influence, the lagoon there being full of delicious fish, crabs and oysters.[103] Crabs were present exactly because of the brackish water at Keta, which also endowed the residents on the south-east end of the lagoon with salt.

Wars of state formation amongst the Akan west of the Volta between the 1670s and 1730s inundated the Ewe of south-eastern Ghana with refugees. Mention has already been made of the effects of Akwamu's wars against Accra and Ladoku between the 1670s and 1702. In 1698 Denkyira crushed Assin's power in the central region of the Gold Coast.[104] Asante's defeat of Denkyira in 1701 also sent a stream of Akan refugees to the lower Volta.[105] Banditry became widespread east of the Volta between the 1670s and the early 1700s, as destabilized groups roamed the area. Keta seemed to be a prime

[99] Greene, History of the Anlo-Ewe, 36.
[100] Grove and Johansen, 'Historical geography of the Volta delta', 1389.
[101] Isert, Letters on West Africa, 56.
[102] Ibid., 60.
[103] Ibid., 75.
[104] Dickson, Historical Geography of Ghana, 107.
[105] Amenumey, 'Brief history', 17.

target, a fact that might indicate that the Keta had begun to exploit their natural resources for commercial gain. Jean Barbot commented in the 1680s that there were few wealthy men in Keta, 'and the generality being very poor, many of them turn strolling robbers about the country, and do much mischief'.[106] Ray Kea has provided an intriguing account of one such group that operated on the western Slave Coast.

> One group of Keta bandits operated along the coastal overland route that linked Keta and Ofra, the main port of Ardra [Allada] kingdom, about 130 km away. The bandits were active between 1675 and 1683. The leader was Aban, and he had about fifty followers. Aban and his men pillaged caravans and murdered travellers, particularly official messengers who travelled from one port to another. They disappear after 1683, but others replace them. One unusual band of piratical brigands specialized in pillaging sloops and other small boats that traded at the ports between the Volta River and the coastal town of Whydah ... At Keta they plundered an English boat and killed many of its crew.[107]

Keta's wealthy men served as provisioners of passing ships and as middlemen in the lagoon trade east of the Volta. They also supplied the important commodities of salt and fish. Law suggests that an African coasting trade, based on a combination of sea and lagoon navigation, had come into place by 1659 along the Gold and Slave Coasts. Gold Coast (Elmina) canoemen, who had become familiar with the Slave Coast from acting as stevedores for European ships, were crucial to this trade. European traders modified the Gold Coast canoe for use on the Slave Coast by raising the prow for the heavy surf. Gold Coast canoemen adopted this technological improvisation in the coasting trade.[108] Fanti canoemen at Anexo provided the crucial switch from the lagoon system to the sea in the westward movement of goods between the Slave and Gold Coasts.[109] Salt and dried fish moved east in exchange for *cori* or *aggrey* beads and cloth from Yorubaland.[110] Keta may have tapped into the east–west trade at an earlier date than Anlo.

Roving bandits, landless refugees, land scarcity, the growing awareness of trade potential and the increasing militarization of the western portion of the Slave Coast altered Anlo–Ewe society in profound ways. The Anlo moved away from an internal distinction between clans in charge of Notsie gods and those in charge of autochthonous ones to an insider versus outsider differentiation. Clans emerged or cohered and first-comers emphasized descent from a related group of ancestors who migrated from Notsie. The Anlo also exhibited a clear preference for clan endogamy to prevent the loss of land from Anlo women marrying strangers.[111] Prior to this, Anlo social

---

[106] Cited in Ray A. Kea, '"I am here to plunder on the general road": bandits and banditry in the pre-nineteenth-century Gold Coast', in Donald Crummey, ed., *Banditry, Rebellion and Social Protest in Africa* (London, 1986), 118–19. Kea points out in this important contribution that banditry was a persistent phenomenon in pre-1800 Gold Coast. Banditry emerged on trade routes with the rise of mercantilism.

[107] Ibid., 119.

[108] Law, 'Between the sea and the lagoon', 227.

[109] Ibid.

[110] See also Robin Law, 'Trade and politics behind the Slave Coast: the lagoon traffic and the rise of Lagos 1500–1800', *Journal of African History* 24, 3 (1983): 321–48; Manning, 'Coastal society in the Republic of Benin'; and idem, 'Merchants, porters, and canoemen in the Bight of Benin', in Coquery-Vidrovitch and Lovejoy, eds, *Workers of African Trade*, 51–74.

[111] Greene, *History of the Anlo-Ewe*, 28–32.

organization may have revolved around patrilineages, similarly to the other Aja peoples of the Slave Coast. Clan membership provided an individual with access to clan lands, gods (*trôwo*) and protection.

Trade opportunities and competition underpinned military rivalry on the western Slave Coast. Anlo and Keta engaged Little Popo in continuous battles from the 1680s. The Accra refugees who established Little Popo, coming from a state with a long trading tradition, quickly recognized the trade potential of the lagoon system that extended along the Slave Coast. They immediately incorporated the Elmina settlement of Anexo into their expanding state and 'wanted to control the trade of the entire area behind the system of lagoons all the way east to the Dahomey coast, and also important coastal markets like Keta'.[112] Anlo in turn also wanted to control the lower Volta basin. Akwamu played an interesting role in the Anlo–Little Popo conflict, propping up the weaker party in these ongoing conflicts to ensure that neither dominated the other.[113] It is possible that Keta may have come to consider the Gen better economic and political allies than their Anlo kinsmen. The valuable lagoon trade lay east of Keta, not west in the direction of Anlo, and Little Popo was crucial to the functioning of lagoon trade on the western Slave Coast. Keta moved into a closer alliance with Little Popo and away from Anlo. It is noteworthy that the kings of Keta and Little Popo promised Bosman security and safe conduct through their lands in 1698 against the threat of banditry.[114] Kea noted a decline in banditry in the Keta–Popo area from the 1690s,[115] and this could have been a result of the joint efforts of Keta and Popo to suppress the banditry that discouraged trade in their area.

In 1702 Akwamu absorbed Anlo, Keta and Little Popo into the Akwamu empire. The year 1708 witnessed the Akwamu conquest of the Krepi of northern Eweland, followed in 1710 by the absorption of the interior Akan state of Kwawu.[116] The exact nature of the Akwamu–Anlo relationship remains contested, and Amenumey has insisted – in contrast to historians such as Wilks, Grove and Johansen, and Greene – that Anlo was an Akwamu ally and not a vassal.[117] Amenumey admits that Akwamu had the wherewithal to annex Anlo, but somehow chose Anlo as an ally. Anlo secured firearms and salt for Akwamu in return for military assistance when required. The defeat of Akwamu by an Akyem–Accra–Akwapim alliance in 1730 loosened or jettisoned Akwamu's control of Anlo. It is striking, though, that Anlo's alliance with Akwamu persisted into the nineteenth century.[118] The presence of Akwamu administrators in Anloga in the early eighteenth century suggests a more formal Akwamu jurisdiction over Anlo.[119] Both Anlo and Keta soon slipped under the hegemony of

[112] Amenumey, 'Brief history', 18. See also Kea, 'Akwamu–Anlo relations', 39–40.

[113] Bosman, *New and Accurate Description*, 306.

[114] Ibid., 307–8.

[115] Kea, 'Bandits and banditry', 119.

[116] Greene, 'Land, lineage and clan', 459.

[117] Amenumey, *Ewe in Pre-Colonial Times*, 32–5; Ivor Wilks, 'The rise of the Akwamu Empire', *Transactions of the Historical Society of Ghana* 3, 2 (1957): 99–136; Grove and Johansen, 'Historical geography of the Volta delta', 1379; Greene, *History of the Anlo-Ewe*.

[118] Kea, 'Akwamu–Anlo relations'.

[119] Greene, *History of the Anlo-Ewe*, 118.

Little Popo in 1741. Anlo overthrew Little Popo's control in 1750, significantly without Keta's cooperation, and Keta remained under Little Popo's influence until the 1770s, when it moved into a closer alliance with Anlo.[120] Even then, Keta opted to be neutral in the 1784 war between Anlo and the Danes. Among the Danish allies was Little Popo, Keta's trading partner and political protector.[121]

The association with Akwamu had provided Anlo with valuable tutelage in military organization. Anlo adopted the wing system of Akwamu, and a three-wing military system – *woe* (right), *lashibi* (left) and *adotri* (centre) – was superimposed on the Anlo clan structure.[122] War chiefs (*asafohene*) emerged, and stools of valour (*kalezi* or *avadezi*) were created for them. Anlo fine-tuned this wing system to suit the geographical outlay of Anlo settlements. Anloga was at the centre, with the settlements to the east providing the core for the right wing – headed by the chief (*asafohenega*) of Woe – and those to the west the core for the left wing, headed initially by the Anyako and later Whuti. The centre was commanded by the *avadada* (war mother), who served as the commander-in-chief of Anlo forces.[123] A land-hungry and security-conscious Anlo waged war north of the Keta Lagoon against the Tefle, Agave and Abolo in the 1730s and 1740s to secure much needed arable land. Some of the Abolo captives were resettled in Anlo and constituted into the Ame clan.[124] In the 1770s, Anlo armies were back in the area north of the Keta Lagoon, this time against Avenor.[125] Anlo were encouraged to relocate to these lands to form a buffer zone, and the settlement of Anyako developed in this way. Anyako is a lagoon island and may have come into use originally as base for Tsiame and Anloga hunters and fishermen.[126] Anyako has the unique feature of possessing all three military wings and their respective *asafohene* in a single town. It made the town a convenient military fulcrum in case of a frontal attack, for it encapsulated the grid system of the Anlo army.[127] Unlike the Akan military system, the Anlo did not need a *kyidom* (rearguard) for the Atlantic Ocean formed its southern boundary. The Keta Lagoon and the Volta River gained new salience as defensive bulwarks.

A more confident Anlo engaged its western Ada neighbours in a series of wars from the 1750s in the bid to dispossess the Ada of their rich salt works based on the Songaw Lagoon and to extend Anlo fishing grounds in the lower Volta. The Anlo also desired to control the Volta River as a trade artery into the interior. The Volta was navigable by canoe as far north as Kete Krachi.[128] An archaeological excavation at the site of Ladoku in 1964 indicated that the Volta was already in use as a conduit of trade

---

[120] Ibid., 37–8.

[121] Isert, *Letters on West Africa*, 59.

[122] Another important influence was the introduction of matrilineal tendencies into Anlo social organization, accounting for the strong element of matrifiliation. See G.K. Nukunya, *Kinship and Marriage among the Anlo Ewe* (London, 1969); idem, 'Social and political organization'; Greene, *History of the Anlo-Ewe*.

[123] NAG, Accra, ADM 11/1/404. Memorandum on Awuna, Addah and Akwamu, 1912 Commission of Inquiry.

[124] Greene, *History of the Anlo-Ewe*, 27, 120.

[125] Amenumey, 'Brief history', 20.

[126] Tobias N. Fiagbedzi, 'Migration and early settlement of Anyako' (BA thesis, History Department, University of Ghana, 1994), 11–12.

[127] Interview with Yao Kumassah, Togbuivi Kumassah and E.K. Keteku, Anyako, 22 April 1997.

[128] Dickson, *Historical Geography of Ghana*, 109.

to the north in the seventeenth century.[129] A contemporary Danish account of the Anlo–Ada rivalry perceptively highlighted the struggle as one over environmental resources:

> From time immemorial the Adas … have been enemies of the Blacks living on the east side of the river. The frequent disputes were mostly because of disagreements about the fishing boundaries … These wars started with small skirmishes, until the parties became so exasperated with each other that war became general. The Adas in particular aroused their neighbours' jealousy partly because they were hosts to the Europeans (namely, our lodge) and partly because of their flourishing saltworks, which bring them the major part of their wealth since they sell the salt so profitably to the Mountain Blacks [Krepis] or to the Assianthees [Asante].[130]

The initial confrontation in 1750 ended in disastrous defeat for the Anlo, but the tide turned and the Anlo notched impressive victories against Ada in 1769, 1770, 1776 and 1780.[131] Anlo's incessant wars explain the interest in a military alliance with Akwamu, even after the collapse of Akwamu suzerainty in 1730.[132] Moreover, Akwamu controlled Krepi, the source of slaves and ivory so central to Anlo's growing long-distance trade in the eighteenth century.[133] Anlo's military victories may have prompted Keta's closer alignment with Anlo. Anlo also controlled the area north of the Keta Lagoon, and burgeoning north–south trade increased Keta's desire to have access to the area north of the lagoon. Keta had the largest army outside Anloga on the littoral between the Volta and Little Popo, and Anlo considered Keta a worthy military ally.[134] The disruption to Danish trade and the immense expense that each Ada defeat cost the Danes in resettling their Ada clients persuaded them to launch a military expedition to subjugate Anlo and Keta. The Danish coalition defeated the Anlo in 1784, resulting in the establishment of Fort Prindsensten in Keta and a technical trade monopoly for the Danes that was never effective. The presence of the Ada, Akyem, Akwapim, Accra, Krobo and Little Popo in the Danish military coalition kindled the Anlo consciousness of being encircled by enemies and prompted a move towards a stronger and more unified Anlo polity, as distinct from the loose confederation of the earlier years.[135] This is ironic as one of the specific stipulations of the Danish–Anlo Treaty of 1784 was to restrict Anlo jusrisdiction to Anlo proper, defining the boundaries of Anlo from the Agave settlements east of the Volta to Tegbi on the coast and to the northern shores of the Keta Lagoon.[136] But the Anlo were unwilling to suffer Danish trade monopoly after experiencing the material rewards of Atlantic trade, and continuous conflicts with the Danes would prompt Danish withdrawal from the Guinea trade. The increasing importance of the Atlantic slave trade in the Anlo area concludes this chapter.

---

[129] Paul Ozanne, 'Ladoku: an early town', *Ghana Notes and Queries* 7 (January 1965): 6–7.

[130] Isert, *Letters on West Africa*, 41.

[131] Amenumey, 'Brief history', 18–19.

[132] Greene, *History of the Anlo-Ewe*, 59.

[133] Kea, 'Anlo–Akwamu relations', 56–61.

[134] Greene, *History of the Anlo-Ewe*, 83.

[135] Amenumey, 'Brief history', 20.

[136] Reindorf, *Gold Coast and Asante*, 136.

African trade networks and the Atlantic slave trade on the western Slave Coast

The western Slave Coast received little attention from the Portuguese during the pre-1630s era of Portuguese domination of the Guinea trade. The difficult crossing at the mouth of the Volta, the heavy surf along the Slave Coast and the absence of natural harbours discouraged Portuguese interest. The Dutch operated on the Slave Coast from the 1630s. The Dutch overthrow of Portuguese control on the Guinea Coast, especially the Dutch capture of the Portuguese fort at Elmina (1637) and the province of Pernambuco in Portuguese Brazil (1630–54), made the Dutch an important player in the Atlantic slave trade. Dutch interest in the slave trade was accentuated when it won the *asiento* from Spain in 1662 to supply the Spanish New World possessions with African slaves.[137] From the mid-seventeenth century, the English, French, Swedes, Brandenburgers and Danes joined the Dutch in the Guinea trade.

Intertwined with the Atlantic trade was the African trade network along the lagoon system of the Slave Coast, which facilitated the assembly of trade goods and fed the Atlantic trade. African trade networks had an independent dynamic though, and they were geared towards supplying African needs – foodstuffs, salt, cloth, *cori* beads. Towns such as Anexo, Jakin and Keta first established themselves as trading centres in this African network, before attracting European attention.[138] Polities of the Slave Coast assiduously promoted free trade. By the late seventeenth century, several states dotted the short coastal expanse between the Volta estuary and the Lagos Channel: Anlo, Keta, Aflao, Little Popo, Great Popo, Whydah and Allada. All became intermediaries in the Atlantic slave-trade, being coastal outlets for inland trading states. But none produced slaves or ivory – items of European demand – in great enough quantities to warrant independent importance as an Atlantic supplier. Promoting free trade at their ports was crucial to their commercial prosperity, and attempts by Allada before 1710 and Dahomey from the 1720s to establish economic control on the Slave Coast were fiercely resisted.[139] The increasing hegemony of Dahomey and its monopolistic trade practices deflected trade to Lagos in the eighteenth century and to Keta, both being at the two ends of the lagoon system and beyond a Dahomey that lacked expertise in lagoon navigation and warfare.[140]

By the late seventeenth century, Keta had attracted some European attention in the slave trade. Its initial role may have been as a provisioning spot, as Keta 'was much frequented during the slave-trade for water and provisions, the former of which is procured without much trouble'.[141] Isert in 1788 described Keta's water as 'better than at any place on the coast of Guinea, and it is available with less trouble'.[142] As Keta had

[137] Albert van Dantzig, *Forts and Castles of Ghana* (Accra, 1980), 11–14; Law, *Slave Coast of West Africa*, 117–21.
[138] Law, 'Between the sea and the lagoon'.
[139] Law, *Slave Coast of West Africa*.
[140] On the rise of Lagos as an Atlantic port, see Law, 'Lagoon traffic and the rise of Lagos'. On canoe warfare in the lagoon system of the Slave Coast, see Smith, 'Canoe in West African history'.
[141] G. A. Robertson, *Notes on Africa; Particularly those Parts which are Situated between Cape Verde and the River Congo* (London, 1819), 232.
[142] Isert, *Letters on West Africa*, 75.

little farming land, the provisions probably came through the lagoon system with Keta serving as an assembly point. Keta's ability to provide European ships with slaves on their provisioning stops gradually gained it European recognition as a player in the Atlantic slave-trade. In 1683, the English Royal African Company reported that one of its ships had obtained a cargo of slaves in its provisioning stop at Keta and hence had not continued to Whydah, its original destination.[143] At the end of the seventeenth century, Bosman described Keta as being able to supply 'a very good number [of slaves], but not yet so many as to lade a ship'.[144] Krepi traders brought these slaves from the north via the Keta Lagoon or down the Volta River.[145] Two important developments strengthened and expanded the economies of the western Slave Coast from the early eighteenth century: Akwamu and Asante expansionism and the Danish decision to concentrate their trading activities in the Volta delta area.

Akwamu's military campaigns in the last quarter of the seventeenth century and the rise of Asante from 1701 destabilized trade on the Gold Coast and shifted European attention east of the Volta. By the 1710s, the Danes, the Dutch, and the English were all making trade stops at Keta.[146] Though European activities were concentrated at Keta, the effects of the expansion of trade were felt throughout Anlo.[147] Asante's wars of expansion in the early eighteenth century against the southern Akan states – Denkyira, Akyem, Assin, Wassa – led to the formation of a coalition to prevent Asante access to firearms and salt through the coastal trade. This embargo was effective between 1729 and 1742, when it collapsed with Asante's conquest of these southern states. But the embargo had the important effect of shifting Asante trading activities east of the Volta for its firearms and salt supplies. The expanded market now made commercially viable the canoe and salt-making technologies introduced into Anlo at the turn of the eighteenth century.[148] The defeat of Akwamu – noted slave-traders – in 1730 and the relocation of the Akwamu state east of the Volta to the Krepi region intensified slave-raiding and trading east of the Volta. The Akwamu traders also brought their slaves to Keta. In the eighteenth century, several coastal towns east of the Volta became important slave ports: Atorkor, Woe, Keta, Adina and Blekusu. Early trade routes between Keta and Krepi to the north now became major arteries.

The Danes had joined the Guinea trade as an extension of the Danish–Swedish wars of the seventeenth century. In 1658 the Danes captured the three Swedish forts on the Gold Coast and went on to construct four new forts in the eighteenth century.

[143] Law, *Slave Coast of West Africa*, 144.
[144] Bosman, *New and Accurate Description*, 307.
[145] Isert, *Letters on West Africa*, 81–2; Reindorf, *History of Gold Coast and Asante*, 131. The major polities in Krepi or northern Eweland included Peki, Ho, Kpandu, Taviefe, Anum and Agotime. J.B. Yegbe, 'The Anlo and their neighbours 1850–1890' (MA thesis, Institute of African Sudies, University of Ghana, 1966), 14.
[146] Law, *Slave Coast of West Africa*, 147–8.
[147] Greene, 'Social change in eighteenth-century Anlo'.
[148] Ibid. Some form of embargo against Asante by Fanti, Akyem, Wassaw and Denkyira persisted into the 1750s, according to Danish reports, and Asante traders still resorted to eastern ports, such as Ningo, in 1749. Fanti, Akyem, Krobo and Akwapim forged a second anti-Asante alliance in the 1770s. This was of short duration as Akyem and Akwapin were brought under effective Asante sway. Ole Justesen, 'Aspects of eighteenth century Ghanaian history as revealed by Danish sources', *Ghana Notes and Queries* 12 (June 1972): 12.

But Danish presence in the Gold Coast was never strong, and Danish forts on the Guinea coast were poorly financed and undermanned.[149] Akwamu depredations adversely affected trade at the Danish Fort Christiansborg in Accra and encouraged the Danes to turn their attention eastward towards the Volta delta area.[150] The initiative was taken under the Danish Governor Lygaard, who in 1710 placed a factor at Keta to sell European liquor.[151] Keta's traditions recollect this commencement of trade with the Danes in an interesting way, which also affirms the importance of liquor traffic in these early Atlantic contacts. Shortly after the ancestors settled at Keta, a ship passed the site and on its return stopped at Keta. An Anlo chief before a colonial commission of inquiry recounted that:

> This was the first time of the Danes coming to the coast. When my grandfathers saw the whiteman they ran and hid themselves in the bush ... It [the ship] came again a few days afterwards. Our fathers ran away again. They [the whites] put rum in a great barrel and put sugar in after this they went back to sea: when our fathers returned they thought it was water and tasted it: They found it sweet and drank all and booze and lie down. When the white man men came back again and found all boozed they took four of them to sea and left the rest. About three years after, they showed them many things and brought them back.[152]

This marked the advent of the Danes and the beginning of Euro-African trade at Keta.

Danish authorities worried about their financial weakness, and they chose the Volta delta because other stronger European powers appeared uninterested in this region. Whereas the Danes yearned for the financial security of a trade monopoly, the Anlo and Keta desired the financial prosperity that came from free trade. This set the stage for a century and a half of tense relations between the Danes and the Anlo–Keta Africans they sought ineffectively to control. The Keta encouraged Danish trade as well as Dutch trade. The Dutch opened a trading lodge in Keta in the 1730s and bought ivory and slaves brought across the Keta Lagoon.[153] The Keta played the Dutch off against the Danes in their endeavour to retain trade autonomy. Probably in the 1730s, the Keta seized the Dutch lodge and offered it to the Danes, presumably in response to Dutch attempts to control trade in the area.[154] But the Keta responded in a similar manner by boycotting the Danish lodge in the 1740s, when the Danes in turn sought to control the flourishing trade of the 1740s.[155]

Increasing participation in the slave trade brought about important social transformations in Anlo society. Anlo and Keta not only funnelled slaves into the Atlantic slave-trade, they became slave holders as well. The preference, as has been demonstrated for much of precolonial Africa, was for female slaves and children.[156] Anlo men used female slaves in the expanding salt-works, to dry fish for the long-distance trade

[149] Georg Nørregård, *Danish Settlements in West Africa 1658–1850*, trans. Sigurd Mammen (Boston, 1966).
[150] Grove and Johansen, 'Historical geography of the Volta delta', 1381.
[151] Nørregård, *Danish Settlements*, 95.
[152] NAG, Accra, ADM 11/1/1661. Evidence of Doviavo, Asafohenega of Denu. Notes of Evidence, 1912 Commission of Inquiry: Awuna, Adda and Akwamu.
[153] Law, *Slave Coast of West Africa*, 147.
[154] Nørregård, *Danish Settlements*, 98–9.
[155] Grove and Johansen, 'Historical geography of the Volta delta', 1387.
[156] Claire Robertson and Martin A. Klein, eds, *Women and Slavery in Africa* (Madison, 1983).

and to produce children that augmented the following of traders. Wealth came to be reckoned in people, and the creation of a stool of wealth or fortune for rich traders (*hozikpui*) marked this important development in Anlo social organization.[157] Wealth derived from the interaction of African trade networks and the Atlantic trade reinforced Anlo's and Keta's autonomy and strengthened their resolve to cultivate European trade, but avoid trade monopoly by any single European power.

A new phase in Danish–Anlo relations ensued with the reverses the Dutch suffered in the Anglo-Dutch war of the 1770s. The English and Danes quickly usurped sections of the Dutch sphere of influence on the Gold and Slave Coasts. With their strengthened position, the Danes began to view the residents in their sphere of influence as subjects and not allies.[158] This, together with incessant Anlo–Ada wars, encouraged the Danes in their bid to establish effective control over Anlo and Keta in the 1780s. The Anlo were defeated in 1784 and a Danish fort was established in Keta. Keta's 'neutrality' in this war revived hostile relations between Anlo and Keta, and the terms of the peace imposed an unwanted Danish monopoly on Keta's trade.

> On the whole, the Keta did not particularly care to become dependents of a fort. But, not having helped the Awuna, their former allies, in the war, they thought it the safest plan to have a refuge, if the Awuna should decide to seek vengeance.[159]

The boot was on the other foot in 1792, when the Anlo were hired by the Danes to discipline the Keta for killing a Danish official of the fort. Commandant Biorn had killed a Keta elder called Dengeni in November 1786. The Keta retaliated in June 1790 by killing Thessen, a Danish official of the fort.[160]

A militarily weak Danish company resorted to Akyem Abuakwa to avenge it. But Akyem Abuakwa was an enemy of Akwamu, and hence of Anlo (Akwamu's ally); thus the Anlo were wary of an Akyem intrusion into affairs east of the Volta. They offered to punish the Keta on behalf of the Danes for monetary reward. The stage was set for an armed conflict between Anlo and Keta in 1792. But the traditions assert that the Anlo had arranged with the Keta to stage a farcical battle with blank ammunition. The Anlo would then burn some huts in Keta and the combatants would share the reward extracted from the Danes. The Anlo would subsequently help the Keta rebuild their town. But something went wrong with the mock battle, which degenerated into a real fight, the destruction of Keta, Agudza and Kpoduwa, and the relocation of the Keta east to found the new state of Some.[161] Anexo and Klikor came to the support of Keta, and the war ended disastrously for Anlo. Relations between Keta and Anlo reached a nadir, and the Keta from this period actively canvassed for the 'complete conquest of Anlo'.[162] The Anlo confederacy collapsed, and Anlo's influence shrank to the core

---

[157] Greene, *History of the Anlo-Ewe*.

[158] Nørregård, *Danish Settlements*, ch. 16.

[159] Ibid., 148.

[160] Amenumey, 'Brief history', 20.

[161] Interview with Togbui James Ocloo IV, Keta, 24 January 1997; interview with Togbui Addo VIII, Klikor, 22 April 1997. For a succinct account, see Amenumey, 'Brief history', 20–1.

[162] Greene, *History of the Anlo-Ewe*, 88–9.

towns that formed Anlo proper.[163] Keta was later rebuilt, but the villages of Agudza and Kpoduwa were replaced by the new settlements at Kedzi and Vodza, formed by Anlo resettlers.

Danish abolition of the slave trade in 1803, followed by the British abolition in 1807, ushered in a new phase in Euro-African relations east of the Volta. Ironically, the slave-trade was abolished just as the Anlo were settling down to a prosperous trade in slaves. The trade had underpinned the accumulation of individual wealth and initiated social transformations that had acquired their own dynamics. For the Anlo, the slave-trade had to continue, and they would persist in the trade into the 1860s. This pitched them against the Danes, who attempted to suppress the slave-trade in their sphere of influence, and especially the British, who had assumed the role of enforcers of abolition along the entire West African coast. European slave-traders, especially Portuguese and Brazilians, moved east of the Volta to the area of Anlo and the Popos, where the slave-trade persisted. To the Anlo, British measures against the slave-trade were an infringement on their right to free trade. Danish endeavours to diversify into plantation agriculture were unsuccessful, and in 1850 they sold their possessions on the Gold and Slave Coasts to the British and withdrew. Anlo's first active contact with the British was as slave-traders, and the conflicts that marked this relationship shaped Anlo relations with the British for most of the nineteenth century.

Conclusion

Anlo migrants from Notsie migrated to the south-eastern coast of Ghana in the mid-seventeenth century. Lacking an aquatic or maritime tradition, the years of early settlement in the aquatic ecosystem east of the Volta were difficult years. Anlo settlement was dispersed, and the early migrants established small farms and harvested nature's bounty. The migrants were compelled to organize quickly in the wake of waves of war refugees that flooded their area from west of the Volta. Canoe and salt-making technologies were acquired from these new immigrants, and the Anlo gradually penetrated the lagoon trading system, which spanned from the Volta estuary east to the Lagos Channel. Anlo social organization underwent important changes in this context, and accumulation and social differentiation were intensified when the area became active in the Atlantic slave-trade. The European abolition of the slave-trade threatened these social processes that had emerged in Anlo and pre-disposed the Anlo to a continuation of the slave-trade. In this endeavour, the lagoon system and the numerous creeks that criss-crossed the Anlo landscape would become valuable assets. Smuggling became an important component of the Anlo economy, a feature that has persisted into the present.[164]

[163] Kea, 'Akwamu–Anlo relations', 45.

[164] Paul Nugent, 'Power versus knowledge: smugglers and the state along Ghana's eastern frontier, 1920–1992', in Michael Rösler and Tobias Wendl, eds, *Frontiers and Borderlands: Anthropological Perspectives* (Frankfurt am Main, 1999), 77–99.

2

Abolition, British Influence &
Smuggling in the Anlo Lowlands
up to c. 1890

Introduction

The Anlo region entered international trade in the eighteenth century as a source of slaves, albeit not on the large scale of Allada, Whydah and, later, Dahomey. Although Anlo slipped technically under Danish rule in the eighteenth century, Danish 'over-rule' rested lightly, and the Anlo and Keta remained autonomous *de facto*. Littoral towns in south-east Ghana prospered from a regime of free trade, engaging in commerce with passing ships of several European nations. Fish and salt from Anlo and Keta also featured prominently in the African coasting trade and in trade between the coast and interior. Danish and British abolition of the slave-trade at the beginning of the nineteenth century moved the focus of the slave-trade from west of the Volta to the less patrolled parts east of the Volta. With its lagoons and numerous creeks, the Anlo landscape was an ideal smugglers' den, facilitating the concealment of slaves and the quick march to the coast when British naval ships were absent. The Anlo would persist in the slave-trade until the 1860s, conniving with the Portuguese and Brazilian slave-traders, who became the major slave-traders in West Africa as the nineteenth century progressed. The slave-trade was succeeded by a booming Anlo trade in European liquor and gunpowder, often smuggled in through German Togoland with its lower customs duties. Important factors underlay Anlo's attachment to the slave-trade: the scarcity of land, which made export agriculture unfeasible; and the Anlo resentment of foreign control, especially by the British, giving the continuation of the slave-trade an element of political protest. But the social transformation of eighteenth-century Anlo society had made slavery an essential component in Anlo, and the dynamics of slave-holding persisted. The petering out of the slave-trade in the mid-nineteenth century and the increasing effectiveness of British control would push the Anlo towards a commercial exploitation of sea fishing and copra, based on the coconut palms that lined the Anlo coastline. By 1890 slave-dealing had become rare, and the lowering of customs duties east of the Volta to equalize those of German Togoland removed the advantage Anlo smugglers had earlier enjoyed in the liquor and gunpowder trade.

Warfare, slaving and Anlo political economy

The Anlo have commented often on the lack of economic resources in their pre-colonial economy. The limited economic base motivated Anlo military aggression against the Ada from the 1750s with the objective of dispossessing the Ada of their rich salt ponds and fishing grounds. Scarce land and the absence of stool lands – Anlo lands were owned by clans and wealthy individuals – made Anlo chiefs dependent on court fines and gifts from resident traders. What was absent was the pattern of slaves toiling on land owned by big men (Twi: *abirempon*), typical of seventeenth-century political economies west of the Volta.[1] And, when the age of militarized territorial states dawned on the Gold Coast from the early eighteenth century, the formidable boundary of the Volta River and Danish support for Ada prevented the Anlo from dislodging Ada in their westward push. Togbui Acolatse aptly summed up the harsh reality of precolonial Anlo's political economy in his testimony before the 1912 Crowther Commission: 'Awuna [Anlo] had no money then ... we were fond of war; kill some and catch some and sell and chop and marry their women; there was no work, we had to sell slaves'.[2] Anlo's constrained economic options help to explain the enduring relevance of warfare, plunder and banditry, slaving and slavery through much of the precolonial period.

Warfare and plunder were instrumental in Anlo's political economy. Anlo militarized early in its settlement on the western Slave Coast. The influx of refugees immediately after Anlo settlement and the early rivalry with Little Popo necessitated this. Little Popo effectively contained any territorial ambitions Anlo may have had to the east, and further east lay the even more formidable power of Dahomey. To the west lay the Volta River, and, in the early years when the Anlo had not gained mastery over lagoon and river navigation, they were indeed grateful for this natural pro-tection. Commenting on Anlo conflicts with the Ada and Accra, Davoji, spokes-person to Awoamefia Sri II, opined before the 1912 Crowther Commission that: 'If it were not for the Volta the Blaos [Ada and Accra] [would] have driven us away.'[3] As the Anlo gained familiarity with their aquatic ecology, but lacked the capacity for territorial expansion, they embarked on brigandage from the late seventeenth century. As the preceding chapter pointed out, poor commoners were the first brigands, and they plundered trading caravans and canoes in the east–west trade and occasionally European ships lying at Keta. These activities reflected Keta's emergence as a trading centre and a locus of wealth.

[1] Ray A. Kea, *Settlements, Trade, and Polities in the Seventeenth-century Gold Coast* (Baltimore, 1982).
[2] Notes of Evidence (1912 Commission); Sandra E. Greene, 'The individual as stranger in nineteenth-century Anlo: the politics of identity in precolonial West Africa', in John Hunwick and Nancy Lawler, eds, *The Cloth of Many Silk Colors* (Evanston, 1996), 115.
[3] Notes of Evidence (1912 Commission).

50

The Anlo Lowlands, to *c.* 1890

Akwamu colonization of the Volta area in the 1700s led to state- or élite-sponsored brigandage in the lower Volta, directed against the Akwamu in the 1710s and 1720s. When Asante hegemony was extended into this area in the 1740s, Asante caravans became the targets of banditry.[4] And, when the Danes became more assertive east of the Volta from the mid-eighteenth century, they in turn became victims of brigands. In the 1780s, Isert complained:

> If we sent any wares with our company slaves, either over land or by the lagoon, to Quitta [Keta], where we had a lodge some 12 miles further away on the east side of the river, they were usually plundered. Our wares, our boats, and even our Blacks were taken.[5]

In fact, banditry persisted on the lower Volta and to the east throughout the eighteenth century. It is certain that these were not the activities of isolated bandits. Anlo was a more organized, militarily strong polity by the late eighteenth century, as witnessed in its successful territorial incursion north of the Keta Lagoon between the 1740s and the 1770s.[6] It had the capacity to impose order within its domains.

But why would the Anlo State perpetrate or condone banditry within its boundaries? Ray Kea provides an astute insight:

> The authorities in the coastal and sub-coastal polities faced mounting economic and political problems. Military defeats meant a loss of political autonomy and reduction to tributary status. This, in turn, meant a loss of control over surplus appropriation and a decline in disposable incomes. Under the circumstances the rulers turned to brigandage to stabilize their losses and, at the same time, to challenge the suzerainty of their political overlords.[7]

Warfare, plunder and booty were popularized and institutionalized in Anlo. These provided a means of accumulation, and the fact that occupants of stools of valour were sometimes also people of wealth underscored this connection. In the 1830s, Gbodzo of Woe, who had created a stool of wealth for himself based on his success in the slave-trade, was raised to the command of the right wing division of the Anlo army when a vacancy occurred.[8] There was no hereditary warrior aristocracy, and leaders were forged in the midst of battle and elevated by popular acclamation. The Anlo army was a voluntary one, and unpopular wars did not attract a large subscription, or were abandoned even in the midst of battle. J.B. Yegbe commented on Anlo's calculating attitude toward warfare:

> Though brave, the Anlo did not fight for fighting's sake. They received no rewards and so fought only in the hope of plunder and slaves. If the war was at the instance of an aggrieved person, the person had to provide some quantity of ammunition to be supplemented either voluntarily by individuals or by the war captains. He provided some rum too.[9]

[4] Ray A. Kea, '"I am here to plunder on the general road": bandits and banditry in the pre-nineteenth-century Gold Coast', in Donald Crummey, ed., *Banditry, Rebellion and Social Protest in Africa* (London, 1986), 123–4.
[5] Paul Erdmann Isert, *Letters on West Africa and the Slave Trade (1788)*, trans. and ed. Selena A. Winsnes (Oxford, 1992), 42.
[6] See Chapter 1.
[7] Kea, 'Bandits and banditry', 123.
[8] Sandra E. Greene, *Gender, Ethnicity, and Social Change on the Upper Slave Coast: A History of Anlo-Ewe*, 73–7.
[9] J. B. Yegbe, 'The Anlo and their neighbours 1850–1890' (MA thesis, Institute of African Studies, University of Ghana, 1966), 8.

51

Anlo decisions to engage in war were based on pragmatic evaluations of expected booty. Anlo's military alliance with Whydah in the late seventeenth and early eighteenth centuries was based on political and economic considerations.[10] The wars with Ada from the 1750s had an economic agenda. The fiasco battle with Keta in 1792 was the botching up of what was conceived as a lucrative business transaction.[11]

In 1865, Anlo waged war against Ada on behalf of a rich, naturalized Anlo trader, Geraldo de Lima. Although Ada was Anlo's traditional enemy, this war was business as usual. Expectations of material gain were paramount:

> Accordingly, when the Anlo were defeated, having lost approximately one hundred men and capturing none of the enemy, they refused to continue to support Geraldo. They saw no profit in such a venture, and they had much to lose. Instead, the majority of the Anlo leaders broke off the campaign and shifted their forces to the east where they had agreed to assist one Kuadzo Landzekpo of Agoue, who was engaged in a conflict with a business partner.[12]

One of the ironies in Anlo's history is that it sought an alliance with its erstwhile ruler, Akwamu, after the collapse of Akwamu domination in 1730. This relationship, initiated from *c.* 1750, coincided with Anlo's defeat by Ada and the need for a stronger military partner. It lasted until the imposition of British colonialism.

Another important reason for the Anlo–Akwamu alliance was Anlo's growing interest in the Atlantic slave-trade and Akwamu control of Krepi, the major source of slaves on the western Slave Coast. This alliance serviced Anlo's trading interests, and the Anlo benefited as middlemen in the Akwamu slave-trade, in addition to selling some of the slaves they acquired as war booty. A Danish factor, Kioge, provided an illuminating description of the slave-trade on the western Slave Coast:

> [T]he Crepee [Krepi] slaves, or the slaves who are purchased on Crepee, are undeniably the very best who can be obtained on the whole Guinea Coast. Crepee lies north-west of Rio Volta, and can in fairness be called the slave coast ... a great number of slaves are sold there yearly, some to the black negro merchants who convey them to Accra, some to Quitta [Keta], Way [Woe] and Augona [Anloga], who bring them to the ships.[13]

Anlo participation and profits from the slave-trade were much enhanced from the 1770s, as Anlo came to control the lower Volta with Akwamu controlling the upper reaches.[14] It was in this context that Denmark abolished the slave-trade in her domains in 1803. The British followed in 1807. The Anlo viewed Danish abolition as sheer interference in Anlo's internal affairs. Trade was booming, and several foreigners, including Portuguese and Brazilians, had moved to Anlo to deal in slaves.[15] Indeed, these were the *awoamefia*'s favourite clients as they lavished gifts on

---

[10] Robin Law, *The Slave Coast of West Africa 1550–1750: The Impact of the Atlantic Slave Trade on African Society* (Oxford, 1991), 248–9.

[11] See Chapter 1.

[12] Greene, 'Individual as stranger', 115–16.

[13] Ray A. Kea, 'Akwamu–Anlo Relations, *c.* 1750–1813', *Transactions of the Historical Society of Ghana* 10 (1969): 56.

[14] Ibid., 57–8.

[15] Yegbe, 'Anlo and their neighbours', 18–19.

him, an important revenue source in a political economy in which subjects paid no tribute to the king. The king's only insistence was that slave-traders should not enslave Anlo.[16] It is perhaps not surprising, then, that the Anlo polity would unite in its opposition to Danish abolition and Danish and British endeavours to enforce abolition in the Anlo area.

Anlo defiance of Danish and British abolition of the slave-trade

The waning years of Danish 'rule'

Danish abolition of the slave-trade in 1803 put the finances of the Danish forts and lodges on the Gold and Slave Coasts in extreme jeopardy. An alternative was sought in plantation agriculture for export, and the surgeon Isert started a pioneer agricultural settlement in Akwapim in the late 1780s called Fredericksnopel.[17] The settlement collapsed with Isert's death in 1789, but was revived by the Danish Governor Schionning from the early 1800s. Schionning's efforts were crowned with some success when he exported 8 tons of coffee in 1810. Asante military incursion into the coast area between 1807 and 1826 destroyed these agricultural activities, and the Danish experiment was aborted.[18] In this weakened state, Danish enforcement of abolition east of the Volta in the early nineteenth century was fitful and inconsequential. By 1807 the Danes had virtually abandoned any involvement in Anlo.[19] Through the 1840s, European anti-slave-trade activities were ephemeral on the Slave Coast. Brazil had won self-governing status in 1822 and had embarked upon expanding her sugar and coffee plantations. Spain was also developing her sugar plantations in Cuba in the first half of the nineteenth century. Both depended on African slave labour, and their demand fuelled the slave-trade until the Anglo-Brazilian treaty of 1845 made the first real dent in slave-trade activities on the Slave Coast.

Danish abolition of the slave-trade in 1803 sent the trade underground. Slave-traders that operated in Keta, such as the Bahian trader Gonzalves Baeta, moved away because of proximity to the Danish fort. Slave-traders who operated outside Keta pursued their activities with confidence.

> But slave-traders like Don José Mora, alias Adohose, a Spaniard, who from 1839–44 was shuttling between Woe, Blekusu and Attoko [Atorkor], Francis Olympio at Blekusu, Convacellos de Lima at Vodza remained at their stations. The natives obstructed the Danes from capturing these daring private individuals.[20]

Atorkor, Woe, Blekusu and Adina became important slave marts in the nineteenth

[16] Ibid., 5.

[17] Isert, *Letters on West Africa*, 5. Editor's 'Introduction'.

[18] Kwamina B. Dickson, 'Evolution of seaports in Ghana: 1800–1928', *Annals of the Association of American Geographers* 55, 1 (1965): 101; Georg Nørregård, *Danish Settlements in West Africa 1658–1850*, trans. Sigurd Mammen (Boston, 1966), 218.

[19] Greene, 'Individual as stranger', 95.

[20] Yegbe, 'Anlo and their neighbours', 19.

century. The strong-arm tactics of the British navy on the Gold Coast encouraged slave-traders to relocate east of the Volta. The slave-trade had thrived in Accra, especially in Dutch Accra, where there was no resident commandant in 1819 and 1820. Reindorf comments that all the influential people in the town were involved in the trade, and Chief Ankra's house became an important rendezvous. The British received intelligence of these activities, and an English man-of-war arrived at Accra in August 1819. The ship bombarded Ankra's house and the immediate vicinity. A repeat expedition by the British navy in February 1820 led to the relocation of slave-traders.[21] As the Danish Governor Carstensen wrote in 1845, several of these Accra slave-traders now shipped their slaves out of Woe in Anlo.[22] The trade received an additional boost from the return of some 4,000 'Brazilians' to West Africa in the 1830s. These were former slaves in Brazil, set free by a law in 1831. Many took up residence on the Slave Coast and, assuming the names of their former masters, became active in trade.[23]

The Anlo themselves were keenly interested in the profits of the slave-trade, for they provided an important means of social mobility. A good example is the career of Amegashi Akofi, a member of the Ame clan, forged from the Abolo captives of Anlo's wars on the northern shores of the Keta Lagoon in the 1730s and 1740s. The son of a fisherman in Alakple, Amegashi Akofi moved to Woe in the mid-eighteenth century. Amegashi Akofi acquired wealth through supplying slaves to the Europeans and Afro-Europeans dealing in slaves in Anlo. This wealth provided the basis of a series of strategic trading alliances, cemented by marriages that ensured the family's prosperity, making it one of the prominent families in Anlo today. Amegashi Akofi married his daughter, Kpetsimine, to his wealthy trading partner from Adangme, Tettega. The offspring was Gbodzo (born c. 1800), whose activities and wealth as a slave-trader are proverbial in Anlo and who is even memorialized in song.[24] Indeed, so seductive were the profits of the slave-trade that leaders of Anlo's most prestigious religious cult, Nyigbla (a war god), could not resist selling female initiates (zizidzelawo) undergoing rigorous training in the Nyigbla forest. The leaders would inform the parents of the death of these initiates, whereas they had been sold to the slave-traders who dealt in the export slave-trade.[25] The sense of insecurity that pervaded Anlo society in the heyday of the slave-trade was captured by Togbui Addo VII, chief of Klikor: 'You returned from the farm and your family had been taken away, probably even by somebody you knew so well'.[26] Many succumbed to the temptation of instant enrichment.

It is significant that the major Anlo slave marts were all located between the lagoon

[21] C.C. Reindorf, History of the Gold Coast and Asante (Basle, 1895) 152–3.

[22] Greene, 'Individual as stranger', 95–6.

[23] Gershon A. Sorkpor, 'Geraldo de Lima and the Awunas (1862–1904)' (MA thesis, Institute of African Studies, University of Ghana, 1966), 21; Patrick Manning, 'Coastal society in the Republic of Benin: reproduction of a regional system', Cahiers d'Edtudes Africaines 114, xxix–2 (1989): 249.

[24] Greene, 'Individual as stranger', 96–8.

[25] Ibid., 98; idem, History of the Anlo-Ewe, 112.

[26] Interview with Togbui Addo VIII, Klikor, 22 April 1997.

and the sea, facilitating the smuggling of slaves along the lagoon and shipping from ports other than Keta, as Danish vigilance was negligible. Yegbe commented on the usefulness of the Keta Lagoon – and its associated creeks – when it came to smuggling.

> Apart from being used for communication it [Keta Lagoon] also serves as a means of protection for the residual peoples who inhabit its shores and islands. It did contribute to the persistence of the slave-trade in the Anlo country; and rendered smuggling easy because it afforded every facility for concealment and distribution of contraband goods.[27]

The aquatic environment lent itself to evasion. British extension of colonial rule to Anlo in 1874 was partly motivated by a desire to benefit from the commercial activity east of the Volta.[28] And the colonial government realized that its endeavour to impose customs duties in Anlo would be futile so long as it did not control the lagoon system.[29] It is noteworthy that mainland Anlo people, who resisted British colonial imposition into the 1880s, were able to do so by situating their camps in the creek area of Tsrekume on the eastern banks of the River Volta. The war that subdued them in 1889 was significantly called the 'Shime (Marsh) War' because it was fought in the marshes.[30]

However evanescent Danish 'rule' had become in Anlo, it could not condone the flagrant flouting of Danish laws in areas of Danish influence. Logistics vitiated the Danish will to enforce abolition, and the situation was worsened when already weak garrisons at Danish forts Fredensborg, Kongesten and Prinsensten were reduced to one soldier each by a royal order in 1834.[31] Danish authorities on the Gold and Slave Coasts launched occasional operations against slave-traders when the resident soldiers at the forts informed the governor at Fort Christiansborg in Accra that the activities of slavers had become blatant.[32] Reindorf records two such events, both involving the Spaniard Don José Mora:

> In 1839 governor Hans Angel Giede was informed that one Don José Mora, a Portuguese [Spaniard] slave-dealer, had established a depot at Bato [Battor] on the bank of the Volta. The governor, at the head of about 60 soldiers and some armed men, the chaplain Mr. Torsloff and Mr. W. Lutterodt marched to Bato to apprehend Don José Mora. He tried to fire a pistol at the Governor but failed and was captured with his weapon. His goods and a few slaves he had bought were confiscated. After promising never to carry on slave-trade again in the jurisdiction of the Danish government, he was set free. Don José Mora shortly after opened the slave-trade at Wei [Woe] in Angula [Anlo]. In 1842 the Danish governor Wilkens with Mr. Wulff, the secretary and treasurer, and 150 soldiers set sail in an American trading vessel to apprehend the malefactor. They landed at night, and marched to attack Don José Mora, who managed, however, to jump

[27] Yegbe, 'Anlo and their neighbours', 4.
[28] D.E.K. Amenumey, 'Geraldo de Lima: a reappraisal', *Transactions of the Historical Society of Ghana* 9 (1968): 71.
[29] Public Records Office (PRO), London, FO 403/12. 'Correspondence respecting differences between Great Britain and France on the west coast of Africa' (1879).
[30] R.S. Rattray, 'History of the Ewe people', *Etudes Togolaises* 11, 1 (1967): 96.
[31] Nørregård, *Danish Settlements in West Africa*, 205.
[32] Greene, 'Individual as stranger', 100.

Photo 2.1 Fort Prindsensten, *c.* 1893 *(Reprinted from Bremen State Archives).*

Photo 2.2 Alley in front of Fort Prindsensten, *c.* 1893 *(Reprinted from Bremen State Archives).*

through a window of his house and escaped. His property and slaves were captured and brought to Christiansborg.[33]

In fact, José Mora was still plying his trade in slaves in Woe in 1844 and was arrested one night when he had the audacity to march his slaves past the fort in Keta. José Mora fired his pistol thrice in an unsuccessful attempt to kill Sergeant J.C. Hesse, commandant of Fort Prindsensten (Photos 2.1 and 2.2). His slaves were seized, but the king of Anlo and his principal chiefs insisted that José Mora's slaves be restored to him. They backed their demands with a siege of the fort, and the frustrated Danish commandant turned the slaves over to the king.[34] It was difficult for a weak European power to enforce abolition on fellow European slave-traders when the indigenous people were against such measures.

Tense relations between the Danes and the Anlo flared up in 1847 in a violent confrontation, which started as a disagreement over the price of firewood supplied to the fort by Chief Dzokoto of Anyako.[35] The fort's soldiers killed an Anlo man in the engagement. The Anlo again besieged the fort and demanded that the culprit be turned over as required by the law of vengeance. Governor R.E. Schmidt hurried from Accra with a significant force of soldiers to relieve the fort. The governor fined his Anlo 'subjects' for their insubordination and felt that they were delaying in making restitution. The governor ordered the arrest of some Anlo chiefs to compel them to pay the fine. Old Akpaku of Keta was arrested, but died of unknown causes when he was brought into the fort, though self-poisoning seems probable. The Anlo immediately paid the fine. Akpaku's family fetched the body and buried him.[36]

That very night the entire Anlo army, some 6,000–7,000 strong, gathered in the precincts of Keta. An attack was launched on the fort the next morning. The governor and his men were only rescued by the providential appearance of a French man-of-war off the coast of Keta. The governor managed to escape to the brig, *Abeille*, and the ship and the fort turned their guns on Keta. The town was destroyed, and the Anlo 'capitulated' to the Danish governor on the 23 October 1847.[37] Worn down by the exactions of her increasingly superfluous possessions on the coast of Guinea, Denmark sold her West African possessions to Britain for £10,000 in 1850 and withdrew. Anlo, technically, came under British influence.[38]

The extension of British influence to Anlo

The Anlo were hostile to the British take-over for they suspected, rightly, that British over-rule would significantly affect their lives compared with the lighter claims

---

[33] Reindorf, *Gold Coast and Asante*, 154.

[34] Ibid., 155–6. Nørregård, *Danish Settlements in West Africa*, 214, reports the same incident but gives 1845 as the date.

[35] Other sources state that Dzokoto had come to sell shells for making lime. See interview with Togbui James Ocloo IV, Keta, 24 January 1997; D.E.K. Amenumey, *The Ewe in Pre-colonial Times* (Accra, 1986), 97.

[36] Reindorf, *Gold Coast and Asante*, 157–8.

[37] Nørregård, *Danish Settlements in West Africa*, 214.

[38] Ibid., 222.

Denmark had made. Britain had more resources, was committed to ending the slave-trade and had interests that went beyond just trade. This hostility was evident from 1850 when Schionning, acting on behalf of the Danish governor, took British Governor Winniett to the four Danish forts and formally informed the chiefs and peoples of the areas that the forts – and 'areas of influence' – had been ceded to Britain. The Anlo were initially uncooperative:

> At each fort he introduced the native chiefs to their new masters and sold the Danish property at auction. East of the Volta River the reception given the new masters was extremely cold. The Awuna accepted the British flags, but refused to give up their Danish and Portuguese flags. Only the utmost liberality on the part of Winniett and abundant rum rations prevented hostilities.[39]

In this initial formal encounter with Britain, the Anlo ascertained the limits of British rule and retained an unexpressed hope that they would be able to continue with the slave-trade. Governor Winniett assured the Anlo of non-interference in their affairs.[40] The king of Anlo and his chiefs made two requests, which tested, implicitly, the British position on the slave-trade in Anlo. The king requested the return of his kinsman Lawson, deported from Anlo for his participation in the slave-trade. Among the Danish–British entourage was the Bahian slave-trader Baeta, who wielded much influence with the Anlo authorities. The Danes had concluded, obviously, that his presence would assuage Anlo fears and ease the transition to British control. The king and his chiefs now requested that Baeta be allowed to remain in Anlo. Winniett agreed to these requests, and the Anlo assumed that 'business' (the slave-trade) could continue as usual. The Anlo then swore allegiance to Britain.[41]

By 1850 several Anlo had themselves become successful and wealthy slave-traders, and their lives and fortunes were intimately enmeshed with the trade. Influential Anlo slave-traders included Tamakloe at Whuti, Bomiklo at Alakple, Ajorlolo and Dokutsu at Atorkor, Gbodzo at Woe, John Tay at Dzelukope and Azaho, Potake and Ahosi at Tegbi.[42] Indeed, several of these slave-traders were also Anlo chiefs. But the times had changed, and the British acquisition of Fort Prindsensten was followed by the appointment of a commandant to the fort and the stationing of a force of Hausa Constabulary at Keta in 1852.[43] Greene describes the consequences for the slave-trade:

> A larger contingent of soldiers was assigned to the Keta fort, which then forced many of the local traders as well as the Brazilian and Spanish merchants still involved in the export of slaves to relocate their businesses. Most moved to the littoral villages of Vodza and Kedzi on the eastern edge of Anlo territory and to the Agbosome coastal towns of Blekusu and Adina, all of which were outside the reach of the British soldiers stationed at Keta.[44]

[39] Ibid.

[40] Yegbe, 'Anlo and their neighbours', 31.

[41] Ibid., 31–2.

[42] Ibid., 35–6; and Felicia E. Akorli-Ayim, 'On the history of Keta with particular reference to its role in the Anlo struggle against European domination' (BA thesis, History Department, University of Ghana, 1972), 23.

[43] D.E.K. Amenumey, 'A brief history', in Francis Agbodeka, ed., *A Handbook of Eweland*, Vol. I: *The Ewes of Southeastern Ghana* (Accra, 1997), 22.

[44] Greene, 'Individual as stranger', 109.

The Anlo Lowlands, to *c*. 1890

The main slave markets in Anlo, such as Woe and Atorkor, ceased to be open markets. The British soon displayed their commitment to ending the slave-trade. The Anlo gradually tempered their brazen defiance of British anti-slave-trade measures:

> In November 1853 the Civil Commandant at Keta, Lt. Cochrane refused to deliver up a runaway slave to Baeta, who was resident at Attoko. Therefore when Dr. Partridge, Staff Assistant Surgeon, stationed at Keta Fort was on his way to Christiansborg, he was arrested by the Attoko people and detained; so that he might be exchanged for the slave or pay the cost of the slave. Dr Partridge had to ransom himself by paying thirty dollars, the price of the slave.[45]

On the advice of Chief Tay of Dzelukope, who correctly anticipated British reprisal, the 30 dollars were returned and a fine paid.

Other British impositions were equally unsavoury to the Anlo. In 1852 the British introduced a poll tax in their domains in the Gold Coast, which by extension now included Anlo. This was problematic as the *awoamefia* refused to recognize the right of the British to legislate for Anlo.[46] The Anlo resisted paying the poll tax after the first collection in 1853, a response shared by the Ga and Fanti in the Gold Coast.[47] They realized that the tax was to support the cost of British administration, not to develop Anloland. The result of this effective British pressure on the slave-trade was to shift trade further eastwards. Again, the lagoon system came in handy: 'From 1860 therefore slaves continued to be brought from the interior by way of the Volta, passed along the lagoons of Anlo and shipped from the sea coast at Dahome.'[48]

Without rich resources in gold or palm oil, which was gradually taking over from the slave-trade, Anlo offered few revenue opportunities for the British. British presence declined from 1856, and the fort at Keta was abandoned in 1859.[49] But the slave-trade was coming to a natural death, and, after a last spurt provided inadvertently by missionaries from the North German Missionary Society (Bremen Mission) in the 1850s and 1860s, it gave up the ghost. The first missionaries of the North German Missionary Society, Wilhelm Dauble and Frederich Plessing, landed at Dzelukope, adjacent to Keta, on 3 September 1853 and established a mission station at Keta. Battered by the Danes in 1847 and still undergoing reconstruction, Keta was 'nothing but a few miserable huts'.[50] With the British virtually gone after 1856, the slave-trade had resumed with some gusto. The German missionaries interceded with good intent, ransoming slaves and bringing them into the mission as freed persons. Between 1857 and 1867 the missionaries redeemed 150 child slaves.[51] Unwittingly, they provided the last slave market in Anlo, as the export trade had gradually dried up. The remaining Brazilians and Spanish, who channelled the slaves

---

[45] Yebge, 'Anlo and their neighbours', 36.

[46] Amenumey, 'Brief history', 22.

[47] Rattray, 'History of the Ewe people', 94; David Kimble, *A Political History of Ghana 1850–1928* (Oxford, 1963), ch. 4; John Mensah Sarbah, *Fanti National Constitution* (London, 1968), 100–3; J. E. Casely Hayford, *Gold Coast Native Institutions* (London, 1903), 160–3.

[48] Yegbe, 'Anlo and their neighbours', 55.

[49] Ibid., 38; Amenumey, 'Brief history', 22.

[50] C. Osswald, *Fifty Years' Mission Work at Keta* (Bremen, 1903), 11.

[51] Sorkpor, 'Geraldo de Lima', 13.

out of Anlo, had died in the 1850s and 1860s, the last significant one being Cerquira de Lima, who died in 1862.[52] By the mid-1860s, the export slave-trade was over in Anlo.

Strikingly, it was the revolt of the Krobo palm-oil producers and Anlo's ideal smuggling facilities that provided the Anlo with an economic opportunity finally to jettison the export slave-trade and to rebuild their economy on 'legitimate' commerce. The German missionaries set the stage in 1857 when, struck by the absence of economic activity, they invited the Bremen firm of F.M. Vietor and Sons to establish business in Keta and to act as the Mission's trading agent.[53] The Vietor Company sent Christian Rottmann to Keta as its representative, and on 3 January 1858 its first ship *Dahomey* arrived at Keta.[54] In 1853 palm oil emerged as the leading export in the Gold Coast, and the Krobo and Shai districts to the immediate west of the Volta were its major producers.[55] In 1861 the Krobo rebelled against British rule and, after being suppressed, were fined £5,125. The colonial government authorized the British firms of F. & A. Swanzy and Messrs Forster and Smith to collect the debt in the form of a monopoly on palm oil purchases from the Krobo.[56] These firms exploited their monopoly by offering a low price for Krobo oil. Amenumey described the Krobo response, whereby:

> To get round the government-sponsored monopoly, instead of sending produce by road to Prampram where the monopolist firms maintained agents, they sent it by river to the seaboard beyond British control where traders like Lima paid higher prices. Because of the competitive prices paid here a regular oil trade was attracted to the area east of the Volta. From 1861 the quantity of oil exported began to rise but the merchants west of the Volta hardly received any of it.[57]

The Volta, the lagoon and the seaboard had proved their usefulness for the Anlo again. Obviously, the British firms and the Ada and Accra traders who operated west of the Volta were resentful of the diversion of Krobo trade to the Anlo coast. The antagonism took shape in the form of a struggle with Geraldo de Lima, the wealthiest Anlo trader from the 1860s and perhaps the dominant figure in Anlo history between 1865 and 1885.[58] A business dispute between Geraldo de Lima and an Ada trader escalated into a full-blown war between Anlo and Ada in 1865–6. De Lima thus came to the attention of the British and came to be viewed by the British as the major obstacle in their desire to reimpose British authority on the Anlo from the late 1860s.

The beneficiary effect of the Krobo palm-oil boycott was immediately evident in the Anlo economy. Several European firms followed the lead of F.M. Vietor and

[52] Greene, 'Individual as stranger', 109.

[53] Chapter 3 provides a detailed discussion of German missionary and trading activities in Anlo.

[54] Yegbe, 'Anlo and their neighbours', 47.

[55] Kwamina B. Dickson, *A Historical Geography of Ghana* (Cambridge, 1969), 143–4.

[56] Louis E. Wilson, *The Krobo People of Ghana to 1892: A Political and Social History* (Athens, OH, 1991), ch. 6; Sorkpor, 'Geraldo de Lima', ch. 2.

[57] Amenumey, 'Geraldo de Lima', 69.

[58] On the career of Geraldo de Lima (a.k.a. Atitsogbi), a former servant of Cerquira de Lima, who inherited his master's business on the latter's death in 1862, see Sorkpor, 'Geraldo de Lima'; Amenumey, 'Geraldo de Lima'; Greene, 'Individual as stranger'; idem, *History of the Anlo-Ewe*, 127–35.

established branches at Keta. The list included other German firms such as Brodecker and Meyer and F. Oloff and Company; French firms such as Regis Ainé; and the British companies of United African Company (UAC) and F. & A. Swanzy. Former Anlo slave-traders, such as de Lima, Quist, Jacobson and Acolatse, also shifted to palm oil. Other West African traders were active in Keta, the most prominent, perhaps, being G.B. Williams of Sierra Leone.[59] This commercial activity revived British interest in Anlo. In 1868, Britain introduced customs duties on imports into the Gold Coast, and it now began to contemplate the extension of these to Anlo – that is, if Anlo could be brought back under British influence.[60] The introduction of customs duties was facilitated by the exchange of forts and lodges on the Gold Coast between the British and the Dutch in 1867, which gave Britain control of the contiguous territory east of the Sweet River, the boundary lying between Komenda and Elmina.[61] As in the 1850 sale of Danish settlements, the Africans were not consulted. Elmina, the Dutch headquarters since 1637 and an Asante ally, refused to go under British suzerainty, and the Dutch had to bombard previously British Komenda into submission.[62] As part of the British–Asante war of 1873–4, the British launched what Amenumey describes as an 'unprovoked attack' on the Anlo in January 1874.[63] Anlo was an ally of Akwamu and Asante, and its relations with Asante had been made explicit when it joined Asante and Akwamu in the Asante invasion of northern Eweland in 1869.[64] Captain Glover thus attacked Anlo in 1874 to prevent Anlo from aiding Asante in the Anglo-Asante war. The unprepared Anlo were defeated, and, by the Dzelukope Treaty of 22 March 1874, Anlo was made part of the British Gold Coast colony. Britain wrongly fixed Anlo's eastern boundary at Adafienu (Elmina Chica), a town in the adjacent Some State.[65]

Colonial imposition was foreshadowed by the gradual British penetration of Anlo's natural defences through superior technology. British warships lying off the coast could easily bombard Anlo's littoral towns. Such was the case in 1847, when the French brig *Abeille* pounded Keta. In one of the Danish occasional flexing of muscles a Danish gunboat bombarded Tegbi and Kedzi later in 1847 to underscore the lesson taught Keta by the *Abeille*.[66] The British vessel, *HMS Pert*, shelled Vodza and Geraldo de Lima's barracoon in 1868.[67] The sea may have served as an effective barrier to other African societies on the Slave Coast, but not to maritime European

---

[59] Yegbe, 'Anlo and their neighbours', 113.

[60] Ibid., 108; Amenumey, 'Geraldo de Lima', 71.

[61] For the text of the Convention that sets out the boundary and the imposition of customs duties in both British and Dutch territories, see G.E. Metcalfe, *Documents of Ghana History 1807–1957* (Aldershot, 1994 [1964]), 320–1.

[62] On the Dutch, Elmina and Asante relations, see Larry Yarak, *Asante and the Dutch, 1744–1873* (Oxford, 1990).

[63] Amenumey, 'Brief history', 22.

[64] See, for example, M. Johnson, 'Ashanti east of the Volta', *Transactions of the Historical Society of Ghana* 8 (1965) 33–59. Asante armies took captive two missionaries of the Swiss Basle Missionary Society, F.A. Ramseyer and J. Kühne, in this incursion and kept them prisoners in Kumasi for four years. For their account of these years, see F.A. Ramseyer and J. Kühne, *Four Years in Ashantee* (London, 1875).

[65] Yegbe, 'Anlo and their neighbours', 109; Amenumey, 'Brief history', 22.

[66] Amenumey, *Ewe in Pre-colonial Times*, 98–9.

[67] Rattray, 'History of the Ewe people', 95.

powers. Anlo complacency was badly shaken in November 1868 when the British steamship *Eyo* crossed the bar of the Volta to become the first steamship to enter the Volta River. Anlo towns could now also be bombarded from the Volta.[68] Even the sense of security of towns on the northern shores of the Keta Lagoon was removed when Anyako was bombarded in 1885 from a flotilla of canoes firing from the Keta Lagoon.[69] Colonial rule had come to stay.

The impact of British colonial imposition on Anlo economy and society

Anlo responses to British colonial imposition varied for different constituencies and changed over time.[70] Those on the seaboard were firmly brought under colonial rule first. The mainland towns were not pacified until about 1890. Anlo's merchants detested British customs duties – in common with European merchants, including the British – and both African and European merchants constantly moved part of their activities just east of the British boundary to evade customs duties. As revenue from tariffs was central to the British return to Anlo, the colonial boundary followed the trading boundary, British jurisdiction was extended eastward in a series of leaps. German colonization of Togoland in 1884 halted the 'kangaroo frontier', but lower customs duties in German Togoland until 1890 still promoted smuggling into Anlo. Two centuries of active slave-trading had also promoted slave-holding in Anlo society. Anlo was not a 'slave society' in the terms defined by Moses Finley, but slave-holding had become important and had altered Anlo society in important ways.[71] Slavery was abolished in 1874 with the imposition of British colonial rule. The Anlo had to adjust to this momentous change. As pillars of Anlo's old economy were deleted, the Anlo turned to a more purposive exploitation of their marine resources.

Smuggling, customs duties and the leaping colonial frontier in Anlo
It has been mentioned that one motivating factor for the Anglo–Dutch exchange of forts in the Gold Coast was to acquire contiguous territories in which to impose customs duties. The convention that endorsed the exchange of forts stipulated that duties would be imposed by both powers on beer, wine and spirits, cigars and imported tobacco and gunpowder and firearms. Under this arrangement, Britain would levy duties of 6d. per old wine gallon on beer, wine and spirits, 1d. on every pound of tobacco, 1d. on every pound of gunpowder and 1s. on each firearm.[72] In

---

[68] Yegbe, 'Anlo and their neighbours', 75.

[69] The British had obviously adopted canoe warfare in the lagoon system on the Slave Coast. On this art, see Robert Smith, 'The canoe in West African history', *Journal of African History* 11, 4 (1970): 513–33.

[70] The flexibility of African responses to colonial rule is highlighted in A.A. Boahen, *African Perspectives on Colonialism* (Baltimore, 1987).

[71] Moses I. Finley, 'Slavery', *International Encyclopaedia of the Social Sciences* 14 (1968), 307–13. A society would be a 'slave society' if the reproduction of élite political power and wealth were dependent on slave labour.

[72] Metcalfe, *Great Britain and Ghana*, 320.

The Anlo Lowlands, to *c.* 1890

1873 British authorities raised the duty on imported beer, wine and spirits to 1s. These duties were only extended to Anlo in 1874, and the colonial government set up revenue posts at Atiteti, Atorkor, Keta and Adafienu.[73] Revenue began to roll into British coffers: £2,369 in 1877, doubling to £5,036 in 1878. Then revenue dropped suddenly the following year to £2,136 (1878). An alarmed colonial government soon discovered the reason.[74]

Both African and European merchants sought to escape import duties and had moved part of their trading activities east to Denu, just beyond the British boundary at Adafienu. Here they could land their goods duty-free and smuggle the goods to their outlets on the littoral and the mainland via the Keta Lagoon. Indeed, foreign traders in Anlo are credited with this manoeuvre. Yegbe reports that:

> In 1879 Denu came into existence as a depot where traders landed duty-free spirits and gunpowder, the import of which was forbidden in Keta. These were then canoed across the Keta lagoon or by a land-route through Some into the protectorate. Thus goods on which no duties were paid could find their way round into what the Administrators regarded as their rightful hinterland. To strike a balance of advantages some business houses in Keta spread their operations by maintaining trading houses in both Keta and in the neighbourhood of the protectorate. Rottmann, a German trader and Agent of the Bremen factory at Keta, and J.B. Williams originated this practice and aptly earned the name of 'founders of Danoe'. The merchants encouraged people to indulge in smuggling, and the result was that the local people became victims of the strong preventive measures the government took against this illegal trade.[75]

These merchants cleverly spread their risks by paying suppliers of produce to their Keta shops with chits to be collected in imported goods at Denu. This put the risk of smuggling the duty-free goods into the British protectorate on local retailers, not the big-time merchants.[76] Smuggling became diffuse in Anlo society. The government could not condone such acts, which encouraged the flouting of colonial law and struck at its revenue base. Official frustration was reflected in the quick turnover of District Commissioners (DCs) at Keta, there being five DCs between 1874 and 1878.[77]

A.B. Ellis was appointed the fifth DC to Keta in January 1878, and he began his duties with a determination to stamp out smuggling in Anlo. His strong-arm tactics have gone down in Anlo traditions. With his Hausa Constabulary as sidekicks, they attacked smugglers – real and imagined – even beyond the protectorate's boundaries. The Hausas benefited financially from their activities and used these opportunities to loot their victims.[78] The Anlo were helpless against the depredations of the Hausa soldiers:

[73] Yegbe, 'Anlo and their neighbours', 112.
[74] PRO, FO 406/67. Firminger to Barrow, Accra, 26 March 1884.
[75] Yegbe, 'Anlo and their neighbours', 113–14. See also Sorkpor, 'Geraldo de Lima', 76–9; Arthur J. Knoll, *Togo under Imperial Germany 1884–1914* (Stanford, 1978), 10.
[76] PRO, FO 403/12. Captain Hay to Lieutenant Governor Lees, Accra, 20 November 1878; Amenumey, 'Geraldo de Lima', 73.
[77] Yegbe, 'Anlo and their neighbours', 115.
[78] Chapter 3 examines in more detail the Hausa and other African immigrants in the social life of colonial Keta.

Very soon the Awunas [Anlo] began to feel the effects of the British administrative machinery in their country particularly the role of the mischievious Hausa soldiers and the new burdensome customs duties. The pressure soon elicited from the Awunas such contemporaneous expressions as 'xexeme egble' (i.e. the world is corrupt).[79]

The governor suspected that Anlo resentment of Ellis was a result of financial losses suffered by ordinary people in seizures, as they attempted to smuggle their payment in contraband goods from Denu to their places of residence.[80] In Ellis's mind, the arch-smuggler was Geraldo de Lima, and his reports on him and his perceived activities against him initiated a British campaign that would end in the arrest of de Lima in 1885 and his detention until 1893. Ellis himself was removed from the Keta district in controversy. In a hunting expedition north of the Keta Lagoon in October 1878, Ellis shot a man, who later died. The circumstances are unclear, though some sources hint that Ellis with his brash attitude may have provoked the incident.[81] Ellis certainly viewed the incident as a prelude to Anlo hostilities, and he, perhaps, sought to pre-empt this through a show of force. He burnt down houses in Kedzi, Keta and Tegbi and sent to Accra for military reinforcement. Anlo chiefs also protested against Ellis's activities, leading to an inquiry. Ellis was transferred from Anlo in 1879.[82]

By 1879 the colonial government had concluded that it needed to counter Anlo's smuggling advantage via the lagoon if revenues were to recover. The Foreign Office set out to revise the Gold Coast's boundaries:[83]

Lord Salisbury will perceive from these papers that the present boundary [Adafienu] is an unsatisfactory one, inasmuch as the inland lagoon which runs parallel to the sea extends during the rainy season somewhat beyond it, and facilities are thus afforded for goods being landed just outside the jurisdiction of the Colonial Government and being smuggled thence into the protected territories.

The extension now proposed is very limited in extent, being only over the small tract of coast-line ... and there is every reason to believe, from the fact that smuggled goods would then have to be conveyed by land at heavy expense and risk, that an efficient barrier to the continuance of the present contraband trade would be created, and that no further acquisition of territory would on this account be required.[84]

Accordingly, the British government signed treaties with the states of Some and Aflao in December 1879 to extend the eastern boundary of the Gold Coast colony to Aflao, and the colonial government paid their chiefs stipends.[85]

But the colonial government underestimated Anlo resourcefulness and the general

[79] Sorkpor, 'Geraldo de Lima', 76–7.
[80] PRO, FO 403/12. Lt Governor Lees to Sir M. Hicks Beach, Accra, 18 December 1878.
[81] Sorkpor, 'Geraldo de Lima', 85–6.
[82] Ibid., 86–7; and Yegbe, 'Anlo and their neighbors', 115–16.
[83] Although Britain had a Colonial Office in London, it was only in charge of settler colonies. It was not until the scramble and partition of Africa was over that the Foreign Office transferred jurisdiction of the newly acquired African colonies to the Colonial Office. Andrew Roberts, 'The imperial mind', in idem, ed., *The Colonial Moment in Africa* (Cambridge, 1990), 26–7.
[84] PRO, FO 403/12. Robert G.W. Herbert to Sir J. Pauncefote, London, 25 June 1879.
[85] Metcalfe, *Great Britain and Ghana*, 395–6. Hicks-Beach to Lees, 13 March 1879.

determination of Keta's merchants. After an initial rise in customs revenue in 1880 to £6,184, customs receipts the following year dipped to £3,771.[86] The trading frontier had hopped again. Yegbe sums it up succinctly: 'As a result of the establishment of a customs port at Denu the traders founded Lome or Bey Beach as a smuggling depot. The race between traders and government continued'.[87] An exasperated colonial government, in fact, blamed the chiefs of Some for founding Lome as a smuggling base with stipends paid them by the colonial government. A colonial official noted that:

[E]arly in 1881, however, the new trading place as Lomeh, or Beh, which had been founded by the Agbosome [Some] chiefs, with their first year's stipend, had become firmly established as a smuggling depot, and as its trade increased the revenue of Quittah [Keta] diminished.[88]

Indeed, Governor Young was proposing to the metropolitan government in April 1884 that the area from Lome to Bagidah be annexed to the Gold Coast. In his opinion:

Smuggling has been persistently and systematically carried on by the Agbosome people and the Afflohoos [Aflao], and until we can acquire the sea coast territory of Beh as far as Bagidah, all our efforts to stop it will be useless … experience has proved that it is a matter of very serious importance, for goods in large quantities are landed without let or hindrance along the shore, and then by means of the lagoon or inland creeks are smuggled into Afflowhoo, Agbosome, and Awoonah [Anlo], and it becomes a grave question how this loss of revenue, which has now been suffered for some years, can be avoided.[89]

This new initiative was forestalled when Germany annexed Bey Beach in July 1884 and the nucleus of German Togoland was forged.

Smuggling thrived in Anlo throughout the 1880s, and colonial judicial records indicate that the brunt of colonial preventive measures fell mostly on small-scale retailers, not on the influential merchants. Hausa forces frequently patrolled the area north of the Keta Lagoon in search of smugglers. The following incident, reported by a Hausa soldier in 1885, is typical:[90]

I was in command of one of the canoes which accompanied the DC to the mainland on the night of 6th Inst[ant]. About six a. m. I saw the prisoner in a canoe and called him to come, the prisoner jumped out of the canoe and tried to escape but some of my men followed him and caught him and I found 19 demijohns of rum concealed in the canoes.[91]

The Hausa soldiers themselves were not models of virtue, and several were indeed as corrupt as their Anlo hosts charged. The following case, reported by Assistant Inspector Freeman, is revealing:

[86] PRO, FO 406/67. Firminger to Barrow, Accra, 26 March 1884.
[87] Yegbe, 'Anlo and their neighbours', 117. On the 'traders' frontier' in the Gold Coast, see also, Kimble, *A Political History of Ghana*, 11–12.
[88] PRO, FO 406/67. Firminger to Barrow, Accra, 26 March 1884.
[89] Ibid. Governor Young to the Earl of Derby, Accra, 29 April 1884.
[90] Although the Gold Coast military and police were called 'Hausa forces' after the Muslim Hausa of northern Nigeria, over time its members were often seldom Hausa or Muslim. The name stuck because of a Hausa contingent that had been brought in to assist the British invasion of Kumase in 1874.
[91] NAG, Accra, ADM 41/4/1. *Regina* v. *Komegah*, Quittah [Keta], 8 October 1885.

On the morning of the 21st I proceeded to Anyako. I seized three canoes containing smuggled rum. I detailed two of my canoes with Houssas [Hausa] to catch the smugglers. On reaching the smugglers' canoes one of the men complained that he had been robbed of some money. I asked him to point out the man. He said he could not do so, but it was a Houssa in the canoe he pointed out. I then ordered the men in it to be searched and found two handkerchiefs containing £2.6.0. in the inside pocket of his shirt. He had previously denied having taken any.[92]

A more permanent solution to the problem of smuggling was imperative for the colonial government, as the preventive forces themselves became tainted with the 'disease'. This was especially pressing, as the random searches conducted in Anlo homes by the Hausa soldiers highlighted the intrusiveness of colonial rule and was bound to provoke confrontations. In towns and villages such as Kedzi, Dzelukope, Denu and Agbosome, soldiers searched houses, confiscating imported liquor and arresting men and women who did not give satisfactory explanation for possessing these.[93]

In 1890 the Gold Coast colonial government decided to lower customs duties on popular items of import – European alcoholic drinks, tobacco, gunpowder and firearms – east of the Volta to render smuggling in Anlo unattractive. The goal was to standardize duties in this part of the Gold Coast with the lower rates in German Togoland and thus to wipe out the relative advantage residents on one side of the Ewe border may have over the other.[94] Consequently, duty on gin was dropped to 6d. a gallon; that on brandy, rum and liqueurs to 4d.; and guns attracted a 1s. tax. West of the Volta the duties were much heavier: 1s. on every gallon of wine, porter or beer; 2s. on brandy, gin and rum; and 2s. on each gun imported.[95] In addition, all goods subject to a 10 per cent *ad valorem* duty west of the Volta were entirely exempted from duty east of the Volta.[96] Smuggling in Anlo declined. In the 1930s, excessively high duties on imported spirits would create a market for illicit distilled gin. The Anlo would become pioneers in the art of distillation, and the lagoon system would again come in handy in the smuggling of illicit gin.[97] The colonial government also dealt with slavery in Anlo, which had been made illegal in 1874. And it is important to consider the role of domestic slavery in nineteenth-century Anlo economy and society to appreciate the transformative impact of early colonial rule.

Internal slavery in nineteenth-century Anlo society
An important result of Anlo's increased participation in the Atlantic slave-trade was the growth in slave-holding within Anlo society. Slaves constituted wealth, just as in other African societies where people were considered wealth.[98] In Anlo, where land –

[92] Ibid. *Regina v. Private Mama Bakasha*, Quittah, 23 September 1885.
[93] NAG, Accra, ADM 41/4/22, Keta Criminal Book. *Regina v. Yetteh*, DC's Court, Keta, 3 August 1889; *Regina v. Ocloo*, 2 September 1889; *Regina v. Korkor*, 11 November 1889.
[94] German Togoland had no customs duties until 1887, and then only on liquor and guns. Knoll, *Togo*, 27.
[95] Gold Coast Colony, *Blue Book, 1890* (Accra, 1891).
[96] NAG, Accra, ADM 5/1/1. Gold Coast, Colonial Annual Report, 1892.
[97] See Chapter 5.
[98] See, for examples, Jane I. Guyer and Samuel M. Eno Belinga, 'Wealth in people as wealth in knowledge: accumulation and composition in equatorial Africa', *Journal of African History* 36, 1 (1995): 91–120;

and fertile land – was extremely scarce, slaves represented an important store of wealth. Influential groups that migrated later to Anlo received no land or were assigned infertile tracts of land that were often subject to flooding.[99] The Anlo exhibited a preference for young women and children as slaves. Slave women were often married to men in the owner's lineage, and slave children – and slave offspring – grew up as junior 'kinsmen'.[100] These slave women were crucial to production and reproduction in Anlo society. Trading families used slaves in the processing of fish and salt, which were sent together with European goods into the interior. These slaves also served as porters, carrying goods to trade marts. A master controlled his slave wife and offspring to a degree that was absent in a marriage to a free Anlo woman.[101] Wealth from long-distance and the Atlantic trade promoted social stratification and competition in Anlo society, sharpening the distinctions between rich and poor, free and slave.[102] Anlo's social structure was aligning to key changes in its material base. For Anlo society, which lacked a landed aristocracy or an endowed nobility, wealth gradually became concentrated in the hands of a few families.

Togbui Gbodzo of Woe's maternal family is a good example of the emergence of affluent families.

> Tettega and Amegashi Akofi, father and maternal grandfather of Gbodzo, were not the only members of Gbodzo's family who were known for their wealth. Gbodzo's mother, Kpetsimine, and his mother's brother, Kuwo Nunya, both had similar reputations in their own right. Nunya acquired enough slaves to create for himself a *hozikpui* or wealth stool. Kpetsimine was also financially well endowed. Her wealth, according to some oral narratives, came from marketing in the Anlo area to the east the beads that her husband purchased, as well as from the wholesale buying of foodstuffs from communities on the northern side of the lagoon, which she then marketed in the Anlo towns on the coast.[103]

Greene suspects that Kpestimine, with her capital, own boats and European contacts, was probably a participant in the Atlantic slave-trade. Her son, Gbodzo, thus had a head start as a trader, and he accumulated wealth that became proverbial:

> Like them, his reputation for great wealth, which he displayed through the creation of his own *hozipkui*, was based on his involvement in the slave-trade. It was Gbodzo who erected the holding cells near the Woe beach on the Atlantic Ocean from which slaves were moved when the European ships anchored off the coast.[104]

Here were three generations of one family, spanning the period from the mid-eighteenth century to the mid-nineteenth century, demonstrating great wealth.

The Anlo possess several powerful national, clan and family gods, and their

[98 (cont.)] Emmanuel Akyeampong, *Drink, Power, and Cultural Change: A Social History of Alcohol in Ghana, c. 1800 to Recent Times* (Portsmouth, 1996), ch. 8.

[99] Greene, *History of the Anlo-Ewe*, 27.

[100] On the 'slave-to-kinship' continuum, see the introduction and essays in Suzanne Miers and Igor Kopytoff, eds, *Slavery in Africa: Historical and Anthropological Perspectives* (Madison, 1977).

[101] Greene, *History of the Anlo-Ewe*, 38.

[102] Ibid., 39.

[103] Greene, 'Individual as stranger', 98.

[104] Ibid., 99.

influential priests were equally keen on expanding their entourage and on demonstrating wealth in people. It appears that, from the late eighteenth century, the priests of powerful shrines, that of the Amlade clan deity Sui in particular, became influential enough to:

> [D]emand from families who sought its services payment in the form of a *fiasidi*, a young woman who remained as a servant associated with the shrine for the rest of her life; if she died, the family had to replace her.[105]

By the early nineteenth century, the national war god, Nyigbla, had begun to make similar demands of those who required its services.[106] These services could be in aid of childbirth, healing, the settling of disputes, or vengeance for wrongs. *Fiasidi* were often young girls, and they occupied an ambivalent position in Anlo society: unfree yet not slave,[107] pledged but not pawns in the typical sense,[108] social persons with genealogical connections to the community.[109] *Fiasidi* became institutionalized and grew in Anlo society over the nineteenth century, and social, political, and religious connections were cemented between patrilineages with powerful gods and the families that gave *fiasidi* in return for their services. With the abolition of slavery, the institution slipped out of the historical record, until a series of *exposés* in the 1990s brought Ghanaians face to face with a forgotten institution.[110]

By the late nineteenth century, slavery was so entrenched that the spiritual needs of the slaves were formally accommodated in Anlo society. The Anlo used the threat of spiritual sanctions to keep slaves quiescent, apart from the usual strategies of finding slave spouses for slaves to give them a vested emotional stake in maintaining the status quo or incorporating the descendants of slaves as junior kinsmen.[111] G.K. Nukunya's biographical profile of Adzo, a young Krobo girl abducted by an Anlo raiding party in the mid-1890s, well after the abolition of domestic slavery in 1874, underscores the spiritual needs and fears of slaves. Nukunya points out that:

> The fact that Adzo had not gone through the *dipo* rite [Krobo puberty rite] had a profound influence on her life. Among the Krobo a girl may not marry unless this rite is performed. Any breach of this custom will incur serious supernatural sanctions. Adzo believed that, despite her physical separation from her people, she was still Krobo. This conviction was probably enforced by the fact that she came from a royal lineage, which inhabited a large palace with a big rock and a metal bowl in its center (probably in the courtyard) where *dipo* rites were performed. After

---

[105] Greene, *History of the Anlo-Ewe*, 64.

[106] Ibid., 87.

[107] Not so atypical considering African 'rights in persons'. Miers and Kopytoff, *Slavery in Africa*, 3–81.

[108] On pawnship, see Toyin Falola and Paul Lovejoy, eds, *Pawnship in Africa; Debt Bondage in Historical Perspective* (Boulder, 1994).

[109] Orlando Patterson, *Slavery and Social Death: A Comparative Study* (Cambridge, MA, 1982), 1–14. Patterson describes slaves, usually cultural outsiders, as 'social non-persons' and 'genealogical isolates'.

[110] See the final chapter of this book for a discussion of this contemporary controversy and for the author's thoughts on how the institution could have survived undetected by the wider nation for this long.

[111] NAG, Accra, ADM 41/4/1. *Buafo v. Quaccoe Duah*, Keta DC's Court (29 October 1889), provides a fascinating case of a former Akan slave in Anlo, who attempted to claim adultery compensation on his wife – also a former slave. The case reveals the tenuousness of slave marriages and the struggle of former slaves to gain social respectability in the post-emancipation era.

68

Adzo passed her puberty her owner wanted her to become one of his wives ... She decided, in any case, that she might escape the supernatural sanctions by not having a legal marriage with full formalities. Thus, she had five children in all, each with a different man.[112]

In spite of Krobo's geographical proximity to Anlo, Adzo never attempted to escape for 'she was convinced that any attempt to go home would cause her death' because the 'Anlo people used supernatural means to tie the slaves to their new homes'.[113] Both Anlo masters and their slaves believed that the ancestral ties of slaves continued to influence their lives in Anlo. By the late nineteenth century, a slave religious order, *Fofie*, was in existence in Anlo to help reconcile the spiritual tensions in slaves' lives. Greene reports that:

According to oral traditions, this order developed in Anlo specifically to meet the spiritual needs of those enslaved men and women who had been removed from their communities and who were said to have become ill because their slave status had prevented them from communicating with and offering sacrifices to their ancestors in their own home areas.[114]

Slave-holding in Anlo society must have progressed to a significant degree to have made masters solicitous of the spiritual welfare of their slaves.[115] This concern strengthened the spiritual control of masters over their slaves, for, if they acknowledged the spiritual influences of the slave's former life in the new Anlo domain, then it made spiritual sense for the runaway slave to expect the wrath of Anlo's gods.

By the mid-1860s, many Anlo traders had turned away from the slave-trade to trade in vegetable oils, rubber, cotton, copra and fish products.[116] An internal slave market continued, and slaves were used in the processing and transport of these new products. When the colonial government abolished slavery in 1874, the Anlo naturally protested. Brodie Cruickshank's mid-nineteenth-century comment on the coastal Akans west of the Volta holds equally true for the Anlo:

Slaves are the only property of many people in the country, and no reasoning can convince them that the forcible taking of them away is not as much a theft and a robbery as if they have been deprived of gold.[117]

Indeed, an important factor in Anlo resentment of the local Hausa Constabulary from the 1870s was that they encouraged slaves who came to Keta as porters to seek refuge in the fort. The timing of British emancipation was particularly painful for the Anlo, for Anlo participation in the volatile vegetable-oil trade had increased

---

[112] G.K. Nukunya, 'A note on Anlo (Ewe) slavery and the history of a slave', appendix to Claire C. Robertson, 'Post-proclamation slavery in Accra: a female affair?' in Claire Robertson and Martin A. Klein, eds, *Women and Slavery in Africa* (Madison, 1983), 243–4.

[113] Ibid., 244.

[114] Greene, *History of the Anlo-Ewe*, 67.

[115] The 'Order of Blood Men', a slave order that developed in mid-nineteenth-century Calabar, emerged in opposition to the disdain of masters for slaves' lives, and not because the masters sponsored or nurtured it. J.B. Webster and A.A. Boahen with M. Tidy, *The Revolutionary Years: West Africa since 1800* (Harlow, 1980), 147.

[116] On the use of unfree female labour in the transition to a cash-crop economy in the Gold Coast, see Beverly Grier, 'Pawns, porters, and petty traders: women in the transition to cash crop agriculture in colonial Ghana', *Signs* 17, 2 (1990): 601–18.

[117] Brodie Cruickshank, *Eighteen Years on the Gold Coast of Africa*, vol. 2 (London, 1853), 233–4.

indebtedness and social insecurity in Anlo society. Pawnship became rife, and it fell unduly on women.[118]

In the unsettled times of the 1870s and 1880s, slaving, brigandage, *panyarring*[119] and pawnship became fused in disconcerting ways. This was not a time for strangers to be in Anlo. As Sri II, *awoamefia* of Anlo (1907–1956), confessed before the 1912 Crowther Commission: 'When they used to kill Hausa man it was only to rob him of his money: they used to do it plenty.'[120] Women were prime victims of *panyarring*, pawnship and slavery. The following case from 1885 is illuminating:

> I am a woman of Afierengbah [Afiadenyigba] a British subject. I was travelling at Fwenyie [Fenyi] about 10 miles from Afflahoo [Aflao] when a company of men came and seized me and brought me to the prisoner who put me in log and in foot irons and sent me to a place called Glapeh Koppe where I stayed a short time still in irons, until the prisoner came and sold me to a man called Amenahkoo to whom I was a slave for two months. About nine days ago the prisoner came and redeemed me and brought me to a man called Folie at Danoe [Denu] who took me to the white officer at Danoe and he sent me here.[121]

In this case, some people at Fenyi owed money to Foli of Denu, and the Fenyi people had arranged to seize some of their own townspeople to pay for their debt to Foli. In 1886 Gbedashi of Afiadenyigba, a native of Agbosome who had been sold by her family into slavery in 1866, was trying to redeem in court the daughter she had had with her master, who had subsequently been pawned by the master/father.[122]

The existence of isolated settlements amidst the lagoons and creeks, and the proximity of German Togoland, where domestic slavery was condoned until 1902, enabled the Anlo to elude colonial vigilance and to hold slaves well after 1874. Indeed, German colonial law in Togo institutionalized *panyarring* in 1896 by recognizing the seizure of a debtor's family in lieu of payment.[123] The Anlo had relations and farmlands in Togoland before the artificial colonial frontier. Masters could simply relocate their slaves to German Togoland.[124] Disputing the date of enslavement also became a heated issue before colonial courts, as masters sought to prove that they had acquired their slaves before the commencement of colonial rule, whereas slaves claimed they had been enslaved after colonial imposition.[125] It was a punishable crime to acquire slaves in the British Gold Coast after 1874, while slaves enslaved before 1874 were simply given the option of freedom. Many, especially slave

---

[118] Greene, *History of the Anlo-Ewe*, 102. On the feminization of pawnship in the Gold Coast, see Gareth Austin, 'Human pawning in Asante, 1800–1950', in Falola and Lovejoy, eds, *Pawnship in Africa*, 119–59.

[119] *Panyarring* was the practice of seizing relatives or even townspeople of a debtor and holding these till the debt was redeemed. Failure to redeem the debt led to the sale of these persons, and their families in turn applied pressure to the debtor to make restitution.

[120] Sri II per Davoji, Notes of Evidence (1912 Commission).

[121] NAG, Accra, ADM 41/4/1. *Fia Fofie v. Bokor Gomashie*, Keta, 3 August 1885.

[122] NAG, Accra, ADM 41/4/21. *Gbedashi of Aferingbah v. Yabua of Accra*, Keta, 11 January 1886.

[123] See Donna J.E. Maier, 'Slave labor and wage labor in German Togo', in Arthur J. Knoll and Lewis H. Gann, eds, *Germans in the Tropics: Essays in German Colonial History* (Westport, 1987), 73–91.

[124] A good example is *Regina v. Attichogbey*, Keta, DC's Court, 31 October 1890. NAG, Accra, ADM 41/4/23.

[125] Ibid. *Regina v. Badago*, 21 November 1890.

women who had children in the master's lineage, chose to stay.[126] The lagoons and creeks also facilitated the abduction and holding of slaves in isolated settlements. Strangers who passed through Anloland were particularly vulnerable. In 1885, Akonyikoo and his wife, Abooya, were abducted while passing through Anlo. They were travelling from Dahomey to Ada, and Agbochie, an Anlo man they met in Keta, offered to guide them to Ada for a fee. It is uncertain whether Agbochie planned from the onset to abduct his charges, but the sudden turn of events merits recounting:

> When we arrived at Jellacoffe [Dzelukope] we took a canoe at the prisoner's instigation. We travelled for three days and I then said to the prisoner, we are a long time reaching Addah. He explained that as I had so much property, it was better to go the way he was taking us. On the 3rd day we arrived at the Mlafie [Mefi] farms on this [Anlo] side of the Volta, we slept at a small village. I heard the prisoner tell the men of the village (which was called Tovie) to seize me and my wife. In the middle of the night plenty of men came and seized me and my wife Abooya and put me in log, the prisoner was present the whole time and directed the men … The prisoner then took us and offered us for sale to a man called Ahinahootor and my wife to another person but she would not agree to be separated from me, so the man Ahinahootor bought us both.[127]

Agbochie obviously appropriated the travellers' property in addition to the money he received from selling them as slaves. What is astounding is the defence of the perpetrator in court: 'I do not know what made me sell them except that I was tempted so it came into my mind'.[128]

The ease with which this transaction had been carried out recalls what Patrick Manning aptly describes as the 'economics of theft' in slaving in African societies.[129] But it also points to the need to explore African cultural concepts of 'chance' or 'luck' in accumulation, though that goes beyond the scope of this present endeavour. Law comments on the prominence of gambling on the Slave Coast in the late seventeenth and eighteenth centuries. He believes gambling was a product of insecurity generated by the expanding money market: 'The drama of enrichment or impoverishment by the vagaries of the market was thus parodied by popular games of chance'.[130] Both Agbochie and Ahinahootor in the above case certainly believed that they had met their lucky day: unplanned, but opportune. But encroaching British power in colonial Anlo was real, and the new power had very defined ideas about legitimate economic activity. As the Anlo settled into the colonial economy, they turned to a more intensive exploitation of sea fishing based on the new fishing technology the European presence had made accessible.

---

[126] This is very much in line with the cases discussed in Suzanne Miers and Richard Roberts, eds, *The End of Slavery in Africa* (Madison, 1988).

[127] *Regina* v. *Agbochie*, Keta, DC's Court, 3 June 1885. NAG, Accra, ADM 41/4/1.

[128] Ibid.

[129] Patrick Manning, *Slavery and African Life: Occidental, Oriental and African Slave Trades* (Cambridge, 1990).

[130] Law, *Slave Coast of West Africa*, 69. See also Thomas Q. Reefe, 'The biggest game of all: gambling in traditional Africa', in William J. Baker and James A. Mangan, eds, *Sport in Africa: Essays in Social History* (New York and London, 1987), 47–78.

The emergence of beach-seine fishing as an Anlo tradition

It is striking that one of the most detailed descriptions of the Anlo area in the eighteenth century made no mention of sea fishing. It is difficult to assume that the author, Isert (1788), missed Anlo sea-fishing activities, as he documented lagoon fishing in the Anloga area, Keta, and at Agudza and Kpoduwa.[131] From Isert's interested account of sea fishing among the Ga of Accra, it is unlikely that similar operations among the Anlo would have gone unnoticed.[132] It appears that the heavy surf still confined Anlo fishing activities to the calmer waters of the lagoon. It is strange, then, that one of the clauses of the treaty the Danes imposed on Keta and Anlo in 1784 was that: 'The Augnas [Anlo] themselves would no longer send canoes out to sea to meet ships, but would trade only with our nation'.[133] Whether this clause proscribed an existing trade or sought to pre-empt any future Anlo dealings is unclear. There is evidence, however, of a growing Anlo familiarity with the sea. Isert mentions that Keta had the best drinking-water on the Guinea coast, which they gained by sinking shallow wells at the beach. What is fascinating was the manner in which barrels of water were transported to waiting European ships: 'The Blacks then swim through the breakers, each one pushing a full barrel with his head, to the point where a ship's boat lies ready to receive them'.[134] If the Anlo or Keta were mariners in the late eighteenth century, they surely would have transported the barrels of water in their canoes. That the Anlo had become strong swimmers is evident when Isert's boat capsized in 1784 on its approach to Fort Prindsensten: 'I was tossed around in the breakers until a Black came swimming from the shore, pulled me on to his back, and thus drew me ashore'.[135] As the Anlo moved tentatively towards an exploitation of the sea's resources from the mid-nineteenth century, copra from the dense coconut trees that lined the Anlo shore entered the commodity market.

Copra had been exported sporadically from the Gold and Slave Coasts since the 1830s. It was only from the 1870s that the Anlo came to treat their coconut trees as an exportable economic product. The Keta and Ada districts were prominent exporters from the start. Dickson provides valuable insights for this pattern:

> The early pre-eminence of Ada and Keta districts in the copra export trade may be accounted for by the absence of profitable alternative occupations. Up to the close of the nineteenth century the coconut tree held its own in the agricultural landscape simply because it did not grow in the same areas with cocoa.[136]

By the 1870s, Anlo religious cults, such as Yewe, were using their members in the collection and processing of copra.[137] Custom bolstered the growing Anlo appreciation of the economic importance of the coconut tree, and the planting of a coconut tree

---

[131] Isert, *Letters on West Africa*, 57, 60 and 75.
[132] Ibid., 126–7, 136 and 142.
[133] Ibid., 71.
[134] Ibid., 77.
[135] Ibid., 88.
[136] Dickson, *Historical Geography of Ghana*, 159–60.
[137] Greene, *History of the Anlo-Ewe*, 99.

at the birth of each child built up Anlo reserves of this valuable resource.[138] By the early twentieth century, the copra industry in Anlo had obtained great importance.

The Anlo experiment with sea fishing was frustrating. By the eighteenth century, a variety of set nets and purse-nets were used on the Gold Coast, together with hook and line and diverse forms of traps and dams in sea, river and lagoon fishing.[139] The Anlo experimented with the purse-net (*agli*) in the first half of the nineteenth century without satisfactory results.[140] A remarkable change occurred in marine fishing methods in the second half of the nineteenth century, and Albert de Surgy has documented the introduction of various nets along the Gold Coast with port towns serving as coastal points of dissemination. Central to the maritime history of the Anlo was the introduction of the technique of fishing from the shore.[141] Sometime between 1850 and 1860, an enterprising Anlo merchant couple in Woe, John Tay and Afedima, introduced a beach-seine net, known locally as *yevudor* ('European net').

> It is generally known in the Keta area that the first yevudor (European net) or seine net was purchased by a Woe woman called Afedima, a wealthy daughter of a prominent local man called Anatsi. Afedima was born around the first quarter of the 19th century and died towards the end of the century. Genealogies and other calculations put the genesis of the seine net at between 1850–60. The numbers of net owners increased gradually and by the beginning of this century no less than fifteen owners, each with his company of operators, were recorded at Woe alone.[142]

The introduction was timely, for contemporary German observers noted the over-fishing of the Keta Lagoon and a decline in fish stocks.[143]

By the early twentieth century, Anlo fishermen had made an effective transition to sea fishing, and they would emerge over the century as the experts of beach-seine fishing along the West African coast. This form of fishing was ideally suited to the Anlo coast with its heavy surf and a sand bar that endangered the approach to the shore. The German missionary, Gottlob Härtter, provides a 1906 description of the operation of a beach-seine net off the coast of Anlo. Greene gives an accurate translation:

> [T]he *Yevudo* ... is 60–100 meters long, 3–4 feet wide and the middle has a sack (*voku*) that catches large and small fish. The net is held with two strong pieces of rope. On one side of the net are attached little weights ... and on the other side are two stakes, *kpotiwo*. On the stakes are attached 300–400 meters of rope. The net itself is reinforced with cotton anywhere from 2–4 times.

[138] J.M. Grove, 'Some aspects of the economy of the Volta delta (Ghana)', *Bulletin de l'Institut Fondamental d'Afrique Noire* 28, 1–2 (1966): 384; Gold Coast, *Report on the Census of the Gold Coast Colony for the Year 1891*, 11. NAG, Accra, ADM 5/2/1.

[139] These are documented by Müller in Fanti country in the 1660s, Adam Jones, *German Sources for West African History, 1599–1669* (Wiesbaden, 1983); for the Ga in the 1780s, Isert, *Letters on West Africa*; Dickson, *Historical Geography of Ghana*, for much of the coast of Ghana since 1700.

[140] Greene, *History of the Anlo-Ewe*, 165.

[141] Albert de Surgy, *La Pêche maritime traditionelle à l'ancienne 'Côte de Guinée': origines et développement* (Togo, 1969), 103–27.

[142] G.K. Nukunya, 'The Anlo-Ewe and full-time maritime fishing: another view', *Maritime Anthropological Studies* 2, 2 (1989): 156.

[143] Greene, *History of the Anlo-Ewe*, 165.

The day of fishing, the boat is prepared and 3–4 men get on board, giving to one man on shore the end of the rope to hold. As soon as the cable is unrolled the net is thrown into the sea and the boat paddled transversely. Once all the net is in the water, the boat is turned around and heads for the shore, with men on shore pulling the net in with the two rope ends. As soon as the stakes are seen, more men rush into the water to hold them under water. Slowly more of the net begins to appear and the concern moves to the sack in the middle of the net. The *voku* is sewn tightly with strong rope. As soon as the *voku* lands on shore, it is emptied.[144]

The wary Anlo had found a way to exploit the fish stocks in the sea without imperilling their lives. Their innovations over the century would improve the facilities of the *yevudor*. The Anlo had become sea fishermen.[145]

Conclusion

The nineteenth century was a period of momentous changes for the Anlo. The slave-trade was abolished at the beginning of the century, just as the Anlo had become established slave-traders. Not particularly blessed with the oil-palm that was replacing the slave-trade, the Anlo persisted in the slave-trade until the 1860s. The lagoons and creeks that stretched inland across Anlo country provided excellent facilities for smuggling. In 1850 the Danes had withdrawn from West Africa, selling their settlements to the British. Anlo slipped, technically, under British influence. Effective British presence in Anlo did not last a decade, for the area did not have the economic resources to support British administration. The North German Missionary Society from Bremen opened a station in Keta in 1853, and their activities, together with those of the Bremen firm of F.M. Vietor, opened a new chapter in Anlo's history. With the revival of trade came the rekindling of British interest in the area east of the Volta. Anlo resistance to the imposition of British colonial rule in 1874 continued in the form of the smuggling of duty-free imported goods. Gradually the British gained control of smuggling and effectively ended domestic slavery within Anlo society. The Anlo, initially resentful about colonial rule, would discover that colonial rule could be beneficial in certain ways. The extension of British jurisdiction east of the Volta accompanied the formalization of Anlo leadership of the Anlo confederacy which had collapsed at the end of the eighteenth century.[146] Keta was declared a colonial surf port, and its emergence as a bustling trading emporium far surpassed anything in its precolonial past. The next chapter examines the economy and social life of this colonial port town.

[144] G. Härtter, 'Der Fischfang im Evheland', *Zeitschrift für Ethnologie* 38, 1–2 (1906): 56–8; trans. Greene, *History of the Anlo-Ewe*, 166.

[145] Detailed discussions of Anlo sea fishing over the twentieth century are provided in Chapters 5 and 6.

[146] See Chapter 1.

3

Commercial Prosperity,
Urbanization & Social Life
in Early Colonial Keta

Introduction

This chapter examines the economy and social life in the colonial port town of Keta. Keta's early prominence on the Slave Coast was as a trading port, a function confirmed and enhanced by colonial rule. Initially one of several surf ports east of the Volta in British Gold Coast, albeit the major one, Keta was made the only surf port east of the Volta in 1916 by colonial fiat.[1] The town became the fulcrum in the regional economy east of the Volta and served as a point for the collection of export products and the distribution of imported goods. Its mercantile class – European and African – expanded with commercial prosperity, and Keta in 1906 was appointed the colonial headquarters of the Keta-Ada District. Keta's spatial growth was unique, for land was extremely scarce, and urban growth was mirrored more in Keta's increasingly prominent role – politically, economically, socially and culturally – than in population or spatial explosion. Though Gold Coast censuses conferred urban status only on areas with over 10,000 residents, Dickson's definition of a town is particularly applicable to Keta, for he defines towns by their 'predominance of cultural, administrative and other non-rural functions, and not necessarily by population size'.[2]

On the four-day cycle market-days, the Keta market attracted huge crowds of people from the Gold Coast, Togoland, Dahomey and Nigeria. In 1900, the District Commissioner (DC) of Keta believed that between £4,000 and £5,000 changed hands daily at Keta.[3] The Commissioner for the Eastern Province (CEP), of which

---

[1] Surf ports describe landing beaches that are not natural or artificial harbours, where goods are loaded on to and unloaded from ships waiting in the roads by canoes moving through the surf zone. See Kwamina B. Dickson, 'Evolution of seaports in Ghana: 1800–1928', *Annals of the Association of American Geographers* 55, 1 (1965): 98.

[2] Kwamina B. Dickson, *A Historical Geography of Ghana* (Cambridge, 1969), 239.

[3] John Fred Kwaku Kumassah, 'Keta: a declining Anlo urban centre' (BA thesis, Geography Department, University of Ghana, 1978), 11–12.

Keta was a part, opined that the Keta market was the largest he had seen in the Gold Coast.[4] Obviously, social relations in Keta became much more complex with a large influx of immigrants: male and female, African and European. Gender, ethnic, race and class relations underwent momentous transformations as people negotiated modernity and urban identity. Modernity is used here to describe the 'spirit of innovation', a willingness to embrace the rapid social change introduced by colonialism with its empowering, alienating and subjugating qualities. Social mobility was a key factor in people's engagement with modernity, and global forces, such as Christianity, Western education and technology, were evaluated and eclectically appropriated in unique ways in local contexts. This spirit of innovation is captured in the Ewe phrase for 'civilization' in the nineteenth and twentieth centuries: *nkuvuvu* ('eye opening'). It celebrates the achievement of new things seen elsewhere (in an era of migrant labour) which are considered worthy of supplementing or even replacing the familiar.[5]

This chapter endeavours to reconstruct urbanization and urbanism in early colonial Keta through census reports, shipping statistics, colonial revenue returns, contemporary missionary reports and photos, and court records from the DC's court at Keta. These court records provide an entry into changing social relations in all of Anlo, which was administered as the Keta District through the DC resident at Keta. Keta's economy is examined within the wider political economy of the Gold Coast, as reflected in the fortunes of its numerous ports.

Economy and society in early colonial Keta

Urbanization in Keta was a gradual process, reflected in Keta's growing pre-dominance in the political, economic and social life of Anlo from the last quarter of the nineteenth century. Two developments were crucial to Keta's prominence: its choice as a mission station by the North German Missionary Society in 1853 and the concomitant presence of German and, later, other foreign merchants; and the explicit role assigned to Keta by the colonial government as the leading port east of the Volta. Up to the 1911 census, Keta's population did not exceed 5,000, though the

---

[4] NAG, Accra, ADM 39/1/173. CEP to Colonial Secretary, 25 April 1911.

[5] Birgit Meyer, 'Translating the devil: an African appropriation of pietist protestantism – the case of the Peki Ewe in Southeastern Ghana, 1847–1992' (PhD thesis, University of Amsterdam, 1995), 65. The exact phrase in Twi, *enibie* ('eye opening'), captures the Akan understanding of 'civilization' or modernity. On modernity, the author has found the following useful for his conceptualization: Jean and John Comaroff, eds, *Modernity and its Malcontents: Ritual and Power in Postcolonial Africa* (Chicago, 1993); Paul Gilroy, *The Black Atlantic: Modernity and Double Consciousness* (Cambridge, MA, 1993); Arjun Appadurai, *Modernity at Large: Cultural Dimensions of Globalization* (Minneapolis, 1996); Kwame Gyekye, *Tradition and Modernity: Philosophical Reflections on the African Experience* (New York and Oxford, 1997); Brian Larkin, 'Indian films and Nigerian lovers: media and the creation of parallel modernities', *Africa* 67, 3 (1997): 406–40. On modernity in Asante before the Second World War, see Emmanuel Akyeampong, 'Christianity, modernity, and the weight of tradition in the life of Asantehene Agyeman Prempeh I, *c*. 1888–1931', *Africa* 69, 2 (1999): 279–311.

Photo 3.1 Keta market-day, *c.* 1893 *(taken by German missionary Ernst Burgi).*

number of people in Keta on market-days far exceeded this amount (Photo 3.1).[6] Land shortage put a premium on real estate, and only indigenes, wealthy traders, colonial officials, the Hausa Constabulary and the civil police and migrant labour (such as the Kru canoemen from Liberia) considered crucial to the reproduction of Keta's port economy found residence in Keta. The rest constituted a floating population that assembled for market-days, and outside traders sojourned for a day or two with trading partners. In contrast to railway and mining towns that sprang up with colonial rule, Keta's population exhibited an even gender balance, and men did not sharply outnumber women, as typical in economies based largely on migrant labour.[7] Indeed, the 1911 census highlights the fact that immigrants in Keta were mostly from Adangme, Dahomey and Togo and that female migrants outnumbered male migrants.[8] An examination of Keta's colonial economy and mission activity provides a necessary context for an analysis of social life and social relations.

[6] Keta's population was listed as 1,887 in 1891, 3,018 in 1901 and 3,630 in 1911. Gold Coast, *Census Report for 1891*; Gold Coast Colony, *Census of the Population 1901* (NAG, Accra, ADM 5/2/2); Gold Coast Colony, *Census of Population, 1911* (NAG, Accra, ADM 5/2/3). The census reports indicate a suspicion, however, that Keta's figures were underestimates. Though Keta's population was smaller than Anloga in 1891 and 1901, Keta's cosmopolitan population is underscored by its thirteen whites and 58 mulattos in 1891, for example, which compared quite favourably with Cape Coast's 39 whites and 216 mulattos – considering Cape Coast's long association with the English.

[7] See Emmanuel Akyeampong, '*Wo pe tam won pe ba* (you like cloth but you don't want children): urbanization, individualism, and gender relations in colonial Ghana, *c.* 1900–1939', in David Anderson and Richard Rathbone, eds, *Africa's Urban Past* (Oxford, 2000), 222–34.

[8] Gold Coast, *Census of Population, 1911.*

The economy of a colonial port town

Chapter 2 underscored the revived British interest in the Anlo region in the 1860s, as trade boomed under German auspices and the Krobo palm-oil boycott diverted palm-oil supplies to Keta and other Anlo ports. Subsequently, British customs duties were extended east of the Volta when Anlo was incorporated into the Gold Coast in 1874. Keta's economy had an inherent weakness: it circulated or distributed goods; it did not produce any minerals; and, outside copra, it produced none of the agricultural exports that replaced the slave-trade. Though copra exports from the Keta-Ada District were not insignificant, copra never became a major export in the Gold Coast's economy. Keta emerged as a major exporter of palm oil in the last quarter of the nineteenth century, but it served only as a collection point, and its attractiveness was based on the low price of European imported goods exchanged for Krobo palm oil. This advantage was a result of the absence of customs duties in Togo and the smuggling of imported goods into Anlo. Hence, in the last half of the nineteenth century, when palm oil exports came to determine the status of ports in the Gold Coast, Keta survived the pruning of surf ports. The forty surf ports in existence in *c*.1800 had been reduced to about twenty-two in 1885. Five of these surf ports were located east of the Volta: Attoko, Dzelukope, Keta, Addafia (Elmina Chica) and Denu.[9] In 1895 there were nineteen accredited ports of entry and twenty-two sufferance wharves where goods could be loaded or unloaded with prior permission.[10]

By the 1890s, the structural weaknesses in Keta's economy were being revealed. In 1887, the German colonial government in Togo introduced customs duties on European liquor, guns and gunpowder, those very items that underpinned Keta's exchange economy.[11] However, these duties were much lower than those of the British Gold Coast, and Keta merchants still possessed a comparative advantage. It was this situation that compelled the Gold Coast colonial government to introduce differential tariffs for the areas west and east of the Volta in 1890. German colonial rule in Togo in the 1890s was shifting from its ad hoc early phase to a more coherent system, and revenue for internal development became an important issue. The government wished to raise customs duties, but feared such a unilateral move would place it at a disadvantage *vis-à-vis* the Gold Coast. In 1894 Togo approached the Gold Coast and suggested the creation of a common customs zone for Togo and the Gold Coast east of the Volta. The Gold Coast government was only too willing to oblige, and a joint tariff system went into effect from 1894, enabling the Gold Coast government to raise duties east of the Volta much higher than the rates fixed in 1890.[12] The result was a decline in Anlo oil-palm exports, as Anlo traders lost their ability to offer Krobo palm-oil producers cheap European goods.[13] Anlo's export economy was further dented by the construction of an excellent road and rail system

---

[9] Gold Coast Colony, *Blue Book, 1885* (Accra, 1886); Dickson, 'Evolution of seaports in Ghana'.

[10] Dickson, 'Evolution of seaports in Ghana', 107–8.

[11] Arthur J. Knoll, *Togo under Imperial Germany 1884–1914* (Stanford, 1978), 26–7.

[12] Ibid., 72–3. The customs union survived until Togo unilaterally abrogated it in 1904.

[13] Sandra E. Greene, *Gender, Ethnicity, and Social Change on the Upper Slave Coast: A History of the Anlo-Ewe* (Portsmouth, 1996), 161.

in German Togo, with Lome as the terminus, between 1904 and 1911.[14] Trade routes from northern Eweland that terminated at Keta were redirected to Lome, especially after the colonial border was firmly defined in 1899.[15] Even road construction in the eastern Gold Coast inadvertently deprived Keta of its middleman role in exports, as these roads linked inland producing areas with coastal outlets. None of the three roads built in the Keta-Ada District in the 1900s had Keta as the terminus: the Anyako–Wute–Sesakpe road, the Afieyingbe–Whenyi road and the Denu–Dokplata road.[16] The Keta Lagoon still acted as an important artery between northern Eweland and Keta, but Pax Britannica also ensured that trade could come safely down the Volta River to Ada for export.

The next phase of challenges would emerge from c.1910 with cocoa's rise as the king of exports in the Gold Coast. Anlo was not a cocoa-producing area, and statistics of cocoa exports in 1910 – the Gold Coast became the world's leading producer of cocoa in 1911 – and 1928 reveal that virtually no cocoa was exported from Keta.[17] Cocoa came to define the status of ports. Accra and Sekondi, with central locations east and west of the colony and the termini of the emerging railway network, became the busiest ports in the Gold Coast. Cape Coast was the only other major port in cocoa exports. The survival of ports was determined by production and trade patterns, and only nine ports showed signs of permanence in 1910: Half-Assini, Axim, Sekondi, Cape Coast, Saltpond, Winneba, Accra, Ada and Keta. These ports pushed neighbouring ports out of existence. East of the Volta, Denu was closed in 1916, leaving Keta's premier position unchallenged.[18]

Keta's pre-eminent role in imports and as the distribution centre in the regional economy east of the Volta compensated for its weakness in exports. The *Annual Colonial Report* for 1892 expressed satisfaction at the increasing government revenue from customs duties in Keta.[19] Indeed, Keta compared favourably with other major ports in a 1894–5 comparison of revenue receipts from liquor imports, the major source of revenue in colonial Gold Coast before the First World War (Table 3.1).[20] Keta had made it into the top ten ports in the Gold Coast as far as import duties were concerned.

Keta's port experienced heavy traffic, and the advent of a steamship service between Europe and West Africa from the 1850s, especially the rise of the Elder Dempster (Liverpool) and C. Woermann (Hamburg) Shipping Lines, ensured a flurry of shipping activity along the West African coast. Shipping statistics between 1885 and 1905 emphasize the large number of British and foreign ships that were cleared through Keta (Table 3.2).

[14] Knoll, *Togo*, 130–1.

[15] See, for example, Donna J.E. Maier, 'Slave labor and wage labor in German Togo', in Arthur J. Knoll and Lewis H. Gann, eds, *Germany in the Tropics: Essays in German Colonial History* (Westport, 1987).

[16] Dickson, *Historical Geography*, 221.

[17] Dickson, 'Evolution of seaports in Ghana', 107–8.

[18] Ibid., 107–9.

[19] Gold Coast, *Colonial Annual Report*, 1892. NAG, ADM, 5/1/1.

[20] On liquor revenue in colonial Gold Coast, see Emmannuel Akyeampong, *Drink, Power, and Cultural Change: A Social History of Alcohol in Ghana, c.1800 to Recent Times* (Portsmouth and Oxford, 1996), ch. 5.

Table 3.1: Customs duties on liquor at Gold Coast ports, 1894–5

District	1894 (£)	1895 (£)	Increase (£)
Axim	4,950.7.6	6,119.12.6	1,169.5.0
Cape Coast	20,258.2.6	20,597.8.10	339.6.4
Salt Pond	16,320.7.6	15,860.12.6	—
Winnebah	14,903.0.0	15,294.15.6	391.15.6
Accra	28,761.18.6	28,946.6.6	184.8.0
Ada	10,569.7.1	11,808.15.0	1,239.7.11
Keta	11,566.14.2	10,532.11.8	—
Other districts	24,931.9.6	26,060.1.3	1,128.11.9
Total	132,261.12.2	135,220.3.9	2,958.17.0

Source: Gold Coast, *Annual Report for 1895.* NAG, Accra, ADM 5/1/4.

Table 3.2: Total number of steamships cleared at Gold Coast ports, 1885–1905

Year	Accra	Ada	Axim	Cape Coast	Denu	Elmina	Keta
1885	40	13	28	39	1	6	125
1890	65	28	44	26	3	8	77
1894	85	16	75	15	10	27	116
1900	111	18	84	37	2	2	101
1905	150	44	163	14	21	—	86

Source: Gold Coast Colony, *Blue Book, 1885* (Accra, 1886); Gold Coast Colony, *Blue Book, 1890* (Accra, 1891); Gold Coast, *Blue Book, 1894* (Accra, 1895); Gold Coast, *Blue Book, 1900* (Accra, 1901); Gold Coast, *Blue Book, 1905* (Accra, 1906).

As the Annual Report for 1895 cautions, the fact that more steamers entered Keta than Accra does not indicate that there was more trade at Keta than at Accra.[21] Axim and Keta occupied unique positions in the economy of colonial Gold Coast as the first major ports on the western and eastern frontiers of the colony. They thus served regional economies and functioned also as watering stations. Axim, moreover, occupied an excellent location. It was situated at the mouth of the River Ankobra, possessed a safe landing beach and was accessible to the gold-producing interior.[22] Keta lacked the natural advantages of shelter and a safe landing beach, but functioned as the centre of distribution for the regional economy east of the Volta. The heavy shipping traffic created a constant hustle and bustle in Keta, adding to its image as a fast, cosmopolitan town.

But Keta also exhibited the features of a mixed economy in the period up to *c*. 1910. Some farmland provided the basis of agriculture, and livestock and poultry abounded. The 1891 census remarked that the barrenness of land had forced the Anlo of Keta District into copra, poultry and, though not mentioned, livestock.[23] The numerous civil suits over crops destroyed by cattle at the DC's Court in Keta underscore Keta's mixed economy. The date 28 May 1887 witnessed James Ocloo

[21] Gold Coast, *Annual Report for 1895* (London, 1897).
[22] Dickson, 'Evolution of seaports in Ghana', 102.
[23] Gold Coast, *Census Report for 1891*.

(soon to be appointed chief of Keta in 1893) suing Mensah Kukubor for the damage done to his crops by the latter's cattle.[24] A similar suit was brought against Quacooboh by J.D. Williams on 18 June 1888 for the destruction of his cassava crops.[25] And on 3 November 1896 J.H. Emmanuel was accusing Mensah Kukubor for stealing his bullocks.[26] The copra industry increased in importance from *c.* 1904 with the discovery in Europe that coconut oil could be used in the manufacture of margarine. The price for copra went up in the early twentieth century, and the Anlo responded by planting more coconut trees between Atiteti and Denu.[27] Fishing in the lagoon and at the seaside continued, and *yevudor* nets were so prized by the 1890s that they became the favourite surety for loans and were eagerly seized even for debts owed by relatives of a *yevudor* owner.[28] Whether in trade, poultry, livestock or fishing, a sharp spirit of acquisitiveness was discernible in Keta, and written contracts regulated all kinds of financial arrangements. Keta owed this utility of literacy to the North German Missionary Society.

German missionaries, German merchants and urbanization in Keta

The North German Missionary Society was founded in Hamburg in 1836 by six Lutheran and Reformed Protestant Churches. The Society sent its first missionaries to West Africa in 1847, and they were eventually referred to Peki (Krepi) by the Basle Mission Society as a possible field of evangelization. Both at home and abroad, the North German Society faced early challenges. Controversies in the mission regarding confessional questions led to the reorganization of the Mission Society as a Reformed Protestant Mission Society in 1851 with Bremen as its headquarters (hereafter referred to as the Bremen Mission). In Peki the early German missionaries also went through their own unique problems – though they were partly an extension of metropolitan difficulties, weak finances and an inability to attract converts. They argued for the convenience of a coastal base instead of the isolated interior and received permission from the Mission Board to set up a station in Keta in 1853.[29]

And thus began the engagement that would have momentous consequences for the social history of Keta in particular, and Anlo in general, as it emerged as a centre of education and Christianity. For the Anlo, the missionaries and the German merchants that accompanied them were the precursors of modernity, generating new needs, images and ideas that were sometimes dismaying to the missionaries them-

---

[24] NAG, Accra, ADM 41/4/2. Keta Civil Record Book (1885–90).

[25] Ibid.

[26] NAG, Accra, ADM 41/4/5. Keta Civil Record Book.

[27] Dickson, *Historical Geography*, 160.

[28] See, for examples, *Regina* v. *Magatse*, DC's Court, 19 March 1891; *Regina* v. *Amegah*, DC's Court, 21 March 1891. NAG, Accra, ADM 41/4/24. Keta Criminal Record Book (1891–2).

[29] For the history of the North German Missionary Society, see Eva Schock-Quinteros and Dieter Lenz, *150 Years of North German Mission 1836–1986* (Bremen, 1989). On its history in the Gold Coast and Togo, see Hans Debrunner, *A Church between Colonial Powers: A Study of the Church in Togo* (London, 1965); Eugene Emil Grau, 'The Evangelical Presbyterian Church (Ghana and Togo) 1914–1946: A study in European mission relations affecting the beginning of an indigenous church' (PhD thesis, Hartford Seminary Foundation, 1964); Meyer, 'Translating the devil'.

selves. It was also significant for the old Keta–Anloga rivalry that the missionaries chose Keta as the site of their station. It was an informed choice, however, for Anloga, the traditional capital, was less open to change, and the power of its two leading personalities – the *awoamefia* and the priest of the war god Nyigbla – was rooted in indigenous religion. Bremen missionaries avidly documented Anloga's 'heathenism' and opposition to missionary work, which, in spite of the propagandist agenda of these writings, captures what was a real confrontation of beliefs and world-views.[30]

Indeed, as late as 1903, when Keta boasted of a boys' primary school, a girls' primary school and a middle school, the Mission still experienced difficulties penetrating the environs of Keta. Dzelukope proved uninterested in the mission until *c.* 1899; mission work began in Attoko only in 1900, and the inhabitants showed no interest in schools; the mission was encountering reverses in stations such as Woe and Whuti; and the return of Chief Tenge Dzokoto of Anyako from exile seemed to have sparked a movement to roll back the advances of Christianity. Yet the mission could boast of 701 Christians and 394 'scholars' in the Keta District.[31] Most of these were based in Keta, and we must turn to Keta to understand the African enthusiasm for mission and what they considered attractive about missionary work.

The Bremen missionaries struggled to win converts in Keta itself until the 1870s and 1880s. When the tide turned, it was at the African initiative, and the Anlo of Keta displayed a strong propensity for individual mobility. The influx of German merchants, other Europeans and literate Sierra Leone traders exposed a new social horizon for ambitious Keta residents. Chapter 2 pointed out that the Bremen Mission invited the Bremen firm of F.M. Vietor and Sons to Keta as its commercial agent. The firm's early years in Keta coincided with the Krobo palm oil boycott, and Keta emerged as an important centre for palm-oil exports. Vietor benefited significantly, and other European merchants followed Vietor's lead to Keta. A special relation was established between the Bremen Mission, Bremen merchants and Keta.[32] When British rule was imposed on Anlo in 1874, Vietor was the most established company in Keta, and it employed forty-five people under the direction of Rottmann, G. Feuerstein and Franz Barenstein. As the firm expanded along the former Slave Coast and into the interior, it was joined by another Bremen company in Keta in 1881, F. Oloff and Company. By 1884, three other Hamburg firms operated between the Gold Coast and Dahomey: Wolber and Brohm, C. Godelt and Max Grumbach.[33] Several Germans came to West Africa to work for Vietor and eventually established their own companies: Luther and Seyffert, Funk and Risch and Alfred Kuhlenkampff.[34] Joined by the French firms of Regis Ainé and C. Fabre, the British

[30] See, for examples, F. Galkowski, *Anloga, eine Hochburg des Heidentums* (Bremen, 1907); Plessing's letters to the monthly bulletin of the Bremen Mission, *Monatsblatt*, October 1854 and February 1855.

[31] C. Osswald, *Fifty Years' Mission Work at Keta* (Bremen, 1903).

[32] Hartmut Müller, 'Bremen und Westafrika', *Jahrbuch der Wittheit zu Bremen* 15 (1971): 45–92. Müller authored a sequel to this first publication, 'Bremen und Westafrica: Part II', and it is bound with the first in the Bremen Mission Archive under the call number 34; AVII.

[33] Knoll, *Togo*, 10.

[34] Müller, 'Bremen und Westafrica: II', 106–8.

Photo 3.2 Wuta-Mission house in Keta, taken by Burgi, *c.*1893 *(Source: Bilder aus dem Gebiet der Norddeutschen Missions-Gesellschaft auf der Sklavenkuste in Westafrika).*

Photo 3.3 Chief James Ocloo's House, Keta, *c.*1893 *(Source: reproduced from Bremen Mission archives held at Bremen State Archive).*

Photo 3.4 Liquor shop in Keta, *c.* 1893 *(Source: Reproduced from Bremen Mission archives held at the Bremen State Archive).*

firm F. & A. Swanzy and Sierra Leonean merchants, such as G.B. Williams, Keta had become a commercial Mecca by the 1880s.

These firms needed clerks and agents for interior and coastal shops, opening up important economic opportunities for literate Anlo. Together with the Bremen Mission, the European and Sierra Leonean merchants became the purveyors of modernity. Architecture, clothing, demeanour, all underwent revolutionary change. Wuta Mission House (Strand House), built by the Bremen Mission in Keta in the early 1870s, constituted a landmark in the architectural history of Keta, becoming a model for successful African merchants (Photo 3.2).[35] The two-storey home of Chief James Ocloo in the early 1890s reflected the new architectural style (Photo 3.3). The European preference for beach warehouses and residences, ostensibly for the cool breeze and to facilitate the offloading of ships, also stimulated affluent African merchants to relocate to the beach front. The Western lifestyle of literate Sierra Leonean merchants – with their European-style houses, European furniture and European clothing – was attractive enough to motivate the wealthy Chief James Ocloo to send his younger brother, Henry William Chapman (a.k.a. Nyaho–Klutse), to Sierra Leone for education.[36]

The demand for education in Keta was on the rise, and missionaries were the only providers. The Bremen Mission gradually withdrew subsidies from education in the 1880s. The German missionary, C. Osswald, points out that the Keta were won over because of their interest in education:

> Later on the clothing, books, and school implements had to be paid for. This caused great dissatisfaction, which openly exploded. The pupils sent their delegates to the missionary to demand their clothes. This being refused, they became defiant at first, but soon gave in and proved more grateful than formerly when everything had been given.[37]

Clothing and literacy were powerful symbols of modernity.[38] The value of education had become self-evident to Keta residents. Female education was catered for, especially from 1884, when German deaconesses took up residence in Keta. Emphasis was on reading, needlework, baking and other domestic sciences.[39] In the early 1900s, Julia Sedode's white European bread was in great demand in Keta.[40] Education opportunities expanded when the Roman Catholics established a mission station at Keta in 1890. The African Methodist Episcopal (AME) Zion Church followed in 1899.[41] Intermarriages among Christian, literate families created a new social class,

---

[35] Osswald, *Fifty Years' Mission Work at Keta*, 12. A flood destroyed Wuta House in 1900.

[36] Interview with Chief James Ocloo IV, Keta, 5 September 1996; Hedwig Rohns, *Zwanzig Jahre Missions-Diakonissenarbeit im Ewelande* (Bremen, 1912), 16.

[37] Osswald, *Fifty Years' Mission Work at Keta*, 17.

[38] For insights on clothing, social identity and individual mobility in Africa, see Phyllis Martin, 'Contesting clothes in colonial Brazzaville', *Journal of African History* 35, 3 (1994): 401–26; Hildi Hendrickson, ed., *Clothing and Difference: Embodied Identities in Colonial and Post-colonial Africa* (Durham, 1996); Laura Fair, 'Dressing up: clothing, class and gender in post-abolition Zanzibar', *Journal of African History* 39, 1 (1998): 63–94.

[39] Interview with two elderly products of Bremen education in Keta: Freda Adabanu and Regina Ayayee, Keta, 20 September 1996.

[40] Rohns, *Zwanzig Jahre*, 265.

[41] For a detailed study, see Theophilus W. Adjorlolo, 'The history of education in Anlo with special reference

and Christianity became an important status symbol. The Bremen chapel often proved too small for worship services in the 1880s and 1890s, necessitating the construction of a 'large, handsome church' in 1900.[42]

It did not matter if some of the African Christians were lukewarm with a reported weakness for brandy.[43] Many had converted in order to gain access to education, for missionaries 'almost always made baptism a condition for [school] attendance'.[44] The Church had become a potent social force in Keta's society. It afforded education, social status and an engagement with modernity. It provided avenues for leisure and social life in early colonial Keta. One mission organization, the Young Men's Christian Association (YMCA), founded in Keta in 1896 by missionary Innes, had an orchestra – courtesy of a gift of trombones from England – and a distinguished choir. The proceeds of the 1903 Golden Anniversary celebration of the Bremen Mission in Keta were used to build a clubhouse, which became the venue for choir rehearsals, soccer and cricket.[45] The reduction of Ewe into writing by the Bremen missionaries further privileged Anlo by choosing Anlo-Ewe as the standard Ewe, hence enhancing Keta's image as a centre of learning in Eweland.[46] The Keta of 1890–1910 had become a complex, cosmopolitan society, rife with racial, class, ethnic and gender conflicts. It is to these that we now turn.

Urbanization, urbanism and social life in cosmopolitan Keta

Social life in Keta was a bewildering amalgam of different social influences: African, Muslim and European. While old patterns of immigration from Adangme and other Ewe groups from Togo and Dahomey continued, new patterns emerged in the second half of the nineteenth century, with the presence of Sierra Leonean traders and the recruitment of Kru canoemen from Liberia. The stationing of a force of Hausa Constabulary at Keta from 1874 added a Muslim dimension with strong representation from Hausaland and the Northern Territories of the Gold Coast. The presence of 186 'Hausa' soldiers in Keta in 1885, when the population was estimated at about 1,700, underscores the significant contribution of this constituency to ethnic diversity and social life in Keta.[47] But this large force reflected the politically disturbed conditions in Anlo in the 1880s, and the Hausa Constabulary at Keta had a strength of thirty in 1900. The decline in military presence in Keta was slightly offset by civil police, several of whom were Fanti.[48] Fanti women also traded in Keta, either

---

[41 (cont.)] to Keta from 1850–1960' (BA thesis, History Department, University of Ghana, 1977).

[42] Osswald, *Fifty Years' Mission Work at Keta*, 16.

[43] Ibid., 12–13.

[44] G.R. Nukunya, *Kinship and Marriage among the Anlko Ewe* (London, 1969), 172.

[45] *Monatsblatt*, February 1909. On Christian missions and sport in Africa, see Phyllis Martin, *Leisure and Society in Colonial Brazzaville* (Cambridge, 1995); Laura Fair, 'Kickin' it: leisure, politics and football in colonial Zanzibar, 1900–1950s', *Africa* 67, 2 (1997): 224–51.

[46] Meyer, 'Translating the devil', ch. 4.

[47] Gold Coast Colony, *Blue Book, 1885*; Osswald, *Fifty Years' Mission Work at Keta*, 16.

[48] Gold Coast, *Blue Book, 1900*.

migrants on their own or wives to the Fanti men, who served as clerks in firms or in the colonial service or as civil policemen. Asante traders frequented Keta, and one Kofi Nti, who claimed to be a 'prince of Ashanti', lived in Keta.[49]

The desire for wealth, social mobility and autonomy and to be 'modern' united many of these immigrants. Modernity in a cosmopolitan town was exhilarating for many indigenes and migrants. One's life options seemed to have multiplied overnight. An ill person might consult an indigenous herbalist or healer, attend the colonial government's hospital, or visit a Muslim healer.[50] Cultural boundaries between gender and generations became blurred, but the spirit of acquisitiveness united all. Young women rejected child betrothals, and their parents looked on askance.[51] The sight of drunken women – including Anlo women – in the street was no longer an anomaly.[52] As women were major retailers of liquor, it was perhaps not surprising that some also took to drink (Photo 3.4).[53] Krobo prostitutes, famous in Sekondi in the early twentieth century, also showed up in Keta.[54]

But the town was also disorientating and alienating, for capitalism and modernity coexisted with the monetization of the economy and the commodification of social life. Literacy lubricated these processes, and early colonial Keta abounded with written contracts, promissory notes and legal suits.[55] Landlords required written contracts from tenants and from those to whom they leased land. Employers and employees both found solace in written contracts, and immigrant Kru men from Liberia clung tightly to their written contracts in case the firms that brought them to

[49] NAG, Accra, ADM 41/4/4. *Rebecca Yankah* v. *G. W. Brew*, DC's Court, Keta, 22 October 1895. Kofi Nti appeared as a witness for the plaintiff.

[50] NAG, Accra, ADM 41/4/5. *Montor Moses* v. *Mama Dagomba*, DC's Court, Keta, 24 January 1896, highlights the availability of several medical therapies in colonial Keta. Medicine in Keta had become very 'cosmopolitan'. Charles Leslie, 'Medical pluralism in world perspective', *Social Science and Medicine* 14B (1980): 191–5. For some important studies of African responses to the multiple therapies of the twentieth century, see John Janzen, *The Quest for Therapy in Lower Zaire* (Berkeley, 1978); Christopher Taylor, *Milk, Honey and Money: Changing Concepts in Rwandan Healing* (Washington, DC, 1992).

[51] See, for example, *Pringle* v. *Gadjekpo*, DC's Court, Keta, 1 August 1896. NAG, Accra, ADM 41/4/5.

[52] *Regina* v. *Atteyshi*, DC's Court, 23 February 1891; *Regina* v. *Awoonatorbey*, DC's Court, Keta, 4 March 1891. NAG, Accra, ADM 41/4/23.

[53] *C.F. Fabre & Co.* v. *Jessie Brew*, DC's Court, Keta, 12 July 1892. NAG, Accra, ADM 41/4/3. Jessie Brew was being sued for money owed on a puncheon of rum.

[54] *Mamley* v. *Kai Odonkor*, DC's Court, Keta, 11 February 1897. NAG, Accra, ADM 41/4/5. On Krobo prostitutes in Sekondi, see Emmanuel Akyeampong, 'Sexuality and prostitution among the Akan of the Gold Coast, *c.*1650–1950', *Past and Present* 156 (August, 1997): 144–73.

[55] Law assumed important ramifications in the colonial era, as a two-tiered legal system came into existence: customary lawcourts and European common lawcourts. Litigants selectively applied to one or the other for redress, depending on the issue at stake and the propensity for the chief's court or the DC's court to be favourably disposed to a matter. The reduction of customary law into writing bolstered the invention of custom and empowered literate court clerks who served in customary courts. See Martin Chanock, *Law, Custom, and Social Order: The Colonial Experience in Malawi and Zambia* (Cambridge, 1985); Kristin Mann and Richard Roberts, eds, *Law in Colonial Africa* (Portsmouth and London, 1991); Roger Gocking, 'Competing systems of inheritance before the British courts of the Gold Coast', *International Journal of African Historical Studies* 23, 4 (1990): 601–18; idem, 'British justice and the native tribunals of the southern Gold Coast colony', *Journal of African History* 34, 1 (1993): 93–113; idem, 'Indirect rule in the Gold Coast: competition for office and the invention of tradition', *Canadian Journal of African Studies* 28, 3 (1994): 421–45.

Keta reneged on agreed conditions. James Ocloo was a frequent litigant, and William Henry Chapman's education seems to have paid off handsomely, for he drafted his elder brother's numerous contracts.[56] Embezzlement was widespread, and European merchants were constantly suing their agents and storekeepers to recover monies.[57] Theft was common, and it became a general practice for men and women to own a locked box in which valuables and money were kept. And crime became more sophisticated as the literate employed their education in schemes to defraud the Post Office and Customs authorities.[58] In fact, trust was a scarce commodity, and, when two friends – John Lamuire and Gilbert Crankson – went shopping at Swanzy's in 1887, the former found it necessary to collect a written debt note from the latter when Crankson ran out of money at Swanzy's and borrowed money from Lamuire. The note came in handy when Crankson proved unable to pay the debt.[59]

The colonial government was clearly aware of the giddy effect of urban life on urban dwellers and migrants: the sense of autonomy, anonymity and empowerment. The modern town held several novel experiences in store, and the colonial government sought to guide the conduct of town dwellers. It laid down clear rules on what it meant to be urban. Urban denizens, after all, were also colonial subjects. These rules were an important source of stress for urbanites. Dogs had to be licensed and sheep and pigs contained and not allowed to roam the town; loud noises were banned; littering was prohibited; it was advisable not to be drunk in public; drums could be played only with a permit; and instruments like the concertina could not be played too loudly. The numerous court cases dealing with the above underscore African resentment of these regulations. Leisure, 'enjoyment', that pleasant category celebrated in towns, was legislated.[60] Flouting leisure regulations could be costly, as Mensah, Quow, Tettey and company found out on 9 September 1890:

> Sgt. Gilbert: I am sergeant of the civil police. Yesterday at about 4:30 p.m. I was going rounds [sic] when I heard a noise in a house. I entered and found the prisoners singing and drunk. I asked for a pass and found none. I arrested them.[61]

Those found guilty were fined 5 shillings or in default seven days in prison.

But it is clear from the experiences and perspectives sampled that many found cosmopolitan Keta a place of opportunity. Indeed, women came from Accra, the capital of the Gold Coast, to Keta in search of suitors. Elizabeth Rhule in June 1891 charged G.P. Brown with assault for pulling her breast in a quarrel. The source of

---

[56] *Chief James Ocloo* v. *Peter Wilson*, DC's Court, Keta, 25 July 1898. NAG, Accra, ADM 41/4/5; *Fiabegi* v. *Padah*, DC's Court, Keta, 4 November 1895. NAG, Accra, ADM 41/4/4.

[57] See, for examples, *A. de Pornian* v. *E.N. Tamaklo*, DC's Court, Keta, 1 March 1894; *Brodecker and Meyer* v. *Christian Agboogar*, DC's Court, Keta, 2 March 1894; *Bremen Factory* v. *Akpawo*, DC's Court, Keta, 22 March 1894. NAG, Accra, ADM 41/4/4.

[58] *Regina per Sgt. Ennin* v. *France de Souza*, DC's Court, Keta, 6 February 1899; *Regina per Sgt. Ennin* v. *William Semakor*, DC's Court, Keta, 8 February 1899. NAG, Accra, ADM 41/4/28.

[59] *John Lamuire* v. *Gilbert Crankson*, DC's Court, Keta, 13 April 1887. NAG, Accra, ADM 41/4/2.

[60] Akyeampong, 'What's in a drink? Class struggle, popular culture and the politics of Akpeteshie (local gin) in Ghana, 1930–1967', *Journal of African History* 37, 2 (1996): 215–36.

[61] *Regina* v. *Mensah et al.*, DC's Court, Keta, 10 September 1890. NAG, Accra, ADM 41/4/23.

the conflict was Elizabeth Rhule's 'maid'. Rhule's daughter, Miss Brew, explained:

> The girl in question was brought from Accra by my mother by the wish of the father, that she might be provided with a man to keep her as soon as possible, the girl left our home and went to prisoner's house. She came back for her things which I would not let her have, the prisoner, his wife and the girl, came and asked for her box, went away and came back again, the prisoner took hold of my mother and pulled her, also threatened to strike her with a club. They took the box with them.[62]

Perhaps the contradiction here is that in the social context of the town, which offers choice and empowers its denizens, Elizabeth Rhule had been commissioned to find a suitor for her guardian in a very traditional way. Perhaps she ignored her ward's choices and desires. In colonial Keta, gender was an acutely contested sphere.

Gender relations in early colonial Keta

Colonial imposition, an expanding cash economy and missionary activity affected gender relations in colonial Africa in significant ways.[63] Women found new economic opportunities in the colonial economy and used these to gain more autonomy.[64] The institution of marriage came under great strain as women sought to redefine marital expectations and obligations. Indeed, some women opted out of marriage entirely, escaping the mechanism by which adult men controlled the labour and sexuality of women. Men often misunderstood the importance women placed on the emotional content of marriage.[65] Individualism and accumulation penetrated gender relations, and male concerns and fears were reflected in a discourse that emphasized the uncontrollability of women, with prostitution and venereal diseases as major themes.[66] Women in colonial Keta insisted on choosing their partners and irregular unions or concubinage became more common.[67] Mothers resorted to colonial courts to bring irresponsible fathers to book and to inject 'commitment' into gender relations.

[62] *Regina* v. *G.P. Brown*, DC's Court, Keta, 3 June 1891. NAG, Accra, ADM 41/4/23.

[63] See, for examples, Margot Lovett, 'Gender relations, class formation, and the colonial state in Africa', in Jane L. Parpart and Kathleen Staudt, eds, *Women and the State in Africa* (Boulder, 1989), 23–46; Jane L. Parpart, '"Where is your mother?": gender, urban marriage, and colonial discourse on the Zambian copperbelt, 1925–1945', *International Journal of African Historical Studies* 27, 2 (1994): 241–71; Jean M. Allman, 'Making mothers: missionaries, medical officers and women's work in colonial Asante, 1924–1945', *History Workshop* 38 (Autumn 1994): 23–47.

[64] For the Gold Coast context, see Penelope A. Roberts, 'The state and the regulation of marriage: Sefwi Wiawso (Ghana), 1900–1940', in Haleh Afshar, ed., *Women, State and Ideology: Studies from Africa and Asia* (London, 1987), 48–69; Jean M. Allman, 'Rounding up spinsters: gender chaos and unmarried women in colonial Asante', *Journal of African History* 37, 2 (1996): 195–214; Akyeampong, 'What's in a drink?'; idem, 'Sexuality and prostitution'.

[65] This is clearly evident in several of the essays in Christine Oppong, ed., *Female and Male in West Africa* (London, 1983). See also Akyeampong, 'Urbanization, individualism and gender relations in colonial Ghana'.

[66] Megan Vaughan, *Curing their Ills: Colonial Power and African Illness* (Stanford, 1991), 129–54; Jean M. Allman, 'Of "spinsters", "concubines" and "wicked women": reflections on gender and social change in colonial Asante', *Gender and History* 30, 2 (1991): 176–89.

[67] Nukunya, *Kinship and Marriage*, ch. 5; Greene, *History of the Anlo-Ewe*, chs 5 and 6.

Old strategies remained salient for young women who sought to escape from arranged marriages. But the changing social context certainly encouraged more young women to assert their autonomy, even if the response took traditional forms. And as the younger generation jettisoned the marriage arrangements made by their parents, parents were sued in Keta's colonial court for their inability to control their daughters. The 1890 case of *Ahetor Tamalekoo* v. *Nyagavie* is typical in this respect:

> About 15 years ago defendant promised her daughter to me in marriage. The girl was quite a child then. In consequence of this promise my mother released the defendant of a debt owing. About four years ago defendant refused to give her daughter and thus broke her promise. I summoned her before the native court, before whom she renewed the former promise. Not long ago I found the girl living with another man, and on questioning the defendant she admitted having given her to this other party in marriage. The original debt which defendant was released by [my] mother was 12/-.[68]

Nyagavie in her defence admitted her debt to the plaintiff's mother, but denied conniving with her daughter's rejection of the arranged marriage:

> I admit having owed plaintiff's mother some money about 10 years ago. Plaintiff's mother came and said she would release me of her debt, it was 9/6, if I promised my daughter, then quite a child, to plaintiff in marriage when of mature age. Later on plaintiff caught her and put her in a house as is the custom before marriage.[69] However, the girl escaped and joined fetish. I never refused the girl being taken in marriage nor did I break my promise as I never gave the girl to any other man.[70]

DC Francis Lamb resolved the matter by instructing that the plaintiff be paid his 9/6 and costs. This was certainly in Nyagavie's favour, for marriage costs had escalated from the late nineteenth century with the expansion of the colonial market economy. Her daughter could certainly attract much more in bride price.

As marriage, divorce and inheritance cases were brought before the colonial court, customary law was reworked and codified. In the above case, the issue at stake was liability for a broken betrothal. In 1897, Adjor sued his 'wife', Hushiejor, for his dowry when she opted out of her arranged marriage:

> When defendant was a little girl she was given to me to marry. I waited until she grew up. I then went and paid her dowry to her mother 26/6 which was handed to the defendant. When I married her I spent £2 on her chop [maintenance] while she was kept in her room for 6 months. She ran away before the 6 months were up and married another man. I called upon defendant's parents. They referred me to the man. He said he did not know the girl was married.[71]

[68] *Ahetor* v. *Nyagavie*, DC's Court, Keta, 20 June 1890. NAG, Accra, ADM 41/4/3.
[69] Nukunya, *Kinship and Marriage*, 91, points out that 'the idea behind the seclusion is to emphasize from the onset the husband's monopoly over her [the bride's] sexual services'. An important part of Anlo marriage ceremonies was for the bridegroom, after the payment of the bride price, to seclude the wife for a period of four to eight months, depending on his wealth. This rite was called *dedexo*. See also interview with Mrs A.B. Godzi, Dzelukope, 17 October 1996.
[70] Joining religious cults, such as Nyigbla and Yewe, was an important strategy for young Anlo women who sought to escape arranged marriages and the rigid control of parents and husbands. See Greene, *History of the Anlo-Ewe*.
[71] *Adjor* v. *Hushiejor*, DC's Court, Keta, 27 April 1897. NAG, Accra, ADM 41/4/5.

In this case DC Gerald Lowie ruled that under native law the defendant was not liable for her dowry but her parents, and the plaintiff could sue the other man involved for seduction. Young women who heard of this ruling would certainly have been emboldened to defy undesirable arranged marriages. In the cosmopolitan context of Keta, it was not only Anlo customary law that was contested. Expert witnesses were often summoned to give evidence on Akan or Hausa customary law. Such was the case when Mina Kaniki sued Mama Lakey in 1898 for £24.7.6 dowry paid for his daughter Zarah. Both had served in the Hausa Constabulary in Keta, where Mina Kaniki married Zarah nine years previously. Mama Lakey in 1898 was a discharged soldier still living in Keta. Mina Kaniki had relocated to Accra with his wife, but the latter abandoned him in 1894 and returned to her father in Keta. The expert witness in this case was Malam Mama, religious head of the Hausa Detachment at Keta:

> I know the marriage custom of the Hausa. The proposed husband sends a friend or relation to the proposed wife's parents to ask her [hand] in marriage. They afterwards were [sic] married at the mosque. It is the custom to pay dowry to the parents. I know that the plaintiff used to send money to the parents of the girl. I was at Kwitta at that time. In this case the plaintiff would pay about £10 dowry to defendant. The plaintiff would also have to pay about £7 expenses of the marriage.[72]

The principle that parents were responsible for the dowry in broken arranged marriages was again upheld in this case, and the plaintiff was awarded £10 damages, as recommended by the expert witness, and costs.

Cross-ethnic relations complicated gender issues, especially as irregular unions became somewhat institutionalized. Nukunya points out that, though irregular unions were based on free will and sometimes evolved into permanent unions, they denied women family support when their men misbehaved, for the marriage ceremonies had not been performed.[73] But Anlo and migrant women in Keta seem to have taken advantage of the presence of migrant men in Keta and the need for female services outside marriage.[74] Material transactions became central to the acquisition of 'sweethearts'. When 'Jack Never Fear' sued for compensation for desertion by his sweetheart, Quaque, he discovered that these material transactions bequeathed little legal claim:

> Defendant's mother gave her to me to marry. I gave her £1 cloths, 4/- handkerchiefs and gave them to her. The mother told me I must make her live in the house. I married her for seven months. Whenever I quarrelled with my wife the mother abused me. The woman left me because she had got belly [pregnant]. I paid defendant 9/- per month in addition to the chop money I gave her. This I did for seven months.[75]

As Nukunya points out, the Anlo marriage payment (*sronu*) involved the giving of cloth, head kerchiefs, liquor and money. But the legality of an Anlo marriage lay not

---

72 Ibid. *Mina Kaniki v. Mama Lakey*, DC's Court, Keta, 21 January 1898.
73 Nukunya, *Kinship and Marriage*, 101.
74 On the commercialization of domestic services in colonial towns, see, for example, Luise White, *The Comforts of Home: Prostitution in Colonial Nairobi* (Chicago, 1990).
75 *Jack Never Fear v. Quaque*, DC's Court, Keta, 17 December 1886. NAG, Accra, ADM 41/4/2.

necessarily in these material transactions, but rather in the powdering of the bride with *eto* (a rite called *togbagba*).[76] 'Jack Never Fear' evidently believed that he had acquired a wife by giving cloth, head kerchiefs – described as handkerchiefs in the legal transcript – and money followed by cohabitation and spousal support. The testimony of Quaque's mother, Gegaqua, is striking in its circumvention of all talk of marriage, drawing a subtle distinction between the position of a sweetheart and that of a wife:

> About seven months ago plaintiff came and asked for my daughter. I agreed. Plaintiff gave her two large cloths and two small ones. Afterwards plaintiff asked me to allow defendant to come and stay at the police station with him. He gave her four more cloths and a handkerchief as is the custom here. Later than that they began to quarrel and last of all someone came and told me that my daughter was in the streets with her load. I went and brought her to my house.[77]

The court was informed during cross-examination that when sweethearts quarrelled and separated, it was the custom for the woman to retain gifts received during the relationship. DC Charles Fraser gave judgment in favour of the defendant.

What rights the relationship of sweetheart granted remained vague. The men provided chop money and other forms of material support for their sweethearts, but discovered to their chagrin that they had no monopoly over their partner's sexuality – for they could not sue for satisfaction in the case of seduction – and could not even take it for granted that their meals would be cooked. A jealous Jonas Kofi stepped out of line when he attempted to 'discipline' his sweetheart in May 1887:

> Prosecutrix is my sweetheart. She lived with another man before she came to me, that is the witness Teshie. One day I saw her sitting at table with Teshie. So I asked her where was my chop. Her mother said she was to stay with her tonight. This vexed me. On Friday I met Prosecutrix near Crepee town with her first sweetheart . . . I told the woman I had not seen her for ten days and asked her to come house [*sic*] with me. She refused. The man ran away. The woman sat down. I was going to pick her up, when she scratched me. I then struck her ears once.[78]

Jonas Kofi did more than strike her sweetheart's ears: he broke her tooth. And he was fined 40 shillings or in default one month in prison for assault.

It was a novel turn of events as wives sued their husbands in Keta's colonial court for the appropriation of their money; pregnant women sued partners for child support for as yet unborn children; and mothers sued men who ruined the careers of their unmarried daughters through seduction. These cases involved both Anlo and non-Anlo and underscored a general trend toward female assertiveness in the colonial urban context. Dadey believed that the fact that her husband had set her up in trade financially did not give him the right to appropriate her money.[79] A pregnant Effuah asserted in 1893 that J.S. MaCauley owed her child support, even if the child was not yet born, when she stated that:

[76] Nukunya, *Kinship and Marriage*, 91–2.
[77] NAG, Accra, ADM 41/4/2.
[78] *Boochey v. Jonas Kofi*, DC's Court, Keta, 3 May 1887. NAG, Accra, ADM 41/4/21.
[79] *Dadey of Croboe v. Dinn*, DC's Court, Keta, 28 January 1892. NAG, Accra, ADM 41/4/3.

I came from Crepee. The defendant saw me in Kitta and said he would like to keep me as his wife. I consented because my real husband died a long time ago. About 8 months ago I went to stay with the defendant at Mr. Jacobsen's … as his wife … I lived with him as his wife till I became pregnant. Then he simply allowed me 1/- a week and I left him and stayed at Nez Holen's house. The defendant then accused me of having connection [sex] with a goldsmith. Since I went to leave with defendant I have allowed nobody to touch me.[80]

The case was dismissed, especially when MaCauley proved that he had been supporting his pregnant sweetheart until he discovered that she was having other sexual liaisons, even while living with him.

Loose women, especially migrants, abounded in Keta, creating some confusion as to who was a prostitute and generating antagonism between Anlo women and foreign women, as will be discussed later under ethnic relations. Suits for defamation of character were numerous, as women resorted to the courts in defence of their dignity and reputation. *Edopen* v. *Yesu* in March 1891 is a good example. Though Ocloo did not know Edopen personally, he showed up at Edopen's house and requested to see her.

I asked him what he wanted, he then saluted me and told me that defendant had informed him that I was a harlot and he (Ocloo) wished to have connexion with me. I had a husband but 14 months ago he left for Elmina. He does not send me any subsistence.[81]

In his defence, Yesu argued that he was aware that the plaintiff's husband had left her and that the plaintiff had come to the house in which he lived and had sex with a man. He thus assumed the plaintiff was in the sex business and referred Ocloo to her when the latter enquired of a prostitute.

The old coexisted with the new in interesting ways in colonial Keta, and much remained about gender relations that was traditional. Colonial law connived with male chauvinism, as evidenced by an 1890 incident:

Yesterday about 2:30 p.m. in Beach Street I found prisoner running after a woman. I asked what was the matter when he told me it was no business of mine. He then slapped the woman. I then told him not to make a disturbance in the street but to flog his wife in his house. He was drunk. After warning him, he again assaulted the woman.[82]

What is interesting about this case is that Policeman Charles Afful, a Fanti, found nothing wrong with the accused, Ada, beating his wife: he should just do it in the private space of his home. Ada's flouting of this warning led to him being cited for disorderly conduct. More interesting is the fact that DC Lamb dismissed the case. A man's control over his wife was upheld by colonial rule, and indirect rule would seek to put women more effectively under the control of men.[83]

---

[80] Ibid. *Effuah* v. *J. S. MaCauley*, DC's Court, Keta, 15 February 1893.

[81] Ibid. *Edopen* v. *Yesu*, DC's Court, Keta, 14 March 1891.

[82] *Regina* v. *Ada*, DC's Court, Keta, 16 October 1890. NAG, Accra, ADM 41/4/23.

[83] Akyeampong, *Drink, Power, and Cultural Change*; Allman, 'Making mothers'; idem, 'Rounding up spinsters'; Lovett, 'Gender relations, class formation, and the colonial state in Africa'.

The stranger in Anlo society:
ethnic and race relations in colonial Keta

Greene has provided detailed evidence of how strangers – individuals as well as corporate groups – were incorporated into Anlo society historically. Corporate groups had more control over the terms on which they were admitted into pre-colonial Anlo. Some constituted themselves into separate clans, such as the Agave and the Amlade clans, and others were consigned to the Blu clan for foreigners in Anlo.[84] Individuals, except wealthy traders, faced a more perilous situation, and Chapter 2 has illustrated how such persons could be abducted and enslaved. Wealthy traders, African, European or Euro-African, were, however, more privileged, and they could influence the terms on which they were incorporated into Anlo society.[85] Colonial rule limited Anlo autonomy in its dealings with strangers in Anlo society, and the large presence of European and African foreigners in Keta had an enormous impact on the Anlo experience of ethnicity, gender and race. The last was a particularly uncertain category, as colonial rule had significantly altered race relations.

The Anlo of Keta were struck by certain anomalies about the colonial situation. Outsiders seemed to wield more power or influence in early colonial Keta than the Anlo themselves: the Hausa Constabulary often rode roughshod over Anlo concerns, and the better-paid clerks were often Fanti. The Fanti had responded enthusiastically to Western education from the eighteenth century, and the Wesleyan Missionary Society had established schools in Fanteland since the 1830s. As was pointed out earlier in this chapter, the Anlo response to mission Christianity and education was quite lukewarm even at the turn of the century. Even apparently manual forms of wage labour, for example canoemen, were dominated by the Kru of Liberia, who were more experienced mariners than the Anlo. These outsiders were privileged groups within the colonial political economy, and the government favoured them with land grants in a land-scarce Keta. Anlo relations with these ethnic outsiders were often tense.

Aboki took matters into his own hands in 1892 when a retired Hausa soldier, Zelenu, was given a piece of land from a parcel the colonial government had set aside for the Hausa.[86] Zelenu started constructing a little hut on a section the chief of the Hausa community had indicated, when Aboki came to destroy the structure. Aboki warned Zelenu that the land belonged to his father and that the colonial government had no land in Keta. DC R.K. Pringle fined Aboki £1 and costs. Apart from these claims on Anlo land, single male migrants seemed to cast covetous eyes on Anlo

[84] Greene, *History of the Anlo-Ewe*.

[85] Sandra E. Greene, 'The individual as stranger in nineteenth-century Anlo: the politics of identity in precolonial West Africa', in John Hunwick and Nany Lawler, eds, *The Cloth of Many Silk Colors* (Evanston, 1996), 91–127.

[86] *Zelenu* v. *Aboki*, DC's Court, Keta, 3 October 1892. NAG, Accra, ADM 41/4/3. In 1884, DC Firminger of Keta had allocated land between the fort and the cemetery for the settlement of discharged Hausa soldiers and civilian Hausa. This followed an old pattern of the creation of *Zongos* ('strangers' quarters') for Muslim strangers in precolonial West Africa. See, for examples, Enid Schildkrout, *People of the Zongo: The Transformation of Ethnic Identities in Ghana* (Cambridge, 1978); William A. Schack and Elliot P. Skinner, eds, *Strangers in African Societies* (Berkeley and Los Angeles, 1979).

women. A large number of rape cases came before the DC's court, several involving foreign men and Anlo women.[87] To Anlo men, the privileged strangers were abusing Anlo hospitality, more so when they happened to be 'empowered' soldiers or police. The following case involving a Fanti policeman, Kwasi Nimpa, and Dohfi in the neighbouring town of Denu is rather obnoxious in its circumstances. Dohfi stated her case of indecent assault (rape):

> I am a native of Denu. I live with police constable Moses Adoo. On the 19th February last, some four days ago, Moses Adoo was away at Quitta with a letter. About midnight I was going to the latrine when Corporal Nimpa the prisoner called me to his hut. I went in and then he caught hold of me and had connection with me by force though I remonstrated with him and told him *I was with child* [emphasis in original]. I called out and resisted and Mr. Ulzen the customs officer came and [prisoner] opened the door and [Mr. Ulzen] asked what was going on. I was naked at the time and I went out naked and prisoner handed me my cloth out [*sic*] afterward also my handkerchief. One of my earrings came out in the struggle. I have not found it yet.[88]

Mr Ulzen, the customs officer, corroborated Dohfi's testimony. It is unconscionable that Kwasi Nimpa could have contemplated raping his Fanti colleague's Ewe wife or sweetheart, especially in the light of her pregnancy. The two assets the Anlo valued most and guarded jealously against outsiders in their precolonial history – land and Anlo women – were under attack.[89]

That these Hausa soldiers and civilian police had more cash than most Anlo worsened matters. Women in Keta were attracted to these male migrants. Ewe proverbs capture male disgust at the rapacity of the women: '*Nyɔnuwo (gbolowo) la amevunolawoe*' ('Women (harlots) are bloodsuckers').[90] When Zoglo assaulted Kenny Grunshie, a Hausa woman-friend of his wife, at his home one night in February 1895, he claimed he mistook her for a thief. She believed otherwise, and her testimony underscored Anlo antagonism towards the Hausa:

> I generally come to Kitta. I live at Afiliubah [?], [and] on my way used to call at defendant to have a drink of water. When the defendant found me in his house with his wife, he said I came purposely to coax his wife, and run away with her so as to give her to the Hausas that caused him to flog me, he flogged me with a native whip.[91]

Court cases documented examples of women eloping with members of the Hausa Constabulary. Ammah Tawiah deserted her husband in Elmina and followed Awudu Grunshie, a Hausa soldier, to Keta in 1894. When she left Awudu Grunshie in June 1895, the latter sued for the return of money and cloths bestowed upon Ammah Tawiah. Ammah Tawiah argued in her defence that these gifts had been given to her by the plaintiff to induce her to 'run away from her husband', but now the plaintiff

---

[87] See, for examples, *Abrewagie v. Amey*, DC's Court, Keta, 28 October 1892. NAG, Accra, ADM 41/4/24; *Regina per R.D. Niezer v. Quacoe*, DC's Court, Keta, 13 March 1894. NAG, Accra, ADM 41/4/25.

[88] *Regina per Dohfi of Denu v. Kwasi Nimpa of Denu*, DC's Court, Keta, 23 February 1886. NAG, Accra, ADM 41/4/21.

[89] On the precolonial context, see Greene, *History of the Anlo-Ewe*.

[90] N.K. Dzobo, *African Proverbs: Guide to Conduct*, vol. II (Accra, 1975), 29.

[91] *Kenny Grunshie v. Zoglo*, DC's Court, Keta, 27 February 1895. NAG, Accra, ADM 41/4/4.

'had no money wherewith to buy food or cloths'. This was an apparent case of poetic justice, and the DC dismissed it.[92]

Some Anlo wives and women found these migrant women irritating for their lack of inhibitions and the liberties they took with their husbands and male partners. Sepenya, an Anlo woman, burst out publicly in a tirade, accusing Harriet Brew of being a 'harlot' and engaging in sexual liaisons with men in Lome despite being married. It did not matter that the outburst was in Ewe, and Harriet Brew did not understand Ewe. The latter's maid translated on her behalf.[93] For her unfriendliness, Sepenya received a fine of 30 shillings with costs for defamation of character. Encounters between Anlo women and migrant women sometimes took on a physical nature. The case of *Mame* v. *Sarpueh* in September 1887 is an extreme example. Anlo wives who suspected their husbands of having affairs with foreign women sometimes took the law into their own hands:

> About four weeks ago defendant met me on the Kedzi road and she took a stick and beat me with it. About three weeks ago I was in my house when defendant came and said she had come to beat me. I said nothing. She spat in my face and tried to kick my belly but some people in the house took me away. About six days ago I was going to the beach to draw water with a pot on my head. Defendant followed me and asked me if it was me her husband followed. She asked me to come and look at him. Saying her husband had slept with me and he had caught venereal [disease]. She then began striking me on the face. She beat me till I fell down and then she threw sand in my face.[94]

Polygamy and sanctioned male superiority in Anlo social life meant that Sarpueh could not vent her anger on her husband for his indiscretion and venereal disease – that is, if Sarpueh's accusation was true – but had to seek out her rival and avenge herself on her. It is also likely that Sarpueh had discovered that Mame (or Maame, an Akan name) was pregnant from her husband, for kicking the stomach of a rival is a common act when that rival is pregnant and the protagonist hopes to induce an abortion. Gender conflict in Anlo dovetailed with ethnic conflict, and the large presence of outsiders certainly reinforced Anlo ethnicity. That these outsiders were often non-Ewe, who dominated the colonial civil service, Hausa Constabulary and the civil police, may have awakened a broader Ewe consciousness of their disadvantaged position *vis-à-vis* other ethnic groups in the colonial political economy.

Such feelings muted race consciousness on the part of the Anlo, especially if cooperating with Europeans enabled them to reverse the gains of other African migrants in Keta's economy. In the following dispute between Kru canoemen and their European employers in November 1897, Keta men acted as 'blacklegs'. Jumnih, leader of this group of Kru canoemen, stated their case: .

> I am headman of Phillis Renner's Krooboys. About 9 months ago J.C. Renner sent a letter to my brother asking for 12 Krooboys to act as canoemen. I brought 14. Three went back. On Friday and Saturday last week Mr. Renner sent us to work for Brodecker and Meyer. He said that we

[92] Ibid. *Awudu Grunshie* v. *Ammah Tawiah*, DC's Court, Keta, 27 June 1895.
[93] Ibid. *Herlet [Harriet] Brew* v. *Sepenya*, DC's Court, Keta, 27 October 1894.
[94] *Mame* v. *Sarpueh*, DC's Court, Keta, 12 September 1887. NAG, Accra, ADM 41/4/21.

should have to work for Brodecker and Meyer if he told us to do so. On Monday last we were working for the same firm, when one of the white clerks struck Davies, one of the plaintiffs. On Monday about 7 o'clock we went by the direction of Mr. Renner to work there again, but we were told that we were not wanted. We went away but at 4 o'clock the same day Mr. Renner sent for us and we again went there. It was then that Davies was flogged. On Monday night Mr. Renner told us that he did not want us and again on Tuesday. When the 'Lounda' came on Tuesday we took the paddles and went to the beach. The defendant sent Kwittamen to take the paddles away from us and they worked the boat. I reported the matter to Phillis Renner and she said if J.C. Renner had said so she would not interfere. I produce an agreement marked 'A'. The other ten plaintiffs are those whose names appear in the agreement.[95]

This rather lengthy quote contains several pieces of important information that illuminate some of the arguments and positions presented in this chapter. The Renners were probably an African trading family of Sierra Leonean extraction, though there is a Renner family in present-day Ghana. As an entrepreneurial class, their interests were closely linked to those of the expatriate European firms, in this case the German firm of Brodecker and Meyer. The female entrepreneur, Phyllis Renner had brought Kru canoemen from Liberia to Keta, using the Renner family network. The canoemen had assumed they were coming to work for the Renner establishment, but discovered that they had been subcontracted to a German firm. Moreover, they were being assaulted and refused work by their employer. It was in their interest that they possessed a written contract, and the colonial court upheld their claims with costs. It is worth noting that the Anlo of Keta were quickly developing adequate sea navigation skills that made it unnecessary, perhaps, to continue recruiting canoemen from Liberia. Desirous of a more central role in the colonial wage economy, they were more than willing to deprive the Kru men of their privileged niche.

But Anlo relations with Europeans could also be demeaning to the former. The following 1894 assault case involving two Anlo men, though amusing in a way, was fraught with racist connotations. Europeans assumed extreme liberties in the colonial context:

Last Saturday I was playing with a white man and after playing with him he used to dash me money. Last Saturday the white man threw water over me and then threw 6d to me. When I was about to pick the money up defendant took it. I went and told the white man ... and he told me to go around and he would throw me another. And a second time the defendant picked it up.[96]

A physical confrontation resulted, in which the defendant throttled the plaintiff. In this case the plaintiff appears to have been mentally ill, but the generally contemptuous attitude of some European merchants and clerks towards their African employees makes it difficult to brush off the above incident as a trivial episode.

The German merchant F. Oloff's relations with his African employees were particularly worrisome. He often hit his Kru men and, in contravention of their work contracts, sometimes withheld their food rations from them.[97] In one bizarre incident

[95] *Jumnih and 10 others* v. *Phillis Renner*, DC's Court, Keta, 20 November 1897. NAG, Accra, ADM 41/4/5.
[96] *Jarkpala* v. *Wugbe*, DC's Court, Keta, 18 April 1894. NAG, Accra, ADM 41/4/2.
[97] Ibid. *West India and his Gang of Men* v. *V.F. Oloff*, DC's Court, Keta, 11 February 1886.

in 1891, F. Oloff found one of his employees, James Glywin, having lunch in the yard of his factory and went over to speak to him. Glywin did not get up when his employer approached, nor did he show the proper signs of subservience expected of him. Then, Oloff discovered a cigar butt Glywin had been smoking. He was now truly incensed, perhaps at Glywin's presumptuousness or social pretensions. Oloff manhandled Glywin into his office, knocked him around and set his dog on Glywin. Oloff's nonchalance is clear in his defence:

> I did not set the dog onto him, but the dog hearing me speaking harshly took it into his mind to go for the plaintiff. I pushed the plaintiff into the office, and told him that I was not satisfied with him, that he had been behaving very badly. I took hold of him by the ears, and he cried out to me for pardon, I got so sick of him that I sent him outside. I did not flog him at all, I had no reason for it.[98]

It is to the credit of the various DCs at Keta that they upheld the written contracts of labourers and protected labourers from unnecessary physical abuse by their employers. In the above instance Oloff was fined 10 shillings with costs.

How did workers interpret their social experiences in a colonial town such as Keta? Were these experiences refracted through the lenses of class? How did they view their labour, work conditions and remuneration? How did they negotiate the social deference that stifled the lives of ordinary people? What did migrant labourers hope to gain from their sojourn in Keta?

Social class, urban identity and migrant aspirations

The politics of deference so pervades numerous court cases in early colonial Keta that one is compelled to strive for some conceptual understanding of social differentiation during this period. The earlier chapters support the fact that social stratification was not novel in colonial Keta; that the accumulation and wealth that accompanied Anlo participation in long-distance and the Atlantic trade had elevated individuals and families in a society that had no aristocratic class. The absence of an inherited aristocracy that lived off the labour of its subjects or by the perquisites of office makes it difficult to talk of 'ranks' as Kwame Arhin does in the case of nineteenth-century Asante and Fanti.[99] Colonial commerce had transformed Keta's economy in significant ways. Keta's economy was a mercantile one that circulated goods and services. But privileged groups had emerged that directed or controlled aspects of this economy. They were literate; African, European or Euro-African; professed Christianity; had a distinct 'Western' lifestyle; and showed a preference for intermarriage. The 'upper classes' conformed very much to the Weberian definition of social class, which emphasizes education and élite intermarriages. The Anlo of Keta, and other African groups, such as the Kru, provided wage labour in this

[98] *James B. Glywin v. F. Oloff*, DC's Court, Keta, 2 September 1891. NAG, Accra, ADM 41/4/3.
[99] Kwame Arhin, 'Rank and class among the Asante and Fante in the nineteenth century', *Africa* 53, 3 (1983): 2–22.

mercantile economy. The politics of deference that characterized relations of production reveals emerging class consciousness among Keta's labouring force.

Knowing one's place was crucial in early colonial Keta. But the social grid was not the old one of valour in war and the generosity of self-made men and women of wealth. The politics of deference revolved around master–servant relations and perceptions of social class that were very 'Western' in their manifestation. *J.W. Yorke v. Jane Williams* in Keta's colonial court in 1896 sharply etches these politics of deference. The Williamses were a Sierra Leonean trading family domiciled in Keta. It appears that Jane Williams's sister or relation had married or entered into a relationship with an employee of the Williams establishment. This was incomprehensible to Mrs Williams, for it lowered the family's social stature. She visited the relative and her husband in the neighbouring town of Blekusu in April 1896. Yorke recounts what transpired:

> She walked round the town and then came to my place. When she came to my house and I offered her a seat which she refused. I then sat down on the seat myself. After I sat down she called my wife and asked my wife if she (the wife) was her (defendant's) sister. My wife did not answer. I told my wife to answer. Mrs. Williams then rose and went away saying good morning to me. I answered good morning. Then she asked me why I did not take off my hat when she said good morning as she was my mistress. Then she took off my hat and flung it on the ground.[100]

Mrs Williams checked out Blekusu before approaching Yorke's house, probably sorry that her sister had consigned herself to this 'uncivilized' town, as Keta was seen by these urbanites as *the* place to live. At Yorke's house, Mrs Williams ignored the norms of decorum: she called out for Yorke's wife instead of requesting Yorke to call his wife, for she assumed the higher authority of consanguinity and social class; and she greeted Yorke as she left his house, not when she entered it as social etiquette required. In her defence Jane Williams confirmed her irritation at Yorke remaining seated with his hat on when she greeted him. The DC awarded Yorke a farthing in damages.

Jane Williams's son, B.R. Williams, was incensed that Yorke had the audacity to sue his mother in court on matters of decorum and dignity. He waited outside the courtroom for Yorke and assaulted the unsuspecting victor:

> I had just got out into [the] passage outside [the] court when the defendant B.R. Williams seized me by the coat and asked what I meant by abusing his mother. He lifted his stick to strike me but the sergeant of police caught hold of his arm and prevented him striking me.[101]

The Williamses were back in court on 9 May for this assault, and Yorke received £5 for damages and the Williamses a warning to discontinue the quarrel or face imprisonment. In suing his social superiors twice, Yorke had stepped beyond his station, in the opinion of the Williamses.

The 'upper classes' in Keta exercised an authority that was commanding, though not sanctioned by traditional office or colonial rule. But it seemed perilous to defy them, or so the 'underclasses' believed. Phyllis Renner was a frequent visitor to the

---

[100] *J.W. Yorke v. Jane Williams*, DC's Court, Keta, 7 May 1896. NAG, Accra, ADM 41/4/5.
[101] Ibid. *J.W. Yorke v. B.R. Williams*, DC's Court, Keta, 9 May 1896.

colonial court. In March 1892 she was in court for 'flogging' Godfrey. Someone threw a stone on Mrs Renner's roof. She saw Godfrey outside and sent her boys to bring him in. Mrs Renner was imperious in her conduct:

> Mrs. Renner slapped my face without asking me any question and scratched me also. Next morning I saw Mrs. Renner. She said did you throw the stone. I said no but I know the party and she told me that I must bring him at five p.m. At 5 I brought the boy and before I entered I took off my hat and behaved respectfully. When she slapped me and told me not to make a noise in her house and took a piece of plank and flogged me with it.[102]

Mrs Renner admitted to flogging the boy and was fined £1 and costs. Mrs Renner's conduct is outrageous, but what is more instructive is that Godfrey felt compelled to call at Mrs Renner's house again, despite her initial mistreatment. And the other boy tagged along, probably quite aware that a beating lay in store for him. But the under-classes also knew when their superiors stepped out of line, as these numerous legal suits underscore.

In the endeavour to understand how migrant workers in the colonial economy perceived wage labour, experienced social class and articulated their social aspira-tions, the author turned to the intriguing nicknames migrants adopted. Patrick Harries's insights on nicknames Mozambican migrant workers assumed on the South African mines between 1860 and 1910 were extremely useful:

> Migrants were required by an 1872 law to register with the police on their arrival at Kimberley, and those who complied with this ruling, perhaps half the black labor force, were given an official European name. These names ranged from terms for local coins such as Sixpence and Shilling, to popular brands of liquor like Cape Smoke and Pontac, to expletives such as Bloody Fool and God Damn. It is tempting to ascribe what we perceive as the absurdity of these names to the practices of racist whites seeking to infantilize blacks and legitimate their exploitation. While there is some truth in this perspective, I believe it ignores the way in which workers constructed their own vision of the world.[103]

There is no evidence in the Gold Coast that migrant workers were required to assume European names. Hence migrant workers in the Gold Coast who took nick-names had more control over the names they assumed, giving them the opportunity to present their vision of themselves, the colonial situation, capitalism, urban life, modernity and their aspirations. Court cases revealed interesting links between nicknames and the situations that brought their bearers to court. This sheds some light on the lives of ordinary people who left few traces in official records.

Patrick Manning mentions that boatmen, who worked at surf ports, were 'reputed to have added to their wages by stealing from the cargoes they were handling'.[104] Placed at an advantageous position in the mercantile economy, these canoemen were exposed to the 'world of goods',[105] which often lay beyond the means of their paltry

[102] *Godfrey v. Mrs. Phillis Renner*, DC's Court, Keta, 10 March 1892. NAG, Accra, ADM 41/4/3.
[103] Patrick Harries, *Work, Culture, and Identity: Migrant Laborers in Mozambique and South Africa, c. 1860–1910* (Portsmouth and London, 1994), 59.
[104] Patrick Manning, 'Merchants, porters, and canoemen in the Bight of Benin', in Catherine Coquery-Vidovitch and Paul E. Lovejoy, eds, *The Workers of African Trade* (Beverly Hills, 1985), 61.
[105] To borrow the apt phrase of Mary Douglas and Baron Isherwood, *The World of Goods* (New York, 1981).

wages. Migrant workers aspired to be 'big men', and were frustrated by low wages in the colonial economy. This created an 'us' versus 'them' mentality in servant–master relations, which apparently justified pilfering as a legitimate subsidy to inappreciable incomes. The Kru canoemen, 'Everyday', 'One Day' and 'Freeman', were arraigned before the colonial court in Keta in March 1892 for stealing two bales containing scarves of a unique design.[106] Did their nicknames reflect their dreams of making it big one day?

Later that year, 'Everyday' was back in court for his involvement in a group fight in the market-place. African traders from the hinterland and coast often came to the Keta market via the lagoon. The market was strategically placed near the banks of the Keta Lagoon. European firms hired 'catchers' on market-days to solicit traders on their arrival at the lagoon side and bring them to their respective warehouses. On this occasion in August 1892, the catchers of Swanzy, the Bremen Factory and Oloff were involved in a row. One of the catchers was nicknamed 'One Day Gentleman'. Urban workers looked forward to 'pay day' when they could go out on the town adorned in their 'Sunday best'. In contemporary Ghana, the term 'one day gentleman' still describes the phenomenon of the occasional spender, geared up in the garb of modernity (Western clothes) on the Saturday after payday. For 'Work for Nothing', a Kru man who had saved enough finally to have a jacket sewn for himself, even this desire was frustrated when a tailor, after he had received a serge cloth worth 9 shillings and a further 5 shillings for services, attempted to defraud 'Work for Nothing' of his 14 shillings.[107] Even the modest hope of being a 'one day gentleman' was threatened. Western clothing was instrumental in the African construction of modern identities, and hats, coats, polished shoes and accessories, such as walking-sticks, were the vital paraphernalia of modernity.[108]

But why would a Kru migrant labourer in Keta name himself 'Work for Nothing'? Was this a daily self-reminder of the unfair wages in the colonial economy? Did it reflect the capriciousness of urban life as revealed in the unscrupulous conduct of the tailor in question? Modernity and capitalism in colonial urban Africa were empowering as well as disempowering in their juxtaposition of autonomy and alienation, wealth and poverty. Increasingly, rural African migrants went into the colonial urban economy, initially propelled by colonial taxes and the decline of rural economies, but staying on in the desire to 'get ahead' in life. This was the 'modern imagination', and its hold was cognitive as well as material. In pursuit of social mobility and the autonomy that came with it, labour migrants and urban workers butted heads with employers, the upper classes and the colonial government. In the supposedly liberating context of the town, they were expected to be subservient in and out of the work-place. Low wages stymied accumulation, and stealing from employers paid them back for their niggardliness. But dreams lived on, and on pay-day workers enacted the lifestyles of the successful.

[106] *Regina per Muller* v. *Everyday, One Day, and Freeman*, DC's Court, Keta, 22 March 1892. NAG, Accra, ADM 41/4/24.

[107] *Work for Nothing* v. *J.H. Freeman*, DC's Court, Keta, 22 February 1894. NAG, Accra, ADM 41/4/4.

[108] For a fascinating description of the clothing of an Asante 'gentleman' in Kumase in 1889, see Richard Austin

Arjun Appadurai recognizes the valid but problematic connections between modernity, consumption, and autonomy. He comments that 'where there is consumption there is pleasure, and where there is pleasure there is agency', even if freedom remains a 'more elusive commodity'.[109] Ordinary Africans in Keta – indigenes and migrants – coveted the goods and autonomy of modernity. Keta's port economy had created enormous employment opportunities within the context of mercantile capitalism. For indigenes and African migrants, the ultimate goal was to become financially independent, ideally as a merchant. This was tied to the fact that capitalism in Africa manifested itself in commerce and not industry. The presence of successful Sierra Leonean and other Gold Coast merchants gave this vision reality. But capitalism and colonialism overlapped in Africa, and capitalist economic relations – even in peripheral areas such as Keta – were not designed to enrich colonial subjects. Wages were insignificant, and accumulation was slow. For ordinary Africans in colonial Keta, hope and frustration intertwined. This was the anomaly of modernity in a mercantilist colonial economy: it created social aspirations in Africans that were out of place in a colonial political economy. They became modern consumers without power. The numerous cases of theft and embezzlement in Keta's courts underscored the desperation of African labourers and clerks to realize their goal of financial self-sufficiency. The majority of Africans bided their time, observed the Western lifestyles of Sierra Leonean and European merchants, acquired cheap Western clothing and other 'perceived' accoutrements of modernity that enabled them to become 'one day gentlemen', and waited for their big break. Theft was an integral part of modernity in the context of colonial mercantilism, for modernity had to be seized.

Conclusion

Keta by 1910 had been transformed into the leading colonial port east of the Volta, a commercial entrepôt with a large expatriate presence, the headquarters of colonial administration in the Keta-Ada District, a centre of Christianity and education and a cosmopolitan town perceived to be on the cutting edge of modernity. What did all this mean in the Anlo imagination? This is an important question because, from the early twentieth century, Keta came under the threat of acute coastal erosion, or 'sea erosion', as referred to in the records. This pitched residents of Keta in a desperate struggle to save their town, as the next chapter explores. What were the stakes for Keta's residents? And how did other Anlo, who did not live in Keta, view Keta's social transformation?

For residents of Keta, Keta was a place of opportunity where the forces of change had unveiled exciting socio–economic possibilities. Participation could bring great wealth to indigenes, as the business activities of James Ocloo I showed. Several African traders took up residence in Keta, the Williamses and the Renners of Sierra

[108 (cont.)] Freeman, *Travels and Life in Ashanti and Jaman* (Westminster, 1898), 368–9.
[109] Appadurai, *Modernity at Large*, 7.

Leone being good examples. Other Gold Coast merchants were attracted by Keta's bustling commerce. Three generations later, descendants of Sarpong, a Kwahu trader who came to Keta in the early twentieth century, remained in Keta and were actively involved in the business he had set up.[110] A small Levantine community developed in Keta from the early twentieth century, and Lebanese families such as the Abdallahs, the Kriams and the Nassers intermarried as well as taking wives from among the Anlo.[111] Expanding commerce raised the demand for literate clerks, and mission schools in Keta increased their enrolment as the Anlo became more appreciative of the economic benefits of education. Early clerks and storekeepers of expatriate firms would become the trading families of Keta as the twentieth century progressed: the Acolatses (United African Company or UAC), the Adadevohs (UAC), the Akligos (John Holt), the Zaneys (G.B. Olivant) and others.[112]

Outside Keta, several Anlo remained suspicious of Keta's engagement with modernity and of the social forces unleashed in Keta. It was mentioned earlier in the chapter that Bremen missionaries as late as the early 1900s still encountered resistance to their efforts to proselytize and establish schools in Anyako, Dzelukope, Woe, Anloga, Whuti and Attoko. For Anloga, the traditional capital of Anlo, the elevation of Keta as the headquarters of colonial administration and the designation of the entire Anlo area as 'Keta District' may have been perceived as an unsatisfactory development. From the early 1900s, the sea began to encroach on the Anlo coastline, selecting Keta as a favourite site in its assault. This ecological threat threw into bold relief Keta's engagement with modernity, fears of the wrath of Anlo's forgotten gods and ancestors and Keta's rivalry with Anloga. The next chapter considers belief and knowledge in Anlo and the Anlo response to coastal erosion and colonial custodianship.

[110] Interview with Yaw Boateng, Keta, 16 October 1996. Yaw Boateng is the grandson of Sarpong, founder of a business concern that had outlets in Keta, Agbosome and Aflao.
[111] Interview with Joseph Abdallah, Keta, 16 October 1996.
[112] Interview with Edward Kartey-Attipoe, Keta, 17 October 1996. See also interview with Enoch Adadevoh, Keta, 4 September 1996; interview with Fred Akligo, Dzelukope, 18 March 1997.

4

Unstable Ecology
Belief, Knowledge & the Enigma of Sea Erosion in Colonial Keta, 1907–32

Bôbôefe tsi to na ('Water flows through places that resist the least').
Ewe Proverb[1]

Introduction

Chapters 1 and 2 examined the Anlo technological transition to the aquatic and marine environment of south-eastern Ghana. This process was facilitated by the introduction of new techniques in salt making, canoe construction and fishing nets. An important dimension to this material transition was a cognitive adjustment to the water world, made possible by the Anlo transfer of or encounter with relevant marine deities and religious cults. This religious innovation or process is reconstructed in this chapter. The chapter also examines the onset of sustained erosion of the Keta coast from 1907 and the Anlo social interpretation of this environmental crisis. An important concept in the Anlo interpretation of environmental disaster is the breach in moral ecology. The Anlo perceived the space they lived in as ecological, social and cosmological. To them ecological disorder also signalled disequilibrium in the social and cosmological realms. This perception of space proceeds from the cultural mapping of the environment, a process by which the environment is invested with social meaning and rendered manipulable through religion and ritual. Knowledge is produced about the environment, and its transmission from generation to generation underpins the successful social reproduction of the community.

Moral ecology emphasizes four tenets in relations between the human, natural and supernatural worlds. First is the idea of symbiosis between humans and nature. The second notion, however, delineates the space of nature and culture – a sense of order. Wild animals stay in the bush or forest, domestic animals in the home or community.[2] Third is the belief that humans and domestic animals should receive their share of produce according to what they have invested. This belief in a 'just return

[1] N.K. Dzobo, *African Proverbs: Guide to Conduct* (Accra, 1975), 117.
[2] See, for example, Robert W. Harms, *Games against Nature: An Eco-cultural History of the Nunu in Equatorial Africa* (Cambridge, 1987), 38–9.

104

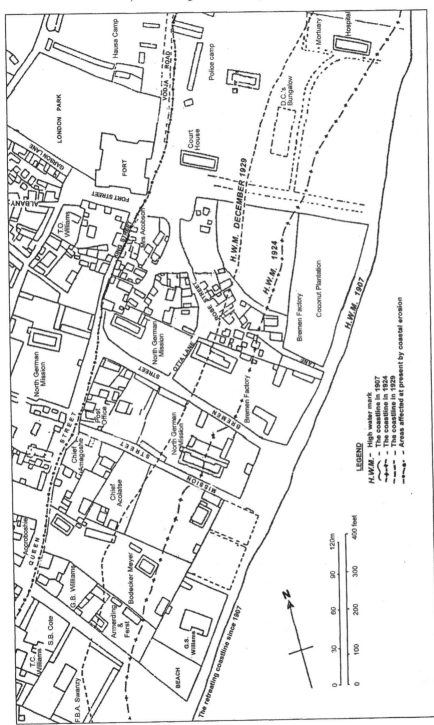

Figure 4.1 High–water mark at Keta Town, 1907–29.

on human investment' is an important aspect of moral ecology and an appeal to the natural and supernatural realms to cooperate with human endeavours for subsistence. Deities and ancestors can endorse or frustrate human attempts at subsistence. Locusts from nature can destroy farms and ruin invested labour. Social cooperation or the codependence of humans is the fourth tenet in moral ecology. Cooperation in the use of resources, labour effort and domestic organization is crucial to community survival. Extreme individualism, rampant greed, witchcraft and the neglect of indigenous religion or ritual are all deprecated as undermining environment and community.

The Anlo believed that their ancestors, in partnership with local deities, such as Mama Bate, caused the sea to retreat, extending the littoral for settlement. For instance, Anlo traditions stress that the Danish Fort Prindsensten was built close to the Keta shoreline in 1784, similarly to most of the forts on the Gold Coast.[3] Figure 4.1 on coastal erosion at Keta reveals the accretion of at least 600 feet of beach land at the Keta shore between 1784 and 1907. The Bate clan claimed responsibility for the land gain, and their perceived spiritual powers – in addition to the retrieval of the *awoame* stool from Notsie — bolstered their claim to the *awoamefia* position in Anlo. The Yewe cult assumed the role of mediators with the sea. It was the major religious cult in Anlo with explicit connections to the sea. Between 1907 and 1932, coastal erosion reversed the coastline at Keta to its 1784 position. By 1907 coastal erosion had assumed alarming proportions and the colonial government began to measure high-water marks at Keta. In 1932 the sea eroded structures of the Evangelical Presbyterian Church and those of the AME Zion, but left the adjacent Catholic Cathedral of St Michael miraculously alone. It was uncanny that the sea chose Keta and its immediate environs for special attention. For many Anlo, this seemed like a divine or ancestral critique of Keta's embrace of modernity – including Christianity.[4] But Christians could also claim the miraculous survival of the Cathedral of St Michael as evidence of their superior faith. In the wake of acute coastal erosion at Keta, Anlo Christians also offered spiritual solutions in the search for a remedy. Sea erosion presented a challenge to Anlo moral ecology for it undermined their understanding of their historic survival in the aquatic environment of south-east Ghana. It served as the context for the review of Keta's social transformation in the preceding decades in the endeavour to establish what went wrong.

Coastal erosion put a new spin on the Keta–Anloga rivalry and revealed the tenuous position of Keta in the colonial political economy as the government declined responsibility for saving Keta. As James Giblin notes, local interpretations of environmental disaster are often closely linked to political ecology.[5] For Keta residents, coastal erosion became an extension of the Keta–Anloga rivalry. And, for the Anlo in general, the colonial government's position that permanent sea defence works far outstripped the value of the land to be saved undermined Anlo loyalty to

[3] NAG, Accra, ADM 39/1/231. Petition from acting Dumega of Keta, Dumega of Dzelukope, and other elders to Governor R. Slater, 13 January 1932.

[4] See Chapter 3.

[5] James L. Giblin, *The Politics of Environmental Control in Northeastern Tanzania, 1840–1940* (Philadelphia, 1992).

the government and the Gold Coast polity. The Anlo resorted to their internal resources of belief and knowledge for a solution to environmental disaster. To enhance our understanding of the Anlo moral ecology, it is necessary that we examine the Anlo religious transition to the marine world.

The Bate clan, Yewe and the sea in Anlo religion and thought

The Bate clan seemed to have a special affinity with water, an affinity initiated when Adeladza encountered the goddess Mama Bate. It is worth remembering that Adeladza was also instrumental in the retrieval of the *awoame* stool from Notsie during the early phase of Anlo settlement. The stool was central to rain-making rituals, and its return ensured the survival of Anlo's ancestors.[6] These circumstances substantiated the Bate claim of special access to the water world. Concerning the Bate priest of Mama Bate, Greene was informed in 1978 that:

> when [the *trônua*, priest] recites a prayer over a calabash of water and pours it on the ground, one would see fish and shrimp jumping out of the water, no matter how small the pool … They never wash their *bisi* cloth with water, but put it in an ordinary flat wooden tray or in a very large calabash. It would immediately begin to rain, and rain so much that [the water which had collected in the container] was sufficient to wash the cloth.[7]

In the new aquatic environment, an ability to 'conjure' fish ensured sustenance, and Bate rain-making powers appeared indispensable in the years of drought that characterized the settlement phase. With their perceived powers over the water world, the Bate clan was in a strong position to claim credit for the accretion of beach land in Anlo. It is instructive that D. Westermann, the Bremen missionary, described the Bate clan leaders as priests, soothsayers and magicians.[8] Strikingly, Bate *awoamefia* tended to highlight the religious nature of kingship during their tenure.[9]

The Yewe cult also emerged as the body with the requisite knowledge to service Anlo's continuing relations with the sea. In charge of rituals to pacify the sea and to ensure bumper fishing seasons, Yewe considered itself the 'champion of the sea' in Anlo society as asserted by Togbui Honi II, custodian of the Yewe shrine at Dzelu-kope.[10] Honi II's ancestor, Honi I, had introduced the first Yewe shrine into Anlo at the beginning of the eighteenth century.[11] Honi I, significantly, was from the Bate clan and was also a grandson of Adeladza I.[12] Thus, Bate and Yewe interests were

---

[6] See Chapter 1.

[7] Sandra E. Greene, 'The past and present of an Anlo-Ewe oral tradition', *History of Africa* 12 (1985): 79.

[8] Cited in Ray A. Kea, 'Akwamu–Anlo relations, *c.* 1750–1813', *Transactions of the Historical Society of Ghana* 10 (1969): 32.

[9] Nii Otokunor Quarcoopome, 'Rituals and regalia of power: art and politics among the Dangme and Ewe, 1800 to present' (PhD thesis, University of California at Los Angeles, 1993), 345.

[10] Interview with Togbui Honi II, Dzelukope, 4 September 1996.

[11] Sandra E. Greene, *Gender, Ethnicity, and Social Change on the Upper Slave Coast: A History of Anlo-Ewe* (Portsmouth, 1996), 95.

[12] Interview with Honi II, Woe, 24 January 1997.

intimately fused, and both mediated Anlo's relations with the sea. As Keta flourished as a seaport and its suburbs, such as Dzelukope and Vodza, became established as centres of sea fishing, the auspicious links between Bate, Yewe and wealth based on maritime occupations may have been self-evident.

The Yewe cult has been described as a 'mixed cult', comprising both sea and sky gods.[13] Although an eastern provenance is assigned to its origins (Dahomey),[14] Herskovits discovered that his Dahomean informants were puzzled by Yewe's western manifestation among the Ewe of Togo and the Gold Coast.[15] The Anlo had borrowed aspects of the worship of sea and sky gods from the related Ewe–Fon–Gun peoples and had fused these in rather novel ways in Yewe.[16] The sea was a complete world in itself, and the Ewe–Fon–Gun held a very defined view of this marine world and its denizens. The 'owner of the sea' was called Hu among the Fon. According to Geoffrey Parrinder, this god was:

> believed to live in a palace under the sea, as sea kings do in many mythologies, and to have his attendants and mermaid wives, lesser divinities, human and fishlike. Rough seas are attributed to the anger of the god, and propitiatory sacrifices were thrown into the sea for him, generally fowls and animals; formerly, human beings were sacrificed on special occasions. He is the protecting god of fishermen.[17]

Law provides an important historical elaboration, which underscores the changing roles of Hu:

> Hu was also in origin a national deity, associated especially with the Hula people of Great Popo, but as the Hula migrated to settle along the coast east of Popo the cult of Hu traveled with them. European sources thus mention the worship of the Sea not only in Great Popo, but also in Whydah and Allada, and the cult was also patronized by the kings of Dahomey after their conquest of the coast [1720s]. This cult must have arisen in importance with the development of trade with the Europeans, since it involved the offering of sacrifices ... to calm the sea in order to facilitate dealings with the European traders.[18]

Sea fishing and European maritime trade underpinned the rise of marine deities on the Slave Coast. The open savannah of the Benin Gap and the lagoon system promoted the dispersion of these marine gods and their associated cults. Significantly, in Anlo 'Hu' refers to the Yewe cult.[19] Yewe and the sea fused in Anlo.

Three deities – Hebieso or Xevieso, Agbui or Avleketi and Voduda or Da – became

---

[13] H. Seidel, 'Der Yewe-Dienst im Togolande', *Zeitschrift für Afrikanische und Oceanische Sprachen* 3, 2 (1897): 161.

[14] Seidel, 'Yewe-Dienst'; Nissio S. Fiagbedzi, 'Sogbadzi songs: a study of Yewe music' (Dip. in African Music, University of Ghana, 1966), 12; Richard Tetteh Torgby, 'A study of the Yewe secret society among the Ewe speaking people of southern Ghana' (BA thesis, Religions Department, University of Ghana, 1977), ii.

[15] Melville J. Herskovits, *Dahomey: An Ancient West African Kingdom*, vol. 2 (New York, 1938), 189–93.

[16] D. Westermann, 'Ein Bericht über den Yehwekultus der Ewe', *Mitteilungen des Seminars für Orientalische Sprachen* 33, 3 (1930): 3.

[17] Geoffrey Parrinder, *West African Religion* (London, 1969), 45.

[18] Robin Law, *The Slave Coast of West Africa 1550–1750: The Impact of the Atlantic Slave Trade on African Society* (Oxford, 1991), 110–11. See also William Bosman, *A New and Accurate Description of the Coast of Guinea, Divided into the Gold, the Slave, and the Ivory Coasts* (London, 1721), 362.

[19] Personal communication from Nissio Fiagbedzi, Accra, August 1999.

prominent in the Yewe cult among the Anlo-Ewe. Although these are perceived as Dahomean or 'eastern' gods, their roles have been redefined among the Anlo. The Fon of Dahomey believed that the universe was created by Nana Buluku, who gave birth to twins, Mawu (female) and Lisa (male), to whom eventual dominion of the world was ceded.[20] Mawu and Lisa's progeny constitute three major pantheons of deities in Dahomean religion: the sky pantheon, the earth pantheon, and the thunder pantheon. Mawu and Lisa head the sky pantheon. Mawu and Lisa gave birth to twins, Dada Zodji and Nyohwe Ananu, and they head the earth cult or Sagbata. Then Mawu and Lisa gave birth to So, god of thunder, who is the progenitor of the gods of the Xevieso pantheon. Mawu and Lisa subsequently had another set of twins, Agbe (male) and Naete (female), who took residence in the sea as man and wife. Agbe and Naete had six children, the sixth and favourite child being Afrekete.

Worship of these deities sometimes overlapped, and important connections linked the thunder pantheon to the marine deities that featured in the Yewe cult. Herskovits was informed that:

> When Agbe had established himself in the sea, he continued to communicate with his parent at the point where the sea and sky meet, that is, at the horizon. Hence is it said that Agbe and his children are both in the sea and in the sky, because their home is where the two meet.[21]

Explicit ties existed between the thunder pantheon, deities that controlled water (including rain), and marine deities, for it was believed that rainfall was drawn from bodies of water such as the sea, lagoons and rivers. This explains why Aido Hwedo, a snake in the sky pantheon who manifests himself as the rainbow, would be associated with Xevieso, for his role is to assist Xevieso (thunder and lightning) in coming to the earth.[22] Xevieso is also described as the 'possessor of the sky'.[23] Aido Hwedo is distinct from Dangbe, the royal python and the tutelary god of Whydah. Both, however, are associated with rainfall and fertility.[24]

Occupational pursuits in the different geographical zones in old Dahomey placed different emphasis on specific deities. In the farming communities north of Abomey, Herskovits noted several shrines to the earth cult, Sagbata.[25] In the coastal or lagoon settlements, such as Whydah, Allada and Great Popo, worship of So and Agbe was prominent. Elaboration of So worship had occurred at Hevie or Xevie, a village between Allada and Whydah, by the 1710s.[26] Thus So was renamed 'Xevieso' in acknowledgement of his ties to Xevie. Xevieso worshippers believed that when Agbe first descended to earth he showed himself at Xwala (Great Popo), where he gave his name and taught them about the deities of the sea.[27] Worship of Agbe and the sea deities diffused from Great Popo along the Slave Coast. Anlo's ancestors had active

---

[20] The following sections on Fon religion are drawn from Herskovits, *Dahomey*, vol. 2, chs 26–28.

[21] Ibid., 152.

[22] Ibid., 108.

[23] Ibid., 150.

[24] Law, *Slave Coast of West Africa*, 110; Bosman, *New and Accurate Description*, 349–51.

[25] Herskovits, *Dahomey*, 144.

[26] Law, *Slave Coast of West Africa*, 111.

[27] Herskovits, *Dahomey*, 157.

contacts with Little Popo, Great Popo and Whydah. Anlo traders brought these deities and cults from the east.

The Yewe cult among the Ewe in Togo and the Gold Coast was prominent in coastal areas, such as Anexo, Porto Seguro, Tsevie, Aflao, Some, Vodza, Kedzi, Keta, Dzelokope and Woe in the late nineteenth and early twentieth centuries.[28] Togbui Honi and his wife Boe brought the cult into Anlo. They brought it from Xoda, on the middle Slave Coast, where Boe had been cured of barrenness by one of the Yewe deities. Togbui Honi established a Yewe shrine in Keta.[29] The Danish bombardment of Keta in 1847 incidentally resulted in the dispersion of Yewe further west along the Anlo coast and the cult grew in popularity as wealthy Anlo became shrine owners.[30] In the Anlo-Yewe context, Xevieso as the thunder god remained the most recognizable deity in his mode of operation. Agbui was certainly derived from Agbe, but the Agbe of Dahomey was male, married to his twin sister, Naete. The Yewe Agbui in Anlo is female, a sex change that facilitated her marriage to Xevieso. This provided a strong fusion of the thunder and sea cults for Yewe worshippers in Anlo. Agbui is also referred to as Avleketi, the deity most favoured by Anlo fishermen. Her magnanimity is tied to bumper seasons, and she receives regular propitiation. But the Dahomean Afrekete was the sixth child of Agbe and Naete, though, again, noted for her generosity to fishermen. Some Ewe Yewe worshippers in Togo claim that Agbui first manifested herself at a town called Avleketi, hence her dual name – Agbui/Avleketi.[31] Then there is Voduda, whose presence in the Yewe cult and close association with Xevieso suggests similarities with Xevieso's relationship with Aido Hwedo. Unlike Dangbe of Whydah, represented by a non-poisonous python, the Voduda of Yewe is symbolized by a poisonous snake. Since both Aido Hwedo and Dangbe are associated with rain and bodies of water, it seems likely that it is this realm of water that ties Xevieso, Agbui, and Voduda together. The presence of snake cults in Anlo underscores the tranmission of cultural influences from related linguistic groups to the east of Anlo. In Anlo, the Amlade clan god Togbi Egbe is credited with the ability to enter snakes and inflict punishment on the adversaries of the god and its followers. Greene points out that the clan's founders came from Anexo to the east in the mid-eighteenth century.[32]

Yewe entered Anlo as the possession of an individual, and individuals bought Yewe and hired priests to supervise it.[33] Yewe was a private acquisition, noted in its introductory years as a fertility god and as a protective charm in war.[34] Its embellishment among the Ewe may be linked to this feature, for it became a platform for acquiring wealth and power. With this probably came the practice of corporal punishment of Yewe devotees, the development of secret languages called Xevieso and Agbui languages – drawing on Fon vocabulary – and the rite of *alagadzedze*. In

[28] Ibid., 58; Westermann, 'Bericht über den Yehwekultus', 49.
[29] Greene, *History of the Anlo-Ewe*, 95.
[30] Ibid.
[31] Westermann, 'Bericht über den Yehwekultus', 45; Herskovits, *Dahomey*, vol. 2, 193.
[32] Greene, *History of the Anlo-Ewe*, 62–3.
[33] Torgby, 'Yewe secret society', i.
[34] Greene, *History of the Anlo-Ewe*, 95.

alagadzedze, an 'insulted' Yewe devotee 'went wild' (was possessed) and could only be restored to normalcy at heavy cost to the culprit.[35] The *alaga* in her wild state was believed to live on the seabed and had to be 'fished' out of the sea after compensation had been paid.[36] Yewe membership afforded protection and prestige. Closely allied with the Afa divinatory system – derived from the Yoruba Ifa – Yewe became central to Anlo life. The rise of European maritime trade and sea fishing provided Yewe with an additional niche in Anlo life, especially with the decline of warfare under colonial rule. Poor fishing seasons necessitated Afa consultation, and Afa would require Yewe to propitiate the sea. Rough seas brought a similar referral to Yewe and their control over water. Exactly when Yewe acquired this role is uncertain. The dispersal of the Bate, caused by the Anloga–Keta war of 1792 and Danish bombardment of Keta in 1847, may have created the need for Yewe to step into the role of public ritual experts.

In the nineteenth and twentieth centuries, the Anlo, noted for their lack of maritime skills through the eighteenth century,[37] acquired a new confidence in their relations with the sea. This was reflected in the cognitive accommodation of the sea in Anlo daily life, religion, and ritual. For the Anlo-Ewe, the sea is sacred space. Although the sea's ordinary name is *atsiafu* or *fu* among the Anlo, its sacred name during rituals is *ahoyo*. The Anlo elder, S.S. Dotse, revealed that:

> When somebody is drowning now, if you mention *atsiafu*, the person will not be washed ashore … But when you mention the name *ahoyo*, then it will vomit the person. Even if you are an Akan, mention *ahoyo* and say whatever you like. Your wishes will be fulfilled. When people are at sea and there is a powerful storm, they break bottles of schnapps against the hull of the boat and mention the name *ahoyo*.[38]

The sea then becomes calm. This 'control' over the sea was certainly crucial in the development of sea fishing among the Anlo. It underpinned the gradual transition from fishing in the calmer waters of the Keta Lagoon to a more intense exploitation of the sea's resources from the mid-nineteenth century. This cognitive shift complemented the technological introduction of the *yevudor* (seine-net) in Anlo.

The sea also served as a custodian of morality, and its sacred power was specifically invoked in the ritual ablutions that separated an Anlo widow or widower from the deceased spouse. Anlo widows observed a period of mourning that lasted sixteen months. Mourning ended with ritual cleansing:

> At the end of this period, there is *ahotsilele*, the ceremonial washing of the widow. In the evening the *ahosi* [widow] is taken to the shores of the lagoon or creek or to the beach to see whether she has been seduced since the death of her husband. This is known as *zumeyiyi*. As they reach the beach she steps into the water. It is said that she will be drowned if she has slept with any man, unless she confesses.[39]

[35] Seidel, 'Yewe-Dienst'; Westermann, 'Bericht über den Yehwekultus'; Torgby, 'Yewe secret society'. 'Insult' covered special categories, such as calling a Yewe devotee an *avu* (dog) or beast (*gbemela*) or to deliberately call the devotee by the pre-cult (*ahe*) name. Personal correspondence from G.K. Nukunya, 28 September 1999.
[36] Seidel, 'Yewe-Dienst', 173–4.
[37] Law, *Slave Coast of West Africa*, 42; J.M. Grove, 'Some aspects of the economy of the Volta delta (Ghana)', *Bulletin de l'Institut Fondamental d'Afrique Noir* 28, 1–2 (1966): 383.
[38] Interview with S.S. Dotse, Keta, 4 September 1996.
[39] G.K. Nukunya, *Kinship and Marriage among the Anlo Ewe* (London, 1969), 207.

Water in general constituted a powerful spiritual fluid in Anlo religion. As a sacred fluid, it facilitated communion with the Supreme Being (*Mawu*), the deities (*trôwo*) and the ancestral spirits (*tôgbenôliwo*). Water symbolized peace, fertility and growth. In all situations where peace was desired, water mixed with maize flour was used in libations.[40] Water's calming effect was so powerful that the spirit of a murdered corpse was enjoined not to drink water in the land of the dead (*tsiefe*) until it had exacted vengeance. The Anlo believed that 'if the dead person reaches the underworld and drinks water, his heart will cool down and he will forget to take vengeance'.[41] Water was an important medium in the rituals of renewal that underpinned Anlo society by banning disease (*dodede*) and reconciling aggrieved parties (*nugbidodo*).[42]

When coastal erosion commenced with intensity at Keta at the beginning of this century, it shook Anlo understanding of the sea and their relationship with the sea. In 1901, the *Gold Coast Chronicle* commented on the serious nature of erosion along the Keta coast.[43] The *Gold Coast Leader* expressed its fears in 1903 that the sea may join the Keta Lagoon at Kedzi in about five to ten years.[44] There were many Anlo outside Keta who had looked on in askance as Keta bravely engaged the forces of social change unleashed by mission Christianity, foreign merchants and other migrants, and the significant presence of colonial officers and civil servants. Had Keta invited environmental disaster through its foolhardiness?

The timing of coastal erosion at Keta was made more awkward by the election of an Adzovia, Sri II, as *awoamefia* of Anlo in 1906. The Adzovia clan nominated Sri II without prior consultation with the Bate clan, the other clan eligible for the paramountcy.[45] Bate clan leaders took exception to this, and it appears that the basis of the alternation and Bate eligibility were questioned by the Adzovia in the resulting exchange. While the Bate clan holds that the alternation of the paramountcy was instituted by Sri I as a permanent arrangement, some Adzovia clan members contend that it was a one-time interruption to reward Adeladza for his service.[46] While the Commissioner for the Eastern Province strove to reconcile the two parties, James Ocloo I of Keta and Togbui Tenge of Anyako (Bate clan leaders) insisted that the record show that the next *awoamefia* would be selected from the Bate clan.[47] The

---

[40] Personal correspondence from Togbuivi Kumassah, Keta, 12 December 1994.

[41] Christian R.K. Bensah, 'Anlo belief in life after death' (BA thesis, Religions Department, University of Ghana, 1979), 11.

[42] Justice M.Y. Amegashie, 'The concept of renewal – a study in Anlo thought' (BA thesis, Religions Department, University of Ghana, 1976).

[43] *Gold Coast Chronicle*, 8 March 1901.

[44] *Gold Coast Leader*, 7 March 1903.

[45] The selecting clan is under no obligation to consult the other clan in its choice of candidate according to Anlo customary law. The other clan is notified after the selection of the candidate. Personal correspondence from G.K. Nukunya, 28 September 1999. In this instance, the Adzovia clan may have delayed unduly in informing the Bate clan of its candidate and news of the *awoamefia*-elect reached Bate clan leaders through third parties.

[46] Interview with Togbui James Ocloo IV, Keta, 24 January 1997; interview with Esther Kwawukume (daughter of Sri II), Keta, 25 January 1997.

[47] Memorandum by the Commissioner of the Eastern Province (CEP), C.A. O'Brien, on the election of Awoamefia Togbui Sri II, alias Kofi Cornelius Kwawukumey, 29 May 1906. NAG, Accra, ADM 41/5/8, Keta District Record Book, 1900–27.

intensification of sea erosion at Keta from 1906 seemed to have provided the opportunity for the Bate clan to vindicate the basis of their original claim to the *awoame* stool by repeating that supernatural event which extended the Anlo coastline. That their failure to do so did not undermine their claim to the para-mountcy indicates that the Anlo put more emphasis on Adeladaza's retrieval of the stool from Notsie as the basis of the Bate clan's eligibility.

The accession of Togbui Sri I as *awoamefia* of Anlo in 1906 marked a significant political change in yet another way. Sri I was a Christian educated in the Bremen Mission schools in Keta. He had been a commercial clerk in Sierra Leone and the German Cameroons in his private life. On being made king, Sri II advocated a new image for Anloga and the *awoamefia* and successfully divested kingship in Anlo of its superstitious cloak.[48] He sought to redefine the old position of the *awoamefia* as a secluded priest-chief.[49] Sri established his imprint as a visible, constitutional monarch who removed his office from the webs of religious constraint. He repealed the ban on wearing European clothing in Anloga and put a stop to the burying of corpses in the deceased's house. Sri opened Anloga to mission education and commerce – the twin forces of change long resisted at the traditional capital.[50] His close personal relation-ship with Francis Crowther, appointed District Commissioner (DC) of Keta in 1912, would facilitate Sri's ambitions. In 1912 Crowther would chair a commission of inquiry that would expand the jurisdiction of the Anlo Tradition State – under the *awoamefia* – to coincide with the boundaries of the informal precolonial Anlo con-federacy.[51] Sri II's physical renovation of Anloga from 1906 and the growing influence of the Anlo Traditional Council gradually made Anloga a credible challenger to Keta for the premier position in Anlo. Keta seemed to be under siege on all fronts.

Sea erosion at Keta: an ancestral critique of modernity?

Several Anlo communities outside Keta remained sceptical of Keta's embrace of modernity and watched with a sense of foreboding at the potential consequences. No doubt there was even a constituency in Keta that shared this view. The heavy mortality among the missionaries, evidenced by the abundant tombstones of the three mission cemeteries at Keta, lent credence to local suspicions that the ancestors disapproved of the missionary presence.[52] It was mentioned in Chapter 3 that, as late as 1903, fifty years after the North German Missionary Society established a station in Keta, the mission still experienced difficulties penetrating the environs of Keta. This opposi-tion to 'modernity' had as one of its major roots a fear of ecological imbalance, a

---

[48] For a good biography, see Napoleon K. Agboada, 'The reign and times of Togbi Sri II of Anlo (1906–1956)' (BA thesis, History Department, University of Ghana, 1984).

[49] See Chapter. 1.

[50] NAG, Accra, ADM 39/1/120. Address by Katsriku Awusu II, Awadada of Anlo, on the occasion of the fortieth anniversary of Togbui Sri II, Keta, 10 December 1947.

[51] Agboada, 'Togbi Sri II', 10; NAG, Accra, ADM 11/1/404, Memorandum on Awuna, Addah and Akwamu (1912).

[52] NAG, Accra, ADM 39/1/177. Missionary tombstones have been preserved at Keta and Anyako.

rupture in the bounded spheres of locality due to uncontrolled change. But locality is far from static, and the 'social activities of production, representation and reproduction … contribute, generally unwittingly, to the creation of contexts that might exceed the existing material and conceptual boundaries of the neighbourhood'.[53] In Anlo, mission, capitalism and colonialism accentuated these social activities. Beneficiaries of the precolonial status quo wanted to keep locality 'fixed', and they used environmental disaster to advance their cause. The centrality of fishing to life in Keta and its environs and the dependence of farmers on rainfall that was often irregular made ecological arguments very powerful. In 1858, when the Keta Lagoon dried up completely, 'the Bremen missionaries at Anyako were blamed for this natural phenomenon as an expression of the displeasure of the gods with the people, for permitting whitemen to stay on their land'.[54] In the 1880s Geraldo de Lima endeared himself to the Anlo when he travelled to a powerful shrine in Notsie with his own money during a drought in Anlo 'and brought prosperity resulting in the abnormal flooding of the Lagoon'.[55]

Sometimes, resistance to Keta's 'disruptive' influences took on a physical nature. Some residents at Whuti sought to physically restrain African evangelists sent from the Keta station. Evangelist Stephen Hiob Kwadzo Afelevo faced several tribulations in Woe and Whuti, especially as he had reneged on the Yewe cult and become a Christian.[56] Heavy rains in 1893 led to flooding by the Keta Lagoon. The German trader, Meyer of Brodecker and Meyer, had some engineering knowledge and decided to cut a canal across the narrow spit of land that separated the lagoon and the sea at Kedzi. The force of the rushing water was unanticipated; the canal quickly widened and swept away people, neighbouring houses and coconut trees. Individual Anlo sued the German firm for the destruction of their property.[57] When a Hausa woman, Addisah, went to the lagoon side to buy fish in December 1893, she was assaulted by a group of Anlo men at the instigation of Abochi, who said 'the whitemen have cut the lagoon and that is why we cannot get fish'.[58] Colonial presence had led to the stationing of a force of Hausa Constabulary in Keta from 1874, and the Hausa community expanded with the immigration of Hausa traders. The Anlo viewed the Hausa as 'associates' of colonial rule, and in Addisah's case she was made to bear the brunt of Anlo frustration at their changing environment – an ecology that was always dynamic.

The year 1906 was momentous in Anlo, marked by drought, earthquake, a fire in Anloga, the nomination of Sri II as paramount chief and the intensification of coastal erosion. Incidentally, 1906 was the year when Anloga elders finally acceded to the Bremen Mission's request to set up a mission station in Anloga. 'Traditionalists'

[53] Arjun Appadurai, *Modernity at Large: Cultural Dimensions of Globalization* (Minneapolis, 1996), 185.

[54] J.B. Yegbe, 'The Anlo and their neighbours, 1850–1890' (MA thesis, University of Ghana, 1977), 4.

[55] Gershon A. Sorkpor, 'Geraldo de Lima and the Awunas (1862–1904)' (MA thesis, University of Ghana, 1966), 90.

[56] *Stephen Hiob Kwadzo v. Coblavie of Wute*, DC's Court, Keta, 2 July 1895. NAG, Accra, ADM 41/4/26. Kwadzo's autobiography formed the core of Westermann's 'Ein Bericht über den Yehwekultus'. See also, G.K. Nukunya, *The History of the Woe Evangelical Presbyterian Church 1887–1987* (Accra, 1987), 15–17.

[57] See, for example, *Kudawoo v. Brodecker and Meyer*, DC's Court, Keta, 30 October 1894. NAG, Accra, ADM 41/4/4. On the cutting of the canal in 1893, see Grove, 'Economy of the Volta delta', 428.

[58] *Addisah v. Abochi et al.*, DC's Court, Keta, 5 December 1893. NAG, Accra, ADM 41/4/25.

were quick to point out the reason for environmental chaos. The Anloga priests of Nyigbla, the Anlo war god, opined in regard to the drought:

> You see, there you go, and this is Nyigbla, because you want the mission and deserve punishment. Look at your fields! Why is everything so dry and dead, your work in vain, the harvest so modest that it may not even satisfy your hunger? Because it does not rain! And why does it not rain? Because Nyigbla does not want it, for you have offended him.[59]

The previous three years stood in sharp contrast, as abundant rains had made the Keta Lagoon navigable and trade, fishing and agriculture flourished. And, when earthquakes shook the Anlo coast on 20 November 1906, some Anloga priests claimed it was the European God shaking his head because he was demanding back the money Anloga elders had received as a gift from the whites.[60]

Ancestral fury seemed to know no bounds when a series of fires ravaged the adjacent towns of Whuti and Anloga in 1906. The conflagrations began in Whuti, and priests in Whuti alleged that Nyigbla had sent the fire because the people of Anloga were aiding the missionaries in the construction of a mission post. Nyigbla's message was clear: stop the construction or fire would be sent to consume Anloga itself. The construction came to a halt as Anloga residents dashed to their homes and removed valuable property to their farming villages. Parents of school pupils forbade their children to assist the missionaries on the construction site, as Nyigbla threatened such accomplices with death. A fire outbreak burnt almost the entire western part of Anloga. The missionaries strongly suspected arson. A sudden downpour of rain prevented the fire in Anloga from spreading.[61]

But modernity was making its advance even in Anloga. The town's elders had granted permission for the mission school to be built because they were convinced by the missionary argument that literate sons would serve Anloga better in the age of colonialism.[62] Indeed, Dzelokope and Keta had appointed literate chiefs familiar with European ways – C.T. Agbozo and James Ocloo I, respectively – and this seemed to facilitate the socio-economic development of these towns.[63] The nomination of Sri II, alias Cornelius Kwawukume, reflected this wind of change. As coastal erosion advanced, residents of the Anlo littoral hoped their identification with modernity and colonialism would predispose the colonial government to come to their rescue. After all, Keta was an important contributor to colonial revenue and the centre of colonial administration in the district. Moreover, missionary education had created the awareness that technology existed in the West to halt coastal erosion. Indeed, local knowledge holds that the German missionaries in the late nineteenth century had predicted the coastal advance of the sea in the Keta area; hence they built with boards and not brick.[64] Keta's leaders confidently expected the expatriate commercial firms in Keta and the colonial government to save the day.

[59] F. Galkowski, *Anloga, eine Hochburg des Heidentums* (Bremen, 1907), 25.
[60] Ibid., 26.
[61] Ibid.
[62] Ibid., 13.
[63] Greene, *History of the Anlo-Ewe*, 137.
[64] Interview with Edward Kartey-Attipoe, Keta, 17 October 1996.

Keta besieged: sea erosion and the politics of colonial trusteeship

From 1907 the colonial government began to record the high-water marks at Keta in order to assess the progress of sea erosion. Hesitancy on the part of the colonial government and the mercantile firms in Keta delayed a concerted response to sea erosion. Key to this confusion was the issue of which party should bear financial responsibility for sea defence. The colonial government's position was that it was not responsible for acts of nature. Indeed, since the mercantile firms were major beneficiaries of Keta's economic boom, they should assume some responsibility in saving it. The merchants and people of Keta looked steadfastly to the colonial government for a solution to sea erosion. They believed that this was part of the obligations of political over-rule. The matter rested there until 1923.

In defence of the colonial government, it must be noted that erosion along the Keta coast was far from predictable. Keta and its environs seemed to be under siege from both the sea and the Keta Lagoon. The Keta Lagoon frequently flooded its banks between 1910 and 1917. In July 1910, the acting DC for Keta reported that:

> the strip of beach on the far side of Kedji [Kedzi] (some 4 miles from Quittah) is now less than 25 yards wide for a distance of a mile or so, and only 2 or 3 feet higher than the lagoon. It is feared that a breach may be made and the lagoon water in that case would be lost and serious trouble would be caused.[65]

Yet the DC could report in 1917 concerning Kedzi that there was 'no occasion to anticipate the lagoon joining up with the sea at Kedji, as the latter has of late years formed a high bank of sand between the two which makes such an event improbable'.[66] Kedzi's situation had reversed, and it was now gaining beach land through the accretion of sea waves. In the 1910s, the danger posed to Keta and its environs through lagoon flooding was as grave as the coastal advance of the sea.

The enormity of the task was daunting to the colonial government. The sea was uncanny in its unpredictability. Although there was movement of sand along the coast between Dzelukope and Kedzi, the points of erosion shifted constantly and were not confined to any definite area. This led the Provincial Engineer in 1923 to assert that any attempt to stop the sand movement 'would be a most expensive job, and might have unexpected results'.[67] But the majority of the government's administrative buildings in Keta were located on the ocean front. Several commercial houses had sited their warehouses on the ocean front also, to facilitate the loading and offloading of ships through canoes. The government had to save its investment, albeit at minimum cost. It hoped the erosion was temporary, and its initial action consisted of relocating affected government offices away from the ocean front. The besieged Keta Hospital was removed further inland in 1913.[68]

[65] Acting DC of Keta to acting CEP, 26 July 1910. NAG, Accra, ADM 39/1/173.
[66] Ibid. DC Keta to CEP, Accra, 5 September 1917.
[67] NAG, Accra, ADM 39/1/231. Report of M.F. Inglis, Provincial Engineer, to the Director of Public Works, 5 February 1923.
[68] Ibid. Address by D. Grieve, Director of Medical and Sanitary Services, at the opening of the new Keta Hospital, 30 October 1934.

Belief, Knowledge & the Enigma of Sea Erosion

In 1923, the destructive nature of the sea galvanized the government into action. European merchants in Keta demanded decisive government intervention. A telegram from Percy Roe, provincial agent for F. & A. Swanzy, set the stage in June 1923:

> Position Quittah [Keta] and Atiteti serious Stop Half Atiteti washed away and large part of Quittah in danger Stop Sea undermining backwall Walkdens premises and with[in] a few feet of Bremen mission ... Would it not be possible to send an agent from the harbour works Stop Hope there will be no delay as the matter is urgent.[69]

By August 1923, the acting Commissioner of the Eastern Province had arranged for the Director of Public Works to erect groynes along a part of the seashore at Keta. He feared that nothing could be done for Atiteti, for the 'works are costly and the nature of the land affected would not justify the large expenses which would be involved'.[70] In short, unlike Keta, Atiteti was no commercial jewel and thus not worth saving. The issue of cost and whether expensive sea defence works were economically justifiable in the coastal areas under siege would become the major factor in the colonial government's considerations.

Timber groynes were sunk at Keta beach from 9 October 1923, with the aim of breaking the force of the sea waves and of facilitating the deposition of sand carried by the sea in its longshore movements. Hope rose when a total depth of 2 feet and 6 inches of sand accumulated under the DC's bungalow by 30 October 1923. Then the sea resumed its unrelenting assault. By August 1926 the groynes had been demolished and the Keta beach was in a worse condition.[71] In 1928 the colonial government acknowledged the need for expert advice. It approached the London based engineering firm of Coode, Wilson, Mitchell and Vaughan-Lee for a technical evaluation of the Keta situation. Since A.T. Coode had already scheduled a trip to Lagos in June 1929, the colonial government arranged for him to stop at Keta on his return from Lagos to England for a first-hand examination of the situation.[72] Coode arrived in Keta on 8 June, and spent the following two days inspecting the shoreline. On the basis of this two-day inspection, Coode issued a report that sealed the fate of Keta for the rest of the colonial period. The report recommended that:

> In all the circumstances such as we have endeavoured to describe, we conclude that the expenditure which would be requisite on a system of groynes or other preventive work could not only be justified by the prospects of success but, moreover, that the value of the buildings and property to be saved does not warrant the very large outlay which would have been incurred.[73]

The question of saving Keta had been reduced to Keta's economic worth.

But the Coode Report was illuminating in explaining the geological factors for the Keta situation. The lie of the coastline at Keta, the sandy nature of the shoreline and the pattern of the prevailing littoral currents were significant features. The coastline

---

[69] Ibid. Telegram from Percy Roe to CEP, 15 June 1923.
[70] Ibid. Acting CEP to Chief Provincial Agent, F. & A. Swanzy, 1 August 1923.
[71] Ibid. Provincial Engineer to acting Director of Public Works, 24 August 1926.
[72] Ibid. Colonial Secretary to CEP, 16 January 1929.
[73] Gold Coast, *Despatches Relating to Coast Erosion in the Neighbourhood of Keta* (Accra, 1929). A. T. Coode to the Under Secretary of State for the Colonies, 15 August 1929.

of the Gulf of Guinea lies in a west-to-east direction, the same direction in which the prevailing littoral currents set. Longshore drift continuously removed sand and replaced it in a west-to-east direction, resulting in a general equilibrium. But there was evidence that the shore around Cape St Paul in Woe had advanced seaward since 1900. This had altered the lie of the Keta coast, and the west-to-east direction from the estuary of the Volta assumed a north–north-east direction after Cape St Paul. The easterly pattern only resumed from Lome.[74] The end result was that the littoral currents continued to remove sand from Keta's beach, but its leeward position – due to the outward projection of Cape St Paul – prevented the replenishment of the Keta coast. The absence of igneous or granitic rocks along the Keta coast accelerated the process of weathering. A bay had been created in the Keta area, and erosion was accentuated by the oblique angle at which waves hit the shore.[75] That the Keta area is subject to land subsidence made it vulnerable to trangression by the sea.[76] The government's uncritical acceptance of the Coode Report shattered the confidence of Keta's residents in government, and henceforth sea erosion assumed a political face for the coastal Anlo. For the colonial government the matter was settled and the issue was now one of resettlement. The people of Keta refused to move. Their resentment of what they considered a superficial examination by A.T. Coode and of the colonial government's ready endorsement of the report provided the context for an Anlo critique of colonial rule.

The scholars and principal citizens of Keta met on 29 March 1930 to deliberate upon the Coode Report. They estimated the value of buildings in Keta to be £800,000, not to mention the value of commercial stocks and goods in the town and properties situated in the hinterland of the town, as well as the townspeople themselves. Were these not worth saving? They refreshed the colonial government's memory of services the Anlo had rendered:

> That the town of Keta (Anlo) which is very important especially in Revenue and stood 3rd or 4th position in the Colony's Revenue statistically, and which during the great European War, had contributed largely and loyally, had supplied volunteers for active service, also carriers showing her loyalty to the British in whom she puts her confidence for protection, and Keta, which is the only sea port, also an eye to the Anlo Nation.[77]

And if the colonial government was not impressed, it could reflect on 'the Bones of our Missionaries [European] who lost their lives here, and the Bones of our Political

---

[74] Ibid.

[75] See Map 1.1, the physical map of Anlo. The author owes David Atta-Peters, a geologist at the University of Ghana, an inestimable debt for his lectures on geological formations and processes. See interviews with Atta-Peters, Accra, 2 December 1996 and 13 December 1996.

[76] Atta-Peters provided the author with an explanation for land subsidence. Tectonically, the entire coastline of Ghana is block-faulted, that is, it has movements. Block faulting can lead to subsidence by creating a lower elevation than the normal heights. This opens an area to invasion by the sea. Apart from faulting, elevation changes can produce subsidence, with the same result of sea transgression. Interview with David Atta-Peters, Accra, 2 December 1996. Cooperativa Muratori and Cementesti, 'Keta sea defence – Ghana' (June 1987), 19, estimated in 1987 that the rate of land subsidence in the Keta area has been in the order of 3 mm per year.

[77] NAG, Accra, ADM 39/1/231. Resolution from Keta Residents, 14 May 1930.

Administrators [British] to be dragged out by the Erosion of the sea, and their Bones eaten up by the deep sea fishes.'[78] The government was not fazed.

The Anlo felt abandoned, not only by the colonial government, but also by the rest of the colony's subjects, who appeared indifferent to Anlo's plight. Politically, the coastal Anlo began to look northwards and eastwards for alliances with other Ewe groups. The Ewe League and the All Ewe Conference became the active champions of this new cause.[79] The Anlo State Council's response in 1939 to the colonial government's appeal for relief funds for earthquake victims in Accra emphasized the Anlo sense of alienation. The DC for Keta reported that:

> The State Council was not interested, and the answer I got was to the effect that as the Accra people have not seen fit to assist the Keta People when 160 houses were washed away in a single night they were not prepared to start a relief in Accra.[80]

Pan-Ewe consciousness and a spirit of self-reliance encompassed the search for a local solution to sea erosion. The Anlo turned to local belief and knowledge in the quest for an internal solution. Did a body of knowledge exist that facilitated the manipulation of nature, including the sea? If so, could it be recovered in the wake of such considerable social change?

Belief, knowledge and moral ecology: a religious solution to sea erosion

The focus now shifted to the Bate clan and the Yewe cult and their alleged control over the sea. The *modus operandi* of the sea's advance seemed to suggest a super-natural design. The period between June and November each year witnessed the sea's unyielding assault.[81] The peak month for coastal erosion was September, the month in which the waters of the Volta also rose and spilled over into the lagoon.[82] In spite of the regularity of the sea's invasion, the impact was nevertheless always unsettling. Christian Gaba noted that: 'Keta suffers regularly and at the same period during the year from sea erosion which the primitive mind among the inhabitants consider naturally inexplicable.'[83] The sea flooded people's houses at night, and the rude awakening from sleep heightened the psychological effect of the sea's invasion. Contemporary personal accounts were filed in October 1931, when the DC of Keta

---

[78] Ibid.
[79] NAG, Ho, Item 209 (KE/C209), 'Unification of Eweland'; D.E.K. Amenumey, *The Ewe Unification Movement: A Political History* (Accra, 1989). See Chapter 7 for a more detailed discussion of the Anlo role and position in Ewe unification.
[80] NAG, Ho, Item 78 (KE/C78). DC Keta to CEP, 25 August 1939.
[81] NAG, Accra, ADM 39/1/232. CEP J.C. Warrington to acting Colonial Secretary, 21 December 1934. These months coincided with the seasonal high tides.
[82] G.K. Nukunya, 'The effects of cash crops on an Ewe community', in Jack Goody, ed., *Changing Social Structure in Ghana* (London, 1975), 59.
[83] C.R. Gaba, 'Anlo traditional religion: a study of the Anlo traditional believer's conception of and communion with the "holy"' (PhD thesis, University of London, 1965), 26.

queried his African clerks for not rushing to the office to save documents when the sea invaded Keta. G.A. Ocloo's written response captures the suddenness of the erosion:

> On the night of the 10th instant I was awakened by the noise of certain people at about 1:30 a.m. and went out to see what had happened. On going outside of my house it was almost under waters. I at once run to see the family house in which my wife and children were living in and found that the whole house was flooded entirely. I at once asked the assistance of some people nearby in removing the children and properties to a certain house near the lagoon. I was in the waters labouring during the whole time up to 4 a.m. At about 4:30 a.m. I left the house and came to the office where I met the keeper of prison who told me that they have already finished with the office.[84]

When lives were at risk, it might have seemed almost insensitive to Anlo such as Ocloo that the DC was concerned about documents. A second clerk, V.A.A. Ashiagbor, woke up at 4.30 a.m. to discover the flood. His first reaction was to proceed immediately to the house of a relative where he kept iron sheets, boards and doors that had been saved when his father's house collapsed from a previous inundation.[85] Nothing seemed to be able to stop the sea. When defences were built high in expectation of a frontal assault, the sea simply removed the mobile sand from the foundations of such structures, and they collapsed, as Keta was built on sand. That was also how the sea demolished houses. The Anlo would have identified with the words of the eleventh-century Chinese mystic, Tao Chung, that 'water is yielding, but all conquering'.[86] The sea's operation may have given rise to the Ewe proverb used as an epigram at the beginning of this chapter. It was crucial that the sea be pacified.

There is strong belief in Anlo that the ancestors possessed the knowledge to manipulate nature. As recently as 1979, the Anlo scholar Charles Mamattah could write that: 'Today, the illiterates are predominantly the custodians of all the wealth of culture and tradition. Should any ill-omen befall the state, they have a secret system for saving the day'.[87] The historical record, oral and written, does not reveal any public endeavour by the Bate clan to find a supernatural solution to coastal erosion in Keta during the period under study, as far as the author has been able to establish. Indeed, some Bate clan members and residents of Keta believed that the Adzovia clan and people of Anloga were secretly rejoicing at Keta's plight.[88] Ironically, Sri II, noted for his 'progressiveness', identified with the modernist spirit of Keta. Sri II opted for European clothing for his inauguration, rode a bicycle through the streets of Anloga, loved ballroom dancing and preferred to stay in Keta.[89] Indeed, his sub-chiefs lodged an official complaint with the colonial government in 1944 that Sri

---

[84] NAG, Accra, ADM 39/1/231. G.A. Ocloo to DC Keta, 14 October 1931.

[85] Ibid. V.A.A. Ashiabor to DC Keta, 13 October 1931.

[86] Michael O'Laughlin, 'Out of the depths' (paper presented at Havard University's Seminar on Environmental Values, 28 October 1997).

[87] Charles M.K. Mamattah, *The Ewes of West Africa* (Accra, 1979), 24.

[88] Interview with L.C.M. Seshie, Dzelukope, 16 October 1996; interview with Freda Adabanu and Regina Ayayee, Keta, 20 September 1996.

[89] Quarcoopome, 'Rituals and regalia of power', 344–5.

spent too much time in Keta instead of residing at Anloga, the traditional capital.[90] Sri II sat on the Legislative Council of the Gold Coast from 1916 to 1938, and the council's debates indicate that erosion at Keta and the development of Keta's infrastructure were issues close to his heart.[91] He led the crusade to reclaim land from the Keta Lagoon after the colonial government rejected the option of a permanent sea defence wall. His private residence in Keta was among the first to be built on reclaimed land.[92] Public memory in Keta appears to have obscured Sri II's crusading role to save Keta.

The Yewe cult was renowned for the efficacy of its sea rituals (*agbodedefu*) for bumper fishing seasons.[93] In Keta district today, these rites underpin the continuing relevance of the Yewe cult. Yaovi Gada, chief fisherman of Abutiakope, explained what this involved:

> When we start doing our rituals, or approach the fetish priest to do this, the person who is in the forefront will list all the types of fish [desired] on a paper and give it to the fetish priest. Then the fetish priest will start his prayers. That [list] will be sent to Avleketi. It will be there for a day. The day you take the sacrifice to the gods there, they will take the names of fishes in accompaniment with the sacrifice, and they will send it to the gods in the sea. So we expect that any type of fish that is on the list, they will send.[94]

According to Yaovi Gada, this sacrifice is usually made every three years in Abutiakope. The external features of the ritual are quite well known, and even Christians interviewed by the author knew that *agbodedefu* involved – among other things – taking a live ram in a canoe far out to sea and dumping the ram there.[95] Indeed, *agbodedefu* means 'sending a ram into the sea'.[96] Fishing communities along the Gold Coast performed similar rites, and the Fanti of Kormantse had sea-fishing rituals, which also involved the throwing of a live cow in deep sea.[97] Ritual is an integral part of fishing, and oral traditions on the introduction of fishing in the Gold Coast comment on the simultaneous transfer of fishing technology and fishing or marine deities.[98] Recently in the Keta district, these rituals have not been performed, because the rank-and-file fishermen refuse to pay their contributions after their

[90] NAG, Accra, ADM 39/1/120. Petition of chiefs and elders of Anlo State to Governor Alan Burns, Anloga, 13 November 1944.

[91] See, for example, Gold Coast Colony, *Legislative Council Debates*, 17 November 1919 and 30 December 1920.

[92] Interview with Esther Kwawukume, Keta, 23 January 1997.

[93] Torgby, 'Yewe secret society', 17.

[94] Interview with Yaovi Gada, Abutiakope, 22 April 1997. See also interview with S.S. Dotse, Keta, 4 September 1996. Keta fishermen Rowena Lawson studied in the 1950s spent an average of 13 per cent of total time on religious rituals. Rowena Lawson, 'The structure, migration and resettlement of Ewe fishing units', *African Studies* 17, 1 (1958): 23. On the importance of religious rituals to fishing, see A.H.J. Prins, *Sailing from Lamu: A Study of Maritime Culture in Islamic East Africa* (Assen, 1965), 254; Bronislaw Malinowski, *Magic, Science and Religion* (New York, 1948), 31.

[95] Interview with Kofi Nyavie, Dzelukope, 16 October 1996; interview with Edward Kartey-Attipoe, Keta, 17 October 1996.

[96] Personal correspondence from G.K. Nukunya, 28 September 1999.

[97] Personal correspondence from Kwame Boafo-Arthur, 7 February 1998.

[98] See, for example, the Fanti introduction of fishing to Accra in A.P. Brown, 'Report on a survey of the fishing industry in Labadi with some reference to Teshie and Accra' (1936). PRO, CO 96/729/12.

leaders have settled the financial arrangements for the rituals with the Yewe priests. There are also other fishermen from Christian families who have lost faith in these sea rituals for bumper seasons.[99]

But the Yewe cult itself was under attack at the very time its services were needed by the Keta community, for Sri II – with the encouragement of missionaries and the colonial government – persecuted Yewe from 1916.[100] Sri II, a Christian, probably did not subscribe to the claims of the Yewe cult, nor did he seem to believe in their ability to manipulate the sea. However, Sri's bias against Yewe did not extend to the more orthodox Anlo gods. In November 1945 Sri II and the Anlo State Council forbade the rearing of pigs in the Atiteti–Wuveme area, as they defiled the shrines or 'tabernacles' of Anlo gods and invited national calamity.[101] Though Sri II had bought a fishing net and formed a fishing company before his installation, it cannot be ascertained if he ever endorsed Yewe fishing rituals.[102] Committed to the idea of a centralized, modern monarchy, he was in fact staunchly opposed to secret societies such as the Yewe cult. Since Yewe dance, music, colourful cloths and social prestige were attractive to young women, Sri moved to deprive the cult of such prospective members. In 1934 the Anlo State Council would rule that:

> a woman below the age of 21 years could not be admitted to the [Yewe] fetish. Any woman from the age of 21 years upwards should not be admitted to the fetish without the knowledge and consent of her parents and husband if any.[103]

Reincarnation became the major means of recruiting members into the Yewe cult during colonial rule. A child believed to be the reincarnation of a dead Yewe member had to be initiated into the cult. Yewe membership was thus perpetuated within certain lineages and families, as lineage lines determine reincarnation.[104] Under siege, Yewe thus lacked the official support to explore a spiritual solution to the sea's advance.

But the cult appears to have held out hope that a supernatural solution to sea erosion was feasible. It may not be coincidental that 1929, the year the Coode Report rejected governmental responsibility for Keta's sea defence, also witnessed a revival of the Yewe cult in the Keta district.[105] The persecution of Yewe may have led to the rise of Mami Water in Anlo, another religious cult linked to sea deities. In the 1930s a Mami Water shrine was in existence at Kedzi under a priestess, Mami Shika.[106] It is noteworthy that Kedzi was, and is, a site of acute coastal erosion. Deities from the Yewe pantheon were prominent in the Adome Mami Water shrine established by an

[99] Interview with Michael Lawson, Dzelukope, 23 April 1997.
[100] Greene, *History of the Anlo-Ewe*, 153–4; and Hans Debrunner, *A Church between Two Colonial Powers: A Study of the Church in Togo* (London, 1965), 146.
[101] NAG, Accra, ADM 39/1/120. Sri II to Amenuda Ahiaku of Atiteti, cc. to Hanua Salah Aklobotu of Atiteti, 16 November 1945.
[102] Agboada, 'Sri II of Anlo', 2.
[103] Greene, *History of the Anlo-Ewe*, 154.
[104] Personal correspondence from G.K. Nukunya, 28 September 1999.
[105] Eugene Emil Grau, 'The Evangelical Presbyterian Church (Ghana and Togo) 1914–1916: a study in European mission relations affecting the beginning of an indigenous Church' (PhD thesis, Hartford Seminary Foundation, 1964), 172.
[106] Personal correspondence from Kathleen Wicker, 10 June 1998.

Avenor Ewe, Adawuso Dofe, who had been initiated in the 1940s by Mami Shika. The entry of the Mami Water cult may have facilitated the survival of Yewe under Sri II.[107]

But did a body of knowledge exist that enabled the Anlo to manipulate the sea in the past, including the flow and ebb of ocean currents? It is evident from oral traditions and interviews the author conducted in Anlo towns that there existed a concept, *gbe* (the spoken word), which operated very much like the Akan *tumi*.[108] As one Anlo elder explained:

> It is believed that God gave [a] certain amount of power to all his creations. This power though universal is not accessible to all. It is true some are born with some uncanny abilities to tap the power given to the other creations. It is also believed that all creations endowed with power have their words of invocation. There are some people who are gifted or able to know these invocations and thereby assume some special powers over them. Power like energy must and could be tapped. However, you need some form of training to be able to tap the power for use.[109]

Gbe could be described as the cumulative knowledge about the supernatural and natural realms, enshrined in the spoken word that endowed its possessors with power.[110] Some of the Anlo ancestors, reportedly, possessed this knowledge. Togbi Tsali of Tsiame possessed uncanny powers such that he 'ended his stay on earth by turning into a god'.[111] He was one with nature, appearing and disappearing at will. The Ewe believed in 'knowledge' or 'wisdom' (*nunya*), the possession of which endowed the gifted or skilled person with control over people and things.[112] There is also 'spiritual knowledge', such as *ta* (to have a 'powerful head') or *adze* (witchcraft).[113] Such knowledge granted the holder the power of transformation (*nusê*). It appears that the Anlo entertained the hope that someone gifted with *nusê* (power) might know the appropriate words (*gbe*) and/or rituals that would halt sea erosion.

No one showed up, and Mamattah's lament highlights the serious breach in Anlo belief and knowledge: 'Today, all that secret power which nature so lavishly had bestowed on Tenge [Dzokoto of Anyako] and other Anlo mystics is lost both to his own family and clan and also to the world'.[114] Christianity has been cited as the adulterating influence on Anlo culture. But Anlo Christians were equally perturbed by coastal erosion, and the spiritual solution perhaps lay in this new faith. In the wake of the Coode Report, an Anlo Christian, E.K. Agbotui of Keta, received a vision from an angel. Agbotui petitioned the angel for a solution to sea erosion in Keta. The angel provided a solution:

[107] Personal communication from Kathleen Wicker. A study of the Adome Mami Water shrine began in 1994 under the direction of Kathleen Wicker and Kofi Asare Opoku, sponsored by Scripps College and the Institute of African Studies, University of Ghana Legon.
[108] Emmanuel Akyeampong, *Drink, Power, and Cultural Change: A Social History of Alcohol in Ghana, c. 1800 to Recent Times* (Portsmouth, 1996), 12–14.
[109] Personal communication from Togbuivi Kumassah, Keta, 12 May 1995.
[110] Interview with Togbui Honi, Dzelukope, 4 September 1996. On *gbe*, see also Law, *Slave Coast of West Africa*, 21–2.
[111] Mamattah, *Ewes of West Africa*, 316.
[112] Quarcoopome, 'Rituals and regalia of power', 66–7.
[113] Personal communication from Nissio Fiagbedzi, Accra, August 1999.
[114] Mamattah, *Ewes of West Africa*, 438.

Photo 4.1 St Michael's Cathedral, Keta, 18 October 1996 *(by author)*.

> If the water from the Dead Sea is taken and sprinkled on the foreshore of the coast of my country [Keta] the sea erosion will cease at once and the sea will have to recede to its original place. That the sea that washes the coast of my country is a living sea and cannot meet with the water from the Dead Sea: so that if water from the Dead Sea is sprinkled on the foreshore it will keep the sea back.[115]

Agbotui's vision, perhaps, possessed spiritual logic: the waters of the Dead Sea will calm the raging waters of Keta's living sea. There is no evidence that this recommendation was treated seriously by the colonial government.

Ironically, confirmation of the power of the spoken word came from an unexpected quarter: a French Catholic priest. Bishop Augustin Herman was appointed as Apostolic Administrator of the Vicariate of Keta in October 1923. In the early 1930s, the Roman Catholic Cathedral of St Michael at Keta was on the verge of being eroded by the sea. Structures to the left and right of the cathedral were swept away by the sea in 1932, including the chapel and deaconesses' house of the Evangelical Presbyterians (former Bremen), and Catholics waited anxiously to see the fate of their cathedral.[116] Some residents of Keta credit Bishop Herman, who has gone down in Keta folklore as a holy man, with the miraculous saving of the cathedral. He is reported to have strolled along the beach in front of the church every morning, praying unceasingly and reading from a small book. Then the sea halted and began to retreat.[117] Kofi Nyavie recounted the episode as he had heard it:

[115] NAG, Ho, Item 177 (KE/C177). 'E.K. Agbotui's vision'. Received at DC Keta's Office, 17 July 1930.
[116] See also Grau, 'Evangelical Presbyterian Church', 172.
[117] Interview with Joseph Kingsley Abdallah, Keta, 16 October 1996; interview with Togbuivi Kumassah, Accra, 9 August 1997.

Wonderfully, the sea just removed all the buildings in that line, including the next one, Mr. Mensah Gawu's house, broke the whole place, and left the Cathedral quietly there, even though all were in line. So we have always attributed his presence, and the presence of his corpse in the Cathedral, as the reason why the Cathedral still stands.[118]

On his death in 1945, Bishop Herman was buried in his beloved Cathedral of St Michael (Photo 4.1). When the author visited the cathedral on 18 October 1996, almost 200 yards of sandy beach separated the cathedral from the sea. For some Anlo, this was a powerful demonstration of the spoken word.

That a similar feat has eluded the Anlo is traced by some to a lack of religious unity. Some blame Anlo disunity on Christianity. Paradoxically, Christianity had its limitations for the Ewe in the event of environmental devastation. Birgit Meyer's comments on the northern Peki-Ewe apply to the southern Anlo-Ewe. She speaks to the disjuncture between ecology and cosmology in changing social contexts:

> The impossibility of presenting God with sacrifices also made it impossible for them to place him under the obligation to do something for them. The subordination of nature gradually resulted in deforestation and devastation, a problem which became apparent in the 1920s. The impossibility of being possessed by God made it difficult to approach the sacred realm.[119]

Torn between two faiths, the Anlo were unable to find a supernatural solution to sea erosion. Their moral ecology had collapsed with the discordant changes in their ecological, social and cosmological realms.

Sea erosion in Keta also constituted a test case for Anlo's successful transition to the marine environment. The previously inland Anlo had not taken to a maritime life until the nineteenth century. The phrase for sea erosion in the Anlo-Ewe language, *tsi de ame* (literally, 'water has married a person'), draws on the experience of water flooding the land – common for inland people – and the imagery of the marital union. The sea, *atsiafu* or *fu*, does not appear in this phrase. The Anlo-Ewe word for 'corrode' or 'wear' – *nyi* – would also be more appropriate for sea erosion. This, the Anlo elder Togbuivi Kumassah points out, may reflect a limited experience and knowledge of sea erosion, a fact portrayed in the limits of Anlo language.[120] It is worth remembering that the Anlo migration to the coast had coincided with beach accretion. For the Anlo, sea erosion is a twentieth-century phenomenon. Anlo belief may propose that supernatural intervention re-created the coastline when the ancestors migrated to the Gold Coast from Notsie. That supernatural intervention may have left no trace in *gbe*.

[118] Interview with Kofi Nyavie, Dzelukope, 16 October 1996. See also interview with Edward Kartey-Attipoe, Keta, 17 October 1996.

[119] Birgit Meyer, 'Translating the devil: an African appropriation of pietist Protestantism – the case of the Peki Ewe in southeastern Ghana, 1847–1992' (PhD thesis, University of Amsterdam, 1985), 156.

[120] Interview with Togbuivi Kumassah, Accra, 9 August 1997. The verb *de* in Anlo-Ewe, besides meaning 'to marry', also means 'to scoop' (as to scoop coconut fruit from the shell) or 'to harvest'. Personal correspondence from G.K. Nukunya, 28 September 1999. That these are terminology from farming lends credence to Togbuivi Kumassah's inference that the Anlo drew on an agrarian tradition to explain sea erosion.

Conclusion

The residents of Keta, now a valuable part of the Gold Coast colony, turned to the colonial benefactor for redress when coastal erosion assumed alarming dimensions from 1907 along the Keta coast. The Anlo found out that there was a limit to what the colonial government could or would do. For the colonial government, Keta was not worth the heavy financial outlay for effective sea defence works. The Anlo resorted to their religion and history in a search for a local solution. This critical review put the limelight on the accredited roles of the Bate clan and Yewe. But the processes of social transformation had taken their toll: there was no consensus on which strategy should be adopted. Anlo Christians had their suggestions; educated Anlo scoffed at superstition; and 'traditionalists' searched for *gbe*, that powerful word capable of reordering nature. By the end of 1932, the Anlo had learned more about the geological factors causing sea erosion, and they had explored several options for solving their environmental problem, but they were no closer to a solution. But two truths had become established: the colonial government was not the benefactor they had envisioned; and economic prosperity and social change had 'weakened' knowledge of moral ecology and impaired the ability to regulate the ecology. Misfortune, it is believed, travels in a cluster. In 1932 coconut plantations in Woe became infected with Cape St Paul's wilt disease. The disease spread rapidly and wiped out the Keta District's copra exports by 1942.[121] Assailed on several fronts, the Anlo were compelled to become more innovative in their use of space and their limited natural resources. Lagoon reclamation, migrant fishing, intensive farming and liquor distillation assumed important places in Anlo life. The next chapter examines the development of these spheres.

[121] Greene, *History of the Anlo-Ewe*, 167.

5

The Search for Space

Land Reclamation, Migrant Fishing, Shallot Cultivation & Illicit Liquor Distillation in Anlo, c.1930–57

Introduction

The Coode Report of 1929 and the colonial government's decision that the residents of Keta relocate to a safer site generated a search for space that was physical and social. The entire economy of Keta and its environs was severely threatened as investor confidence declined and expatriate companies relocated their factories. Coastal erosion destroyed beaches and even reduced sites conducive for beach–seine fishing. Lagoon reclamation aimed at replacing land lost to the sea, and the town of Keta expanded in the opposite direction away from the sea. Attempts to halt sea erosion were not abandoned but seemed increasingly half-hearted. The coconut wilt disease intensified the search for alternative economic pursuits in the Keta District. Massive emigration – often perceived as temporary – was one important response. The population of Keta town declined from 9,839 in 1921 to 6,392 in 1931, and the 1931 census report opined that the low figures were 'due to the absence of thousands of young males who leave their homes in the dry season for work in the fishing industries on the Volta River, and as far east as the Nigerian waters'.[1] Thus began the tradition of migrant fishing, and the Anlo of the Keta District would be described in the 1960s as pan-African fishermen.[2] Shallot cultivation in Anloga, noted as an export in the nineteenth century, was intensified after 1930.[3] The 1948 census observed that on the Keta peninsula 'a species of onion is cultivated on a comparatively large scale in more systematic fashion than is normally to be found among cultivators in the Gold Coast'.[4] The islands in the Volta River and the lagoon and creek country of Anlo also became havens for the illicit distillation of *akpeteshie* (local gin) from the 1930s.[5]

[1] A.W. Cardinall, *The Gold Coast, 1931* (Accra, 1931), 161.

[2] Hill, 'Pan-African fisherman'.

[3] J.M. Grove, 'Some aspects of the economy of the Volta delta (Ghana)', *Bulletin de l'Institut Fondamental d'Afrique Noire* 28, 1–2 (1966): 391–3.

[4] Gold Coast, *Census of Population 1948: Report and Tables* (Accra, 1950), 29.

[5] Emmanuel Akyeampong, *Drink, Power, and Cultural Change: A Social History of Alcohol in Ghana, c. 1800*

The Search for Space

The Anlo search for *Lebensraum* and strategies of economic survival were often individualized. Education and the acquisition of artisan skills were crucial to the quest for social space. By 1916 the Bremen Mission had thirteen schools in the Keta Circuit. The number declined to eleven in 1926, as the expulsion of the German missionaries during the First World War resulted in cut-backs in mission education.[6] The period from 1900 to 1925 witnessed great expansion in educational facilities in Anlo in general and in Keta in particular. The AME Zion Mission opened fifteen schools in Anlo in this period. The first batch of Standard VII leavers graduated from the Bremen Mission school in Keta in 1906. Three secondary and business schools were founded in Anlo (in Keta and Anloga) in the 1930s: the Anlo State School (1934–5); the New African University College (1937), later renamed Zion Secondary School; and the First Century Gospel Business College (1939), now the Keta Business College.[7] The new emphasis on the importance of education and artisanship is reflected in the careers of the two *awoamefia* of the twentieth century, Togbui Sri II (1907–56) and Togbui Adeladza II (1956–98). The first was a product of the Bremen Mission school in Keta and learnt tailoring as a vocation.[8] The second completed his middle school education in 1948 at the Anloga Ewe Presbyterian Senior School (formerly Bremen Mission) in Anloga, furthered his education at the Zion College of West Africa, and worked as a pupil teacher and postal clerk.[9] The huge carpentry industry at the 'Anloga' suburb in Kumasi in this century is a product of the dual Anlo strategy of artisanship and emigration.

Keta survived the economic depression of the 1930s and entered into a new phase of economic prosperity in spite of coastal erosion. Key to this renaissance was the centrality of Keta market to the regional economy. As long as the market thrived, Keta flourished. Keta had also emerged as an educational centre for the region, and Anlo and non-Anlo students were enrolled in Keta's schools. By the 1948 census, Keta's population stood at 11,380, registering a gain of almost 5,000 over its low 1931 figure.[10] The town had reversed its decline in population.

Resettlement, lagoon reclamation and sea defence works in the Keta District

The colonial government set up a committee in 1931 under the chairmanship of the Commissioner for the Eastern Province to consider Keta's future and to choose a site for resettlement. The terms of reference reflected the government's position that resettlement was the only real option:

[5 (cont.)] *to Recent Times* (Portsmouth, 1996), 100.
[6] Gold Coast, *Report on the Direction of the Former Bremen Mission of the Government of the Gold Coast from June, 1916 to March, 1926* (Accra, 1927), 9.
[7] Theophilus W. Adjorlolo, 'The history of education in Anlo with special reference to Keta from 1850–1960' (BA thesis, University of Ghana, 1977), 22, 33.
[8] Rev. F.K. Fiawoo, 'Togbi Sri II Awoamefia of Anlo' (May 1956).
[9] Anlo Traditional State, *Funeral Rites for the Late Togbui Adeladza II* (Accra, 1998).
[10] Gold Coast, *Census of Population 1948*.

Land Reclamation, Migrant Fishing, Shallot Cultivation & Illicit Distillation

> To consider the problem caused by the continuous erosion of the sea at Keta, an erosion which appears certain to lead to the total disappearance of the town in the not too distant future and which cannot be prevented except at prohibitive cost and even then with no certainty of success, and to make recommendations as to the best site on which a new Keta could be built having due regard to all the interests concerned.[11]

The committee included Sri II and two other members of his state council. Denu to the east of Keta was chosen as the site for relocation. Port facilities were to be constructed at Denu in its new function as the only port east of the Volta. Though the State of Some, with its town of Denu, was founded by Keta emigrants, the people of Keta proved unwilling to relocate *en masse* as their fortunes were tied to Keta market and the rich fishing grounds in this area. That relocation meant the closure of Keta's port further dissuaded Keta's residents from moving, as the port serviced Keta's market. Keta acted as a central point for the collection of goods produced east of the Volta and for the distribution of imported commodities landed at Keta.

An early intimation that the town's residents would resist relocation is contained in a petition addressed to the governor by Anlo traders in 1932. Forwarding the petition, District Commissioner (DC) Judd of Keta observed:

> Most of the signatories to this petition are independent traders whose business would be ruined if Keta is closed as a port as they would have no facilities to import at Denu. In my opinion the bulk of the population of Keta will never move to Denu and persons whose buildings have been washed away by the sea already have either built at Dzelukope or on the edge of the lagoon. In one or two cases plots have been reclaimed from the lagoon.[12]

Expansion to Dzelukope just west of Keta, and seen as a 'suburb' of Keta, enabled Keta's residents to remain *in situ*, benefiting from the access to more land, yet maintaining the privileges of a famous market and rich fishing-grounds. The colonial government's decision not to open the Denu port until Keta's relocation confirmed the residents of Keta in their determination not to move and have Keta's port closed.

The government went on with its plans to relocate government buildings from the administrative headquarters of Keta to Denu. In 1932 the government earmarked the following facilities as necessary for the new administrative and port functions of Denu: the DC's court and offices, customs offices and warehouse, police barracks, a prison, a post office, a native hospital and a Public Works Department.[13] Plans were also laid for road construction to improve the economic potential of Denu as a port. The chiefs, elders and people of Keta and Dzelukope responded quickly with a petition to the governor in June 1932 expressing their preference in the relocation site:

> We are firmly therefore suggesting with our comment on these grounds to Government that the continuous erosion of the sea, may it be of good upbuilding without any upheaval to remove the Court House, the Steamers' Anchorage, Medical Department (Hospital), Education Department, and all other public offices which are available to Jelukope Area, which space is advantageous – and will cost Government so less a sum in building these houses almost with their usual materials.[14]

---

[11] PRO, CO 96/751/2. Governor Arnold Hodson to W.G.H. Ormsby-Gore, Accra, 5 February 1938.

[12] NAG, Accra, ADM 39/1/231. DC Judd to Commissioner for Eastern Province (CEP), Keta, 27 June 1932.

[13] Ibid. See, for example, Acting CEP to Colonial Secretary, Accra, 18 July 1932.

[14] Ibid. Petition of Dumega of Keta-Dzelukope to the Governor, 13 June 1932.

The governor acceded to the wishes of the residents of Keta and Dzelukope, and the plans to relocate Keta's facilities and inhabitants to Denu were shelved. Eventually, most of the government buildings were rebuilt at Dzelukope, after health surveys and a planned layout of Dzelukope.

Erosion put great pressure on land in Keta, and reclaiming land from the shores of the Keta Lagoon was an important possible solution. *Awoamefia* Sri II took a pioneering role in encouraging this option from the 1930s. The lack of government support vitiated the endeavour, and the reclamation of lagoon plots was mostly undertaken on an individual basis. To ensure that reclamation was undertaken in an orderly fashion, Sri II alloted plots from the lagoon edge to be reclaimed by individuals. The process was expensive and tedious. W.S. Chapman Klutse, an eyewitness to these efforts, commented on the process in 1984:

> Land reclamation was carried out in the past by manual collection of material from the dry lagoon bed. Several individuals did this reclamation along the town's lagoon water front but the process ceased when the Keta Lagoon no longer dries up.[15]

The fluctuating waters of the Keta Lagoon made the process of land reclamation tenuous. In 1934, for example, all attempts to reclaim land were rendered futile because of heavy rains and a full lagoon. Moreover, reclaimed plots had to be walled to prevent the lagoon waters from moving in when the water level of the lagoon rose. A conservative estimate in 1934 put the cost of walling a plot using cheap prison labour at £60. And the colonial government regarded the titles granted by the paramount chief to reclaimers of lagoon land as well-intentioned but dubious, as it was doubtful that the *awoamefia* had the 'power to grant titles to such plots'.[16]

Sri II in 1935 sought government assistance for individuals desirous of reclaiming land from the Keta Lagoon. It had become apparent that the process was beyond the means of several individuals. He informed the colonial government that:

> At Keta land is very scarce, and, even if a small piece is available it is of prohibitive value. Consequently the majority of the people whose houses have been demolished by the sea, cannot afford to negotiate for the purchase of a plot at these depressed times. On the contrary they can with a minimum of financial assistance reclaim a portion of the lagoon for erection of dwelling houses in replacement of those demolished by the sea.[17]

Sri II hoped that the government would extend some gratuity to those who had lost houses to sea erosion to enable them to rebuild on reclaimed lagoon land. Even as the DC for Keta forwarded the petition, he advised against governmental assistance in individual efforts to reclaim lagoon land. The DC did not believe that the people of Keta were destitute, and he opined that reclamation could be pursued without external financial assistance. In addition, were the government to consider financial assistance, 'numbers of people would undoubtedly try to take advantage of the

[15] W.S. Chapman Klutse, *The Keta Coast Erosion and Dredging for Development; and some Landmarks for Anlor History* (Accra, 1984), 17.

[16] NAG, Accra, ADM 39/1/231. DC Keta to CEP, 28 September 1934.

[17] NAG, Accra, ADM 39/1/232. Petition of Sri II, Paramount Chief of Anlo to Governor Arnold Hodson, 15 January 1935.

government'.[18] It was an interesting paradox: Keta was not economically valuable enough to warrant expensive sea defence works, according to the Coode Report; yet its residents were not poor enough to justify government subsidies for lagoon reclamation.

Lagoon reclamation continued piecemeal as an individual enterprise.[19] The commencement of internal self-government within the Gold Coast in 1951 under the Convention People's Party (CPP) and local government reform introducing local councils changed the political climate and rekindled hopes among the Anlo of governmental assistance in lagoon reclamation and sea defence works. The Keta Urban Council was formed in 1952. Its chairman, Chapman Klutse, led a delegation to see the representatives of the new African government. The delegation had a discussion with the Minister of Works and Housing, N.A. Welbeck (appointed in 1954), who commissioned the London engineering firm of Sir William Halcrow and Partners to undertake the survey of a pilot reclamation scheme and submit a report. William Halcrow and Partners submitted its report in 1956. African politics dogged this new initiative, and the Halcrow Lagoon Land Reclamation Project was stillborn. An African road surveyor in the Public Works Department, Aryee, managed to edge out his expatriate superiors, who were qualified engineers, and had himself appointed Officer-in-Charge of the Keta District Public Works Department. Qualified engineers usually held this position. Aryee's attempt to implement the Halcrow Project was an abysmal failure. His endeavour in 1963 to cut a canal at Kedzi (dubbed locally the 'Aryee Canal') to let out the waters of the swollen Keta Lagoon into the sea resulted in disaster. The unanticipated force of the water quickly widened the canal and swept away coconut trees, houses, people, and Aryee, who was supervising the construction. Aryee's body was never found.[20]

Though the colonial government had ruled in 1929 that nothing could be done to save Keta from the sea's onslaught, the refusal of Keta residents to relocate made it impolitic for the government to abandon any attempt at least to slow down erosion. The perception of the Anlo that the Coode investigation was cursory and that revenue from Keta port was being diverted for development in other areas of the Gold Coast under the excuse that Keta could not be saved soured Anlo relations with the colonial government. Strikingly, DCs at Keta sympathized with the Anlo view and believed that the government should make some effort to contain coastal erosion as long as the residents remained in the town of Keta. DC Bratton of Keta summed up the situation in a 1931 report:

> Experience gained by recent erosion, seems to have impressed on the public that Keta can be saved at no great expense for an indefinite period by the construction of a retaining wall along the seaward side of Keta. With this opinion, I am in entire agreement and I consider that a retaining wall of no great height would go a long way towards lengthening the life of Keta.[21]

Nothing came of this proposal. The Anlo consternation at colonial neglect was

[18] Ibid. DC Keta to CEP, 22 January 1935.
[19] By one estimate, about 50 per cent of the town of Keta in 1984 stood on land reclaimed from the Keta Lagoon. Klutse, *Keta Coast Erosion*, 59.
[20] Ibid., 16–17.
[21] NAG, Accra, ADM 39/1/231. Acting DC Bratton to CEP, Keta, 19 October 1931.

expressed at a meeting between Sri II and his chiefs with the Commisisoner for the Eastern Province and the DC of Keta in April 1938. The Anlo representatives referred to successful sea defence works at Lagos and in Holland. Indeed, groyning had been quite effective in containing erosion at Sekondi and Lome. Why had the government dismissed Keta's plight?[22]

The Anlo State Council in 1938 decided to take matters into its own hands and build a retaining wall along the shore at Keta. The wall was to be constructed from old iron rails, purchased from the railways in Takoradi, and coconut trees. The State Council, with the approval of DC J. E. Miller of Keta, voted a sum of £70 for the purchase of the iron rails. The commercial firm of John Holt magnanimously offered to ship the 200 iron rails from Takoradi to Keta free of charge.[23] The outcome of this experiment is summed up in the quarterly report for the Keta District:

> The District Commissioner experimented on the Keta foreshore to try and check the erosion. He built a wall of railway lines and palm trees near the Ewe Presbyterian Mission, but the whole work was washed away. The experiment cost the State Council about seventy pounds. It is interesting to note that the local people, when asked for palm trees to build the wall, and for labour and help in the construction, failed to supply either in this pitiful attempt to save their town.
>
> The sea on the whole is still encroaching but the main point of erosion appears to be moving along the coast towards Vodja. There has been a considerable area of sand replaced opposite Messrs John Holt's and the Roman Catholic Mission.[24]

It is unlikely that the residents of Keta were uninterested in saving their town. Perhaps they viewed the whole experiment as a superficial or token gesture. Bate leadership in the town of Keta was itself divided in the aftermath of James Ocloo I's death (1931), as the Amegashie family made a bid for chieftaincy in Keta.[25] Old claimants to the Keta stool, the priestly Amegashie family had, in consultation with Awoamefia Amedor Kpegla, appointed a stool family member James Ocloo I *dufia* of Keta in the early colonial period because of his long association with Europeans.[26] The struggle for leadership in Keta could have vitiated the town's contribution to the sea wall in 1938. It is uncertain whether this struggle in part reflected a desire for more spiritual leadership in Keta.

Though the colonial government continued to record high water marks at Keta, the next serious endeavour to check sea erosion was in 1951. This was at the initiative of the new African government. The sum of £8,000 was voted for anti-erosion work at Keta, and the Officer-in-Charge of the Public Works Department at Keta constructed a number of temporary groynes, with plans for permanent groynes once the necessary pile-driving equipment arrived from Britain.[27] By December 1951, all the necessary materials required for the construction of permanent groynes were on

[22] NAG, Accra, ADM 39/1/550. Meeting of CEP, DC Keta, Sri II and his chiefs, and members of the Ewe League, Keta, 24 April 1938.
[23] NAG, Accra, ADM 39/1/232. Acting DC Keta to CEP, 15 August 1938.
[24] NAG, Accra, ADM 39/1/303. Report for the Keta District for the quarter ending 30 September 1938.
[25] NAG, Accra, ADM 39/1/469.
[26] Sandra E. Greene, *Gender, Ethnicity, and Social Change on the Upper Slave Coast: A History of the Anlo-Ewe* (Portsmouth, 1996), 137.
[27] NAG, Accra, ADM 39/1/712. Quarterly Report for the Keta District, April–June 1951.

site at Keta. Pile driving commenced in January 1952. This experiment also failed. The quarterly report for April–June 1952 conveyed the unfortunate news:

> One of the new pile-driven groynes was washed away early in May and erosion in the neighbourhood of the Roman Catholic Mission is serious. The pile driver previously made available has been transferred to Weija. A new machine has been ordered from the United Kingdom but is unlikely to arrive for several months.[28]

Though anti-erosion work resumed with the receipt of a new pile driver in September 1952, the sense of gloom was heavy.

Migrant fishing assumed an important dimension against this context of severe coastal erosion, land shortage and fitful attempts to reclaim land from the Keta Lagoon. Sea fishing at Keta was of the beach-seine type, and coastal erosion had littered the ocean floor with debris from collapsed buildings. This tore the expensive seine-nets. Victor Nyadanu and Peter Afabegee, two Keta fishermen, explained the impact of coastal erosion on sea fishing:

> Sea erosion has affected fishing in so many ways. First, the erosion has caused many buildings to fall down and these have become debris in the sea that become obstacles especially to drag net operation. Second, the erosion has made us come inland so much that it has reduced sea fishing. How the sea has eroded the land, the site we used to fish from at first has become so deep for our nets. When it happens like this, the currents also change. The current becomes swift, making it difficult to catch fish. The sea has become more shallow at the shore and deepens sharply as one moves out to sea. This has affected the way we use our nets.[29]

Seine fishing cannot be practised at any beach site. It is noteworthy that at the Ga fishing town of Labadi in the 1930s, only one site was considered suitable for beach-seining, and only one net could be shot from this site at a time.[30] Erosion compelled improvisation at Keta, and offshore fishing with purse-seine nets, or *watsa*, and motorized canoes has grown in importance since the 1950s.

The development of migrant maritime fishing among the Anlo

Anlo's sandy beach accelerated coastal erosion, as mobile sand presents no resistance to the sea. But the sandy beach and the absence of a foul bottom on the approach to the shore also made the Anlo beach ideal for beach-seine fishing. As mentioned earlier, Afedima, a female entrepreneur at Woe, introduced the beach-seine net or *yevudor* between 1850 and 1860. Its use in Anlo spread between Woe and Kedzi to the east, where fishing was actively practised. The Anlo coastline narrows significantly north-east of Dzelukope and Keta, making arable land extremely scarce. The major economic pursuits in this area, traditionally, were fishing and salt making. The urbanization of Keta gradually eliminated the little farm and grazing land available, and Keta's economy from the late nineteenth century lost the mixed features described in Chapter 3. Land was increasingly put to residential and commercial use,

[28] Ibid. Quarterly Report for the Keta District, April–June 1952.
[29] Interview with Victor Nyadanu and Peter Afabegee, Keta, 19 September 1996.
[30] PRO, CO 96/729/12. A.P. Brown, 'Survey of the fishing industry at Labadi' (1936).

and farmers who combined farming or animal husbandry with fishing must have been pushed to concentrate on lagoon or sea fishing. Considering the possibility that the Keta Lagoon was overharvested by the 1870s, sea fishing was primed to become an important pillar in the local economy.[31] In an insightful article on the development of full-time maritime fishing among the Xwla (Pla or Hula) and the Anlo – albeit limited in its endeavour to formulate a universal sociological law on full-time maritime fishing – Paul Jorion points to the link between ports of international trade and the deliberate specialization in sea activities, including maritime fishing.[32] Nukunya confirms this observation in his comment that a tradition of beach-seine fishing did not develop in Anloga because of Anloga's proverbial resistance to European trade and presence.[33]

Anlo fishermen cite a decline in fisheries in Anlo waters as the reason for their migration along the coastal waters of Ghana and West Africa. Nukunya informs us that:

> Up to about the 1920s everything seemed to have worked smoothly with the [Anlo] economy. But round about that time, however, the population pressure began to tell on land (and the sea) resulting in large-scale migratory movements from the area. Scores of Anlo fishermen started to migrate in search of fresh and richer waters. Some settled permanently in Abidjan in the Ivory Coast and Badagri in Nigeria, but others were content to spend periods of up to three years before returning home.[34]

Indeed, pressure on land was so great that George Benneh claimed cemeteries were being put under cultivation in coastal Anlo in the twentieth century.[35] The inference from the above quotation was that there was a similar pressure on fishing resources. The increased population meant more active fishermen, and beach-seine fishing requires beach space. Jorion discounts the fishermen's claim that fish stocks have declined:

> There is no big mystery as to why Anlo-Ewe and Xwla turned in large numbers to full-time maritime fishing: their countries of origin – although somewhat distant (some 80 km between Blekusu and Grand Popo) – were subjected to exactly the same process of land erosion through sea action, erosion which has narrowed dramatically the portion of land between beach and lagoon, reducing it in places to a single sandy dune.[36]

In Jorion's opinion, Anlo and Xwla fishermen were forced into full-time maritime fishing because they had no economic alternatives. Nukunya ably contests this proposition, and he accurately depicts the viable alternative economic pursuits in Anlo. Some Anlo adopted full-time maritime fishing because of the lucrative financial

---

[31] William Forbes McLaren, a Glasgow trader who travelled to Ada via the Keta Lagoon in 1873, commented on the proliferation of fish dams and basket traps in the Keta Lagoon. There was just sufficient space for the passage of the canoe. William Forbes McLaren Private Papers, Rhodes House (Oxford University), Mss. Afr.s.710.

[32] Paul Jorion, 'Going out or staying home: migration strategies among Xwla and Anlo-Ewe fishermen', *Maritime Anthropological Studies* 1, 2 (1988): 134.

[33] G.K. Nukunya, 'The Anlo-Ewe and full-time maritime fishing: another view', *Maritime Anthropological Studies* 2, 2 (1989): 170–1.

[34] G.K. Nukunya, 'The effects of cash crops on an Ewe community', in Jack Goody, ed., *Changing Social Structure in Ghana* (London, 1975), 61.

[35] G. Benneh, 'Land tenure and Sabala farming system in the Anlo area of Ghana: a case study', *Research Review* 7, 2 (1971): 74.

[36] Jorion, 'Migration strategies among Xwla and Anlo-Ewe fishermen', 134.

rewards and a love for sea fishing. He argues, importantly, that over the course of the twentieth century the Anlo have become people of the sea. He addresses the centrality of the sea in Anlo life:

> Sometimes even the financial aspect becomes either secondary or irrelevant. Their occupations have become part and parcel of their lives. One has to remember that many of those who become fishermen along the Anlo coast virtually grow up with the sea. By about age ten, they have already mastered the art of swimming and acquired the skills to join the fishing expeditions.[37]

The Anlo have successfully forged a maritime tradition over this century, and it is reflected in the proliferation of fishing skills even among schoolboys, who may rent a canoe and a net and go sea fishing over the weekends.[38]

Anlo migrant maritime fishing predated the onset and intensification of coastal erosion, which Jorion considers the reason behind Anlo full-time fishing, and the 1920s landmark identified by Nukunya. Albert de Surgy dates Anlo migrations from the Keta area to the late nineteenth century. These Anlo maritime fishing expeditions were eastwards along the Ewe coast to 'points well-known to them, to which their ancestors had migrated, and in which other Evhé lived'.[39] Seine fishermen from Adafienu, a Keta settlement, founded the village of Ablogame in Togo around 1880.[40] Polly Hill conducted oral interviews with Anlo seine fishermen in 1963 that confirmed that the fishermen have been aware of the dangers of overfishing from the Anlo beach for many decades and this lay behind migrant fishing from the late nineteenth century.[41]

Jorion would argue that these early moves eastward along the Ewe coast were 'seasonal moves' and not 'migration'. A good example of a seasonal move is that practised by Anlo beach-seine fishermen from Srogboe, who regularly move to Muniano in the central province of the Gold Coast every August and return to Srogboe in April.[42] Jorion defines migration as:

> the temporary settlement of a family-based crew or of a 'company' at one or at a number of places … sufficiently distant from the original homebase to prevent any return to it for at least a number of years. A distinctive feature of a migration is that while in seasonal moves the boat normally travels at sea, in the case of a proper migration the canoe is usually transported on board a steamer, the crew and accompanying family travelling to the port of destination either by road … or often nowadays, by air.[43]

Based on this rather dubious distinction, Jorion considers Anlo moves to Togo and the Republic of Benin coast as 'seasonal moves', and only moves to Ivory Coast, Sierra Leone and Liberia as real migrations. This obscures the internal dynamics of Anlo migrations, as well as the technological handicaps in seafaring along the Gulf of Guinea. Jorion obviously considers Anlo moves to the Ewe coast and along the Gold Coast as no

---

[37] Nukunya, 'Anlo–Ewe and full-time maritime fishing', 158–9.

[38] Interview with George James Ocloo, Emmanuel Cobblah Doe, Eugene Awunyo and Francis Segbawu, Keta, 15 October 1996.

[39] Albert de Surgy, *La Pêche maritime traditionnelle a l'ancienne 'Côte de Guinée': origines et développement'* (Kara, Togo, 1969), 130–1.

[40] Ibid.

[41] Polly Hill, *Talking with Ewe Seine Fishermen and Shallot Farmers* (Cambridge, 1986), 11.

[42] Robert Wyllie, 'Migrant Anlo fishing companies and socio-political change: a comparative study', *Africa* 39, 4.

[43] Jorion, 'Migration strategies among Xwla and Anlo-Ewe fishermen', 142.

Photo 5.1 Horse-mackerel catch, Adzido beach, 18 September 1996 *(by author)*.

radical breaks in the cultural and geopolitical contexts to warrant the term 'migration'. This author classifies moves out of Anlo waters as migrations for Anlo fishermen.

The *yevudor* from its introduction was an expensive net. Made initially of European-manufactured cotton twine for net, lead sinkers and cork or calabash floats, and with long ropes attached to its side wings, the entire contraption could be 300 yards long.[44] The Anlo elaborated on the *yevudor*, and net sizes increased in length. Even the smaller seine nets in use along the Ga beach cost between £48 and £68 in the mid-1930s by A.P. Brown's estimation.[45] Anlo seine-nets were much larger.[46] Different nets have different mesh sizes. The fishing season in Anlo waters peaked between July and December. From July to August was the herring (*Sardinella aurita, Sardinella cameronensis*; Anlo-Ewe: *vetsimu, adruku*) and anchovy (*Engraulis encrasicholus*; Anlo-Ewe: *abɔbi*) season. This season required nets with a smaller mesh size. The movement of particular fishes also influenced the nature of the nets used, and the *agli* (*ali* among the Ga) surface drift-net was ideal for herring fishing. From September to December was the *afafa* or horse-mackerel (*Caranx hippos*) season. The horse- or jack mackerel is a fairly big fish and adults may weigh between 10 and 20 pounds (Photo 5.1).[47] This required a *yevudor* with a larger mesh size, known locally as the *afafa* net. *Afafa* nets were huge and could extend for a mile.[48] In regard to the jack or horse-mackerel, F.R. Irvine commented in 1947 that:

[44] Wyllie, 'Migrant Anlo fishing companies', 36.
[45] Brown, 'Survey of the fishing industry at Labadi'.
[46] Polly Hill, *Studies in Rural Capitalism in West Africa* (Cambridge, 1970), 34.
[47] Nukunya, 'Anlo-Ewe and full-time maritime fishing', 165–6.
[48] Gold Coast, *Colonial Report 1950* (London, 1952), 19.

A specially large and strong seine-net is used at Keta, where the season is from October to December, and as many as 1000 to 2000 fish are sometimes taken at a single haul, which includes comparatively few other fishes. These fish are split, dried or smoked, and then sent up country.[49]

Rowena Lawson estimated in 1958 that a new *afafa* net could cost as much as between £1,000 and £1,500.[50] Although maritime fishing continued in the off-peak seasons, the catch was not as remunerative as between July and December. Considering the large investment in a *yevudor* or *afafa* net, it became economically unfeasible to restrict its use to particular seasons of the year.

The early Anlo migrant maritime fishermen were entrepreneurs motivated by profits. They followed the movement of fishes into neighbouring waters to maximize the use of their nets over periods that transcended the fishing seasons in Anlo waters.[51] Nukunya records that a 'mass exodus of [Anlo] fishermen for Badagri took place in the 1920s with the peak years put at 1925–6'.[52] Anlo movement west of the Gold Coast was a later development with initial moves to Ivory Coast in 1935. In 1964 there would be thirty-one Anlo fishing companies in Ivory Coast, seven at Monrovia and eight at Freetown.[53] And, as 'fish production increased with the spread of new fishing equipment, marine canoe fishing increasingly became a commercial and market oriented activity'.[54] As a new class of accumulators, *yevudor* owners were renowned for their wealth in towns such as Keta, Vodza and Kedzi. Hill observed in 1963 that the 'hard core of net-owners consists of owners of the large contractor-built houses in Keta, Kedzi, Vodza and elsewhere, whose fathers owned *yevudor* before them'.[55] She provides several examples. Gidiglo Sewornu, the alleged 'inventor' of the *afafa* net, lived in a pink two-storey house in Kedzi at a time when cement or concrete houses were rare. His canoes operated in distant places in Togo and the current Republic of Benin.[56] Fedevi Awuye lived in an elegant two-storey building on the lagoon side in Blekusu. His father was a migrant maritime fisherman long before 1914 and had made an expedition to Lagos with a *yevudor* and an Ewe company.[57]

[49] F.R. Irvine, *Fishes and Fisheries of the Gold Coast* (London, 1947), 140.

[50] Rowena Lawson, 'The structure, migration and resettlement of Ewe fishing units', *African Studies* 17, 1 (1958): 22–3.

[51] On the movement of shoals of herring on the Gulf of Guinea, see Jorion, 'Migration strategies among Xwla and Anlo–Ewe fishermen', 136.

[52] Nukunya, 'Anlo–Ewe and full-time maritime fishing', 156.

[53] Hill, *Studies in Rural Capitalism*, 33. On Anlo fishing in waters west of the Gold Coast, see also Jorion, 'Migration strategies among Xwla and Anlo–Ewe fishermen'; Nukunya, 'Anlo–Ewe and full-time maritime fishing'. On Fanti fishermen in Liberia and Sierra Leone, see Elizabeth Tonkin, 'Creating Kroomen: ethnic diversity, economic specialism and changing demand', in Jerry Stone, ed., *Africa and the Sea* (Aberdeen, 1985), 37; Melvin K. Hendrix, 'Technology and maritime fisheries on the Sierra Leone peninsula, *c.* 1600–1980', in Stone, ed., *Africa and the Sea*, 73–4. Such coastal moves along the West African coast were promoted by the availability of steamship service, and, especially after 1914, by the control of most of the coast by just Britain and France. Ironically, African independence and political differences between African governments have militated against such migrations in more recent years. See Wyllie, 'Migrant Anlo fishing companies', 396.

[54] Ragnhild Overa, 'Partners and competitors: gendered entrepreneurship in Ghanaian canoe fisheries' (PhD thesis, University of Bergen, 1998).

[55] Hill, *Studies in Rural Capitalism*, 39.

[56] Hill, *Ewe Seine Fishermen and Shallot Farmers*, 13.

[57] Ibid., 19–21.

Anlo migrant maritime fishing thus developed as a profit-making venture. The growth of mining, railway and cocoa towns from the turn of the twentieth century expanded markets for fish and provided an important incentive for increased fish harvests. Perceptions of well-being and profitability determined how long migrant fishermen stayed away from their home bases. The erosion of Anlo beaches, crucial to beach-seine fishing, and the glut in fishermen operating from the limited landing beaches encouraged further migration. This fascinating pattern of migrant maritime fishing had emerged with innovations in nets from the late nineteenth century. A discussion of changes in net technology and how this in turn shaped canoe construction and led to the emergence of that unique economic organization, the 'fishing company', follows.

New nets and the revolution in maritime fishing on the Gold Coast

The post-1890 period witnessed an explosion in net innovation in the Gold Coast with the Fanti, the Ga and the Anlo as pioneers and disseminators. Prior to this date, much of the innovation in fishing technology had been restricted to canoes. The extension of the prow, and how this facilitated the passage of canoes through rough surf, has been mentioned.[58] Another innovation in the nineteenth century was the adoption of the 'iron paddle' or the long steering sweep. Here again, the pioneers were Gold Coast canoemen who had worked for Europeans on surf boats and had learned the advantages of the long steering sweep.[59] Fishing gear prior to the mid-nineteenth century consisted of lines, cast-nets operated from shore and from canoes and a series of small wall nets used for catching big fish and shark.[60] Three new nets would alter the nature of fishing in the Gold Coast from the late nineteenth century: the beach-seine net, the drift-net and the purse-seine net. Their first impact was in size, and the volume of catch was unprecedented. Moreover, these nets required less skill in their operation compared with the cast-net, opening up the profession of marine fishing. Secondly, with large nets came the need to increase the labour force required to haul these nets and larger canoes to carry fishermen and their equipment.[61] The result would be the birth of the 'fishing company'.

The Fanti remained the pioneers in marine fishing through the end of the nineteenth century. Innovations in canoe and net technology were often credited to the Fanti. The Ga of Accra report that a Fanti fisherman introduced the *ali* net to Accra around 1870. Migrant Fanti fishermen visited Accra annually during the herring season, and the *ali* net was designed especially for herring.[62] The history of the *ali* net, however, is a bit confusing. Its use on the Anlo coast was reported before the mid-nineteenth century.[63] The Fanti may have been the transmitters here as well.

[58] See 'Introduction'.

[59] Brown, 'Survey of the fishing industry at Labadi', 4.

[60] Ibid.

[61] On improvements in canoe technology, see Kwamina B. Dickson, *A Historical Geography of Ghana* (Cambridge, 1969), 317–18.

[62] Claire C. Robertson, *Sharing the Same Bowl: A Socioeconomic History of Women and Class in Accra, Ghana* (Madison, 1984), 86–7.

[63] See Chapter 2.

But A.P. Brown in his survey of fishing in Labadi, Teshi and Accra gave a different account of the net's origin on the Ga coast. At the cutting edge of fishing innovation was Male Akro of Teshi, who in 1890 introduced a bottom drift-net called *tengiraf*. This net stretched in the sea like the telegraph lines on land – hence its name.[64] Male Akro introduced another drift-net:

> Shortly after this Male Akro and his half brother Habel K. Nmai went to Nigeria. Nmai was a bricklayer and Akro went as his mate. There at Moledge near Zundu they saw a herring drift net. When they returned they made a similar net but were not allowed to use it for fear that it should kill all fish. They had brothers at Nungua [to the immediate east of Teshie] and there the net was first used. There was no opposition.[65]

This was the *ali* net, and several fishermen and traditional rulers fiercely opposed its use, for it caught fish indiscriminately and the *ali* net operators then threw the small fish or fry back into the sea. Other fishermen believed the dead fry caused a stench and drove other fish away, thus threatening their livelihood. Indeed, it took a high court ruling in 1898 in favour of the use of the *ali* net to quell the resistance of traditional rulers in Ga and Efutu coastal towns.[66] Brown's account that the *ali* net was borrowed from Nigeria does not necessarily contradict the version crediting the Fanti with its development. As late as 1950, Gold Coast fishermen were reported to be the only fishermen engaged in sea fishing on the Nigerian coast, as the Nigerians restricted themselves to inland waters.[67] These Gold Coast fishermen in Nigeria certainly included Fanti, who used *ali* nets. What remains problematic is the date of the net's entry into Accra, and later research may resolve the difference between the 1870 and 1890 dates. It should be mentioned, however, that an earlier account of the fishing industry in the Gold Coast gives dates for the introduction of these new nets that tally with Brown's report.[68]

A series of other bottom and surface drift-nets were introduced into the Gold Coast in the early twentieth century, but perhaps the next most influential net was the purse-seine – referred to as a cast-net by the Anlo – popularly known as *watsa*. Male Akro and his associates remained the pioneers of fishing technology:

> In 1917 Male Akro at Teshi evolved Kokole Ali, a net like Ali but with a larger mesh for catching Kokole (shad) and taking the place of a cast-net Dzane; the next year his half brother Habel Nmai answered him with a Watsa, a version of Kokole Ali made with much stouter twine, and which has become one of the most used nets during Harmattan. Kokole Ali was brought to Labadi from Teshi by Amatsu and Malefio in 1920, Watsa by Kokowe in 1924. Accra got them from Teshi in 1927–8 and 1929 respectively.[69]

[64] Brown, 'Survey of the fishing industry at Labadi', 4.

[65] Ibid., 5–6.

[66] NAG, Accra, ADM 11/1471. Fishing industry, 1900–24.

[67] PRO, CO 554/220. Report of Dr Hickling (Fisheries Adviser, Colonial Office) on his tour of West Africa, October–December 1950.

[68] *Gold Coast Advocate*, 12 January 1907.

[69] Brown, 'Survey of the fishing industry at Labadi', 7. Though Brown's authoritative study records the spread of *watsa* along the Ga coast between 1918 and 1929, Ragnhild Overa cites an account of *watsa*'s origin that credits Robert Ocran, owner of Mankoadze fisheries, with modelling the *watsa* net on a prototype he had seen at the FAO-sponsored World Gear Congress at Hamburg in 1957. Overa, 'Partners and competitors', 96–7.

The *watsa* would be elaborated upon over time, and the coastal erosion of Keta's beaches and the introduction of the outboard motor would promote the adoption of *watsa* fishing along the Anlo coast from the 1960s.

But it was the beach-seine net that ushered in the Anlo as maritime fishermen. In its adoption and development, the Anlo were far ahead of other maritime fishermen along the Gold Coast. Polly Hill points out that seine-nets date back to biblical times:

> The Ewe seine net is not a species of indigenous technology: known as *yevudor* (literally European net) it was presumably a copy of a European-owned net, possibly a type which was first introduced by the Portuguese in the region of Congo and Angola.[70]

This net could have spread west via the African coasting trade discussed in Chapters 1 and 2. The Anlo seem to have been the first to utilize the beach-seine net in the Gold Coast. Indeed, Fanti and Ga entrepreneurs went to the Anlo coast to recruit Anlo fishermen for migrant companies that specialized in beach-seine fishing. This method of fishing was spread to the Ga and Fanti coast through Anlo annual migrations.[71] The beach-seine net gained patronage in Accra and Teshi only in 1907, and Ada migrant fishermen – neighbours of the Anlo – pioneered its use there.[72] But the Anlo had also established themselves as experienced users of the *ali* net. In March 1907 a dispute raged between the neighbouring Fanti fishing towns of Great Kormantine and Saltpond, for the latter had hired Anlo *ali* fishermen in local waters.[73] The DC for Keta in 1908 reported on the active use of four different nets in Anlo maritime fishing: *yevudor, nekpeli* (a beach-seine net with a half-inch mesh), *agli* and *dogbledi* (similar to the *agli* net, but often left in the sea overnight).[74] Much of Anlo sea fishing was on the immediate continental shelf and not in the deep sea. The continental shelf is narrower on the Anlo coast – 9.8 miles off Cape St Paul, compared with 58 miles off Elmina. So the Anlo coast had a concentration of coastal, littoral and pelagic fish[75] within a short distance from its shores.[76]

The toll of these large nets on fish was immediately apparent. The beach-seine net, for instance, caught fish that swam on the surface and at the bottom of the ocean.[77] It caught adult fish and the fry of fish that migrated to shallow waters to spawn. C.R. Curling, Commissioner for the Eastern Province, was filled with dismay at this development. He recorded his sentiments in 1908: 'On my return from Keta I passed putrifying heaps of tiny fish which had been thrown on the land as not worth troubling about – there were thousands of fish about an inch long.'[78] In the 1940s F.R.

[70] Hill, *Ewe Seine Fishermen and Shallot Farmers*, 8.

[71] Lawson, 'Structure, migration and resettlement', 22–4.

[72] Brown, 'Survey of the fishing industry at Labadi', 7. Robert Wyllie discovered in 1969 that several migrant fishermen and their relatives from the Anlo town of Srogboe left annually for the coastal village of Muniano (near Winneba) to practise beach-seine fishing. Wyllie, 'Migrant Anlo fishing companies'.

[73] NAG, Accra, ADM 11/1474. 'Memorandum on the use of *ali* nets and local fishing industry'.

[74] Ibid. DC Keta to CEP, Ada, 18 November 1908.

[75] Fish that occupy the upper layers of the ocean up to 100 fathoms. See F.R. Irvine, *The Fishes and Fisheries of the Gold Coast* (London, 1947), 1–2.

[76] The 100-fathom line marks the continental shelf.

[77] Irvine, *Fishes and Fisheries*, 5.

[78] NAG, Accra, ADM 11/1474. C.R. Curling to Colonial Secretary, Akropong, 8 October 1907.

Irvine also commented on the great number of fry caught in seines.[79] The Anlo's growing efficiency at sea and inland fishing had its destructive elements. Profits drove Anlo entrepreneurs, and the thorough harvesting of Anlo waters may have compromised the long-term viability of local fisheries. The colonial government expressed its alarm in 1937–8 at Anlo fishing methods in the River Volta:

> Unfortunately there has grown up in the course of the last few years a method of fishing which if not checked may lead to as rapid a depopulation of fish, as there has been of game.
>
> The Awuna [Anlo] people have introduced a type of net which is anchored between the bank of the [Volta] river and the many islands. These nets are designed to catch both surface and deep water and are believed to prevent the migration of fish coming up the river to spawn.[80]

The government responded with the 'Rivers (Fishing) Regulations Ordinance (1938)', which prohibited the use of nets in the colony's rivers other than cast nets with a circumference of not more than 15 yards.[81] In the early 1960s Hill described the short Anlo coast as more heavily fished than any other coast in West Africa.[82] The Anlo have complained about the depopulation of fishes in local waters; they may have contributed to this trend.[83]

'Fishing companies' were formed on the Anlo coast to handle these huge nets. Net owners, as the sole investors of capital in the company, owned these companies. The rest of the company members were wage-labourers, though some held more skilled positions. Company members were paid by day or at the end of the fishing season. Marine fishing had become a major capitalist endeavour and clerks, teachers and traders invested in nets as part of their pension plans.[84] The exorbitant cost of the new sea-fishing nets restricted net owners and put many in the class of wage-labourers. Whereas an *afafa* net could cost £1,000 in the 1950s, a freshwater fisherman could equip 'himself with a canoe, a set net, basket traps and lines for less than £50'.[85] A typical beach-seine company working an *afafa* net comprised an average of sixty core members, thirty each pulling on the two ropes attached to the net.[86] Casual labourers could always be hired at the beach when and as needed. As Hill points out, the size of a company depended on net size, the number of nets operated by the company and the availability of casual help.[87]

The net owner appointed a 'bosun' or captain, and a 'second', as the immediate supervisors of the fishing operation. The 'bosun' determined when it was auspicious to cast the net and where to deploy the net. He was instrumental in the hiring of company members, and the composition of the company changed seasonally. The 'second' was the immediate assistant to the 'bosun'. When a company operated more than one net, the 'second' was in charge of the deployment of the other net. Each company had a

[79] Irvine, *Fishes and Fisheries*, 6.
[80] PRO, CO 96/739/2. Annual Report on the Eastern Province of the Gold Coast Colony, 1937–8.
[81] Dickson, *Historical Geography of Ghana*, 316.
[82] Hill, 'Pan-African fisherman'.
[83] See Chapter 6 on Anlo reasons for this phenomenon.
[84] Hill, *Studies in Rural Capitalism*, 35.
[85] Lawson, 'Structure, migration and resettlement', 26.
[86] Ibid., 22.
[87] Hill, *Studies in Rural Capitalism*, 36.

secretary or clerk, who recorded the expenditure and income of the fishing company.[88] The adoption of the name 'company' and the formal titles of 'bosun', 'clerk' and so on seem to have postdated the First World War and appear to be a conscious emulation of the commercial companies that proliferated in the Gold Coast from the late nineteenth century. The 'company' also reflects the heavy infusion of capital by net owners, who were not necessarily fishermen. An old Anlo fisherman who worked his father's *yevudor* off the coast of Togo in 1914 asserted that the word 'company' was not used at that time and the titles of 'bosun', 'secretary' and 'clerk' did not exist although these functions were exercised by some company members.[89] The records kept by the company secretary or clerk were crucial to the sharing of catch or revenue at the end of a fishing day or at the end of the fishing season. The net owner claimed the largest share in the division of income based on his capital investment. The share system, though not uniform in Anlo or on the Gold Coast, had certain commonalities. The total fishing revenue or catch was divided into shares and the net/canoe owner claimed about a third of the proceeds. Company members received roughly equal shares, with some bonuses for those with special skills, such as the 'bosun' and the 'second'. The advent of outboard motors from the 1950s increased revenue differences between net owners and company members, as net owners now claimed about 50 per cent of total revenue for the canoe, net and outboard motor. The rest of the company shared the other 50 per cent.[90] Social mobility in canoe fisheries – from wage earner to net owner – became more limited.

Fishing companies and fish wives: gender complementarity in canoe fisheries
Women played an important role in the fishing company and in the fishing industry. There were female members of the fishing company, and these women carried the ropes attached to the fishing nets after the net had been pulled in and supplied drinking water to the men during the operation of the net. Ragnhild Overa informs us that:

> Women are also employed in the companies. They are called *kakorviwo* – 'those who carry the rope', and *tsikuviwo* – 'those who fetch water'. They coil up the rope as the men haul, they fetch water for the men to drink, or dig a hole in the sand to fetch fresh water from ground water level.[91]

These women are in the fishing company as distinct from women of the company. Each company has a group of women attached to it known as 'fishwives'. As Overa points out, a fishwife 'is not necessarily a wife; she is a fish processor and trader on a relatively minor scale'.[92] The processing and marketing of fish is entirely a female

[88] On the structure of fishing companies, see Hill, *Studies in Rural Capitalism*; idem, *Ewe Seine Fishermen and Shallot Farmers*. See also interview with Wilson Pillow (and Daniel Defor), net owner and head of Defor Fishing Company, Atiteti, 19 March 1997; interview with Yaovi Gada, chief fisherman, Abutiakope, 22 April 1997.
[89] Hill, *Ewe Seine Fishermen and Shallot Farmers*, 16–17.
[90] Overa, 'Partners and competitors', 98.
[91] Ibid., 243–4. See also interview with Togbuivi Kumassah, Woe, 3 September 1996; Yaovi Gada, Abutiakope, 22 April 1997; Michael Lawson, Dzelukope, 23 April 1997.
[92] Ragnhild Overa, 'Wives and traders: women's careers in Ghanaian canoe fisheries', *Maritime Anthropological Studies (MAST)* 6, 1/2 (1993): 110. See also Irene Odotei, 'The migration of Ghanaian women in the canoe fishing industry', *MAST* 5, 2 (1992): 88–95.

domain. Overa states succinctly: 'When the canoe is emptied, and the fish has been put into carrying pans and is sold, the fish has entered a female domain'.[93] Fish is either sold fresh or processed through drying, smoking or frying. Woman hold several roles in the fishing industry as 'standing women' or regular fish buyers at the beach; as 'carriers' who convey fish for standing women in their own head pans or baskets; as fish processors; and as fish traders, sometimes with networks extending to interior towns. Women also own canoes or nets.[94]

Fish wives are either married to members in a fishing company or are related to fishermen. Ties of marriage and kinship enable these women, sometimes with very little capital, to buy fish on credit from fishing companies and to make some profit through the selling of fish. Overa describes their position in the Anlo town of Dzelukope:

> Wives of the company members are entitled to buy fish from the beach seine. They come with their head pans to the beach when the *yevudor* is approaching the seashore. The wives are not members of the net company as such, but through marriage they are entitled to buy fish from the company where their husband works.[95]

C.R. Edelsten, a policeman stationed at Keta in 1947, provided a vivid account of the landing of a beach-seine:

> Men and women, with gay cloths tucked around their thighs, mill around and scoop up basins full of fish from the net. The owner of the catch does a great deal of shouting and bargaining with the men and women as they push and shove, trying to get a full basin. The basins are emptied on the beach in a shower of silver. Soon there is [a] shimmering, flipping heap of fish. The owner then starts to sell to the crowd of women; a full basin being sold at 5/- or 6/-.
>
> The basins are then emptied into wicker baskets and when full the baskets are lifted by helpers on to the heads of the women, who carry them off to the nearby dry bed of the lagoon which lies behind Keta. The fish are then scattered, so that the sun can dry them in a few hours. When dried the fish are swept into heaps, put into the wicker baskets and taken to the market, or they are put on a lorry and sold up-country at a fair price.[96]

Edelsten's account captures the various roles of women in the fish industry: standing women, carriers, processors and traders. Women were responsible for the movement of fish from beaches to the cooking pots of homes. They were indispensable in the complementary gender relationship between fishermen and 'fishwives'.

As fishing companies migrated, they took along the fishwives. These women cooked for the company, processed and sold the fish, and acted as bankers for the fishing company. Indeed, several women and skilled artisans accompanied a fishing company in its migration. Fishing companies were mini-economies that generated spin-off occupations. As one Anlo informant told Hill in 1963 about migrant fishing companies

---

[93] Overa, 'Partners and competitors', 101.

[94] Overa, 'Wives and traders', 126.

[95] Overa, 'Partners and competitors', 245. See also Hill, *Studies in Rural Capitalism*, 38.

[96] Charles Richard Edelsten Private Papers, Rhodes House, Mss. Afr.s.506. G.K. Nukunya suggests that the wicker baskets were actually baskets made from oil palm, as these were used to carry both fresh and processed fish even in the late 1940s. Wicker baskets were used to convey lagoon crabs. Personal correspondence, 28 September 1999.

in the early twentieth century, 'any woman who feels to can go'.[97] The complex social structure of a migrant fishing company is captured in Albert de Surgy's study of fishing in the Ivory Coast in the 1960s.

> Statistics collected by M. de Surgy, relating to 389 Anlo seine fishermen in the Ivory Coast showed them to be accompanied by 336 women – as well as 449 children, some of whom would be old enough to assist the fishermen.[98]

And as sea fishing became increasingly commercialized, accumulation among fish-wives led to the emergence of 'fish mammies', and a distinction between them and other 'fishwives'. Fish mammies were large-scale standing women, often the wives of net owners or independently wealthy fish traders from fishing communities. They acquired enough wealth to become company owners themselves or the financiers of male net owners.[99] They were indispensable as financiers in the transition to motorized fishing.[100] Instructively, not many Anlo women emerged as owners of fishing companies. The few examples were often of Anlo women based in non-Anlo towns. Overa cites patrilineal ideology and an inheritance system that favours transmitting fishing equipment to sons as strong reasons for this pattern.[101]

Though fish mammies existed in Anlo, they were subordinated to the interests of patrilineages. Several migrated in order to exercise their entrepreneurial freedom.[102] For Anlo women around Anloga and Woe, the preference was for farming, and some were active pioneers in the shallot industry. It is to this industry that we now turn.

Shallot farming in Anlo

Greene documents important transformations in Anlo social relations where land tenure and household organization are concerned between the seventeenth century and the nineteenth century.[103] A general pattern was the increasing marginalization of women, especially younger women, in their access to clan lands and in their ability to choose their marriage partners. In regard to land, the Anlo traditionally acquired land from the patrilineages of both parents. Daughters received parcels of land from their fathers, and women bequeathed land to their daughters and granddaughters.[104] Husbands allocated lands to their wives. Women generally had the use of marginal

---

[97] Hill, *Ewe Seine Fishermen and Shallot Farmers*, 16.

[98] Cited in Hill, *Studies in Rural Capitalism*, 50.

[99] Overa, 'Partners and competitors'.

[100] See James B. Christensen, 'Motor power and woman power: technological and economic change among the Fanti fishermen in Ghana', in M. E. Smith, ed., *Those who Live from the Sea: A Study in Maritime Anthropology* (St Paul, NY, 1977), 71–89; Emile Vercruijsse, *The Penetration of Capitalism: A West African Study* (London, 1984); and Overa, 'Wives and traders'.

[101] Overa, 'Partners and competitors', 252–3.

[102] See, for example, interview with Yorkor Amedoyor, Tegbi, 23 April 1997.

[103] Greene, *History of the Anlo-Ewe*.

[104] Ibid., 28; Benneh, 'Land tenure and Sabala farming', 78; G.K. Nukunya, 'Land tenure, inheritance and social structure among the Anlo', *Universitas* 3, 1 (1973) 72–3. Daughters received smaller parcels of land than sons did.

patrilineal lands close to the Keta Lagoon, and they harvested reeds and wickers here for their basket weaving.[105] It was on these small parcels of land that women cultivated vegetables – including shallots – for household use and for sale to subsidize the household budget. By the late nineteenth century, women's access to land was further restricted by the abolition of the slave-trade and an increased shift of Anlo men to farming. This trend was intensified by the growing demand in the Gold Coast and Europe for shallots, copra and sugar cane.[106] As the Cape St Paul wilt disease wiped out coconuts and the copra industry from the 1930s, more Anlo men turned to commercial farming and appropriated even the marginal lands available to women.

Benneh dates shallot (Anlo: *sabala*) cultivation in Anlo to the eighteenth century, though he gives no evidence for this date.[107] It is striking that Isert, with his keen interest in natural science, noted the cultivation of plantain, yam, banana and sugar cane in Anloga in 1784 but not shallot.[108] However, this does not indicate that shallot was unknown in the Anlo area. One of the earliest references to shallot cultivation in Anlo was a ship account of buying shallots in baskets anchored off the coast of Keta in 1877.[109] When Stein, the agricultural officer stationed in the Keta District, reported on valuable agricultural exports from the Keta-Ada District in 1930, he did not include shallots.[110] Grove highlights that shallot cultivation was unimportant outside the Anloga–Woe area until the mid-1930s, when the coconut disease promoted the spread of shallot cultivation between Tegbi and Anyanui.[111]

Edward Ahiabor – an agricultural science teacher at Anlo Secondary School and a large-scale vegetable farmer – narrated the beginnings of the shallot industry:

> Well, as you move from the main road towards the lagoon, you encounter some underlying clay. Meaning, from a point on that side, it is all black heavy clay. But from the main road to the sea, it is all sand. What has supported agriculture in Anlo is the perch of underground fresh water, which is easily tapped by farmers to irrigate. Otherwise farming would not be possible here. In the past, the main cash crop here was coconut. Then somewhere along the line, the coconut trees were attacked by the Cape St Paul's wilt disease. Folks here had to switch to something. Of course, in the past, they were growing cassava for home use. Somewhere along the line, some-body by name Dzisam brought some of these shallot bulbs from Anexo in Togo, and surprisingly it did well when it was planted in the sand. That was the beginning of the shallot industry in Anloga.[112]

Edward Ahiabor placed Dzisam's introduction of shallot seeds into Anloga in the nineteenth century. This account was also reproduced in the first study of the shallot industry in Anloga. S.T. Quansah, the author and an agricultural officer, placed Dzisam's introduction of shallots from Anexo at the beginning of the nineteenth

[105] Greene, *History of the Anlo-Ewe*, 4–5, 162.

[106] Ibid., 161.

[107] Benneh, 'Land tenure and Sabala farming', 74.

[108] Paul Erdmann, *Letters on West Africa and the Slave Trade (1788)*, trans. and ed. S.A. Winsnes (Oxford, 1992), 56.

[109] Grove, 'Economy of the Volta delta', 392.

[110] Ibid. Stein listed coconuts, palm kernels and palm oil.

[111] Ibid., 392–3.

[112] Interview with Edward Ahiabor, Anloga, 20 March 1997.

century.[113] Even today, shallot seeds are replenished with imports from Togo and the Republic of Benin.[114] An important success story in Ghana's agrarian history this century has been the ability of the Anlo to transform their infertile soil with irregular rainfall into an oasis of vegetable cultivation based on heavy manuring, hand irrigation and the sanding of clay beds near the lagoon side to facilitate percolation. Indeed, the only environmental factor the Anlo have been unable to control in this process is the erratic flooding of the Keta Lagoon and other low-lying areas in periods of heavy rainfall. The result is a regime of permanent cultivation with three seasons of shallot a year. And the Anloga–Woe area has emerged as the centre of shallot cultivation in Ghana. Ministry of Agriculture figures for shallot production in Anlo, based on the returns of ferry depots and customs posts, indicate a rise in output from 322 tons in 1941 (estimated value £3,457) to 1,268 tons in 1955 (estimated value £149,480).[115] As Nukunya rightly points out, these figures reflect neither the quantity of shallots kept as seed for subsequent plantings nor the amount consumed locally.[116]

Land tenure and inheritance rules are crucial to an understanding of the shallot industry, especially as Nukunya estimated in 1973 that in 'Anloga over 90% of the farmers are dependent on family land rather than that acquired by themselves or their parents, although many farmers have bought additional plots themselves'.[117] Shallot cultivation is carried out on very small parcels of land fashioned into beds with individual holdings seldom exceeding one acre, and an examination of Anlo inheritance rules sheds light on this feature. Land tenure in Anlo has unique developments in that the emergence of highly commercialized horticulture has promoted several tenurial arrangements enabling those without access to clan or lineage lands to acquire land through leasing, pledging, sharecropping and even outright purchase. And the history of land use in Anlo facilitates a better understanding of the role of Anlo women in shallot cultivation – and marketing – in spite of the insistent claims by Anlo men that Anlo women 'are not farmers'.[118] But often there has been a tendency for men to appropriate cash crops or their proceeds and to relegate women to subsistence farming, such as vegetable cultivation, even where female labour was crucial to cash crop production.[119] The disputed role of Anlo women in shallot

---

[113] S.T. Quansah, 'The shallot industry: incorporating a recent survey of the Anloga growing area', *New Gold Coast Farmer* 1, 2 (1956): 45, as cited in Margaret Adzo Agbodzi, 'The impact of shallot farming on the socio-economic status of women in Anloga' (BA thesis, Sociology Department, University of Ghana, 1986), 13.

[114] Benneh, 'Land tenure and Sabala farming', 86.

[115] Grove, 'Economy of the Volta delta', 403.

[116] Nukunya, 'Effects of cash crops', 66.

[117] Nukunya, 'Land tenure', 73.

[118] This claim was reiterated in Nukunya's personal correspondence with the author (28 September 1999). He states that Anlo women may own farms or shallot beds, but men usually do the hoeing and planting – the essence of farming in the Anlo context. Empirical evidence from Africa indicates that women dominate farming in hoe cultivation. See Jack Goody, *Production and Reproduction: A Comparative Study of the Domestic Domain* (Cambridge, 1976), ch. 4. The insistence that Anlo women do not farm may be part of a gender discourse underpinning differential access to land.

[119] See, for examples, Christine Okali, *Cocoa and Kinship in Ghana: The Matrilineal Akan of Ghana* (London, 1983); Jane Guyer, 'Household budgets and women's income' (Boston University, African Studies Center Working Paper 28, 1980); Beverly Grier, 'Pawns, porters, and petty traders: women in the transition to cash

Photo 5.2 Shallots at Anloga market, 1996 (by author).

farming may reflect the transition of shallot from a local condiment with some sale value to the major commercial crop in coastal Anlo from the 1930s. Their continued presence as shallot farmers and farm labourers underscores important historical continuities.[120] And women control the marketing of shallot, for they have the distribution network as in the distribution of fish. Anloga shallots are marketed in local markets, such as Keta and Anloga, and in long-distance markets at Togo, Accra, Koforidua and Kumasi (Photo 5.2).

The basis of Anlo-Ewe claims to land is settlement, and the legal right to land is vested in clans or lineages as exercised by local families.[121] To quote A.K.P. Kludze on the Ewe land tenure:

> In Eweland, as among the Akan, the basis of land acquisition in the ancient times was settlement; the difference is that the Ewe settlement was not by virtue of apportionment by the political authority. Land became available for settlement either because of war, because of the discovery of unoccupied land or because of cession of territory by way of a gift. Once the lands became available, acquisition on behalf of the family was simply through occupation and use by individual members of the families.[122]

Although Kludze draws his case studies mostly from the northern Ewe of Ghana, the statement above holds true for the Anlo. No empty land existed in twentieth-century Anlo. Indeed, as Greene argues, land was scarce very early in Anlo history.[123] With

119 (cont.) crop agriculture in colonial Ghana', *Signs* 17, 2 (1992): 304–28.

120 See, for example, Agbodzi, 'Impact of shallot farming'.

121 See Chapter 1.

122 A.K.P. Kludze, *Ewe Law of Property* (London, 1973), 109.

123 Greene, *History of the Anlo-Ewe*.

clan and lineage membership in Anlo comes access to land use. Lineage heads periodically allocated land:

> Within the lineage itself formal demarcations are made, roughly once in a generation, which determine the portion of lineage property an individual may cultivate without let or hindrance from any other member of the group. Before this formal demarcation all descendants of the previous user as well as his close relatives such as brothers and sisters have access to his land.[124]

Land use was restricted to usufruct, and land alienation was rare until the late nineteenth century.[125] Land and lineage are thus closely tied in Anlo history, and not all Anlo clans even possessed land.

Anlo inheritance rules tended to fragment land, as the deceased's landed estate was parcelled out among his children. Nukunya states:

> The Anlo are patrilineal, with property passing from father to sons and daughters as the case may be. As a rule, sons take precedence over daughters, though the latter are not entirely excluded from the system. When a plot of land cultivated by a deceased person is to be divided among his children the portion received by the daughters is much smaller than that of the sons.[126]

This custom was greatly altered in reality, as Nukunya documents for the twentieth century:

> Case histories and genealogies support the view that the right of daughters to inherit their father's property was clearly recognized in the past. Many current instances have also confirmed this view. However, there seems to be a growing tendency among many Anlo now to regard the claim of daughters as only a privilege and not a right to be enforced before a court of law.[127]

This development is a result of the increasing scarcity of land and the fear that land granted to daughters may be lost to the patrilineage. The outcome is the very small parcels of land on which shallot is cultivated. Though this inheritance pattern ensures access to some land for landed lineage members, land sizes are often unviable and large landholders are few.[128] Enterprising shallot farmers thus acquire lands through various means: inheritance through patrilateral and matrilateral lines, purchase, lease and pledge. An individual farmer's shallot beds are often scattered.

Polly Hill, an expert on farming systems in West Africa, marvelled at Anlo ingenuity in regard to tenurial arrangements in shallot farming. She considered the system of *dame* or 'farm renting' as unique in the West African context.[129] Under *dame*, 'the shallot harvest is divided equally between the bed-owner and tenant, after the deduction of expenses, which may have been incurred by either party'.[130] There are actually two systems of sharecropping: *dame* and *fame*. Nukunya distinguishes between these two with further clarification:

---

[124] Nukunya, 'Land tenure', 69.

[125] NAG, Accra, ADM 5/3/9. *Report upon the Customs Relating to the Tenure of Land in the Gold Coast* (London, 1895), especially George E. Ferguson to Colonial Secretary, 11 July 1895, and H.M. Hull to Colonial Secretary, 31 August 1895. See also Kludze, *Ewe Law of Property*, 126–8.

[126] Nukunya, 'Land tenure', 72.

[127] Ibid., 73.

[128] See the case of the shallot-producing family in Dornnorgbor near Anloga in Benneh, 'Land tenure and Sabala farming'.

[129] Hill, *Ewe Seine Fishermen and Shallot Farmers*, 40.

[130] Ibid.

In the case of *dame* the owner of the unprepared plot grants it to another to cultivate and the produce is shared between the two in the ratio of two to one in favor of the tenant. In the *fame* [system] a farmer who has already prepared his beds but finds that he cannot get sufficient seeds for all, hands them to another who provides the seeds, sows them and maintains the plot. The harvest is often divided into moieties.[131]

The system described by Hill is apparently the *fame* system. Other tenurial arrangements enabled those without land to acquire land and landowners to increase their holdings. Those in debt but in possession of beds could pledge (*do woba*) these as mortgage for a loan. The pledgee is allowed use of the land while the loan is outstanding, the use of the land constituting the interest on the loan.[132] Others have acquired shallot beds as gifts (*fiabo*) from their fathers or even masters. *Fiabo* was generally awarded for diligent service.[133] Then there is the renting of beds (*bodada*), referred to as 'leasing' today.[134] Hill stated that in 1963 this was usually for no more than a year or two.[135] Today bed leases run generally for five years, and land scarcity together with the profitability of the shallot industry has put a premium on land values in the Anloga area.[136] The prosperity of shallot farmers has led to a decline in sharecropping. David Fianu, President of the Woe Benevolent Shallot Farmers Association, explained: 'Nowadays, when they see the farmers putting up buildings, they don't want to do the sharecropping anymore. They think the farmers are cheating them. Formerly, that is what our fathers used to do. Now landlords are not interested'.[137] The preference nowadays is for leasing for a specified term or outright sale of land.

The shallot farmers the author interviewed in 1997 owned beds from various sources, which mirrored the complexity of Anlo social relations. Whereas inheritance seemed to have been the major source of beds according to studies conducted in the 1960s and 1970s,[138] there has been a shift to leasing and purchase. Inheritance and pledging are still important, but there has been a notable decline in gifts (*fiabo*), especially from husbands to wives and from parents to daughters.[139] Minawo Dovor acquired her beds from her deceased husband with whom she farmed and by leasing. In 1997 she had 100 beds and was the largest shallot farmer in Woe.[140] Dovi Kponor

---

[131] Nukunya, 'Land tenure', 76.

[132] Ibid., 77; Hill, *Ewe Seine Fishermen and Shallot Farmers*, 44; Benneh, 'Land tenure and Sabala farming', 80.

[133] Nukunya, 'Land tenure', 75.

[134] The farm (*agble*) is distinct from the shallot bed (*bo*).

[135] Hill, *Ewe Seine Fishermen and Shallot Farmers*, 46. Hill mentions that written lease contracts executed by letter writers were common. Ibid., 44.

[136] Interview with Madam Minawo Dovor, shallot farmer, Woe, 20 March 1997; interview with David Fianu, shallot farmer, Woe, 20 March 1997; interview with Edward Ahiabor, shallot farmer, Anloga, 20 March 1997; interview with Madam Dovi Kponor, shallot farmer, Anloga, 20 March 1997. In 1997, twenty beds, measuring on the average between 5 and 7 feet in width and 50 and 70 feet in length, could fetch 3 million cedis, then the US dollar equivalent of $1,500, for a five-year lease.

[137] Interview with David Fianu, Woe, 20 March 1997.

[138] Hill, *Ewe Seine Fishermen and Shallot Farmers*; Benneh, 'Land tenure and Sabala farming'; Nukunya, 'Land tenure'; idem, 'Effects of cash crops'.

[139] See Agbodzi, 'Impact of shallot farming', 20.

[140] Interview with Minawo Dovor, Woe, 20 March 1997.

of Anloga inherited a few beds from her grandmother. Her brothers took all the land when their father died, and she received no land from her father's estate. Married to a man in Woe, she actually 'leased' beds from her husband.[141] She had recently moved back to Anloga from her marital home in Woe. Her ties with Anloga had more salience where accessibility to beds was concerned. Contrast these women's experiences with Edward Ahiabor, son of a deceased farmer, who was also the largest shallot farmer in Anloga. His father's holdings totalled 1.5 hectares in the depressions by the seashore and 2 hectares in the uplands away from the seashore. Each hectare can be partitioned into 120 beds, making Edward Ahiabor's father's holding a total of 420 beds. Much of this he had acquired through unredeemed pledges. Edward, with a Masters degree in agricultural science, inherited his father's holdings – and responsibilities – and has automatically emerged as one of the largest and most innovative shallot (and vegetable) farmers in the Anloga–Woe area.[142]

Anloga and Woe men often stated that their women were not farmers like the men. A male shallot farmer in Anloga told Hill in 1963 that: 'Even if women own shallot beds they are not themselves real farmers, but have to be helped by men'.[143] In 1997 Edward Ahiabor affirmed this position:

> To start with, inheritance in this area is patrilineal. In the past land was held by men, except some few women. So the very few women in farming in this area are those whose mothers owned land and passed them on to their daughters. That is why you don't have a lot of women going into vegetable farming.[144]

But the large presence of women in the agrarian labour force – as well as the few female bed owners – and the location of many of these shallot beds suggest a historical subtext that needs to be unravelled. All that can be offered here for the moment are intuitive suggestions based on a close reading of the historical sources. Much of the shallot farming in Anloga and Woe is conducted on marginal lands bordering the Keta Lagoon, which were considered unproductive before the nineteenth century and often occupied by women. To quote Nukunya:

> Much of the shallot growing area bordering on the Keta Lagoon between Tegbi and Anloga falls within this category. Because of its marshy nature its importance as a farming area was not realized until the introduction of sugar cane and shallots in the 19th century. Before then, women basket weavers claimed them for growing reeds and wickers. The plots indeed passed down in the female line until men found use for them they remained in the hands of the male offspring. Land traced to a woman in this way is referred to as *mamanyigba*, grandmother's land.[145]

In places such as Tegbi and Woe, where lagoon and sea fishing were important but farmland available, wives farmed vegetable plots to supplement the fish their husbands brought home and the maize that could be purchased on the market. And the wives of farmers also planted vegetables, such as okra and pepper, on their

---

[141] Interview with Dovi Kponor, Anloga, 20 March 1997.
[142] Interview with Edward Ahiabor, Anloga, 20 March 1997.
[143] Hill, *Ewe Seine Fishermen and Shallot Farmers*, 43.
[144] Interview with Edward Ahiabor, Anloga, 20 March 1997.
[145] Nukunya, 'Land tenure', 70.

husbands' farms for subsistence.[146] It is possible that these wives pioneered shallot cultivation on their 'useless' plots by the lagoon side. There are Anlo traditions that place the cultivation of shallots in the eighteenth century.[147]

Thus, behind the firm pronouncements by Anloga and Woe men that women are not farmers – not even just shallot farmers – may lie a story of dispossession. The process of carting sand from the seashore and mixing this with the heavy clay soil of the lagoon side to promote percolation could have been an early female experiment. Grass from the lagoon side, such as *gbekle* (*Paspalum vaginatum*), was cut and used to shore the borders of the beds (*gbekoke*) to prevent the beds from being washed away in heavy rains.[148] It was from this very site that women obtained reeds and wickers for weaving baskets. Manure to aid the fertility of these marginal lands comprised bat guano, fish manure and cow dung. Chemical fertilizers are utilized, but this was probably a later development. Indeed, the crop regime practised by shallot farmers in the Woe–Anloga area today is reminiscent of the female domain: shallot intercropped or alternated with tomatoes, okra and pepper. Women feature prominently in the agrarian labour force today, and their skills are preferred over those of men in watering, the harvesting of shallot and the preparation of shallot seeds for the next planting. Men are used in the carting of sand from the seashore to the lagoon side, preparing the beds and manuring. But these are heavy duties due to the expanded scale of shallot farming – hence male labour was preferable.[149] By the late nineteenth century, when colonial officers commented on the neat shallot beds in the Keta District, Anlo men had practically taken over vegetable farming.[150] This process may have begun with the effective ending of the slave-trade in the 1860s and the gradual realization of the commercial value of shallots in the search for economic alternatives.

Sugar cane also gained commercial importance in the late nineteenth century, grown on marshy marginal lands, and it would constitute the base for local distillation in colonial Anlo.

Liquor distillation in colonial Anlo

Sugar cane, the basis of local distillation in Anlo, flourished on Anlo farms as far back as the late eighteenth century.[151] In the 1920s, colonial officers suggested the establishment of a sugar mill in the Keta District to tap this reservoir of sugar cane.[152] Local gin, *akpeteshie*, often referred to in Anlo as *kele* or *sodabi*, is made from either

[146] Interview with Obed Nutsugah (Economic Planning Officer, Keta District) and Fred Akligo (Assemblyman for Afiadenyigba), Dzelukope, 18 March 1997; interview with Esther Kwawukume, Keta, 23 January 1997.

[147] Benneh, 'Land tenure and Sabala farming', 74; Agbodzi, 'Impact of shallot farming', 13.

[148] Benneh, 'Land tenure and Sabala farming', 88.

[149] Interviews with Minawo Dovor, Woe, 20 March 1997; David Fianu, Woe, 20 March 1997; Dovi Kponor, Anloga, 20 March 1997; Edward Ahiabor, Anloga, 20 March 1997.

[150] NAG, Accra, ADM 5/3/9. H.M. Hull (Travelling Commissioner) to Colonial Secretary, Accra, 31 August 1895.

[151] Isert, *Letters on West Africa*, 56.

[152] See NAG, Accra, ADM 39/1/207. Sugar cane industry (Keta District).

sugar cane or palm wine from the oil-palm, and Anlo had both in significant quantities. Chapter 2 highlighted the importance of imported liquor in the Anlo economy in the precolonial and early colonial eras. A series of colonial liquor laws between 1928 and 1930 raised the fees for liquor licences, reduced the hours of sale for spirits, banned the sale of spirits on credit, hiked up the duties on spirits and stipulated that gin and geneva imports – the most popular spirits among Gold Coast Africans – be phased out over a ten-year period (1930–40). These stringent liquor laws were a response to temperance agitation in the Gold Coast and Britain. The colonial government passed the laws as an appeasement gesture, but hoped that the proverbial demand for liquor in the Gold Coast would stymie these liquor regulations. Customs duties on imported liquor were central to colonial government revenues in the Gold Coast.[153] But the new liquor laws coincided with the economic depression of the 1930s, and the reduced purchasing power put imported liquor beyond the reach of most Africans in the Gold Coast. The pinch was felt more in Anlo, with its local economy already under siege in the 1920s and 1930s. It is perhaps not surprising that Anlo, in search of economic alternatives in the 1930s, took up liquor distillation with a vengeance. It would record the greatest number of arrests and convictions as the colonial government rallied to halt illicit distillation. And as the numerous lagoons and creeks aided Anlo evasion of colonial surveillance, the government reluctantly came to the conclusion that it could not eradicate illicit distillation.

Liquor played an important role in the Anlo economy and social relations. When the colonial government was contemplating the substantial increase in liquor duties and the gradual abolition of gin and geneva in 1929–30, Sri II, paramount chief of Anlo, cautioned:

> I have consulted my State Council and we are of the opinion that any attempt to control the importation of spirits still further would be undesirable unless the French adjust their tariff. We wish the situation to remain as it is at present. I do not want to turn my people into smugglers and see them get into trouble. A great number of my people are fishermen and they require a little stimulant as their calling is a difficult and dangerous one.[154]

The role of liquor in the fishing industry, especially in employer–employee relations, was documented by Hill. She interviewed a Keta fishing company owner in 1963, who was heavily in debt. Hill reported that:

> This debtor had earlier shown us a file full of accounts, making it clear that he spent huge sums on drink. He provided Ghana gin when his men came back from sea. He employed daily laborers as net-repairers and paid them with cash and Ghana gin. An item in the account had read: 'Tins of drink for repairing the net and finding people £10'.[155]

Liquor had an equally important role in Anlo farming communities, as it lubricated social relations: patron–client relations, funeral wakes and other rites of passage, festivals and judicial processes.

[153] For a detailed treatment of temperance and liquor policy in the Gold Coast, see Akyeampong, *Drink, Power, and Cultural Change*, chs 4, 5. The discussion here is restricted to the Anlo context. On the alcohol industry in Ghana, see Emmanuel Akyeampong, 'The state and alcohol revenues: promoting "economic development" in Gold Coast/Ghana', *Histoire Sociale* 27, 3 (1994): 393–411.

[154] PRO, CO 96/692/657. Notes of Evidence, 1930 Liquor Commission Report.

[155] Hill, *Ewe Seine Fishermen and Shallot Farmers*, 34.

Land Reclamation, Migrant Fishing, Shallot Cultivation & Illicit Distillation

In 1930–1 the colonial government discovered six cases of illicit liquor traffic, and eleven persons were convicted.[156] These initial cases were from the Volta River District. The Inspector General of Police, Bamford, was supercilious in his comments on this alleged new threat:

> I do not in any way wish to belittle the gravity of the offence, loss of revenue, danger to health and so forth but I am convinced that no illicit distillery could be in existence for long in this colony without information reaching my police and a scrutiny of each case dealt with so far supports the view.[157]

Colonial complacency is revealed in the confident opinion of the comptroller of customs in March 1926 that the art of distillation was largely unknown in West Africa except Liberia.[158] Illicit liquor traffic offences jumped a hundred times from the reported six in 1930–1 to 558 cases between 1 April 1933 and 31 March 1934.[159]

The colonial government was truly astounded and implemented strong measures to curtail this new threat to colonial revenues and colonial order. But the government underestimated the tenacity of determined Gold Coasters like the Anlo and the suitability of the Anlo environment for smuggling. Evidence that the Volta River District had become the den of illicit distillers was forthcoming:

> In January 1934, a highly successful raid was made by police in force between the villages of Kpong and Amedica, where 50 Bush Stills, 40 gallons of distilled spirits and 500 gallons of palm wine were seized and destroyed. Fines to the aggregate of £375 were imposed in respect of this raid but nothing was paid. This raid revealed the fact that the Volta River Islands afford suitable shelter for the distillers which accounts for the numerous cases of possessing trade spirits reported in the Akuse and Ada Districts.[160]

In Anlo illicit distillation from sugar cane was established in Woe on the littoral, on lagoon islands, such as Alakple, and at Atiavi and other towns and villages on the northern shores of the Keta Lagoon.[161] This industry thus drew on the mixture of mud and clay lying close to the lagoon shore and suitable for sugar cane cultivation. In 1938–9 the Keta-Ada District still held the record for the highest number of illicit distillation cases reported.[162] Already in 1935, Governor Arnold Hodson of the Gold Coast was informing the Colonial Office in London that nothing could stamp out illicit distillation.[163]

How did the Anlo emerge as pioneers in distillation? It is not exactly certain when local knowledge of distillation became available in the Gold Coast. It is likely, however, that this knowledge may have existed in restricted circles, at least, by the early nineteenth century. Dutch traders in the Gold Coast experimented with commercial distillation from the early nineteenth century.[164] Though the Dutch jealously guarded

[156] Akyeampong, *Drink, Power, and Cultural Change*, 98.
[157] PRO, CO 554/89/4495. 'Illicit distillation of spirits'. Minute by IGP Bamford, 25 January 1932.
[158] Akyeampong, *Drink, Power, and Cultural Change*, 98.
[159] Ibid.
[160] Ibid., 100.
[161] Grove, 'Economy of the Volta delta', 391; Sophia Amable, 'The 1953 riot in Anloga and its aftermath' (BA thesis, University of Ghana, 1977), 11; and Greene, *History of the Anlo-Ewe*, 162–3.
[162] Akyeampong, *Drink, Power, and Cultural Change*, 100.
[163] PRO, CO 554/98/33522. Governor Hodson to the Secretary of State, Accra, 3 May 1935.
[164] Akyeampong, *Drink, Power, and Cultural Change*, 106–7.

their trade secrets, their African assistants could have learned by observation. Such a process of observation and independent experimentation took place among Anlo-Ewe labourers on the Basle Mission cocoa plantations in Akropong. The Basle Missionary Society had introduced cocoa seedlings into the Gold Coast in 1858. Anita Mensah, a distiller from a family of distillers, narrated how her family had learnt the art of distillation:

> Two of my grandfather's brothers were taken as labourers for the Basle Mission from Eweland to Akropong. These Europeans instructed my grand uncles in distillation. My grand uncles would supervise the fermentation of cocoa beans. They would then connect a pipe between two receptacles and distill. The vapour from the fermented cocoa beans turned into gin. My grand uncles developed an interest in this gin as the Europeans used to give them some to drink, although they were paid labourers. So immediately after the cocoa season in Akropong, my grand uncles would ferment some of the beans and distill it. But the Europeans used to rectify their distilled gin. But that part of the process they did not let my grand uncles witness or learn. So my grand uncles would just do the initial distillation and drink their gin. The gin aided them in their agricultural labour and it livened their social moments.[165]

As the Ewes left Akropong for other areas, they took their interest in distillation with them. The Ewes later discovered that fermented palm wine and sugar cane juice had the same qualities as fermented cocoa beans.[166]

Illicit gin was pervasive in Anlo social life.[167] Its origins remain vague though some believed it predated colonial rule in Anlo. Dotse recalled the colonial days:

> In fact, we cannot say exactly when *akpeteshie* started. Formerly, we were calling it *kpôtomenui* ('something hidden in a coconut mat fence') because people started brewing [distilling] this thing even before the white men came. Because of its high alcoholic content, they found out that it was not good for health. Our contention was that the drink the white man brought is the same as ours. The white men's contention was that ours was too strong ... Before the white men came, we were using *akpeteshie*. But when they came they banned it, probably because they wanted to make sales on their own liquor. And so we were calling it *kpôtomenui*. When you had a visitor, whom you knew very well, then you ordered that *kpôtomenui* be brought. That is *akpeteshie*, but it was never referred to by name.[168]

Before *akpeteshie* came to the notice of the colonial government in 1930–1, A.J. Beckley, senior collector of customs, reported that he had heard from several sources that the Anlo 'cooked rum', but had been unable to obtain a sample.[169] Illicit liquor, and the poisoning that sometimes resulted from it, was so prevalent in Anlo that the Catholic Mission of the Keta District was the only mission body that asked for the relaxation of the stringent liquor laws when the colonial government sponsored a review of liquor policy in 1934.[170]

[165] Interview with Anita Mensah, Takoradi, 5 March 1992.

[166] Ibid.

[167] Though fictionalized, Kofi Awoonor, *This Earth, My Brother* (Portsmouth, 1972), contains valuable information for the social historian of alcohol. He includes detailed descriptions of daily life in the Anlo inland village of Deme in the 1930s and 1940s.

[168] Interview with S.S. Dotse, Keta, 19 September 1996. Another Anlo nickname for *akpeteshie* was *vevetô*, the 'smelly one'. Personal correspondence from G.K. Nukunya, 28 September 1999.

[169] Notes of Evidence, 1930 Liquor Commission Report

[170] Gold Coast, *Correspondence and Statistics Relating to the Consumption of Spirits in the Gold Coast* (Accra, 1934).

Land Reclamation, Migrant Fishing, Shallot Cultivation & Illicit Distillation

As demand for local gin grew, sugar cane cultivation spread to the drier parts of the Keta Lagoon. Anlo schoolboys could easily buy *akpeteshie* at Anyako in the 1930s.[171] Dzodze with its considerable oil palm plantations has featured as an active centre of *akpeteshie* distillation right into the postcolonial period.[172] Illicit liquor traffic was profitable and the profits encouraged the brave. But the vicissitudes of the trade are captured in the life story of 'Tailor' in Kofi Awoonor's *This Earth, My Brother*. Tailor had sought quick riches through the smuggling of illicit gin:

> He was middle-aged, and as he himself said, had been rich once upon a time. He had worked with the famous District Commissioner, John Miller, to build the road from Keta to the Volta River and beyond. He had been strong once. After that he made money smuggling akpeteshie, the local gin which the colonial government declared unwholesome. One day a lorry carrying a large quantity of his gin was arrested at the riverside. The drink was poured into the river; he himself was arrested at Fiaxo where he had taken refuge. After two years in prison he came back home, broken. His three wives had married other people, three of his sons had gone up country into the cocoa area, the other two had joined a fishing company in Abidjan. His daughter Amavi took the mammy truck and vanished to Accra.[173]

Though fictionalized, Tailor's life account above sums up socio-economic strategies in Anlo in the 1930s and 1940s: migrating to cocoa areas as agricultural labourers and farmers; migrant maritime fishing; and, for women, trading and more beneficial marriage arrangements. *Akpeteshie* thrives as an important industry in Anlo. Once distillation was legalized in independent Ghana, the first liquor factory was established at Adutor in the Keta-Ada District, drawing on the sugar cane plantations in the area for its raw material.[174]

An important paradox in Anlo history is that Keta maintained its prosperity into the 1960s, postponing the decline that was inevitable following sustained coastal erosion and the weakening of Keta's ability to serve as the point of distribution in the regional economy. As residents of Keta and its immediate environs draw their livelihood also from sea fishing and salt making, the continued viability of these industries generated a false sense of economic continuity and security. When decline came in the 1960s, it followed the wake of certain economic decisions made by the independent Ghanaian government, giving Keta's imminent decline a political face. Let us now examine the reasons for Keta's continued prosperity in the face of ecological disaster in the 1930s up to the mid-1950s.

A stay of execution? Continued economic prosperity in Keta

The period between 1930 and 1957 showed that Keta's – and Anlo's – economy hinged on its famous market. This was in spite of repeated failures in the fishing season in the 1930s and 1940s. The fishing season was poor from September 1938 to June

[171] Interview with Freda Adabanu, Keta, 20 September 1996.
[172] NAG, Ho, KE/c.846.
[173] Awoonor, *This Earth*, 71.
[174] Ghana, *Report of the Committee Appointed to Enquire into the Manner of Operation of State Distilleries Corporation* (Accra, 1968), 5.

1939. The quarterly report for the Keta District in June 1939 bemoaned the fact that: '[Instead] of as many as a hundred lorries, loaded with dried fish, leaving Keta every market day, there are now a mere thirty to forty. Most of them are carrying corn and other produce'.[175] The *afafa* season was again unsatisfactory in the last quarter of 1939.[176] Though the fishing seasons from 1945 to 1949 were considered relatively good ones in the Gold Coast,[177] the Keta District continued to have bad spells. The 1947 *afafa* season ended abruptly. The DC noted that:

> The Afafa season ended early in December. It was the worst in quantity for many a year, though the fishermen did not lose much, as the price of the fish was very high owing to scarcity. A freak storm in mid-November did considerable damage to their nets. Two were lost completely each of the approximate value of £600. Neither was insured.[178]

The years from 1949 to 1954 were considered poor fishing seasons in Gold Coast waters.[179] These bad seasons no doubt underpinned the increased migration of Anlo maritime fisherman to neighbouring coastal waters. Salt making in the Keta District also underwent setbacks in the period covered by this chapter. In 1950 the natural process of salt crystallization north of the Keta Lagoon ceased abruptly. Hill reports that though annual salt production had always varied, 'there is no local recollection of previous total failure over such a long time'.[180] Salt making appears not to have resumed its normal regime until the mid-1960s.

Table 5.1: Imports and exports, 1948–50 (tonnage handled by Gold Coast ports).

	Takoradi	Cape Coast	Winneba	Accra	Keta	Total
Imports						
1948	443,797	9,396	4,885	185,513	3,481	645,072
1949	555,754	15,275	13,056	273,386	6,681	864,152
1950	584,577	22,260	20,930	244,815	8,116	880,698
Exports						
1948	1,179,309	7,493	16,195	55,583	—	1,258,580
1949	1,318,617	6,227	12,733	65,206	2	1,402,785
1950	1,279,538	8,039	18,792	66,164	—	1,372,533

Source: PRO, CO 554/465. Office of the Government Statistician, 'Notes on the future port requirements in the Gold Coast' (31 May 1951).

Yet Keta market thrived. It continued its distribution role, and market revenue totalled £5,000–£6,000 a year in the early 1950s.[181] But the focus was equally – if not more – on distributing goods produced in the subregion, and not just imported European merchandise. Keta market was patronized for Anloga shallot and Agbozume

[175] NAG, Accra, ADM 39/1/303. Report on the Keta District, June Quarter, 1939.
[176] Ibid. Report on the Keta District, December Quarter, 1939.
[177] Colonial Office, *Report on the Gold Coast 1954* (London, 1956), 50.
[178] NAG, Accra, ADM 39/1/303. Quarterly Report on the Native Affairs of the Keta District for the Quarter Ended 31 December 1947.
[179] Colonial Office, *Report on the Gold Coast 1954*, 50.
[180] Hill, *Studies in Rural Capitalism*, 32.
[181] NAG, Accra, ADM 39/1/712. Quarterly Report, Keta District, January–March 1953.

Kente textiles, as well as Keta fish. Ships continued to call at Keta port, though not in the numbers that characterized the early twentieth century.[182] Statistics on shipping imports and exports between 1948 and 1950 underscored the weakened position of Keta's port, especially when compared with the four other ports in the Gold Coast (Table 5.1). Only two ships called at Keta port in the quarter from April to June 1952. The numbers were up slightly in January–March 1953, and six ships called at Keta port and landed 3,380 tons of cement and 47 tons of general cargo.[183]

Awoamefia Sri II and his chiefs affirmed the market's centrality to the Anlo economy in a 1943 petition to the Secretary of State:

That our existence as a state and, particularly, the hopes we entertain for a better future – politically, educationally and commercially speaking – centre around the town of Keta within which is situated a market that, unsurpassed by any other local one in the volume and worth of trade done, attracts commercial adventurers and others from such widely scattered places as the Western Province of the Colony, Ashanti and the Northern Territories, French Dahomey and even Lagos, not to mention the enormous overseas trade in imported goods carried through the town in peace time, to which the cluster of stores of all sizes around the extensive market area bears convincing testimony.[184]

And Keta market would continue to play an integral role in the Anlo economy into the 1960s. As late as 1976, Chapman Klutse could, with a little stretching of the imagination, describe Keta as a 'nodal town and the market here flourishes, despite the housing problem, flooding, etc'.[185] Yaw Boateng, grandson of a Kwahu trader who settled in Keta, captured for the author what Keta market-day was like in the 1960s:

Today is the day before market-day. In the 1960s, this entire place would have been a hive of activity with articulators [cargo trucks] parked all over, bringing goods. They would buy *abɔbi*, the 'Keta schoolboys' [the Ghanaian nickname for anchovy]. All these small stores that line the side of the market would be full of Zamarama [Zabrama] people [northern traders].[186] The lorry station would be still bustling with people at midnight and the Zamarama shops would still be open. In the 1960s, I would not have had time to sit and talk with you like this. We would open the store at 5.30 a.m. or 6.00 a.m. on market days and stay open until 8.00 p.m. or even 9.00 p.m. You sold goods continuously. Prices were not expensive too. Those behind the lagoon, Anyako and other places, they would come here on market-day. When you went to the lagoon side, boats would have drawn up all along the market edge. We would come early in the morning to find these traders or customers actually sitting in front of the bank waiting for us to come and open the shop. So business started right from the moment we opened up shop. One did not even have the time to eat, so I would buy roasted ripe plantain and snack in between helping customers.

---

[182] See Chapter 3.

[183] Office of the Government Statistician, 'Notes on the future port requirements in the Gold Coast' (31 May 1951). Quarterly Report, Keta District, April–June 1952; Quarterly Report, Keta District, January–March 1953.

[184] PRO, CO 96/770/1. Petition by Togbi Sri II and others to Secretary of State, 21 September 1943.

[185] Klutse, *Keta Coast Erosion*, 17.

[186] In the 1860s Songhai-speaking Zabrama horsemen came from the region of modern Niger to serve the ruler of Dagomba in what became the Northern Territories of the Gold Coast. Today, 'Zabrama' and 'Hausa' have become loose categories for describing non-Ghanaians of northern origin. See Daniel M. McFarland, *Historical Dictionary of Ghana* (Metuchen, 1985), 196.

The market was huge and filled with people. Children always got lost in the maze of the market, and we would go through the market announcing that so-and-so's child is lost, and the finder should bring the child to our shop.[187]

The author often stood gazing at the empty stalls of Keta market during fieldwork in 1996 and 1997. He wondered what had made it special. Yaw Boateng put it simply: 'what made it [Keta market] big was the people'.[188] And, as long as people came to Keta on market-days, Keta and Anlo thrived.

Conclusion

This chapter has traced Anlo socio-economic strategies of survival in the wake of pernicious coastal erosion at Keta and the rather half-hearted attempts by the colonial government to halt the sea's onslaught. As far as the colonial government was concerned, the issue was closed: effective sea defence works would be too expensive and the solution was for Keta residents to relocate. Residents of Keta refused to budge for what was often labelled sentimental reasons. But in truth, Keta's economy and prosperity were based on salt, fish and its market and, as long as these three remained viable, the incentive to remain was great. Anlo strategies of survival from 1930 included migrant maritime fishing, intensive commercial cultivation of shallots and the distillation of illicit gin. Underpinned by its famous market, Keta continued to prosper and was indeed made the regional capital for the new Volta Region on independence when the country was divided into administrative regions. When Keta's economy stumbled in the 1960s and began its effective decline, it was associated with certain decisions in political ecology. First was the decision to close Keta's port in 1962. A second deep-water harbour had been opened in Tema in 1962, and the government considered this sufficient for handling imports and exports for the eastern half of the country. The government closed the surf ports at Keta, Accra, Winneba and Cape Coast. This was followed by the disastrous Kedzi canal of 1963, which sought to release waters from the swollen Keta Lagoon into the Atlantic Ocean. The result was to render dangerous the approach to Keta market, and traders were unwilling to risk their lives. People ceased coming to Keta market and Anloga market emerged as a viable alternative. The Anlo blamed these inimical economic developments and what was believed to be a noticeable decline in lagoon and maritime fishing on the government and on development projects that had altered the Anlo hydrology. The next chapter examines harbours and dams and their impact on the Anlo environment.

[187] Interview with Yaw Boateng, Keta, 16 October 1996.
[188] Ibid.

158

6

Harbours & Dams
Economic Development & Environmental Change
in the Lower Volta Basin, 1957 to the Present

Introduction

James Giblin's study of the politics of environmental control in north-eastern Tanzania between 1840 and 1940 emphasizes the importance of political authority in shaping environmental and demographic processes.[1] Local networks of patronage, redistribution and trade had enabled residents of Uzigua District to survive and even prosper despite their harsh environment. These facilitated continued residence and the control of vegetation, which kept disease vectors and famine at bay. German and British colonial policies destroyed these networks and reorientated existing trade patterns. Famines became severe and, as migration vitiated control of vegetation, trypanosomiasis and theileriosis epizootics became rife. This chapter examines the development of harbours and dams and why the Anlo viewed these as adversely affecting their environment. Emphasis is placed on these local perceptions of environmental change, though sometimes contradicted by scientific evidence, because they shed light on the social interpretation of environmental change. The Anlo also considered as evidence of political and economic marginalization the fact that these development projects were all sited west of the Volta. This pattern unified the peoples of the lower Volta basin in a concerted protest against the political economy of colonial and independent Ghanaian governments and obliterated old enmities, such as that between Anlo and Ada.

The Anlo have explicitly linked artificial deep-water harbours and the construction of hydroelectric dams on the Volta River to intense erosion of the Anlo coast, as well as to a decline in fish stocks in both lagoon and maritime fishing. The abundance of mosquitoes in Anlo and the spread of schistosomiasis in the lower Volta below the dam are some of the epidemiological changes wrought by the construction of the Akosombo Dam in the mid-1960s and the Kpong Dam in 1982. These

[1] James L. Giblin, *The Politics of Environmental Control in Northeastern Tanzania, 1840–1940* (Philadelphia, 1992).

159

developments have been worsened by frequent migrations in a depressed economy, as weeds grow prolifically around the Keta Lagoon and provide breeding places for mosquitoes and constant mobility renders disease transmission cycles difficult to break. The importance of development projects, such as harbours and dams, to national governments have tended to minimize their deleterious impact on the environment, health and the livelihoods of those displaced by these projects. Feasibility studies that precede such projects often discount the environmental and health implications. Manning cites the example of the deep-water port at Cotonou. The port altered the hydrology around Cotonou:

> At the end of the colonial era, the construction of the deep-water port at Cotonou, though modernizing the Atlantic commerce, compromised life on the lagoons. The port's breakwater interrupted the eastward transport of sand and caused the lagoon's opening to the sea to become permanent, thus sharply increasing the salinity of Lake Nokoue and causing the yield of fish to decline.[2]

Likewise, the interconnectedness of the hydrological regime of the lower Volta basin – the river, lagoons and the Atlantic Ocean – gave alterations in the hydrology unforeseen consequences. Traditionally, dams and irrigation schemes have been associated with malaria, schistosomiasis, trypanosomiasis and onchocerciasis. These may be associated with the lake created by the dam or the river section below the dam.[3] Though not all Anlo claims about the causes of their environmental collapse can be scientifically verified, they point to a subtle awareness that political authority is a major influence on environmental and demographic processes.

Harbours and sea erosion in Anlo

The British annexation of gold-rich Asante in 1896 boosted investor confidence and led to the granting of several mining concessions in Asante and the Western and Central Provinces of the Gold Coast colony. This coincided with the growth of the cocoa industry, and together they created the need for adequate port facilities and an internal transport network. Mechanized mining required that heavy machinery be offloaded at a suitable port and transported to the interior mines, and cocoa and other products needed to be conveyed to the ports for export. In 1898 the colonial government began the construction of a railway network from Sekondi, and Sekondi and Accra would become the coastal termini of the railway system. Surf ports proved inefficient in the Gold Coast's shift to mechanized mining, cash-crop exports and expanded commerce. Ocean-going vessels could not be serviced, the offloading of

---

[2] Patrick Manning, 'Coastal society in the Republic of Benin: reproduction of a regional system', *Cahiers d'Etudes Africaines* 114, xxix–2 (1989): 251–2.

[3] See, for examples, L.E. Obeng, ed., *Man-Made Lakes* (Accra, 1969); William H. McNeill, *Plagues and Peoples* (New York, 1977), ch. 3; Ralph K. Klumpp, 'A study of the transmission of *Schistosoma haematobium* in Volta Lake, Ghana' (PhD thesis, London School of Hygiene and Tropical Medicine, 1983); M.B.K. Darkoh, ed., *African River Basins and Dryland Crises* (Uppsala, 1992); and Helmut Kloos, ed., *The Ecology of Health and Disease in Ethiopia* (San Francisco, 1993).

heavy equipment was inconvenient, damage to merchandise was common and the numerous ports of call made freight expensive.

The need for a deep-water harbour was felt by the late nineteenth century. In 1895 Joseph Chamberlain (Colonial Secretary) authorized the London firm of civil engineers, Messrs Coode, Son and Matthews, to advise on the siting of two harbours in the Gold Coast and to investigate the constantly shifting sand bar at the mouth of the Volta in Ada. The report was completed in 1897. Its findings would lead to the construction of the Gold Coast's first deep-water harbour:

> It recommended Takoradi Bay as the site for a deep-water harbour. Though this was not to be started for another twenty-five years, it was never questioned as the best site. In the east of the country, it recommended a breakwater, and a jetty with steam cranes, for Accra.[4]

The report was unfavourable in respect of Ada as a site for a deep-water harbour. The improvements at the Accra port were put into immediate effect. The volume of trade continued to expand, and the colonial government in 1900 decided to make the then open roadstead of Sekondi a lighter port. Breakwaters and jetties were constructed at Sekondi to enable lighters to work alongside ocean vessels, which lay at anchor in the open seaway. The early twentieth century coincided also with a world demand for manganese, of which the Gold Coast had respectable reserves, so lighters loaded manganese and offloaded mining machinery, coal for the railway engines and other goods. Heavy surf at times required the use of surf boats to load cocoa and offload general merchandise, and these worked alongside the lighters.[5] When Governor F.G. Guggisberg assumed the office of governor of the Gold Coast in 1919, he took up the need for a deep-water harbour in his ten-year development plan.

Guggisberg was an engineer, and providing the colony with a decent socio-economic infrastructure was central to his administration and his vision of a prosperous Gold Coast. His development plan was ambitious:

> This was to involve a total expenditure of £25 million; £2 million was earmarked for the construction of a harbour, £14.5 for railways, £1 million for roads, £1.9 million for water supplies, £1.9 million for town improvements and drainage, £2 million for hydraulic and electric works, £1 million for public buildings including Achimota [college], £90,000 for posts and telegraphs, and £200,000 for maps and surveys.[6]

The engineering firm of Messrs Stewart and McDonnell was appointed as a consultant to survey the coast and choose a suitable site for the deep-water harbour. The firm confirmed the earlier choice of Takoradi in its 1920 report and also provided useful information on the geology of the entire coastline of the colony:

> Saltpond is geographically the most central point of the coast line, but from that point eastward to the boundary of the colony (with the exception of the Volta mouth which is dealt with separately) and westward to the entrance of the Prah river into the Shama Bay, the coast is

[4] James Moxon, *Volta, Man's Greatest Lake: The Story of Ghana's Akosombo Dam* (London, 1984), 40. This is a highly readable reconstruction of the history of the Volta River and the Volta River Project.

[5] PRO, CO 554/104/9. West African Harbours. See Chapter 3 for a brief history of Gold Coast surf ports up to the early twentieth century.

[6] A.A. Boahen, *Ghana: Evolution and Change in the Nineteenth and Twentieth Centuries* (London, 1975), 110.

unsuitable. The shore is practically one continuous sandy beach shoaling very gradually from deep water.[7]

The engineers opined that any breakwater constructed in this part of the shoreline would form a sand trap, 'since the stilling of the water would tend to cause precipitation of any sand entering the protected area, and at the same time to prevent any equalising process of erosion from wave action'.[8] This useful piece of information would come in handy in the 1950s when the site of the Gold Coast's second deepwater harbour became a hotly contested issue.

Takoradi harbour was built between 1921 and 1928 under the technical supervision of Messrs Rendall, Triton and Palmer and was opened officially on 3 April 1928. Its total cost was about £3.4 million, almost double the initial estimate, but the end result was gratifying. J.H. Thomas, who attended the harbour's opening ceremony, described the engineering feat:

> Accommodation is provided for nine ocean going vessels, excluding ships engaged in loading manganese, and there are twenty sets of moorings for smaller craft. The area contained within the two breakwaters is approximately two hundred and twenty acres. In provision of equipment, of public buildings, of roads of access and of railway facilities, every care has been taken to meet the requirements of modern traffic, and we may fairly claim that the port is worthy of those who have been responsible for its design and construction.[9]

The party of distinguished guests that graced the opening of the harbour drove along the concrete drive that runs the entire length of the main breakwater and were suitably impressed. The new governor, Ransford S. Slater, informed the Colonial Office:

> From this point the harbour presents, perhaps, its most impressive appearance, and the sight of that huge sheet of unruffled water, protected from the storms and breakers of the Atlantic by massive blocks of granite, is one that cannot fail to evoke admiration.[10]

But it is the construction of these admirable breakwaters – the taming of the waves – that the Anlo claim has altered wave patterns and the littoral drift of sand, thus aggravating erosion along the Keta foreshore.

In a 1994 television documentary on the history of coastal erosion at Keta, an eighty-two-year-old Keta educationist, Nathaniel Tamakloe, recollected the onset of coastal erosion at Keta and how this coincided with the construction of Takoradi harbour.[11] He was a school pupil when the Takoradi harbour was under construction. He noted that shortly after the building of Takoradi harbour the sea began to pose a greater danger to old Keta. Much of present-day Keta stands on land reclaimed from the lagoon. Elderly Anlo appear to be convinced of the connection between Takoradi

[7] PRO, CO 554/465. 'Opinions concerning the site of a new harbour for the Gold Coast'.
[8] Ibid.
[9] PRO, CO 96/677/13. Address of welcome presented by the Legislative Council of the Gold Coast to the Right Honorable J.H. Thomas (MP) on the opening of Takoradi Harbour, 3 April 1928.
[10] Ibid. Governor Slater to L.S. Amery, Accra, 7 April 1928.
[11] Ghana Broadcasting Corporation (GBC), 15 July 1994.

harbour and intensive erosion at Keta. The late Togbui James Ocloo IV informed the author that severe erosion at Keta dates from the commencement of work on Takoradi harbour in 1921. He had been a pupil at the Society for the Propagation of the Gospel school in Sekondi and had been an eyewitness to the effect of the new breakwaters. The breakwaters diverted the wave pattern and erosion intensified in neighbouring Sekondi. A sea defence wall was put in place in Sekondi. This protection diverted the force of the waves eastward, and erosion was reported at Accra. This necessitated sea defence works at James Town. Again the force of the waves was diverted eastward and erosion progressed in the area of Ada and Anlo.[12] The Anlo had made astute connections between successive sea defence works east of Takoradi and the construction of the harbour. In the opinion of Anlo, the colonial government failed to halt the situation in Keta by implementing similar sea defence works.

Though the author lacked technical expertise, it struck him as a bit far-fetched that a harbour at one end of the colony could influence coastal erosion at the other end of the colony. The Anlo geographer, Togbuivi Kumassah, offered an explanation:

Harbour construction is a way of taming the waves so that there will be calm water for ships to come into. Meanwhile, a wall is constructed into the sea. So it affects the normal movement of tides, the drifts, the waves along the coast. Instead of the waves perhaps depositing themselves here, they have been forced out of that area to break at another point, and who knows the distance they could cover before breaking on the point? What people have cited as evidence that the two harbours – Takoradi and Tema – were partially responsible was that the rate at which the waves were destroying the coast appeared quickened from 1927 when Takoradi harbour was constructed [opened to traffic]. Now, if the construction of these harbours contributed to [coincided with] the quickening of the pace of destruction, the people will easily conclude that these harbours are also responsible for the destruction of the coastline.[13]

David Atta-Peters, a geologist at the University of Ghana, provided further illumination. The question was whether the combination of deep-water harbours and sea defence works west of the Volta could influence wave patterns and erosion east of the Volta. Atta-Peters confirmed that breakwaters divert waves along the coastline. Judging from the distance between Tema and Keta, he doubted that the force of waves diverted from Tema would extend that far. And Takoradi is even more distant from Anlo than Tema. Sea defence projects are built to face the angle at which the ocean waves strike the coast. Similarly, these waves are diverted eastward in the Gold Coast and may accentuate coastal erosion. But the distance between the sea defence works in Sekondi and Accra and the Anlo coast again makes it unlikely that these have a direct bearing on erosion along the Anlo coast.[14] Yet Togbui James Ocloo IV and many others are firmly convinced that the construction of a deep-water harbour at Takoradi and a dry dock at Tema actually worsened erosion at Keta.

Tema harbour is a particularly sore point in the Anlo interpretation of political ecology. It reminded communities of the lower Volta basin of years of neglect by colonial and postcolonial governments. In the late 1930s, a South African engineer,

[12] Interview with Togbui James Ocloo IV, Keta, 4 September 1996.
[13] Interview with Togbuivi Kumassah, Woe, 3 September 1996.
[14] Interview with David Atta-Peters, Legon, 13 December 1996.

Duncan Rose, developed a complex scheme to establish a hydroelectric dam on the Volta. The scheme included building an alumina plant to transform bauxite from deposits in Kwahu and Asante into alumina, a smelter and a deep-water port at Ada to facilitate the export of aluminium and the import of heavy machinery. He intended to dredge the Volta from the estuary to the dam site at Ajena (a distance of 72 miles) to improve water transport. The states of Anlo, Ada, Osudoku, Akwamu, Peki and the Tongu Confederacy were delighted. At last, 'development' had come to the lower Volta basin. The decision to relocate the new harbour to Tema (near Accra) was a major disappointment for these states. The ancillary industries that were associated with the hydroelectric scheme were also sited at Tema, the new industrial town. But a discussion of Tema harbour and its significance for Anlo is best carried out within the context of the hydroelectric scheme on the River Volta.

Hydroelectric dams and economic development

The history of the Akosombo Dam goes back to 1915 when A.E. Kitson, Director of Geological Survey in the Gold Coast, explored the Volta River and commented on the suitability of Akosombo (near the Ajena gorge) for a hydroelectric dam. The Volta River in the Gold Coast represents the merger of four major rivers: the Black, White and Red Voltas, with their source in Burkina Faso, and the Oti River, which rises in the Republic of Benin as the Pandjori. The Volta takes its recognizable form at the merger of the Black and White Voltas just north of Bui. The Volta then flows for 300 miles southward into the sea, as the Red Volta and the Oti join it. The volume of water and the velocity of the Volta in the Gold Coast make it ideal for damming, especially at its two gorges at Bui and Ajena.[15] In 1914 Kitson had established the existence of extensive bauxite deposits on Mt Ejuanema in Kwahu, and he now mooted the idea of building an alumina plant and smelter based on cheap hydroelectric power.[16] In 1924–5 Kitson submitted a report or bulletin to the Gold Coast government. He proposed an integrated development plan for the Volta basin, which involved the transformation of bauxite into alumina and the smelting of aluminium from alumina based on the waters and hydroelectric power of the propounded dam. Kitson also recommended the creation of a canal on the lower Volta and the irrigation of the Accra plains. But Governor Guggisberg, already saddled with his ten-year development plan, decided to shelve Kitson's proposals for the time being.[17] The project was revived in the late 1930s by private initiative and with the additional feature of a deep-water port at Ada. The alumina plant and smelter were to be established near the dam.[18] The Gold Coast government appropriated the Volta River Project in the late 1940s and shed the features desired by the Voltaic states – for

[15] Moxon, *Volta*, 23–4.
[16] Kwamina Barnes, *Economics of the Volta River Project* (Tema, 1966), 1.
[17] Gold Coast, *Development of the Volta River Basin: A Statement by the Government of the Gold Coast on the Volta River Project and Related Matters* (Accra, 1952); Moxon, *Volta*, 49–50.
[18] PRO, CO 96/825/5. Press release, 'Development of the Volta River basin', 3 February 1950.

instance, the harbour at Ada and siting the alumina plant and smelter near the dam, that is, in Akwamu territory. Though the government's actions were based on geological and entomological surveys and recommendations, the Voltaic states felt victimized and unified in a coherent critique of the colonial government and the first African government.

In November 1938 Duncan Rose, the South African engineer, read Kitson's bulletin in a Johannesburg public library. He was intrigued by Kitson's proposals and arranged a visit to the Gold Coast in February 1939. The Second World War was imminent, and Rose appreciated the value of a sterling source of aluminium. He went back to South Africa and formed the African Aluminium Company, which included Christopher St John Bird, a geological engineer. Rose and Bird returned to the Gold Coast in May 1939: Rose to secure bauxite concessions from the colonial government in Mpraeso (Kwahu) and Yenahin (Asante), and Bird to conduct a geological survey of the Ajena gorge.[19] Bird confirmed the suitability of Ajena gorge for a dam, and his evaluation of the project revised Rose's modest project, with an estimated cost of £2.5–£3.5 million, to a much larger project, with a cost estimate of £6.5 million. Rose met the relevant chiefs whose lands abutted the crucial 7-mile Ajena gorge where the dam would be sited, and arranged to secure rights over the gorge. The Second World War intervened and the entire project was postponed until 1944.[20]

By the time Rose and Bird returned to the Gold Coast in 1944–5, the aluminium project in the Gold Coast had attracted international attention. There was a strong demand for aluminium on the world market, and larger concerns were interested in Rose's newly formed West African Aluminium Limited.[21] In June 1949 the Aluminium Company of Canada secured a 25 per cent interest in Rose's company. The British government, through the British Aluminium Company Limited, was exploring prospects for producing aluminium in North Borneo. It was doubted that the sterling community needed two large aluminium producers, and a joint commission comprising the British and Canadian aluminium companies was established to investigate the Gold Coast and North Borneo schemes and recommend one. Britain and Canada agreed to collaborate on either North Borneo or the Gold Coast scheme, whichever was selected.[22] By this time even the United States had become interested in the Gold Coast aluminium project and wanted to be part of the action.[23] Bird's report appeared in September 1949, and it highlighted the fact that the dam at Ajena would create an artificial lake covering an expanse of over 1,000 square miles. It was apparent to the Gold Coast government that a scheme of this magnitude would require the delicate handling and resettlement of several displaced communities. The potential of the scheme for the colony's economic development was also immense. This was not a project for a private company; the Volta River Project had to become

---

[19] Moxon, *Volta*, 52–3. Large deposits of bauxite were discovered at Awaso in the Western Province and informed the post-Second World War development plans for the Gold Coast.

[20] Ibid., 53.

[21] Barnes, *Economics of the Volta River Project*, 2.

[22] PRO, CO 96/825/5; Gold Coast, *Development of the Volta River Basin*.

[23] Ibid. Memorandum by Sir Hilton Poynton of a conversation with Ervin Anderson (US Economic Corporation Administration), London, 18 January 1950.

a public concern.[24] In late 1949 the British and Gold Coast colonial governments commissioned the London engineering firm of Sir William Halcrow and Partners to 'examine the proposed power scheme and report on the wider aspects of the development of the Volta River Basin in respect of health, navigation, and communication'.[25] The *Manchester Guardian* reported on 6 January 1950 that five engineers from Halcrow were departing for the Gold Coast the following day to commence the survey of the Volta River Project for the Gold Coast government.

Halcrow's preliminary report was ready in July 1950, and it confirmed the possibility of Ajena gorge as a feasible site for the dam and the alumina plant and smelter as crucial if such a large dam was to be economically viable.[26] But, pending geological studies, the report did not give Ajena a definitive endorsement. Halcrow's report differed from the Rose scheme in its choice of a port, and its rejection of Ada removed the necessity of making the portion of the lower Volta between Ajena and the estuary navigable:

> Our view is that the cost of the works and necessary maintenance would not be justified by the traffic and the port of Ada would prove of little strategic or economic value to the Colony itself.
>
> The Gold Coast has at present only one large port, Takoradi, and a second modern and well-equipped port further east would greatly benefit the economy of the Colony. For various reasons Accra is an unsuitable site for such a port and we recommend detailed consideration of Tema which appears to hold favourable prospects, or alternatively, of Teshi.[27]

Halcrow, in a private communication to the Colonial Office, also expressed concern that a breakwater at Ada could accentuate coastal erosion on the Anlo coast, considering the constantly changing profile of the sea and river bed. He opined that:

> Erosion is already seriously affecting the Keta coastline, east of the river mouth and the construction of a breakwater will aggravate this. This erosion will form, in addition, a threat to the stability of the proposed works for closing the river mouth, which form an essential part of the scheme.[28]

This appears to confirm Anlo observations about harbours and coastal erosion, though in this case Ada was close enough to the Anlo coast to cause legitimate concern.

The entomological survey conducted as part of the Volta River Project eliminated the choice of Ada as a port. The extensive mangrove swamp and the *Paspalum* marsh at Ada made it the ideal breeding place for the *Anopheles gambiae melas*. The health and financial implications of selecting Ada as a port were thus enormous:

> If Ada is selected as the harbour site, extensive control measures will be required to protect the permanent personnel, as well as the crews of ships which dock in the harbour. The location in a

---

[24] Moxon, *Volta*, 57, 62; Barnes, *Economics of the Volta River Project*, 2.

[25] Keith Jopp, *Volta: The Story of Ghana's Volta River Project* (Accra, 1965), 11.

[26] PRO, CO 96/825/5. Government of the Gold Coast, by Sir William Halcrow and Partners, *Preliminary Report on Development of the River Volta Basin* (July 1950).

[27] Ibid.

[28] PRO, CO 96/828/7. William Halcrow and Partners to C.G. Eastwood (Colonial Office), London, 22 March 1951.

veritable marsh will mean that control will be costly, as considerable drainage and larviciding will be required.[29]

The entomologist, an American named Lewis Berner, also recommended either Tema or Teshi. The report of the Joint Commission set up to examine the relative advantages of the Gold Coast and North Borneo aluminium projects also came out in favour of the Gold Coast in March 1951, and all seemed set for the commencement of the Volta River Project.[30]

The Voltaic lobby was filled with dismay at the rejection of Ada as a port by the Halcrow report. Whereas subsequent geological studies under the auspices of Halcrow eventually approved Ajena as an ideal site for the dam,[31] Halcrow's final report, in August 1951, strongly recommended Tema as the port site and suggested that the smelter be located in Tema also.[32] Even the towns to be served with electricity from the new dam included none east of the Volta, as the economics of the project favoured mining towns and larger cities such as Accra, Sekondi-Takoradi and Kumasi. The paramount chiefs of the lower Volta basin – Nene Dake II of Ada, Nana Kwafo Akoto II of Akwamu, Awoamefia Sri II of Anlo, Kwadzo Dei X of Peki, Kwaku Animle IV of Osudoku and C.K. Anipati III of the Tongu Confederacy – cabled the Colonial Secretary in London condemning Halcrow's choice of Tema and reiterating their support for Ada as a harbour site.[33] Economic expediency had muted old hostilities that pitted Ada and Osudoku against Anlo and Akwamu.[34]

In the interval between Halcrow's preliminary and final reports, political conditions in the Gold Coast had changed dramatically. The surge of African nationalism had resulted in general elections in January 1951 to form the first African government. The Convention People's Party (CPP) led by Kwame Nkrumah emerged victorious and the new African government displayed a keen proprietary interest in the ongoing Volta Project Survey as part of its broader industrialization plans. In 1952 the Gold Coast government published a white paper accepting Halcrow's proposals and initiated a feasibility study at Tema.[35] The government's position had been foreshadowed in December 1950, when Nkrumah announced in the Legislative Assembly that the government intended to proceed with plans for a harbour at Tema irrespective of the final outcome of the Volta River Survey. It cited congestion at Takoradi and Accra ports as evidence that a new modern port was necessary.[36] The response of the Voltaic constituency was immediate. The paramount chiefs of the lower Volta region met at Dodowa to pass a resolution. In this they lamented the insensitivity of the Gold Coast government to their repeated petitions on the harbour question. The chiefs cited the support of the West African

[29] Lewis Berner, *Entomological Report on Development of the River Volta Basin* (Westminster, 1950), 26.

[30] Moxon, *Volta*, 59.

[31] PRO CO, 96/828/6. Frank E. Fahlquist, *Progress Report on Geology Volta River Project Dam, Gold Coast Colony* (London, 1950).

[32] For the full report, see PRO, CO 96/828/7.

[33] PRO, CO 554/506. Cable of chiefs from the lower Volta basin to the Colonial Secretary, 14 November 1951.

[34] See Chapters 1 and 2.

[35] Gold Coast, *Development of the Volta River Basin.*

[36] PRO, CO 554/465. Press release no. 1539/51.

Aluminium Company and shipowners such as Elder Dempster and John Holt for Ada as a harbour and highlighted Halcrow as the lone voice in support of Tema. They considered it unconscionable that the Volta basin was to be exploited to the detriment of local communities and that none of the Voltaic towns were even to benefit from the electrification programme. The chiefs asserted that this was part of a deliberate neglect of the Gold Coast Volta region, which dated back to the British assumption of Danish influence in 1850. The chiefs stated that this resolution should serve as a final warning to the government 'not to interfere with our lands and the Volta River which we hold in sacred trust for our people and generations yet unborn'.[37] The divide between Gold Coast east and west of the Volta had been drawn in a rather belligerent fashion, but the cards were stacked against the communities east of the Volta. It seemed unjust that, to those who had much, more would be added, while the Volta region remained undeveloped. But the distribution of cocoa and mineral deposits had determined this pattern at the turn of the century, and the lines were only being etched more deeply.

A subsequent petition by the same signatories to the Colonial Secretary, Oliver Lyttelton, on his visit to the Gold Coast in 1952 revealed an awareness of how cocoa had restructured the Gold Coast economy to the detriment of the lower Volta basin. The chiefs remembered not so long ago when palm oil and palm kernels had dominated Gold Coast exports and the lower Volta area had been a valued contributor to the colonial economy. The advent of cocoa and railways ousted the palm oil and palm kernel trade, and trade was diverted to towns along the railway. The reorientation of trade 'seriously shook this Region to its foundation and it has ever since been miserably sinking down in desolation'.[38] The Duncan Rose scheme promised economic salvation for the area, but this had been sabotaged by the Halcrow report. The Volta chiefs pleaded that the Colonial Secretary should reinstate the Rose plan and site the dam at Ada with its attendant benefits or at least give instructions for a further study of the issue.

The British government did not want to derail the peaceful political transition in process in the Gold Coast. In light of the caution Messrs Stewart and McDonnell had expressed in 1920 about harbour works east of Saltpond, the Colonial Office suggested that the Gold Coast government agree to a second investigation of Tema. The firm of Messrs Coode, Vaughan-Lee, Frank and Gwyther were asked to examine the suitability of Tema.[39] Anlo hearts may have been filled with trepidation at the choice of Messrs Coode *et al.*, remembering the firm's investigation of coastal erosion at the Keta foreshore in 1929 and its damning report. D.C. Coode visited Tema in early February and, in its report of March 1952, Messrs Coode, Vaughan-Lee, Frank and Gwyther endorsed the choice of Tema.[40] The Anlo felt doubly let down.

[37] PRO, CO 554/506. Resolution passed by the Natural Rulers of the Lower Volta Region on 5 April 1952 at Dodowa.

[38] Ibid. Petition presented to Oliver Lyttelton, Secretary of State for the Colonies, by the paramount chiefs and chiefs of the Lower Volta Region of the Gold Coast Colony.

[39] PRO, CO 554/465. Telegram from the Secretary of State to the Governor of the Gold Coast, 18 December 1951.

[40] PRO, CO 554/465. Press release no. 377/52. Issued by the Ministry of Development, 28 March 1952.

The Lower Volta Basin, 1957 to the Present

But the same nationalist political processes in the Gold Coast that bred caution in the colonial government also made international capital wary about investing huge sums in the Volta River Project. Halcrow's estimate for the Volta River Project stood at £144 million, and prospective foreign investors sought certain assurances from the Gold Coast government that their interests would be protected. The British government and the British and Canadian aluminium companies pressed the Gold Coast government to set up a Preparatory Commission to re-examine in greater detail the Volta River Project and to report on its economic feasibility. The commission came into being in 1952 and submitted its report in 1955, again confirming the economic feasibility of the Volta River Project, but revising Halcrow's 1952 estimate of £144 million to £231 million.[41] This was enormously expensive, especially in the mid-1950s when the world demand for aluminium had dipped.[42] In March 1958 the Aluminium Company Limited of Canada announced that it was withdrawing its interest in the Volta River Project. Funding proved difficult, as Ghana had gained its independence in 1957 and investors preferred a wait-and-see attitude. Nkrumah turned to the United States for funding, and Ghana and the United States agreed to finance a reassessment of the project. Henry J. Kaiser Company of the United States was retained as a consulting engineer, and its report in 1959 selected Kitson's earlier choice of Akosombo as the dam site and recommended smaller dams at Kpong and Bui in the future as Ghana's power needs increased. They recommended siting the smelter at Tema. A pruning of the original plans resulted in a cost estimate of £130.7 million, and the Volta River Project materialized in the 1960s with funding from the governments of the United States, Britain and Ghana and the International Bank for Reconstruction and Development (World Bank). The smelter was built and operated by a private American company called Volta Aluminum Company (VALCO), and the Ghana government pledged not to appropriate it.[43] The dam and the administration of electricity were put under a public body called the Volta River Authority. Between 1977 and 1982 a smaller dam was built at Kpong, downstream from Akosombo, to augment the power supply from the Akosombo Dam.[44] Pilot irrigation schemes were launched in the endeavour to harness the stored water for agriculture on the Accra plains.

The environmental impact of dams

William Ackerman, Gilbert White and E. Worthington highlight the paradox that: 'Artificial lakes are symbols of economic advancement and also of dismay'.[45] Dams represent the greatest source of hydrological interference by humans.[46] Dams rapidly

[41] Barnes, *Economics of the Volta River Project*, 4–6; Moxon, *Volta*, 82–3; Jopp, *Ghana's Volta River Project*, 12.

[42] Jopp, *Ghana's Volta River Project*, 12.

[43] Ibid, 13–16.

[44] Moxon, *Volta*, 258–62.

[45] William C. Ackerman *et al.*, *Man-made Lakes: Their Problems and Environmental Effects* (Washington, DC, 1973), 3.

[46] Hassan A. Abdel Ati, 'The damming of the River Atbara and its downstream impact', in Darkoh, ed., *African River Basins*, 21.

transform terrestrial and riverine conditions into aquatic and lacustrine ones with immense implications for health and livelihood. Thus, the benefits of dams are heatedly contested, especially since other sources of power have become available.[47] The Volta Lake created by the Akosombo Dam is the largest human-made lake in the world and also one of the most studied in all its aspects.[48] The lake began to fill in 1964, and it eventually extended to a length of 250 miles upstream from the dam site, covering 3,275 square miles and with a shoreline of over 4,500 miles. In the process 738 villages were drowned and 80,000 people displaced. These were resettled in fifty-two new towns (Map 6.1).[49] Ironically, technical reports of the Volta River Project in the early 1950s had anticipated a less dramatic transformation:

> The submersion of the area of the [Volta Lake] reservoir would inundate very little of economic value; a recent enquiry into the effects of the proposed flooding has shown that the population likely to be displaced would number about 18,000, and that about 4,000 acres of cocoa would be submerged. A few Forest Reserves, created to preserve climatic conditions, would be affected in the area of the Afram plains. Little other disturbance to the normal life of the area north of the dam would be caused.[50]

The Volta Lake constitutes a mixed blessing for those who live around the lake and downstream from the dam. Considering the intricate links in the Anlo coastal hydrology, such an intrusive alteration of the Volta's flow was bound to affect the Anlo environment.

The Keta Lagoon is badly drained and hence floods its banks often. Its main sources of water are from the Volta and Todzie Rivers through the interconnecting channels and rainwater. It discharges its water slowly through the connecting channels back into the Volta and the sea or by evaporation. The lagoon sometimes overflows the sand bank into the sea.[51] The Volta is tidal up to Sopwe and the river feeds the connected lagoons brackish water, with the salt content becoming stronger during the dry season. Coincidentally, 1963 was an extremely wet year, and the Keta Lagoon flooded its banks with disastrous consequences for Anlo farmers. The following year the Volta was artificially interrupted to enable the Volta Lake to fill. For two years the Volta was virtually cut off below the Akosombo Dam, affecting the flow of water into the Angaw, Avu, Keta and other smaller lagoons in Anlo. In that interim, the flora and fauna of the lagoons were wiped out or drastically changed. Most of the lagoons supplied by the Volta have lost 50 per cent of their fauna since the 1960s.[52] Dams regulate a constant supply of water downstream, hence technically

[47] Ibid.

[48] See, for example, Obeng, *Man-made Lakes*; Moxon, *Volta*; Jopp, *Ghana's Volta River Project*; Barnes, *Economics of the Volta River Project*; Klumpp, '*Schistosoma haematobium* on Volta Lake'; R.K. Klumpp and K.Y. Chu, 'Ecological studies of *Bulinus rohlfsi*, the intermediate host of *Schistosoma haematobium* in the Volta Lake', *Bulletin of the World Health Organization* 55, 6 (1977): 715–30; K.Y. Chu, H.K. Kpo and R.K. Klumpp, 'Mixing of *Schistosoma haematobium* strains in Ghana', *Bulletin of the World Health Organization* 56, 4 (1978): 601–8.

[49] Moxon, *Volta*, ch. 16; Richard Ashong, 'A historical study of hydro electricity in Ghana' (BA thesis, History Department, University of Ghana, 1993), 19.

[50] PRO, CO 96/828/7. *Volta River Circular*, 25 January 1951.

[51] See Chapter 1 on Anlo's hydrology.

[52] Interview with A.K. Armah, oceanographer, Accra, 14 August 1997.

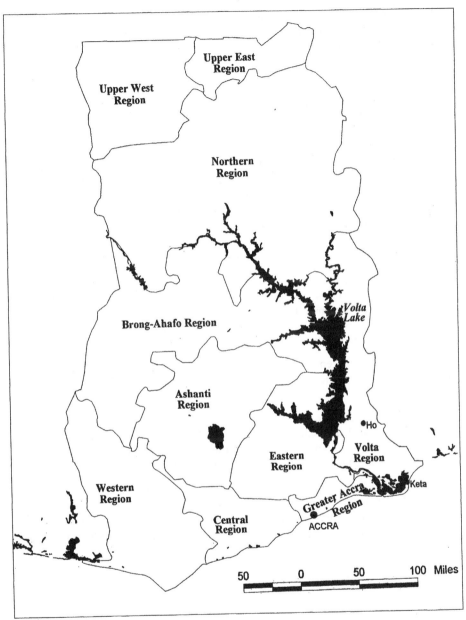

Map 6.1 Ghana showing administrative regions and Volta Lake.

the Volta dam would have ensured a steady flow of water downstream, minimizing the variations between the wet and dry seasons. But the 1970s and 1980s turned out to be extremely dry decades in West Africa, with frequent droughts. Between 1971 and 1983 the influx of the Volta River fell below average in nine years out of twelve. In 1982 the Volta recorded its lowest influx of water for forty-seven years, and 1983 turned out to be lower still.[53] Silting has been accelerated in the lower Volta and in the Avu and Keta Lagoons.[54] The drainage system in Anlo had thus been severely affected, and the extension of marsh and ponds in between houses in Keta, Adzido and Vodza bears strong evidence of an impaired drainage system (Photo 6.1).

Abdel Ati's study of the downstream impact of the Khashm El Ghirba Dam on the lower Atbara River in Sudan underscores the adverse environmental effects. The dam was constructed in 1964, and the discharge of the dam has continuously declined because of the dry spell in climate. Here again, minimum rainfall was recorded in the mid-1980s. The lower Atbara has suffered a severe drop in the amount of water passing downstream, erosion of the river channel, siltation and a decline in fish stocks.[55] Ati comments on how dams alter the habitat of fish:

> Ecologists point out several adverse effects of irrigation dams on downstream fish. The hindrance of up- and downstream movement of fish, obstruction by turbines, alteration of the river regime thus disturbing the breeding and feeding systems, the alteration of natural sedimentation rate which influences nutrients and dissolved oxygen levels, and the change in salinity and chemical structure of the river waters, are some of those adverse effects.[56]

Similar effects have been manifested downstream of the Volta dam, although the large artificial lake itself has become a major source of fish. According to one account in 1993:

> The formation of the lake brought in the wake an enormous increase in fish production. Currently the Volta Lake produces 40,000 metric tons of fish a year which is at least 10% of the national fish requirement. Among the most delicious species of fish inhabiting the lake are Nile Perch, Tilapia and mud fish. The number of people employed in the industry is about 20,000.[57]

The boom in fishing is countered by the disease epidemiology associated with water development projects. In particular, numerous studies highlight that schistosomiasis (bilharzia) becomes endemic in non-endemic areas after dam and irrigation projects.[58] The Volta is also plagued by onchocerciasis (river blindness),[59] and the

---

[53] Moxon, *Volta*, 290; Ashong, 'Hydro electricity in Ghana', 19.
[54] Interview with A.K. Armah, Accra, 14 August 1997.
[55] Ati, 'Damming of the River Atbara'.
[56] Ibid., 31.
[57] Ashong, 'Hydro electricity in Ghana', 29.
[58] For a good review of the literature, see Klumpp, '*Schistosoma haematobium* in Volta Lake', Ch. 1.
[59] See Stephen Younger and Jean-Baptiste Zongo, 'West Africa: The Onchocerciasis Control Program', in R. Bheenick, ed., *Successful Development in Africa: Case Studies of Projects, Programs, and Policies* (Washington, DC, 1989), 27–46; Della E. Macmillan, *Sahel Visions: Planned Settlement and River Blindness Control in Burkina Faso* (Tucson, 1995). On the Onchocerciasis Control Programme in Ghana, see interview with Alex Adza, entomologist, Hohoe, 17 January 1997; interview with Nicholas Opoku, medical practitioner, Hohoe, 17 January 1997.

Photo 6.1 Flooded houses in Keta, September 1996 *(by author)*.

extended shoreline of the lake provides ample breeding places for mosquito larvae. Tsetse flies nest in the shade provided by vegetation around the lake perimeter, increasing the incidence of trypanosomiasis. Disease epidemiology has also changed downstream, with increased incidence of schistosomiasis below the dam and at the estuary and what has been described as an increase in the mosquito population in Anlo's littoral towns. The next section examines the disease epidemiology of the lower Volta after the dam, followed by a discussion of changes in fishing seasons on the lower Volta and Anlo coast.

The Volta dam and disease epidemiology in the lower Volta basin

The Volta dam has affected epidemiology downstream in both beneficial and adverse ways. The same cannot be said for communities living around the Volta Lake, for their health conditions have become more precarious. Aware that water development projects created new disease pools, entomological surveys were an important part of the Volta River Survey. In 1950 the American entomologist Lewis Berner was retained to conduct a survey of the potential hazards of the Volta Lake where malaria, onchocerciasis, schistosomiasis and trypanosomiasis were concerned.[60] Another

[60] On the association of these diseases with dams and irrigation projects, see Helmut Kloos, Abdulhamid Bedri Kello and Abdulaziz Addus, 'The health impact of the 1984/85 Ethiopian resettlement programme: three case studies', in Darkoh, ed., *African River Basins*, 147–65.

American entomologist, Elmer G. Berry, arrived later to undertake a special investigation into schistosomiasis in the Volta valley. Berner's report was published in 1950, and he anticipated that the dam would actually eliminate onchocerciasis in the dam area and downstream, as the blackfly vector, *Simulium damnosum*, thrives only in fast-flowing rivers and streams. Trypanosomiasis was not a major threat in the lower Volta, and he did not expect the situation to change with the dam. Berner was more worried about malaria and schistosomiasis:

> Following impoundment of the Volta, ecological and biological changes in the river will be profound, as the riverine flora and fauna will be converted into lacustrine types. Naturally, mosquito populations will be affected favourably and there shall be an even greater number of the pests produced than is now present. With the cessation of flow, the banks of the new lake should become overgrown with fringing trees and bush and the littoral zone will be invaded by vegetation characteristic of standing water.[61]

Berner pointed to the presence of *Schistosoma haematobium* in the lower Volta and expressed concern that the slowing down of the river's flow would increase the presence of schistosomiasis. Already in 1938 the Gold Coast Medical Department reported high rates of schistosomiasis at Ada at the Volta estuary and upstream at Akuse.[62]

Berner's concern about schistosomiasis was substantiated. Its prevalence and intensification around the Volta Lake was documented by the World Health Organization Schistosomiasis Control Project, which ran in Ghana from 1971 to 1978. Ralph Klumpp's research in over thirty Volta lakeside villages established that *S. haematobium* infection rates in the snail host *Bulinus rohlfsi* were among the highest in the world.[63] Moxon's evaluation of health conditions in the first four years of the dam project is alarming:

> Within the space of four years – between 1960 and 1964 – the dreaded bilharzia (urinary schistosomiasis) spread from a mere 5 per cent incidence in riparian children to an outrageous 90 per cent amongst lakeside children, and today virtually the whole 4,000 mile shoreline is infected where there are people.[64]

A more recent study of health conditions around the Volta Lake remains rather bleak in its assessment.[65] Health care and other social amenities are negligible, and these lakeside communities in the absence of water transport remain inaccessible to the outside world. It was only in 1990 that the Ghana government redesignated a ferry-boat ordered by the Ghana Highway Authority to serve as a medical boat for the Volta lakeside communities. Named 'MV *Onipanua*', its services are welcome but inadequate for the 1,000 communities that have sprung up around the Volta Lake.[66]

[61] Berner, *Entomological Report*, 19.

[62] Ibid., 71.

[63] Klumpp, '*Schistosoma haematobium* in Volta Lake', 2. See also the file on 'Epidemiology of Lake Volta', in David Scot's Private Papers, Mss. Brit.Emp.s.461, Rhodes House.

[64] Moxon, *Volta*, 276.

[65] Winfred N. Amanu, 'Coping with ill-health in riverine communities along the Volta Lake' (BA thesis, Sociology Department, University of Ghana, 1994).

[66] Ibid.

The Lower Volta Basin, 1957 to the Present

Downstream from the Volta, the dam has slowed the flow of the river and has eliminated onchocerciasis from areas such as the Kpong and Senchi rapids. The rapids have disappeared with the dam, and so has the simulium fly, which bred in the fast waters of the rapids. Moxon has highlighted the beneficial effect of the dam in the case of Atimpoku:

> Thus in the village of Atimpoku, near to the Adomi Bridge, 68 per cent of the population was found to be infected including 92 percent of the adult males. The effect of the lake of course has been to eradicate entirely breeding grounds in that area, but recent research has shown that these flies are also capable of resettling themselves and are already congregating in a number of streams and water courses all around the lake.[67]

Onchocerciasis has also decreased in the area around the lake, where the disease was prolific before the creation of the slower-moving lake.[68]

Ironically, the area downstream of the dam shed onchocerciasis in exchange for schistosomiasis, as the slow flow of the river is ideal for the host snail of schistosomiasis. It has been mentioned that the Volta River was tidal up to Sopwe in the pre-dam days, and saline water from the sea penetrated that far. The dam has minimized this tidal effect, as sedimentation has increased and the shifting sand bar at the mouth of the Volta has become more permanent. Instead of the river cutting through the sand bar during its annual floods between September and November, the river now meanders slowly around the sand bar and joins the sea. The implications for water-borne diseases are intriguing. A.K. Armah, the oceanographer, explained:

> Diseases that are associated with pure fresh water upstream have now migrated downstream because the salinity regime has moved down to a few hundred metres from the sea, which used to go all the way up to Sogakope. So the people of Ada, for example, are not safe from bilharzia.[69]

The extension of fresh water has resulted in an overgrowth of weeds close to the estuary. These weeds would not have thrived in saline water.[70] The weeds provide food material for the snail host of schistosomiasis, and Klumpp's study underscored the close connection between the aquatic weed, *Ceratophyllum*, and the *B. rohlfsi* snail. Thus, schistosomiasis has extended further south on the Volta River.[71]

Cross-infection of schistosomiasis by Ewe and Ada fishermen between the Volta delta and the Volta Lake area threatens to make schistosomiasis endemic in the lower Volta. Tongu-Ewe fishermen have long dominated riverine fishing in Ghana, and they annually migrated upstream of the Volta, returning to their homes between August and November when the Volta was in flood.[72] The creation of the Volta Lake and its immense fishing opportunities accentuated this trend, and Tongu, Anlo and Ada fishermen migrated to the lake area to fish. In pre-dam studies the Volta delta displayed the greatest concentration of *B. rohlfsi*, and high rates of schistosomiasis

---

[67] Moxon, *Volta*, 157.
[68] Interview with Nicholas Opoku, Hohoe, 17 January 1997.
[69] Interview with A.K. Armah, Accra, 14 August 1997.
[70] Ibid.
[71] Klumpp, '*Schistosoma haematobium* in Volta Lake'.
[72] Rowena Lawson, 'The structure, migration and resettkement of Ewe fishing units', *African Studies* 17, 1 (1958): 25.

have already been mentioned for Ada and Akuse.[73] The influx of thousands of Ewe and Ada fisherfolk from the delta area where the *B. rohlfsi* strain dominated started an epidemic of urinary schistosomiasis in almost every part of the newly formed lake.[74] Thus, in spite of the availability of effective drugs against schistosomiasis, ambilhar in the 1960s and more recently praziquantel, reinfection of treated patients who return to contaminated waters makes the cycle of transmission difficult to break.[75] Tongu fishermen have been viewed as prime culprits in this process.

> In spite of planning precautions to site new townships away from the lakeside, the Tongu fishermen did what fishermen the world over do – they settled at the water's edge and, ignoring elementary health measures, have infected the water-snail vector in the vicinity of human habitation with bilharzia, and in return infecting themselves.[76]

Breaking the transmission cycle of schistomiasis may involve halting the migratory patterns of Ewe and Ada fisherfolk along the Volta, and this may be impossible.

Environmental deterioration in Anlo, accelerated by the construction of the Volta dams, seems to underpin the increased presence of mosquitoes in the Anlo littoral. The transmission of malaria in Ghana is linked to three species of mosquitoes: *Anopheles gambiae gambiae, Anopheles gambiae melas* and *Anopheles funestus. Anopheles gambiae melas* is primarily a coastal species and is associated with brackish water. The Angaw, Avu and Keta Lagoons are thus ideal breeding places for this mosquito. *Anopheles gambiae gambiae* also inhabits a great variety of breeding places, such as puddles, shallow ponds, animal footprints and the edges of lakes and swamps.[77] The proliferation of puddles and ponds from lagoon flooding and rains in low-lying Anlo has increased breeding places for this species. The presence of mosquitoes does not necessarily imply the presence of malaria if there are no malaria-infected persons, but Ghana is an endemic malaria zone and a positive correlation may be safely assumed.[78] A 1996 report on the Keta District indicated that malaria accounted for about 40 per cent of reported disease cases. This was attributed to the numerous stagnant pools of water scattered throughout the district, which provide breeding grounds for mosquitoes. Waterborne diseases made up another 10.9 per cent of reported disease cases, making environmentally related diseases the leading disease category in the district.[79] Instructively, the first gift the author received from an Anlo during his first week's sojourn in Anlo was a can of insecticide spray. It must be mentioned, however, that this benefactor worked in a Mobil petrol station, which also sold insecticides, and it was therefore a convenient gift to give.

[73] Klumpp, '*Schistosoma haematobium* in Volta Lake', 36.

[74] Ibid., 45.

[75] Hermon Ghermay, 'Contaminated waters: resettlement and schistosomiasis in Ethiopia (1956–1988)' (History 1912 seminar paper, Harvard University, 1999).

[76] Moxon, *Volta*, 261.

[77] Berner, *Entomological Report*, 13–16.

[78] On the long history of malaria in West Africa in general and Ghana in particular, see Sheldon Watts, *Disease, Power, and Imperialism* (New Haven, 1997), 213–68; A. Norman Klein, 'Towards a new understanding of Akan origins', *Africa* 66, 2 (1996): 248–73.

[79] Keta District Assembly, 'Medium Term (5 Year) Development Plan (1996–2000) for Keta District' (May 1996), 52–3.

The Lower Volta Basin, 1957 to the Present

The Anlo themselves comment on the abundant presence of mosquitoes in present-day Anlo. Some ascribe this to the breakdown in moral ecology. Anlo oral traditions are revealing in this respect. Mosquitoes were present in Anlo right from its settlement period. Indeed, Dodi, custodian of the Kli god, got his alias 'Fuga' from the numerous mosquito bites he received in a hunting expedition with Adeladza I.[80] The people of Glidzanu are reputed to have had a means of controlling mosquitoes, and mosquitoes did not bite people in Glidzanu. Togbui Honi II recalled that:

> They had two pots in the forest. When the rainy season came, the people of Glidzanu would catch a mosquito and put it into the water-filled pots and say: 'Here is your home, don't go anywhere to bite anybody.' So mosquitoes did not bite anyone there. This was even there when I was young [1940s]. We went to spoil these things. I was among myself. Now mosquitoes come to destroy us rather.[81]

Youthful irreverence for custom is, in this instance, seen as the cause of the collapse of mosquito control. Nukunya confirms the use of religious ritual to eliminate mosquito infestation along the Anlo coast and at settlements fringing the Keta Lagoon.[82]

Less mystical causes also underpin the increased presence of mosquitoes in Anlo, and these are a combination of environmental and human factors. Lagoons, lakes and other bodies of water are associated with mosquitoes, and Anlo abounds in these. But what may have made the presence of mosquitoes more conspicuous today may be linked to the extension of grass and mud pools around Anlo's lagoons with the reduction of the influx from the Volta and the dry cycle in the past two decades or more. Mosquitoes do not actually breed in the open water of the lagoon, but rather in the very shallow parts where the growth of grass protects the larvae from fish.[83] Indeed, the reported decline in fish stocks in the Keta Lagoon may have contributed to the presence of mosquitoes, as certain fishes feed on mosquito larvae and thus serve as a form of natural control.

Irvine lists that among 'the Gold Coast fishes known to feed on mosquito larvae are the toothed carps (*Cyprinodontidae*), the goby (*Eleotris lebretoni*) and the young of the Cichlidae'.[84] Emigration from the Keta area from the 1960s has also reduced the population size and its ability to control peripheral mud pools and the vegetation that grows around the lagoon and provides breeding places for mosquito larvae. The 1970 census marked a decline in Keta's population from 16,719 to 14,446, and the decline has continued to the point that only the elderly and the young are mostly found in central Keta today.[85]

Apart from the epidemiological ramifications, the Anlo attribute changes in fishing

[80] Interview with Togbui Honi II and Togbuivi Kumassah, Woe, 24 January 1997.

[81] Ibid.

[82] G.K. Nukunya, personal correspondence, 28 September 1999.

[83] When mosquitoes plagued Accra in the 1920s, a scheme was proposed in 1929 to reduce the size of the Korle Lagoon and to ensure that the entire lagoon was always filled with water. PRO, CO 96/689/2. 'Accra (Korle) Lagoon Reclamation and Deepening Scheme'.

[84] F.R. Irvine, *Fishes and Fisheries of the Gold Coast* (London, 1947), 18.

[85] In contrast, Anloga's population, underpinned by the shallot industry, grew from 11,038 in 1960 to 14,032 in 1970.

regime and a decline in fish stocks to the Volta dam. As 60 per cent of the people in the Keta District derive their livelihood from fishing, the dam then significantly affected the district's economy.[86]

The Volta dams and fishing in the lower Volta and on the Anlo coast

The damming of the Volta had immediate and long-term impact on riverine, creek, lagoon and coastal fishing in the lower Volta. Freshwater fishing is conducted in the Volta and its associated creeks and ponds. Creeks may form when rivers are obstructed and break into distributaries. During the rainy season, the river may overflow its banks and create creeks. Also, rivers become sluggish in the dry season and tend to meander, finding the path of least resistance. The river returns to its original channel in the rainy season, and the sections that are cut off become creeks. Ponds are produced in a similar manner, though smaller, but can also be man-made.[87] Anlo hunters and fishermen discovered several of these creeks east of the Volta in what is Agave country from the eighteenth century and settled family members around the creeks to secure possession.[88] Indeed, it was in this creek country on the eastern bank of the Volta, in places such as Tsrekume, that Anlo 'nationalists' led by Tenge Dzokoto II of Anyako fought the last battle against colonial imposition in 1889.[89] Creek fishing is seasonal, as the creeks are filled with water and fish when the Volta floods its banks. The fish are trapped in the creeks in the dry season when the river retreats, and that is when they are harvested.

The immediate effect of the Akosombo Dam, as the Volta Lake filled, was to cut off water to the lower Volta and to these creeks and ponds that received water and fish in the Volta's annual floods. Moxon described the impact:

> But while the lake was filling the creeks have obviously remained empty and this particular source of fish, has quite literally, dried up. Their future too is uncertain. With a steady river flow of 38,000 cusecs in the future some of the creeks and lagoons will be inundated again, though not as fully as in bygone flood seasons. Others, with a little deepening perhaps, may also continue to be good fishing grounds. But undoubtedly creek fishing has had its hey day.[90]

Moxon lamented the fate of the clam fishing industry concentrated in the 35-mile stretch of relatively shallow water between the Kpong rapids and Tefle:

> Curiously, the harvesting of the clams [*Egeria radiata*] is exclusively a female occupation and is pursued for six or seven months a year whilst the river flow is relatively slight. Mostly the

[86] Interview with Obed Nutsugah (Economic Planning Officer, Keta District) and Fred Akligo (Assemblyman for Afiadenyigba), Dzelukope, 18 March 1997.

[87] Interview with Togbuivi Kumassah and E.K. Keteku, Woe, 18 September 1996; interview with David Atta-Peters, Accra, 2 December 1996.

[88] Interview with Togbui Honi II and Togbuivi Kumassah, Woe, 24 January 1997; guided tour of selected Anlo towns and villages by Togbuivi Kumassah, 22 April 1997.

[89] J.B. Yegbe, 'The Anlo and their neighbours 1850–1890' (MA thesis, University of Ghana, 1966), 129.

[90] Moxon, *Volta*, 190.

women dive from canoes into one or two fathoms of water and pick the clams out of the sand. But when the river is very low they stand in the water and pick the clams out of the sand with their toes.[91]

Moxon did not believe the clam industry would survive the immediate cut-off of the Volta's flow. Theoretically, the Volta dam would regulate the flow of the water downstream after the lake filled, and, though the clam industry might continue on submerged sand banks, the water flow would be too swift and great for the women to dive for clams as in the past. The impact of the dry cycle in the past two decades on the clam industry is yet to be examined in detail. But the current review appears to indicate a decline in overall fishing downstream of the dam. The clam fishery has gone down, for it requires a certain amount of salinity to thrive. Clams used to be caught at Akuse and Sogakope, but now they are found downstream at Ada on the estuary. Shrimp production even in the estuary has declined.[92]

The Volta dam also affected the lagoons connected to it, especially the Keta Lagoon, through the process of sedimentation. Sedimentation accelerated when the dam slowed the Volta's flow with a consequent reduction in the volume of water in the Volta. One result has been the extension of marshland in the Volta delta area. Before the dam, the annual floods of the Volta brought nutrients favoured by fishes into the creeks and lagoons and also broke the sand bar at the estuary. Sea water then penetrated the Volta, promoting a culture in the estuary that favoured estuarine fishes that thrived in brackish water. At this time the Volta fed the Avu and Keta Lagoons brackish water. The Volta with its inland freshwater tributaries also flushed out the water in the Avu and Keta Lagoons and hence limited the salinity levels. The dams impaired this hydrological regime. The sand bar at the mouth of the Volta has become more permanent and quickly re-forms when it is blasted. The channel that connects the Volta to the Avu has silted up. The Volta does not feed the lagoons the regular inputs of brackish and fresh water. The Keta Lagoon receives fresh water from the rains and salt water when the sea transgresses the narrow sand spit at Kedzi and enters the lagoon. The changed culture of the Keta Lagoon has reduced fish stocks.[93]

The interchange between the Volta, the lagoons and the sea in the pre-dam days meant that both freshwater and marine fishes could be found at the estuary and in the Avu and Keta Lagoons. Marine fishes appearing at the estuary, included the tarpon (*Megalops*), the shad (*Ethnalosa dorsalis*), the barracuda, some members of the herring family, the two jacks or horse-mackerels (*Caranx hippos* and *Caranx crysos*), the grey mullet and the catfish.[94] Freshwater fishes, such as those of the cichlid family, also entered the estuary. The cichlid *Tilapia hendeloti* is also a lagoon favourite and features in the Keta Lagoon. Marine fishes found in lagoons, especially the young, included tarpon, shad, the young of two snappers and two sea perches and three species of grey mullets. These are especially found in the lagoons in the rainy

---

[91] Ibid., 191.
[92] Interview with A.K. Armah, Accra, 14 August 1997.
[93] Ibid.; interview with David Atta-Peters, Accra, 13 December 1996.
[94] Irvine, *Fishes and Fisheries*, 9.

season when the sea, the Volta and the lagoons are in active contact.[95] The Keta Lagoon was also rich in shrimp, but this is now restricted to the estuary.[96] Fred Akligo of Afiadenyigba complained about the decline of fish variety in the Keta Lagoon:

> It was in 1961, when they started the Volta dam project. Around 1964 the thing materialized. Ever since, the fishing patterns have changed. Fishes that responded to the Volta current have ceased to come. Some sea fishes were caught in the Keta Lagoon when the Volta flooded its banks. Since the two dams at Akosombo and Kpong, this has stopped. Now it is only tilapia that is caught in the Keta Lagoon. Every day tilapia![97]

Crabs appeared in the Keta Lagoon, as they prefer brackish water and use the saline water to form their own shells.[98] Now crabs are available in the Keta Lagoon only when the sea overflows the sand spit. The result captures the paradox of life in the Keta area: residents are alarmed at the threat to life and property when the sea transgresses, but they are rewarded with crabs from the lagoon.

And the dams have affected maritime fishing along the Anlo coast, or so the Anlo claim. Indeed, some Anlo claim the dam intensified erosion along the Anlo coast, as the force of the Volta used to mitigate the power of the ocean waves in the area.[99] Though not scientifically proved yet, the logic of their arguments is clear. The exchange between the Volta and the sea lies at the centre of the Anlo argument, for fresh water from the Volta's floods used to penetrate deep into the sea and signal the rendezvous of fishes at the estuary to feed and spawn. A major casualty of the dam, in Anlo opinion, is the *afafa*, or horse-mackerel, season. Chapman Klutse explains:

> This was because the *aflu* vegetation which floated down the River into the sea at the Volta estuary during floods would be blocked by the Dam. The *afafa* is said to be a rapacious fish inhabiting the deep Atlantic Ocean. During the pre-Dam yearly flood of the Volta River, the *afafa*, the herring and the anchovy instinctively found a common rendezvous at the Volta estuary. The small fish went there to feed on the *aflu* vegetation which the river seasonally emptied into the sea at the estuary while the *afafa* descended from the deep Atlantic to feed on these small fish. As the flood subsided and the movement of the *aflu* downstream slowed down, the small fish moved upstream in search of the *aflu* feed. In effect, they were pursued by the *afafa* to as far as about the vicinity of Sogakope where the rendezvous broke up on the disappearance of the *aflu*. The *afafa* were then seen moving downstream towards the estuary. In the general process of climbing back into the Ocean, the well fed and presently weighty *afafa* drifted into the Keta bay and were caught in great numbers.[100]

---

[95] Ibid., 10.

[96] Interview with A.K. Armah, Accra, 14 August 1997. In 1996 shrimp became available in the Keta Lagoon when the sea breached the sand spit and entered the lagoon. Interview with Yaw Boateng, Keta, 16 October 1996.

[97] Interview with Obed Nutsugah and Fred Akligo, Dzelukope, 18 March 1997.

[98] Interview with David Atta-Peters, Accra, 13 December 1997.

[99] Interview with Togbuivi Kumassah, Woe, 3 September 1996. Coastal erosion was noted at Cape St Paul in the 1960s. The Coode Report of 1929 had observed that the cape had been extending seaward from at least the early twentieth century (see Chapter 4). An architectural study in 1971 concluded that the recent erosion at Cape St Paul 'may be connected with the fact that the Akosombo Dam on the Volta River built in the sixties retains the highest part of fluvial deposits which were formerly washed into the sea'. Faculty of Architecture, *Keta Study* (University of Science and Technology, Occasional Report No. 15, *c*. 1971), 39.

[100] Chapman W.S. Klutse, *The Keta Coast Erosion and Dredging for Development, and some Landmarks for Anlo History* (Accra, 1984), 11.

The Lower Volta Basin, 1957 to the Present

Irvine, in his authoritative work on fishes and fisheries in the Gold Coast, confirmed that the jack mackerel does ascend into fresh water from the sea.[101]

Though the author received independent corroboration of the *afafa*'s ascent into the Volta from several Anlo – fishermen and others – it remained unclear whether this was just to feed or also to spawn, as some Anlo claim. E.K. Keteku provided one version:

> Later [after the anchovy season] the horse-mackerel migrate, as they move towards the fresh water to spawn. When they are going, the horse-mackerel are fat, and they have a lot of energy to withstand the sea. Thus they swim far from the shore. When they go and spawn and are returning, they escort their young ones through the shallow parts of the sea. That is the time our people catch them or are supposed to catch them. They are closer to the shore. These days, because they are using very powerful outboard motors, they intercept them when they are on their way. So we now complain that we don't have fish. But when they are going to spawn so that we [can] have more fish, it is then that we catch them.[102]

Local observers had informed Irvine that the *afafa* spawned in the Volta, but he had no scientific proof. He advocated the protection of the horse-mackerel in the river systems if this was substantiated.[103] Equally interesting is the claim of some Anlo fishermen that the horse-mackerel now responds to the fresh water of the Mono further east, hence its diminished presence at the Anlo coast.[104] Keteku's account above suggested that Anlo fishermen practising *watsa* actually caught the egg-heavy horse-mackerel on its way east to spawn. The spawning habits of the horse-mackerel in Ghana are still unresearched, and the oceanographer A.K. Armah could not endorse or disprove the Anlo observations. He confirmed that he had observed huge horse-mackerel at the Volta estuary, but could neither prove they came up the Volta to spawn nor confirm that the horse-mackerel was now responding to the Mono further east. He valued the wisdom of local knowledge, however, and advised the author not to discount the observations of local fishermen, whose families have often fished for generations.[105]

Anlo and non-Anlo scholars who have examined maritime fishing off the Anlo coast have reported Anlo views on the impact of the dam on fishing. Nukunya observed in 1989 that:

> [T]he [*afafa*] seasons are not always good and for the past twenty-five years the amount of catches has gone down considerably, a fact which has been blamed on the Akosombo Dam whose construction has been said to have adversely affected the spawning habits of the fish. Today with even bigger nylon nets good catches could exceed the former maximum of 15,000, but they are rather few and far between with more modest catches of between 500 and 2,000 a time more common.[106]

Overa in her 1998 account also reported a decline in *afafa* catches as a result of the Volta dams:

---

[101] Irvine, *Fishes and Fisheries*, 11.

[102] Interview with Togbuivi Kumassah and E.K. Keteku, Woe, 18 September 1996. For a fisherman's corroboration of this version, see interview with Michael Lawson, Dzelukope, 23 April 1997.

[103] Irvine, *Fishes and Fisheries*, 18–19. See also interview with Victor Nyadanu and Peter Afabegee, Keta, 19 September 1996.

[104] Interview with Michael Lawson, Dzelukope, 23 April 1997.

[105] Interview with A.K. Armah, Accra, 14 August 1997.

[106] G.K. Nukunya, 'The Anlo-Ewe and full-time maritime fishing: another view', *Maritime Anthropological Studies* 2, 2 (1989): 166.

The environmental changes following the big dam project of Volta Lake (completed in 1966) had a detrimental impact on the fish species that used the lower areas of the River Volta as a spawning ground. *Afafa* and other fish stocks have thus been reduced.[107]

That fish catches have declined off the Anlo coast cannot be doubted.[108] In 1962 the Fisheries Department commented on the decline of *afafa* catches in recent years and commenced biological studies to ascertain the causes for the decline.[109] Some blame trawlers that fish off the Anlo coast.[110] Others opine that fish stocks have not decreased *per se*, but rather the population fishing Anlo waters has increased, and improved nylon nets and outboard motors facilitate a more thorough harvesting of the sea than in the past. What is thus missing is the old sense of 'surplus': refrigeration and long-distance markets have erased this surplus.[111]

The timing of the fishing seasons also appears to have become a bit unpredictable. A concerned S.S. Dotse enlightened the author in rather dramatic terms on how erratic the seasons could become. In June 1996 the Keta area experienced a bumper harvest when they least expected one. Then the season ended abruptly. Retrospectively, the Anlo tried to explain the calamity. Certain fishes, such as the *adzaduvi* (the fingerling of the Spanish mackerel) appeared prematurely in June, and this was not a good sign. Before the main fishing season commences in June–July, there is a bluish tinge to the sea waves as they come to the shore. Fishermen then rush to fish. In June 1996 as the bluish waves approached, they reversed and went back. No one understood why, but the fishing season was a disaster. Dotse mused over the precariousness of depending on nature for a livelihood.[112] The Anlo hydrology has always been a dynamic one. But, as Armah pointed out, overall it was 'predictable' and often 'beneficial'. In the altered hydrological regime, fish seasons have become unpredictable and catches are often poor.[113] This has reinforced old patterns of migrant fishing.

Port closures, floods and the decline of Keta in the 1960s

When Keta's economy, especially Keta market, faltered in the 1960s, it was in the wake of certain environmental and political developments. The cumulative effect of these developments, however, undermined the position of Keta as the distribution point in the regional economy. Fred Kumassah, in an insightful study in 1978,

---

[107] Ragnhild Overa, 'Partners and competitors: gendered entrepreneurship in Ghanaian canoe fisheries' (PhD thesis, University of Bergen, 1998), 240.

[108] Interview with A.K. Armah, Accra, 14 August 1997.

[109] NAG, Ho, KE/c.585. Circular letter from secretary to the Regional Commissioner to DCs of Keta, Agbozume, and Anloga, 6 November 1962.

[110] Interview with Michael Lawson, Dzelukope, 23 April 1997; interview with Yaovi Gada, Abutiakope, 22 April 1997. Both fishermen were active members of the Ghana National Association of Farmers and Fishermen (GNAFF) and were reporting on deliberations at these meetings. Ghanaian companies, such as State Fishing Corporation and Mankoadze Fisheries, introduced refrigerated trawlers into Ghanaian seas from the 1950s.

[111] This is the position of Togbuivi Kumassah. Interview with Togbuivi Kumassah and E.K. Keteku, Woe, 18 September 1996.

[112] Interview with S.S. Dotse, Keta, 4 September 1996.

[113] Interview with A.K. Armah, Accra, 14 August 1997.

examined the role the closure of Keta's port in 1962, the cutting of the Kedzi canal in 1963, the relocation of the regional capital to Ho in 1968 and the Aliens Compliance Order of 1969 played in Keta's decline.[114] He does not discount the importance of sea erosion in Keta's decline, but points out rightly that Keta achieved its apogee in spite of the commencement of active erosion from 1907.[115] The four factors outlined above shook the foundations of Keta's market. That all were essentially political decisions lent Keta's collapse political causes.

Tema harbour was opened in 1962, and, with this, the last surf ports at Keta, Cape Coast and Winneba were closed. The era of surf ports was over, and an attempt to reopen Denu port in 1962 elicited the response 'that the cabinet has recently decided against the re-opening of such ports'.[116] The government believed that the two deep-water harbours at Takoradi and Tema could adequately handle the country's trade. An improved road and rail network would ensure an efficient distribution of goods throughout the country. The Gold Coast and Ghanaian governments financed both Takoradi and Tema harbours from external sources and closed adjoining surf ports to ensure that competition did not render the new harbours unprofitable.[117] Sea erosion had also rendered operations at Keta's surf port hazardous. Goods when landed were often wet. The closure of Keta's port in 1962 was followed in 1963 by the serious flooding of the Keta Lagoon. These developments undermined the redistributive role of Keta market. Kumassah commented on the consequences:

> The closure of the surf-port had serious implications for the growth and development of Keta especially for the business community. The town felt the discomfort of the closure. Its position as the central market for the sub-region and its commercial relations with the outside world and dependence on external resources for raw materials and foodstuff made it impossible for the town to escape unscathed from the economic consequences of the closure.
>
> With the closure of the surf-port, the remaining major force of attraction became the market. Thus in 1963 when the floods of the Keta Lagoon threatened its existence, the elders of the town in consultation with the resident engineer of the Public Works Department decided to apply a bad solution to a worsening problem and this led to the cutting of the now unpopular Kedzi Canal in 1963.[118]

The impaired drainage system of the Keta Lagoon after the Volta dam did not augur well for the heavy rains of 1963. Major flooding occurred in the Keta District and the ill-advised Kedzi or Aryee canal has already been mentioned earlier in Chapter 5.

The Kedzi canal changed the currents on the approach to Keta market and endangered lagoon transport. The result was to redirect trade to neighbouring markets:

> Many people who attempted crossing the canal in boats to attend the market had their boats driven into the sea by the strong currents generated by the lagoon waters running into the sea. This led to emigration of many traders to markets east of the canal such as Denu, Aflao, Dzodze and Agbozume. As a result of this emigration the Keta Kente market was transferred to

[114] John Fred Kwaku Kumassah, 'Keta: a declining Anlo urban centre' (BA thesis, University of Ghana, 1978).
[115] Ibid., 2.
[116] NAG, Ho, KE/c.464. Secretary to the Volta Regional Commissioner to DC Agbozume, Ho, 25 July 1962.
[117] On developments after the opening of Takoradi harbour, see PRO, CO 96/677/10. Axim and Saltpond ports were closed in the 1930s. Kwamina B. Dickson, *A Historical Geography of Ghana* (Cambridge, 1969), 255, 297.
[118] Kumassah, 'Keta', 14.

Agbozume and also the corn market went to Denu where they have remained ever since. The traders who left also managed to secure stores and stalls in these new markets and when the canal was later closed and life returned to normal were reluctant to return.[119]

Floods had exposed the non-productive base of Keta. Keta's urban status and land shortage had eliminated farming early in the twentieth century, and fishing was progressively pushed to adjacent villages and towns, such as Adzido, Vodza and Kedzi to the east and Abutiakope and Dzelukope to the west. Salt production had declined since 1950, and active salt-ponding progressed only north of the Keta Lagoon in places like Afiadenyigba. Anloga shallots had ceased to come to Keta market in significant quantities from 1953, when the latent hostilities between Keta and Anloga exploded into a violent confrontation over the issue of direct tax. Although a colonial imposition, the tax was viewed by many Anloga residents as emanating from administrative Keta with the intention of benefiting Keta.[120] In the aftermath of the riots, Anloga town leaders banned shallot traders from taking Anloga shallots to Keta market. Anloga also fixed its market-day on Keta market-day, putting the two markets in direct competition.[121] With the exposed underbelly of Keta market making it vulnerable in the early 1960s, these littoral markets gradually emerged in their own right, some surpassing Keta market in prominence.

Subsequent political decisions further weakened an already tottering Keta. Pernicious erosion and the absence of land for development or expansion weighed heavily against Keta's ability to function adequately as the regional capital. In 1968 the military government of the National Liberation Council (NLC) decided to relocate the Volta regional capital from Keta to Ho, where there was abundant land for development. Administrative offices and personnel were moved from Keta, diminishing Keta's urban status and cultural prominence as the leading Ewe town of Ghana. Commercial houses closed their branches at Keta and opened new ones at Ho to benefit from the bustling trade that characterizes administrative capitals. Then on 18 November 1969, the new Progress Party government that had succeeded the NLC promulgated an Aliens Compliance Order, expelling all aliens in Ghana without residence permits. This ruling affected the Hausa and Zabrama traders in Keta, who dominated the Kente trade and featured largely in retail trade also. Their stores lined the perimeter of Keta market with the exception of the side that bordered the lagoon. In the aftermath of the Aliens Order their numbers in Keta dropped from 1,915 to 536, and most of the stores and stalls they occupied remained empty in 1978 and even in 1996–7 when the author conducted fieldwork in Keta.[122]

Today the residents of Keta are left with memories of their once famous market.

[119] Ibid.

[120] Interview with L.C.M. Seshie, Dzelukope, 16 October 1996. For an excellent treatment of the Anloga riots, see Sophia Amable, 'The 1953 riot in Anloga and its aftermath' (BA thesis, University of Ghana, 1977). See also Rudolph K. Sebuabe, 'The life and work of T.S.A. Togobo 1900–1984' (BA thesis, History Department, University of Ghana, 1997). On Anloga–Keta relations in the period immediately preceding the riots, see NAG, Accra, ADM 39/1/120. Anlo State Native Affairs (1944–51).

[121] Interview with Esther Kwawukume, Keta, 23 January 1997; interview with Freda Adabanu and Regina Ayayee, Keta, 20 September 1996.

[122] Kumassah, 'Keta', 16.

There is a partial revival of the Keta market on market-days, but this is nothing compared with its past. As Keta residents looked optimistically to successive Ghanaian governments to implement an effective sea defence project that would save their town and help them reclaim land for settlement, they hoped also for a renaissance of their market and their focal role in the economy of the subregion.

Conclusion

Anlo residents single out deep-water harbours and hydroelectric dams on the Volta River as major reasons for the intensification of coastal erosion and the deterioraton of their environment. The decline of fish stocks in the Keta Lagoon and low catches in Anlo maritime fisheries are also blamed on these developmental projects. This chapter has reviewed the Anlo arguments against the available scientific evidence, but also in their own context as the local interpretation of environmental change and as a significant critique of colonial and postcolonial political economy. Instructively, these projects and the ancillary industries were sited west of the Volta to the detriment of communities east of the Volta.

By independence, over half of Keta lay under the sea, and the sea continued its progressive assault. It seemed as if the relocation of the regional capital to Ho removed any incentive to save Keta. Official rhetoric often centred on relocation to an inland site. This is unacceptable to residents of the Keta area. S.S. Dotse complained: 'How can we go and start anew there as farmers whilst we are fishermen?'[123] This is an interesting turn in history for the successful transition to an aquatic ecosystem in large parts of Anlo had undermined the agrarian tradition brought from Notsie. And, for the Anlo of Keta District, nature continues to be unpredictable: the sea robs them of their houses and property and rewards them with fish. It is a cynical cycle that keeps the Anlo trapped in Keta, Vodza and Kedzi in spite of the sea's ravages. The strategy of many has been to acquire dwelling places at Dzelukope, where paradoxically accretion of shoreline is occurring, while pursuing their fishing vocation in the eroded sites. The Anlo turn to each successive government with cautious optimism that something might be done about coastal erosion at Keta. Indeed, official responses to coastal erosion and lagoon flooding in Anlo would become a measuring stick for evaluating the responsiveness of Ghanaian governments to Anlo's environmental and developmental concerns. Successive disappointments crystallized a world-view in which Ghana east of the Volta was perceived as forgotten terrain. The image of a separate and unique landscape east of the Volta informed the movement for Ewe unification in the first half of the twentieth century. And, in the second half of the twentieth century, environmental issues would become crucial in the Anlo perception of political inclusion and exclusion in the Ghanaian nation-state. The next chapter examines these links between environment and political identity.

[123] Interview with S.S. Dotse, Keta, 4 September 1996.

7

Coastal Erosion, Political Ecology & the Discourse of Environmental Citizenship in Twentieth-century Anlo

Chapters 4 to 6 examined the contextual sources of environmental change, some rooted in geological processes, others related to state policies (especially hydroelectric dams) and global capitalism. This is an important component of the framework of Third World political ecology outlined by Raymond Bryant. He sees this emerging field as comprising the contextual sources of environmental change, locational struggles over the environment and the political ramifications of environmental change.[1] Bryant highlights 'the important effects of environmental change on socio-economic and political relationships'.[2] It is these effects of environmental change on socio-economic and political relationships that this chapter seeks to explore. Sea erosion has loomed large in the history of twentieth-century Anlo. The educated constituency in Anlo mobilized itself from the 1920s to inform the broader community on the causes and course of sea erosion and to lobby the state for sea defence works. Drawing on an intimate local knowledge of the environment, Anlo intellectuals engaged the colonial and postcolonial state on its environmental policy concerning coastal erosion in Anlo. Anlo's intellectuals critiqued state policies and offered – indeed, sometimes experimented with – local solutions to coastal erosion. A veritable 'citizen science', or folk environmental knowledge, had emerged in Anlo on coastal hydrology and fisheries.

Even in 1929 the estimated £1,000,000 stated by A.T. Coode as required for permanent sea defence works in Anlo was ruled out as exorbitant by the colonial government. The government suggested relocation from Keta and its environs; the residents refused. The progression of coastal erosion over the twentieth century further damaged the Anlo environment and made the required sea defence works more extensive and expensive. The destruction of socio-economic infrastructure also necessitated the resuscitation of the Anlo economy. By the second half of the

---

[1] Raymond L. Bryant, 'Political ecology: an emerging research agenda in Third World studies', *Political Geography* 11, 1 (1992): 12–36.
[2] Ibid., 14.

186

twentieth century, the finances required for sea defence and economic revival in Anlo had exceeded the resources of independent Ghanaian governments. It had become necessary to seek international financial assistance. As various Ghanaian governments procrastinated over committing to such an expensive financial endeavour, the Anlo became acutely aware of how environmental issues had pushed them to the margins of the nation-state.

The Anlo began to frame questions and notions of political inclusion and exclusion in a discourse on the environment. Independent Ghanaian governments were evaluated on their policies towards Anlo's environmental crisis. These governments got off on a bad footing, as the framework of environmental policy inherited from the colonial government concentrated on forests. The current focus in Ghana's environmental and agrarian policy is on the forest agrarian sector and the revival of the declining cocoa industry.[3] Deforestation remains a key issue, and the timber industry has come under elaborate regulation. The declining world price for cocoa, however, underpins the continued viability of the timber industry, putting it second after gold in the country's export sector.[4] But an important link exists between cocoa cultivation – which thrives only in the forest belt – and deforestation. The contradictions involved in continuing colonial economic policies throw into bold relief the conflicting roles of the state as 'developer, and as protector and steward of the natural environment'.[5] And since most developing countries are currently implementing environmental policies framed and funded by the developed West, Anlo's coastal erosion problem had to be put on an international agenda to be redressed.[6]

Scholars have examined the changing conceptions of polity and ethnic identity in Anlo.[7] This chapter inserts the importance of the environment and environmental issues into conceptions of polity and identity in Anlo. It examines the use of landscape in the Ewe unification movement. Landscape became a powerful image in the Ewe advocacy for a separate Ewe polity. The chapter also analyses the centrality of environmental issues in Anlo's relations with independent Ghanaian governments, ending with a discussion of the importance of environmental issues in the general elections of 1992 and 1996. Emphasis is placed on the 1996 elections, during which the ties between environmental issues and political inclusion or 'citizenship' were made explicit.[8] The period immediately before and after the elections witnessed newspaper accounts and allegations of Ewe ethnicity and references to the landslide victory of the reigning National Democratic Congress (NDC) in the Volta Region in the 1992 elections. Ewe politicians were prominent in the NDC, and the government

---

[3] Kojo Sebastian Amanor, *The New Frontier. Farmers' Response to Land Degradation: A West African Study* (London, 1994).

[4] Ibid., 48–9.

[5] K.J. Walker, 'The state in environmental management: the ecological dimension', *Political Studies* 37 (1989): 32.

[6] Amanor, *New Frontier*, 7.

[7] Sandra E. Greene, *Gender, Ethnicity, and Social Change on the Upper Slave Coast: A History of the Anlo-Ewe* (Portsmouth, 1996); and D.E.K. Amenumey, *The Ewe Unification Movement: A Political History* (Accra, 1989).

[8] The author's archival and fieldwork in Ghana in 1996–7 coincided with an election year and the general elections of 7 December 1996.

was nicknamed the 'Dzelukofe Mafia' in recognition of the important Anlo component.[9] The President of Ghana, J.J. Rawlings, is a son of Keta. The Ewe were accused of insularism, and fears were expressed that a repeat performance of the 1992 elections would recur in the Volta Region.[10] A supposed titanic struggle between the Ewe and the Akan was documented in some newspapers, and the 1996 election cast in terms of the Ewe versus the Akan.[11]

But the ethnic map of the Volta Region is more complex than these newspaper accounts admitted. In 1996, daily broadcasts in Twi – the language of the Akan – on the newly launched Radio Volta emphasized the existence of Akan constituencies in the Volta Region from at least the eighteenth century.[12] History also informs us that other non-Ewe political parties have thrived in Anlo, the Convention People's Party (CPP) and the United National Convention (UNC) of 1979 being good examples. Though not discounting the ethnic card, it is important, as emphasized by Paul Nugent, that we examine the manner in which ethnicity and history interact and are contextualized at the local level.[13] And here the Anlo perception of political marginality under post-CPP governments is key.[14] The prominent Ewe presence in the NDC certainly made it attractive to the Anlo. But the NDC was also viewed as the 'party of development', and the 'environmental platform' gained immense support in Anlo as the NDC government combined permanent sea defence works with a broad economic package in the Keta Basin Integrated Development Project. This project has become the blueprint for socio-economic redemption for Anlo. It might be more useful to examine the allegations of 'Anlo-Ewe tribalism' within the more meaningful discourse of 'environmental citizenship'.

Landscape in the Ewe unification movement

The construction of landscape featured prominently in the movement for Ewe unification in the first half of the twentieth century. Landscape is about the physical land, the people on it and the culture through which they mediate their access to and use of the land. Landscape is a historical process constantly undergoing change. The world between the Volta and Mono Rivers constituted the landscape for Ewe

[9] 'Talk shop column', *The Ghanaian Chronicle* (21 November 1996).
[10] See, for examples, *Ghanaian Chronicle* (21 November 1996); (4 December 1996).
[11] See *Weekend Statesman* (20–26 December 1996) for the statement of Agyenim Boateng, Secretary General of the National Patriotic Party.
[12] Radio Volta Premier was launched by students of the Ho Polytechnic in June 1996. *Ghanaian Voice* (1–3 July 1996). On the ethnic composition of the Volta Region and its complex politics, see Paul Nugent, '"A few lesser peoples": the central Togo minorities and their Ewe neighbours', in Carola Lentz and Paul Nugent, eds, *Ethnicity in Ghana: The Limits of Invention* (forthcoming). The author is grateful to the authors for allowing him to see the manuscript in press.
[13] Paul Nugent, 'Living in the past: urban, rural and ethnic themes in the 1992 and 1996 elections in Ghana', *Journal of Modern African Studies* 37, 2 (1999): 307–8.
[14] See, for example, Stevens. K.M. Ahiawordor, 'A study of the 1996 presidential and parliamentary elections in Ghana: the case of Ketu South and Ketu North constituencies', in Joseph R.A. Ayee, ed., *The 1996 General Elections and Democratic Consolidation in Ghana* (Accra, 1998), 475.

unification. The initial move for unification focused on the coastal stretch. This territory exhibited common environmental features. It was located in the Benin Gap; it was marked by sandy, unfertile soils; and its coastline featured an extensive lagoon network. Moreover, this territory was occupied mainly by Ewe-speakers, unified in a regional economy. Increasingly, the Anlo would emphasize the natural unity of this landscape – environment, culture and economy – and advocate that logic dictated political unity also. Politics would extend this bounded world to include the northern sections of the Volta in the unification movement. Humans shape landscape; hence the social boundaries of landscape are very permeable.

Ewe-speaking communities dot the coastal stretch between the Rivers Volta and Mono. The precolonial era witnessed intense political, economic, social and cultural exchanges in this region. Competition as well as cooperation was exhibited in the long feuds that characterized relations between the Anlo, Keta and Little Popo, and the lagoon and coastal trade on the Slave Coast.[15] In association with Akan allies – Akwamu and Asante – Anlo launched military invasions among the Krepi (northern Ewe) in the mid-1830s and in 1869. Eweland was certainly not a homogeneous political unit. Colonial imposition and colonial boundaries drastically revised the politics of Anlo identity.

Artificial German and British boundaries reinforced kinship and cultural ties among the Ewe and underscored the disabilities of forced partition. From the defeat of Germany in Togo in 1914, the Anlo became advocates of Ewe unification, a novel concept. Anlo scholars would spearhead a cultural renaissance from the 1940s that underpinned a burgeoning Ewe nationalism by popularizing the Ketu–Tado–Notsie traditions and the homogeneity of the Ewe people. But the political terrain was far from simple, and some Anlo would lend support to the competing call for the unification of Togoland and a Gold Coast nationalism from the 1950s that sought the integration of British Togoland and the Gold Coast.[16] Anlo positioning in the politics of identity shifted constantly, but had certain continuing themes: protecting Anlo's distributive role in the economy east of the Volta; environmental decline from the 1920s; and marginalization within the wider political economy of Gold Coast/ Ghana. It is against this backdrop that the 'naturalness' of Ewe ethnicity was forged, an 'essentialist' paradigm that was a historical construct. The influence of landscape and the environment on the Anlo politics of identity persists in the postcolonial period.

---

[15] See Chapters 1 and 2.

[16] On the Ewe unification movement, see D.E.K. Amenumey, 'The pre-1947 background to the Ewe unification question', *Transactions of the Historical Society of Ghana* 10 (1969): 65–85; idem, *The Ewe Unification Movement*; Claude Welch, *Dream of Unity: Pan-Africanism and Political Unification in West Africa* (Ithaca, 1966); Greene, *History of the Anlo-Ewe*, ch. 5. On the politics of partitioned ethnic groups in Africa, see A.I. Asiwaju, ed., *Partitioned Africans: Ethnic Relations across Africa's International Boundaries, 1884–1984* (Lagos, 1989). This chapter avoids a detailed discussion of the political history of Ghana, as this is adequately covered by several studies. Good analyses are offered in David Kimble, *Political History of Ghana 1850–1928* (Oxford, 1963); Dennis Austin, *Politics in Ghana 1946–1960* (London, 1964); A.A. Boahen, *The Ghanaian Sphinx: Reflections on the Contemporary History of Ghana, 1972–1987* (Accra, 1989); Kevin Shillington, *Ghana and the Rawlings Factor* (London, 1992); Paul Nugent, *Big Men, Small Boys and Politics in Ghana* (Accra, 1995).

Coastal Erosion, Political Ecology & Environmental Citizenship

The impact of colonial boundaries on Anlo economy and society

German colonization curtailed active Anlo trading at Bey Beach (Lome) and other places along the Togo and Dahomey coast. Reference was made in Chapter 2 to the leaping traders' frontier and how traders in Keta founded Denu and Bey Beach as smuggling centres in their endeavour to elude British customs duties. On the eve of colonization, Ewe border settlements in the Gold Coast, such as Aflao, had residents who possessed farmlands in what became German Togoland. Intermarriages ensured a fluidity of movement before the colonial boundary was erected between 1884 and 1890. Colonization imposed a severe burden on Ewe communities in the Gold Coast and Togoland in the restrictions placed on their mobility. Several Krepi states, such as Adaklu and Waya, protested against artificial partition, but were silenced by German force. Ewe territory was split into two: Anlo, Some, Klikor, Peki and Tongu became part of the Gold Coast; and the other Ewe states were acquired by German Togoland.[17]

David Kimble made an astute observation on the unifying force of colonialism among colonized peoples:

> The arrival of Europeans had revealed to Gold Coast Africans – as it might have done to West Africans over a much wider area – how much they had in common concerning religious beliefs, political institutions, social customs and family traditions. The basic difference of colour, not initially regarded as of fundamental importance, but later exacerbated by false notion of superiority and inferiority – on both sides – did much to awaken national feeling.[18]

This later development was in sharp contrast to the disunited African response to colonial imposition.[19] The different colonial policies of Britain and Togo underscored for the partitioned Ewe the discriminatory nature of colonial rule. Divine Amenumey, historian of the Ewe unification movement, noted that:

> The incidence of colonial rule on the Ewe subtribes in Togoland was therefore quite harsh. The [German] government exacted compulsory labour, resorted to severe punishments, imposed a host of direct taxes, restrained the people's freedom to trade and infringed on their right to the land. The power of the traditional authorities, the chiefs, was effectively curtailed.[20]

British colonial rule in the Gold Coast was no blessing, but rested much more lightly in comparison with German colonialism. Direct taxation was not effectively introduced until the 1930s; indirect rule preserved a semblance of chiefly authority; and the indigenous peoples retained their right to land. Several Togolese evaded harsh German rule by emigrating to the Gold Coast, in spite of the prison terms that awaited those apprehended.[21] Awareness of Ewe disabilities under German – and later French – rule in Togo established the parameters of Ewe unification for the Anlo in the colonial period: Ewe unification under British auspices.

For the Anlo the imposition of the German boundary assailed trading relations in Eweland and the privileged position of Keta as the regional emporium. Colonial archives document the numerous frontier cases that arose from colonial restrictions on

---

[17] Amenumey, 'Ewe unification question', 67.
[18] Kimble, *Political History of Ghana*, 506.
[19] A.A. Boahen, *African Perspectives on Colonialism* (Baltimore, 1987).
[20] Amenumey, 'Ewe unification question', 67.
[21] Ibid., 68.

mobility between the Gold Coast and Togoland.[22] The boundary affected Ewe traders, farmers and families that were domiciled on both sides of the border. This partly explains the unique feature that calls for Ewe unification from the 1910s were mostly among coastal Ewe communities, especially those with commercial interests.[23] An important demand of Ewe traders was for free trade between the Gold Coast and Togoland.

Soon after his installation as *awoamefia* in 1907, Sri II pledged his support to the British in any adventure that would dislodge the Germans from Togo. Sri assisted the British force that entered Togo in August 1914 through information about German defence systems in Lome and the interior. He also organized carriers for the troops to Togo, and supplied the British forces with food and water. At short notice, Sri managed to enlist 1,200 Anlo into the colonial army.[24] The Anlo thus contributed substantially to the British war effort and entered Lome in August 1914 not as conquerors but as liberators of their kinsmen. Sri II and James Ocloo I received the King's Medal for African Chiefs (KMAC) in recognition of their services during the Togo campaign. The temporary partition of Togoland between the British Gold Coast and French Dahomey placed western Togo with much of the colony's Ewe population – including Lome – under British rule. The Anlo were elated and lobbied for the remaining Ewe peoples in the French section of Togoland to be incorporated into the Gold Coast on a permanent basis in the much-anticipated postwar settlement.

As the war drew to a close in late 1918, leading Ewe traders and chiefs in Togoland sent a number of petitions to the British government expressing their desires in the postwar settlement for German Togoland. In a delegation to the British commander in Togo on 19 November 1918, prominent traders, such as Octaviano Olympio, A.D. Mensah (brother of the chief of Porto Seguro) and Augustine de Souza, explicitly stated their wish to be incorporated into the Trans-Volta District of the Gold Coast under British administration.[25] Sri II supported these demands for the amalgamation of the Ewe in Togo and the Gold Coast. But French diplomacy was also active. The French government made representations to Britain requesting a territorial settlement of Togo after the war that would bequeath the port of Lome and its hinterland to the future French Togo. The Gold Coast had numerous surf ports so Britain decided to concede to the French request. The League of Nations in 1919 asked Britain and France to formally demarcate their boundary in the partitioned Togoland, and under the Simon–Milner Agreement of June 1919 Britain transferred two-thirds of British Togoland, including the districts of Lome and Misahohe, to French Togoland.[26] The two Togos became mandated territories under League of Nations trusteeship.

The Anlo and Togolese Ewe were aghast at the cavalier dismissal of their expressed sentiments on the settlement of their future. The Ewe had now been partitioned between the three separate political administrations of the Gold Coast, British Togoland and French Togoland. Sri II, a member of the Gold Coast Legislative

[22] See, for example, NAG, Ho, KE/c.19. Frontier incidents (1909–14).
[23] Amenumey, *Ewe Unification Movement*, 1.
[24] Ibid., 9–10.
[25] Ibid., 11.
[26] Ibid., 20.

Council since 1916 and familiar with the politics of deputation then in vogue in the Gold Coast, involved himself in shuttle diplomacy between the Gold Coast and Togoland in a bid to reverse the inimical Simon–Milner Agreement. In October and November 1919, Sri II paid several visits to Lome. He met leading Ewe chiefs and traders, advocated for the unification of Ewe-speaking peoples and canvassed for support to send an Ewe deputation to the League of Nations. Within the Legislative Council in the Gold Coast he sought the support of outstanding politicians, such as Casely Hayford and Nana Ofori Atta, in his bid to pressurize the British government to retain Togo. Though British officials in Lome and the Gold Coast were sympathetic to the Ewe lobby and obviously flattered by the adamant rejection of rival French rule, a directive from the Colonial Office on 10 December 1919 ended local British vacillation and emphasized that the Simon–Milner settlement was final.[27]

Geographical and cultural unity: removing artificial colonial borders
It is striking that chiefs like Sri II, and not the educated élite, spearheaded the movement for Ewe unification in the 1910s and early 1920s. The movement subsided in the 1920s and 1930s until another world war raised Ewe hopes for an agreeable settlement of their situation in the more sensitive and representative United Nations. Sri II was intensely disappointed at the outcome of the French–British partition of Togo. A colonial report in 1921 described Sri as 'conspicuously loyal to Government', and that he had borne his disappointment at the partition of Togoland 'with dignified resignation'.[28] But what was the Anlo position on Ewe unification? Why did Sri II and his State Council champion the Ewe cause?

Anlo chiefs have often been astute traders and they resented the restrictive trade policies in colonial Togo.[29] In arguing for the removal of colonial boundaries in Eweland, they presented the territory between the Volta and Mono as a bounded landscape, unified by geography and culture. Though Sri II's recorded position on Ewe unification comes from the 1940s, his long-term advocacy suggests some continuity in his stand. On 21 September 1943, the Anlo State Council petitioned the Secretary of State for the Colonies for the removal of the frontier between Atiteti and Grand Popo (settlements marking the Volta and Mono Rivers). The 'original unity' of the peoples between the Keta District and the Mono River, the Anlo State Council argued, had been artificially divided by colonial boundaries. The Council hoped for a more desirable political adjustment of the boundaries on the termination of the Second World War.[30] Instructively, the region between the Volta and the Mono also formed the core area that patronized Keta market. Anlo was not rejecting colonial rule, but rather demanding a free trade zone that predated the imposition of colonial frontiers.[31] The emphasis here was on free mobility, not a separate polity for Eweland.

[27] Ibid., 16–17.

[28] NAG, Accra, 11/1/404. Anlo Native Affairs.

[29] See Chapter 2.

[30] Amenumey, 'Ewe unification question', 77–8.

[31] The Anlo elder, L.C.M. Seshie, affirmed in an interview with the author that Keta people were involved in the Ewe unification movement because of an interest in the welfare of their kinsmen in French Togoland and the desire for free movement. Interview with L.C.M. Seshie, Dzelukope, 16 October 1996.

Sri II amplified his position on Ewe unification in a recorded discussion with the Senior District Commissioner (DC) of the Trans-Volta District in 1948. His views revealed a new phase in the Ewe conception of polity, no doubt influenced by the political conditions of the post-1945 era and the demands of the several Ewe and Togoland political organizations that emerged from the 1940s. Sri echoed several of his earlier demands. The Senior DC sought written confirmation of Sri's views on 26 April 1948:

> I understand your views to be:
>
> (a) Complete freedom of movement of Ewe people and their personal goods across the Anglo-French frontier is desirable.
>
> (b) The Anlos do not wish to lose their status as British subjects nor do they wish to sever in any way the connection they have had with the British Empire for many years and in especial the connection with the Gold Coast colony.
>
> (c) The Anlos wish to obtain all the benefits of a conventional zone designed to remove all disabilities resulting from the customs frontier between British and French territory but subject to their not losing their British status as in (b).
>
> (d) The Anlos wished to ensure that the same individual is not taxed in both territories.
>
> (e) The Anlos generally do not wish to be identified with peoples other than Ewes in Togoland under British and French Trusteeship.[32]

These were rather specific demands on the economic promotion of the Anlo and other Ewe-speaking peoples between the Volta and the Mono Rivers, which assumed the continuity of colonial rule and expressed a preference for British administration. But the last demand was a radical departure from Sri's expressed position in 1943. Anlo now advocated for a separate political entity for Ewe-speakers, albeit under colonial rule. The northern Ewe in old Krepi were included in the Anlo scheme.

Indeed, the Anlo had sought closer ties with the northern Ewe in the Gold Coast, particularly from the 1930s when the British colonial government abdicated responsibility for sea defence along the Anlo coast and prompted an Anlo search for a local and/or spiritual solution to sea erosion. This process involved a plumbing of the Anlo past, which emphasized historic ties to the northern Ewe as co-migrants from Notsie. The migrations of Anlo maritime fishermen along the Gold Coast and the hostility that was sometimes expressed by some coastal communities seem to have deepened Anlo consciousness of their common ties with the northern Ewe *vis-à-vis* other Gold Coast peoples.[33] The wider neglect of the Trans-Volta District within the Gold Coast economy nurtured the tentative links being forged between the northern and southern Ewe in the Gold Coast. The fears of the Gold Coast government that the mandated territory might be restored to Germany seemed to have discouraged some governors from investing in the development of the Trans-Volta District.[34] The boundaries of Ewe ethnicity – and landscape – were being extended.

The Second World War severely affected the economy of the Ewe of French Togo,

---

[32] NAG, Ho, KE/c.209. Senior DC to Togbui Sri II per DC Keta, 26 April 1948.

[33] Sandra E. Greene, 'The past and present of an Anlo-Ewe oral tradition', *History in Africa* 12 (1985): 82-5. Quoting R.W. Wyllie, Greene states that: 'From childhood Fanti learned to view the Anlo as thieves, kidnappers, sorcerers, and ritual murderers.' Ibid., 83.

[34] PRO, CO 96/776/5.

British Togo and the Gold Coast. The defeat of France in 1940 and the establishment of a collaborationist Vichy regime resulted in two competing French governments: the Vichy and De Gaulle regimes. French West Africa stayed loyal to the Vichy regime, while French Equatorial Africa went over to the De Gaulle regime. French Togo thus came under Allied blockade from 1940 to 1942, and the border between French and British Togoland was closed. The mobility of Ewe traders was curtailed and French Togolese lost access to 'commodities like salt, cloth, and dishes which had hitherto been acquired from Keta'.[35] The capitulation of French West Africa to the De Gaulle government led to the incorporation of French Togo into the Allied war effort and imposition of demands for raw materials and food. Wartime hardships rekindled Ewe dissatisfaction with the frontiers that partitioned Eweland and with French administration. The proliferation of literate associations in the Gold Coast and Togoland and the emergence of an educated Ewe élite – keenly attuned to international developments and the changing global balance of power – underpinned the resuscitation of the Ewe unification movement in the 1940s. The Ewe educated élite hoped that the postwar political dispensation, especially the United Nations (UN), would be more sympathetic to Ewe unification aspirations.[36]

Several organizations were formed to champion the cause of either Ewe unification or Togoland unification, and one in particular, the All Ewe Conference (AEC), with its important Anlo and Peki membership and its organ, the *Ewe News-Letter*, was prominent in its manipulation of landscape in the cause of Ewe unification. These new organizations sprang up in French Togo, British Togo and the Gold Coast. In French Togo, the Comité d'Unité Togolaise (CUT), founded in 1941, was the champion of Ewe unification.[37] It is perhaps not surprising that Anlo and Peki scholars would be at the forefront of the unification movement and essentially provide it with an ideology. Peki and Keta had been sites of Bremen Mission education from the mid-nineteenth century and constituted important education centres in Eweland. French Togolese desirous of providing their children with English education sent them to Keta. Bremen missionaries had chosen Anlo-Ewe as the written form of Ewe, equipping the Ewe with an important nationalist asset – a written language – and confirming the leadership role of Anlo in Eweland.[38]

An important educated constituency existed in Anlo from the early twentieth century, and their prominence in the community discussions of the Coode Report in 1929–30 emphasized the fact that they possessed some organizational form or the nucleus of one.[39] By the 1930s, the Anlo educated constituency had formed an 'Ewe

[35] Amenumey, *Ewe Unification Movement*, 36.

[36] Ibid.

[37] 'The Special Report of the first visiting UN Mission to the Trust Territories of Togoland under British Administration and Togoland under French Administration on the Ewe problem' (1950) provides valuable profile information on the various organizations advocating for either Ewe unification or the competing Togoland unification. NAG, Ho, KE/c.209. See also Amenumey, *Ewe Unification Movement*.

[38] See Chapter 3; Birgit Meyer, 'Translating the devil: an African appropriation of pietist Protestantism – the case of the Peki Ewe in southeastern Ghana, 1847–1992' (PhD thesis, University of Amsterdam, 1995). Benedict Anderson, *Imagined Communities: Reflections on the Origin and Spread of Nationalism* (London, 1983), highlights the importance of a written, shared language and newspapers in the imagining of community.

[39] See Chapter 4.

League', which sought to influence the policies of the Anlo State Council.[40] This decade also saw the existence of literate Ewe associations in other cities, such as the Ewe Unionist Association in Accra.[41] In May 1945, D.A. Chapman, an Anlo university graduate and a geography teacher at Achimota Secondary School, launched a monthly paper, the *Ewe News-Letter*, partly in response to a CUT request for assistance in publicizing the cause of Ewe unification.[42] The 1940s witnessed an Ewe cultural renaissance and the *Ewe News-Letter* was key to the dissemination of literature and culturo-historical information, which fed the growing Ewe cultural nationalism. The paper aimed at stimulating Ewe cultural consciousness, overcoming divisions within Ewe society and spearheading the unification cause.[43] The very first issue of the *Ewe News-Letter* provided a standardized version of Ewe history, tracing Ewe successive migrations from Ketu, Tado and Notsie and eventual dispersion within Togo and the Gold Coast. It emphasized the connectedness of the Ewe people and served as historical fact supporting an identity that was being actively constructed in the twentieth century.[44]

The vision of a shared landscape – environment, people, culture – between the Rivers Volta and Mono was presented in the second issue of the *Ewe News-Letter*:

> No one who knows anything about the Ewe people can pass from the British to the French side of the frontier without being struck by the absurdity of the frontier arrangement. This frontier cuts indiscriminately through villages and farms. A man's house may be on the British side while his farm is on the French side, and vice versa. The real truth of the matter is that it is impossible to set up a satisfactory frontier anywhere between the lower Volta in the Gold Coast and the lower Mono on the western boundary of Dahomey. One village has close family ties with the next, and so on all the way from the River Volta to the River Mono.[45]

Settlements and kinship networks were portrayed as intricately fused all the way from the Volta to the Mono. To argue for a single Ewe polity was to play for high stakes. To use landscape as a factor for separation from the Gold Coast would make it difficult to rearticulate a unified vision with the Gold Coast if Ewe unification failed, especially since the Akan majority ethnic group lived mostly west of the Volta.[46] A solid organization was crucial if the bid for Ewe unification was to succeed. In June 1946 Chapman engineered a conference in Accra of Ewe chiefs, notables and associations from the two Togos and the Gold Coast. The conference resulted in the

---

[40] NAG, Accra, ADM 39/1/550. Keta District Native Affairs (1936–46).

[41] Amenumey, 'Ewe unification question', 81.

[42] Ibid.

[43] Amenumey, *Ewe Unification Movement*, 39.

[44] *Ewe News-Letter* (May 1945), 1.

[45] *Ewe News-Letter* (June 1945), 2. The author's interviews elicited the fact that several Anlo had relations in Togo. See, for examples, interview with Freda Adabanu and Regina Ayayee, Keta, 20 September 1996; interview with S.S. Dotse, Adzido, 21 March 1997.

[46] A 1947 estimate put the number of Ewe and Ewe-speaking people in Togoland and the Gold Coast at 800,000 with 330,000 in the south-eastern Gold Coast, 126,000 in British Togoland and 290,000 in French Togoland. 'Special Report of the first visiting UN Mission' (1950), 1. The Gold Coast's population in 1948 was estimated at 4,118,450, making the Ewe an estimated 8 per cent of the total population of the Gold Coast. Gold Coast, *Census of Population 1948: Report and Tables* (Accra, 1950), 10.

formation of the AEC to coordinate the efforts of the various organizations for Ewe unification and to provide the movement with a central fund.

Chapman's successor as editor of the *Ewe News-Letter* and general secretary of the AEC, the Peki scholar E. Amu, continued to highlight landscape as a factor in Ewe unification. In the pages of the newsletter Amu argued the naturalness of Ewe unification, painting the area between the Volta and the Mono as a single geographical zone:

> Lome is not only a seaport town and capital of French Eweland, but it has also a good harbour. But Accra, which is a seaport town and the capital of the Gold Coast, has no harbour. Lome is therefore of greater economic importance than Accra. By far the greater part of Eweland – British and French, is nearer to Lome than to Accra. Furthermore traffic over the two main motor roads that lead from Eweland to Accra must be ferried across the Volta. Until this has been bridged, every part of Eweland is, for all practical purposes, nearer to Lome than Accra.[47]

The separate worlds east and west of the Volta had been cast in stark terms. It argued an eastward orientation – geographically and economically – for the region east of the Volta, overriding the accident of history that had included the area east of the Volta in the Gold Coast colony.

The demise of the Ewe unification movement

The hostility of the British and French governments, the rise of other organizations advocating Togoland unification and opposed to Ewe unification and a burgeoning Gold Coast nationalist party (CPP) that actively sought the incorporation of British Togoland derailed the Ewe unification movement. The prominence of the Gold Coast Ewe in commerce, education and the church generated unease among the other Ewe and non-Ewe speakers in British Togoland.[48] A group of mostly non-Ewe teachers in British Togoland formed the Togoland Union (TU) in 1943 to oppose Ewe unification and work rather for the unification of the two Togos. TU went into temporary abeyance, but was revived in 1947 with the advent of the AEC. It actively opposed the AEC and its claim to speak for Ewes in the three territories of French Togoland, British Togoland and the Gold Coast.[49] In 1951 it was incorporated and succeeded by the Togoland Congress (TC), which competed in Gold Coast elections from 1954, and was the major party advocating for separation from the Gold Coast. The lack of progress on the unification fronts – both Ewe and Togoland – prompted a meeting of the AEC, TU, French Togoland organizations pushing for Ewe unification and Togoland chiefs at Agome Palime on 7 January 1951. The separate movements decided to unite their fronts and advocate for the unification of the two Togolands and independence.[50] This new note intensified the opposition of the French and British governments and the CPP.

The French government did not want to relinquish its hold on French Togo and had every intention of incorporating it into the French Union. It did not encourage the demands for Ewe unification and actually sponsored two parties in French

---

[47] *Ewe News-Letter* (December 1946), 20.
[48] 'Special Report of the first visiting UN Mission', 10; Nugent, 'Central Togo minorities', 11.
[49] NAG, Accra, ADM 39/1/675; Amenumey, 'Ewe unification question', 83–4.
[50] Amenumey, *Ewe Unification Movement*, 124–5.

Togoland – the Parti Togolais du Progrès (founded 1946) and the Union des Chefs et des Populations du Nord (founded 1951) – to challenge the influence of CUT in French Togo politics. Official persecution gradually undercut the CUT and ensured the ascendancy of the government-supported parties.[51] The British government after initiating decolonization in the Gold Coast from 1948 was not interested in remaining as the administrative authority of British Togoland on the attainment of Gold Coast independence. For different reasons, both administering authorities thus opposed the Ewe unification movement. They struck an important blow against the movement in 1947, when in a joint memorandum to the UN they pointed out that the Ewe in the Gold Coast lay outside the UN trusteeship system hence Gold Coast Ewe could not petition the UN on the status of the two Togos.[52] Both colonial powers worked to isolate the Ewe in the Gold Coast. The CPP and Nkrumah's broad vision of political inclusiveness would provide a path to the reincorporation of the Gold Coast Ewe into the Gold Coast nationalist movement.

It was CPP nationalism that enticed members of the AEC and the TU and divided the unification parties. The adoption in 1951 of independence as a goal for a unified Togoland brought the unification movement into direct competition with the CPP's independence drive for the Gold Coast. With his pan-Africanist ideals and his hope to forge a West African government, Nkrumah could not be reconciled to the severance of British Togoland. Moreover, his identification with the Volta River Project, which encompassed both banks of the Volta (i.e. British Togoland and the Gold Coast), made it imperative that an independent Gold Coast control both banks of the River Volta.[53] Aware that the unification argument was in part an underdevelopment argument, the CPP ensured that development funds were directed towards the Trans-Volta–Togoland Region from 1952.[54]

Importantly, the CPP development package included the building of a suspension bridge over the Volta (the Adomi Bridge) to replace the crossing by ferry at Senchi.[55] This would minimize the geographical separation between the Gold Coast east and west of the Volta. The 1953 Van Lare Commission of Enquiry into Representational and Electoral Reform, by assigning the Trans-Volta–Togoland Region thirteen seats in an enlarged Gold Coast legislature of 104 seats, compelled the parties of British Togoland to compete against the CPP in Gold Coast elections from 1954. With its image as the 'commoners' party' and its patronage as an incumbent government, the CPP made rapid inroads into British Togoland. Nkrumah expressed his position on British Togoland in his autobiography:

I had never for one minute contemplated excluding that part of Togoland under United

[51] Ibid., 156–65.
[52] 'Special Report of the first visiting UN Mission', 2.
[53] Amenumey, *Ewe Unification Movement*, 171. On the politics of the Volta River Project, see Chapter 6.
[54] Kimble commented on how the unevenness of economic development can produce political discontent in the colonial context. Kimble, *Political History of Ghana*, 556. On the crucial impact of economics on the Gold Coast nationalist movement, see Richard Rathbone, 'Businessmen in politics: party struggle in Ghana, 1949–1957', *Journal of Development Studies* 9, 3 (1973): 391–402.
[55] Austin, *Politics in Ghana*, 234.

Kingdom administration from my political organisation of the Gold Coast, for it was my aim to bring about a united country embracing all four regions – the Northern Territories, Ashanti, the Colony and Trans-Volta/Togoland.[56]

Nkrumah urged the British government to make a statement in the UN announcing that the independence of the Gold Coast was imminent and that the Togoland issue must be resolved soon, as Britain did not intend to remain as the administering authority after the Gold Coast's independence. Indeed, the British government went a step further and suggested that: 'the objectives of the Trusteeship would be achieved if Togoland attained self-government as an integral part of an independent Gold Coast'.[57]

Even before the 1956 UN-organized plebiscite that resolved the political future of Togoland, several leading members of the AEC and the TU had taken their place within the ranks of the CPP. F.Y. Asare and Gerald Awuma of the TU and D.A. Chapman, F.K. Fiawoo and Philip Gbeho of the AEC were part of this important contingent.[58] Paradoxically, the CPP managed to adopt both the Ewe and Togoland unification causes. The formation of the Trans-Volta–Togoland region presented in nucleus the Ewe unification the AEC sought. Considering the UN position in 1947 that the Ewe within the Gold Coast fell beyond UN trusteeship and the Togoland question, the unification of the Ewe in the Gold Coast and the southern section of British Togoland in 1952 was as good as it could get. Leading members of AEC joined the CPP and the bandwagon for Gold Coast independence. After all, founding members of the CPP included an Anlo son, K.A. Gbedemah, whose father had been a founding member of the AEC.[59] The CPP also stated that after Gold Coast independence, which would include British Togoland, it would then broker a union of some sort with French Togoland. So TU members did not feel out of place within the CPP. The 1956 UN plebiscite revealed that the unification party was limited to the southern British Togoland. Fifty-eight per cent of the votes cast in British Togoland supported integration with the Gold Coast, while 42 per cent was for separation from the Gold Coast and the continuance of UN trusteeship.[60] British Togoland joined the Gold Coast in an independent Ghana on 6 March 1957. The unification cause went underground for another hiatus.

Independence, political ecology and the discourse of environmental citizenship

The history of the Ewe unification movement and the landscape argument the Ewe intellectuals had utilized would continuously intrude into party politics in independent Ghana. Not only did the region east of the Volta remain socially separate from the west, despite the construction of bridges across the Volta, the loyalty of the Ewe to the Ghanaian nation-state was often queried. And, as independent nation-states

[56] Kwame Nkrumah, *Ghana: The Autobiography of Kwame Nkrumah* (New York, 1976 edn), 260.
[57] Ibid., 261.
[58] Nugent, 'Central Togo minorities', 11–13; Amenumey, *Ewe Unification Movement*, 165–7.
[59] Ibid., 137.
[60] Ibid., 266–70; Nkrumah, *Ghana*, 262.

jealously guarded their colonial boundaries, the prospect of a unified Eweland became less and less certain. Ghana's relations with Togo have often been tense in the independent era, each accusing the other of supporting dissident political groups and of entertaining territorial ambitions. Tensions have not eased even under the Ewe-led NDC government, and the international border has frequently been closed. It is incontestable that independent Ghanaian governments have privileged the region west of the Volta in development projects. As coastal erosion devastated parts of the Anlo coast and the issue of relocation remained in abeyance, Ghanaian governments made little effort to repair or improve the impaired physical infrastructure of the Keta District.

Anlo opinion is unified on how Ghanaian governments have failed to address Anlo's environmental problems. With the exception of the CPP, most of the post-1966 governments were portrayed as insensitive to coastal devastation and socio-economic decline in Anlo. Though Ghanaian governments have intervened to check the sea's onslaught on the Anlo coast, the Anlo questioned the commitment of these governments to a permanent resolution of coastal erosion. The Anlo critique of Ghanaian governments was also a discourse on marginality and the politics of inclusion and exclusion. That this discourse was framed in oblique environmental terms is perhaps a legacy of the old landscape argument in favour of the naturalness of Ewe unification. In an independent Ghana, the Anlo have eschewed political rhetoric that might portray them as separatists. Irwin points out that 'environmental citizenship raises many familiar questions of power and equality in a relatively new setting'.[61] It represents pressure 'from below', a discourse on citizenship or political inclusion not dictated by the framework of the state.[62] The advantage of the discourse of environmental citizenship for the Anlo is that it enabled them to highlight their environmental crisis, symbolizing their powerlessness, and criticize governments in terms that did not resurrect the image of a separatist Ewe. Whereas the landscape argument was 'secessionist' and had advocated for a separate Ewe polity, environmental citizenship is about 'inclusion' and a critique of Ghanaian governments for pushing the Ewe out of the nation-state.

With prominent Anlo sons in the CPP, the Anlo were optimistic that the CPP government would find a final solution to coastal erosion and environmental deterioration in Anlo. The Anlo could also count on the accelerated economic development promised by the CPP government. Anlo disappointment under the CPP and successive Ghanaian governments where these objectives are concerned has transformed environmental policy into the yardstick by which governments are reviewed, and has encouraged the Anlo perception that their powerlessness reflects the Anlo absence in government. The financial considerations of the colonial government continued to inform the evaluations of independent Ghanaian governments. Though rarely stated, the decline in Keta's revenue earning potential seemed to weaken the resolve of independent governments to embark on expensive sea defence projects in

[61] Alan Irwin, *Citizen Science: A Study of People, Expertise and Sustainable Development* (London and New York, 1995), 177.
[62] Ibid., 178.

the area. Several governments initiated 'surveys', which seldom translated into effective action. The impact of political ecology was to sharpen Anlo–Ewe ethnicity, especially as the only governments that appeared concerned with Keta's plight were those with prominent Ewe members. And the politics of neglect by successive Ghanaian governments built the foundation of Anlo and Ewe commitment to the Provisional National Defence Council (PNDC)/NDC governments of the post-1981 era, for this was the first government to seriously tackle Keta's myriad environmental and economic problems.

The CPP days: an era of hope

Several educated Anlo had been early supporters of the CPP. As L.C.M. Seshie informed the author, the Keta constituency supported Kwame Nkrumah in his 1949 break from the United Gold Coast Convention (UGCC) to form the CPP. Seshie, an old member of the UGCC, became the district secretary for the CPP in Keta.[63] K.A. Gbedemah was a founding member of the CPP, while Daniel Chapman became one of Nkrumah's trusted confidants in the early years of CPP power.[64] Residents of Keta believed such loyalty would be rewarded by the CPP with a permanent sea defence wall. Their wish took a while to be fulfilled. Between 1951 and 1957 the old ineffective remedy of timber groynes was tried once again. The sea destroyed the groynes.[65] In 1958 the CPP government was actually contemplating a forcible relocation of Keta town and its residents 'to a site near Akatsi on the ground that the sea was on the verge of breaking into the Keta lagoon and swallowing up Keta'.[66] Keta's residents resisted relocation, and their loyalty to the government in power eventually paid off. As Togbuivi Kumassah surmised:

> During Nkrumah's time, ironically Keta was a CPP town and Anloga a UP [United Party, formed in 1957] town. Government wanted to satisfy Keta people for supporting the proper government. Also one of the citizens of the area became the Finance Minister of the Nkrumah regime, that is Gbedemah. So, by and by, an approach was made to save Keta from sea erosion.[67]

The Public Works Department conducted a technical survey in 1960 on the dual problem of coastal erosion and lagoon flooding in the Keta area and developed a phased project.[68] It was decided to construct a longitudinal sea wall initially along the beach of Keta town. Rocks were non-existent in the area, and steel sheet piling was

[63] Interview with L.C.M. Seshie, Dzelukope, 16 October 1996.

[64] Nkrumah, *Ghana*.

[65] Cooperativa Muratori and Cementisti, 'Keta sea defence – Ghana' (Draft Project Document, June 1987), 20. Steven Selormey, the District Coordinating Director for Keta District, kindly shared this valuable document with the author.

[66] Chapman W.S. Klutse, *The Keta Coast Erosion and Dredging for Development, and some Landmarks for Anlor History* (Accra, 1984), 24.

[67] Interview with Togbuivi Kumassah, Woe, 3 September 1996. Both Keta and Anloga were initially in the CPP camp. The Anloga riots of 1953, and the imposition of a curfew on Anloga, led to Anloga's political switch. Anloga blamed the nascent CPP government for the curfew. Keta and Anlo united in their support of the same parties after the CPP's overthrow in 1966. Personal correspondence from G.K. Nukunya, 28 September 1999.

[68] Public Works Department, *Report on Coastal Sea Erosion, Sea Defences and Lagoon Flooding at Keta* (Accra, 1960).

used as a substitute.[69] Togbui James Ocloo IV in 1960 drove a low-loader or long vehicle for the State Transport Corporation, and it gave him deep satisfaction to deliver some of the sheet piling from Accra to his native Keta.[70]

Divisive party politics at the local and national levels sabotaged Keta's sea defence project. In the fever to Africanize the civil service, an unqualified Ghanaian road surveyor (Aryee) managed to capture the top position in the Public Works Department in the Keta District. His inefficiency sabotaged the sea defence project and resulted in its temporary abandonment, while a personal rift between Nkrumah and Gbedemah ensured that the project was never resumed – or so the Anlo believe.[71] Chapman Klutse provides an account of Aryee's debacle:

> The Road Surveyor presently ordered a deviation of the sheet piling seaward, out of the planned bearing, for reasons, I understood, best known only to himself. The piles got into deep water and instability set in. The pile concrete tops which should never have been built on at that stage were frantically built on in the hope of stabilizing the piles. Top heaviness resulted. The concrete tops soon started to collapse together with the sheet piles. By the time this 'construction' reached the Keta fort, everything looked hopeless but dragged on for some distance and ended just beyond the Zion Mission Chapel. This was virtually the end of the project, evidence of which is at the Keta beach today.[72]

Today the remnants of this ill-fated project constitute a hazard to swimmers and beach-seine operations on this section of the Keta beach. The project had ignored the hard lessons of the colonial experiments: the sandy nature of Keta's beach did not provide a solid foundation for such constructions as the iron sea wall.[73] Common sense should have indicated, moreover, that the salt water would have corroded the sheet piling. However, it must be conceded that this was conceived as a temporary measure.

A decline in the world market price for cocoa – Ghana's leading export – created financial difficulties for the CPP government from 1961 and put a brake on the party's developmental plans. Corruption, nepotism and faction fighting over spoils within the CPP prompted Nkrumah to carry out an internal purge of his party. Advocating his own brand of socialism, Nkrumah expelled many senior members of the CPP – including Gbedemah – to strengthen party discipline.[74] Gbedemah's independent mind lay at the core of his falling out with Nkrumah. As Minister of Finance, a portfolio he held from 1954 to 1961, he objected to Nkrumah's image being put on the Republic's new banknotes.[75] He resigned as Minister of Finance and

---

[69] Klutse, *Keta Coast Erosion*, 14.

[70] Interview with Togbui James Ocloo IV, Keta, 4 September 1996.

[71] Aryee similarly bungled the attempt to cut a canal at Kedzi and release the flooded waters of the Keta Lagoon into the sea. See Chapter 5.

[72] Klutse, *Keta Coast Erosion*, 16. See also interview with Edward Kartey-Attipoe, Keta, 17 October 1996; interview with Nancy Dovlo, Keta, 20 March 1997.

[73] See Chapter 4. A similar verdict was handed down in the Faculty of Architecture, *Keta Study* (University of Science and Technology, Occasional Report No. 15, 1971), 104. This study further opined that effective seashore protection at Keta was possible and desirable. Togbui James Ocloo IV made a copy of this 1971 study available to the author. Such optimistic reports sustained the hopes of Keta residents for an eventual resolution of their environmental problems.

[74] Shillington, *Ghana and the Rawlings Factor*, 11.

[75] Daniel M. McFarland, *Historical Dictionary of Ghana* (Metuchen, 1985), 88.

was reassigned to the Ministry of Health. In September 1961 Nkrumah expelled Gbedemah, E.K. Dadson, Kojo Botsio and several leading members of the CPP for amassing large personal fortunes. Gbedemah protested his innocence in a spirited speech in the National Assembly, in which he criticized Nkrumah's dictatorial tendencies. He went into self-exile after this remonstration.[76]

Residents at Keta observed with apprehension the immediate consequences of the rift between Nkrumah and Gbedemah. Togbui James Ocloo IV, installed as chief of Keta in January 1961, was alarmed when Nkrumah ordered the removal of the sheet piling from Keta to Tema later in 1961. A port was under construction in Tema and the materials were needed there. Chief James Ocloo IV intervened and was informed that the sheets would be replaced when sheets arrived for the Tema project. The closure of Keta's port on the opening of Tema harbour in 1962 heightened the Anlo sense of political persecution, though this in reality had nothing to do with the Nkrumah–Gbedemah quarrel.[77] That was the end of sea defence in Keta under the Nkrumah regime.[78] Yaw Boateng, an infant in 1961, recounted the local version of this sad development:

> Gbedemah was then the Minister of Finance. It is said that Nkrumah gave him money to go abroad and bring experts to examine the Keta area and also plan for a harbour. But Gbedemah misappropriated the funds. So they came to build a sea defence wall. It had cement foundation with metal sheet walls. The sea corroded the metal sheets. Maybe the harbour would have benefited us better. Or had he [Gbedemah] found qualified experts, they may have come up with a permanent solution. Now we are still besieged by the sea. Gbedemah is from Anyako. He didn't see Keta as his hometown, so maybe he was not motivated to assist Keta.[79]

This account is very partial on historical fact, but expresses a strong need to come to terms with deep local disappointment.[80] The Anlo had come to the conclusion that the cost of effective sea defence and the technology involved made it necessarily a government project. This was not a project for private initiative.[81] Each successive government would be petitioned to resume sea defence works at Keta.

Keta on hold: 1966–81

An acute drop in declining cocoa prices in 1965–6 precipitated an economic crisis and served as the immediate backdrop to the military overthrow of the CPP government in February 1966. Three Ewe officers (Kotoka, Harlley and Deku) and two Akan officers (Afrifa and Ocran) spearheaded the coup.[82] A National Liberation Council (NLC) was formed and the pivotal role of an Anlo son, Colonel E.K. Kotoka, renewed Anlo hope for a solution to their environmental problems. Kotoka took

[76] Austin, *Politics in Ghana*, 406–7.

[77] See Chapter 6.

[78] Interview with Togbui James Ocloo IV, Keta, 4 September 1996.

[79] Interview with Yaw Boateng, Keta, 16 October 1996.

[80] Gbedemah had stayed with his grandmother in Keta as a child. He won the parliamentary seat for Keta in 1951 and again in 1969 under his National Alliance of Liberals (NAL). Kojo T. Vieta, *The Flagbearers of Ghana: Profiles of One Hundred Distinguished Ghanaians*, Vol. 1 (Accra, 1999), 76–85.

[81] Interview with Edward Kartey-Attipoe, Keta, 17 October 1996.

[82] David Brown, 'Who are the tribalists? Social pluralism and political ideology in Ghana', *African Affairs* 81, 322 (1982): 56–7.

command of the Ghana Armed Forces after the coup and was also in charge of the portfolios of Defence, Health, Labour, and Social Welfare.[83] Unfortunately, some junior Akan officers killed Kotoka in an unsuccessful coup attempt on 17 April 1967. Akan interests seemingly dominated the NLC now in the person of the Asante soldier, A.A. Afrifa. The NLC considered itself a custodial government, and implemented little in the nature of development policy. As head of the NLC, Afrifa supervised general elections and the return to civilian rule in 1969. The CPP was explicitly banned from competing in this election, though an exception was made for Gbedemah's National Alliance of Liberals (NAL). In a rather uneven contest, the government-favoured Progress Party (PP), under K.A. Busia, swept up 105 out of the 140 seats in the National Assembly. The successor of the UGCC–UP tradition, the predominantly Akan opposition was now in power.

Some studies of politics in Ghana comment on the play of the ethnic card in the elections of 1969 and during the brief PP tenure from 1969 to 1972. Kevin Shillington, for example, argues that the voting patterns and the support base of the PP and the NAL in the 1969 elections reveal an Asante–Ewe ethnic animosity that was apparent even in the military regime of the NLC.[84] Though Shillington provides little historical evidence in support of this Ewe–Asante divide, other political commentators note the increasing ethnic polarization in the politics of the Second Republic. It is not insignificant that Gbedemah's NAL won fourteen out of sixteen parliamentary seats in the Volta Region, the two exceptions being the Akan-dominated areas of Nkwanta and Krachi.[85] An important contributor to the perceived Ewe–Asante rivalry may have been the 1967 Akan-led coup, which eliminated Kotoka and two other senior Ewe officers.[86] Victor Owusu, a leading Asante PP member, did not help matters when he unwisely described the Ewe as nepotistic and inward-looking in a public speech.[87] David Brown has pointed to the Ewe–Akan rivalry in Ghanaian politics of the 1960s and 1970s, and he expresses the conviction that embattled Ghanaian governments have often scapegoated the Ewe in an era of continued economic decline.[88] He examines the 'myth of Ewe secessionism' and how governments from the colonial era up to 1981 have perpetuated this view.[89] These studies often reify the Ewe–Asante rivalry, portraying it as long-standing and ignoring the fact that ethnicity is 'situational, flexible and manipulable' and the historical evidence of an Asante–Anlo alliance for most of the nineteenth century and well into the twentieth century.[90]

[83] McFarland, *Historical Dictionary of Ghana*, 107.

[84] Shillington, *Ghana and the Rawlings Factor*, 17.

[85] Vieta, *Flagbearers*, 84. As a note of caution against taking ethnic analysis to extremes, it is worth mentioning that an Asante royal, J.H. Cobbina, was chairman of NAL. Mike Oquaye, 'The Ghanaian elections of 1992: a dissenting view', *African Affairs* 94, 375 (1995): 272.

[86] Brown, 'Social pluralism and political ideology', 57.

[87] David R. Smock and Audrey Smock, *The Politics of Pluralism: A Comparative Study of Lebanon and Ghana* (New York, 1975), 247.

[88] Brown, 'Social pluralism and political ideology', 37–69; idem, 'Sieges and scapegoats: the politics of pluralism in Ghana and Togo', *Journal of Modern African Studies* 21, 3 (1983): 431–60.

[89] Brown, 'Social pluralism and political ideology'.

[90] Carola Lentz and Paul Nugent, 'Ethnicity in Ghana: a comparative perspective', in idem, eds, *Ethnicity in Ghana*, 3, 12–13. On the malleability of ethnicity, see, in general, the essays in Leroy H. Vail, ed., *The Creation*

They also subsume Anlo interests within Ewe politics and that of the Volta Region, but these did not always overlap.

It suffices to state that nothing much happened during the NLC and PP eras where Keta's environmental problems were concerned. In 1968 the NLC, in what seemed to be a token nod to Keta's environmental problems, commissioned a West German firm to undertake a survey of lagoon flooding and land reclamation in the Keta Lagoon basin. The resulting Wakuti Report (1969) was quietly shelved.[91] The NLC's relocation of the Volta Region capital from Keta to Ho in 1968 further undermined Keta's declining urban status and distributive role in the economy east of the Volta. Togbuivi Kumassah informed the author that: 'During the Busia time, when the appeal for the [sea defence] construction was made ... that was the end. They did not take the matter up so seriously'.[92] Indeed, the Busia government unwittingly kicked aside one of the props of the Anlo economy through its Aliens Compliance Order, which deported the Hausa and Zabrama traders, who underpinned Keta's Kente and retail trade. Then, in 1970, the Busia government also proposed the relocation of Keta town. The town's residents again declined the invitation to move to a new site.[93] The further decay of the Ghanaian economy made economic redress and recovery a necessary step to any meaningful development policy. In pursuit of this, an increasingly unpopular PP government devalued the Ghanaian cedi by 40 per cent at the end of 1971.[94] This provided the immediate cause for the military coup of Colonel I.K. Acheampong in January 1972 and the advent of the National Redemption Council (NRC).

For a government that lacked direction and was constantly embroiled in political and economic crises, the formation in 1972 of the National Liberation Movement of Western Togoland, which sought a union with French Togo, provided a convenient scapegoat for some of the country's woes. It did not matter that the movement attracted little support even within the Volta Region.[95] It is not certain whether this development and the virulent government criticism of 'Ewe tribalism' made the Anlo reticent to approach the government on their coastal erosion problem. Acheampong's dismissal of several Ewe military officers for an alleged coup in 1975, believed to have been 'manufactured' by the regime itself, certainly convinced the Anlo–Ewe that they were not exactly in the government's good books.[96]

It was not until early 1978, after the sea broke the front of the Keta fort on the evening of 25 January 1978, that the Anlo sought the assistance of the Acheampong

---

[90 cont.] *of Tribalism in Southern Africa* (London, 1991).

[91] Klutse, *Keta Coast Erosion*, 24.

[92] Interview with Togbuivi Kumassah, Woe, 3 September 1996. The record shows, however, that timber revetments were constructed along the Keta beach in 1971. As before, this experiment failed. Cooperativa Muratori and Cementisti, 'Keta', 19.

[93] Setriakor Kobla Nyomi, 'A pastoral theological perspective on ministry to persons dealing with loss to natural disasters in Ghana' (PhD thesis, Princeton Theological Institute, 1991), 93.

[94] The Ghanaian pound replaced the pound sterling (in use from 1889) at par value on independence in 1957. A new currency, the cedi, was introduced in 1965 at the rate of C2.40 to the Ghanaian pound.

[95] Brown, 'Social pluralism and political ideology', 61.

[96] Brown, 'Sieges and scapegoats', 455.

Photo 7.1 Collapsed front of Fort Prindsensten, Keta, 4 September 1996 *(by author)*.

government (renamed the Supreme Military Council (SMC) in 1975) on a sea defence wall (Photo 7.1). The sea subsequently eroded the Keta–Denu road at Vormaworkofe and Adzido. The besieged citizens of Keta hurriedly formed the Keta Lagoon and its Littoral Problems Association in January 1978, and petitioned the SMC government. The Volta Regional Commissioner and the Commissioner for Works and Housing met the Anlo at the Anlo District Council Hall in Keta on 31 January 1978, and unveiled a C300,000 government plan to protect the Anlo shoreline through stone works.[97] The stones would be obtained from stone quarries at Dzodze and transported to the project site. The government later raised this amount to C450,000 and a contract was awarded to Messrs Marine Salvage Works Limited to perform the required work. Messrs Marine Salvage implemented the project in a desultory manner and in August 1978 the disillusioned residents of Keta called for an official investigation of the company and the very process that awarded it the contract. The company claimed to have expended almost all the allocated government funds, and yet the project was far from complete.[98] Meanwhile the sea continued to pound the Keta coastline. Marine Salvage lacked an adequate number of tipper trucks to speed up its work, and much of the required heavy equipment in the country was in a deteriorated state. An inept government and a collapsed economy made external financial institutions unwilling to honour import licences with letters of credit.[99] The Keta project had become a casualty of a weak Ghanaian economy.

The country's economic indices were disheartening: inflation had increased from 3 per cent in 1970 to 116.5 per cent in 1977, and the country's credit lines were

[97] Klutse, *Keta Coast Erosion*, 27–34.
[98] Ibid., 35.
[99] Ibid., 42–5.

Figure 7.1 High-water mark at Keta Town, 1907–87 *(Source: Cooperativa Muratori and Cementesti, 'Keta', 25).*

blocked by July 1979 because of an inability to pay past arrears.[100] A farcical government attempt to defuse calls for a civilian government through a 'Union Government' scheme engendered civilian unrest and sparked a palace coup in July 1978. Acheampong was removed as head of state, and Lieutenant General Fred Akuffo, the new head of state in a revamped SMC government, promised a general election on 18 June 1979. A successful army mutiny by the middle and lower ranks of the military intervened on 4 June 1979. The leader of the Armed Forces Revolutionary Council (AFRC), Flight Lieutenant John Jerry Rawlings, committed the new government to the existing transition programme and proceeded to conduct a 'house-cleaning exercise' to rid the country of corruption. Elections came on as planned and the victorious People's National Party (PNP) formed a new civilian government. The persistence of official corruption and the apparent lack of direction in the new government provided the pretext for Rawlings to intervene again in a military government on 31 December 1981. This time Rawlings declared that he had come to stay, and his PNDC launched a national revolution on a socialist platform.[101]

'Our own government': the environmental platform in Anlo politics, 1981 to the present

By the early 1980s, two-thirds of Keta lay under the sea, and it was with a sense of desperation that the Anlo turned to the PNDC in the hope that the Keta-native head

[100] Boahen, *Ghanaian Sphinx*, 9–10.
[101] On these revolutionary days, see Kwame A. Ninsin, *Political Struggles in Ghana 1967–1981* (Accra, 1985); Shillington, *Ghana and the Rawlings Factor.*

of state would be their saviour. Figure 7.1 indicates the high-water mark at Keta up to 1987. The prominent Ewe contingent in the PNDC government was reassuring: the Tsikata brothers from the Anloga–Whuti area, Dan Abodapki from Keta, Steve Obimpeh from North Dayi, Obed Asamoah and Kwabena Adjei from northern constituencies in the Volta Region. The PNDC, more than any government, would understand the environmental crisis along the Anlo coast, and how this had come to symbolize political marginality for the Anlo. A representation of Anlo chiefs, including Togbuivi Kumassah, went to Accra to plead their case before the head of state.[102] But there was little the PNDC could do in its early years in office managing a collapsed economy on a vague platform of diffuse socialism.[103] Severe economic hardships compelled the PNDC to abort its socialist platform and to adopt an Economic Recovery Programme in 1983 under the auspices of the International Monetary Fund and the World Bank. Implementing the stringent measures of what became known as the Structural Adjustment Programme won the government the grudging respect of the capitalist West. A respectable growth rate of 5 per cent in gross domestic product (GDP) between 1985 and 1990 signalled the arrest of economic decay and the revival of the Ghanaian economy.

From 1985 the PNDC began to tackle the problem of coastal erosion. Coastal erosion plagues countries of the Bight of Benin, and the huge investment required in coastal protection and management and the potential impact of beach protection on the adjacent coastline suggested regional cooperation as a line of action. Ghana – under the auspices of the Organization of African Unity's Scientific Technical Research Commission – hosted a meeting of Ghana, Togo, Benin and Nigeria in Accra in September 1985, to discuss and formulate a blueprint for coastal protection. The European Economic Community (EEC) supported this regional endeavour and sponsored the next meeting of the four countries in Togo in April 1987.[104] EEC funding for the project seemed likely, but somehow the regional discussions dissipated and national solutions have been adopted instead.[105] In 1986 the PNDC had commissioned a group of consultants headed by Professor J. Mawuse Dake to study the problem of coastal erosion in Ghana and advise the government on strategies for the implementation of relevant measures.[106] That there were twenty-two active spots of coastal erosion along Ghana's 370-mile coastline made coastal erosion a major national concern.[107] Of these twenty-two erosion spots, the most pernicious area was Keta.

The years of coastal devastation by the sea and frequent flooding by the lagoon had destroyed the physical infrastructure and economy of the Keta subregion. What was needed was not just sea defence or lagoon-flooding control, but an entire package designed to physically protect the subregion and rehabilitate its economy. Around 1986 the PNDC retained the Italian firm of Cooperativa Muratori and Cementisti to design an integrated plan for sea defence, lagoon-flooding control and economic

---

[102] Interview with Togbuivi Kumassah, Woe, 3 September 1996.

[103] For a perceptive analysis of the political economy of the PNDC, see Nugent, *Big Men, Small Boys*.

[104] Cooperativa Muratori and Cementisti, 'Keta', 31.

[105] Interview with Steven Selormey, Dzelukope, 17 October 1996.

[106] Cooperativa Muratori and Cementisti, 'Keta', 31.

[107] *Weekly Spectator* (30 November 1996).

rehabilitation. The firm's June 1987 report has been cited frequently in the preceding pages. The integrated development project for the Keta area would involve sea defence works at Kedzi, Vodza and Keta town, lagoon-flooding control, construction of access roads, lagoon reclamation and agricultural development, a shrimp industry based on the Keta Lagoon, the building of a fishing harbour and tourist facilities.[108] The entire package would require donor inputs of an estimated $44,148,000 and a Ghanaian government contribution of $488,000 and C634,420,000.[109] Though expected funding from the Italian government did not materialize, the 1987 report remained an important blueprint for the government as it canvassed other sources of funding. Internal and external pressure pushed the PNDC in 1990–1 to consider a transition to a democratically elected civilian government. Ghanaian governments are notorious for abrogating the policies of previous governments, especially as military governments would deprive themselves of justification if they continued the policies of the predecessors. As the country approached democratic elections in 1992, it made great sense for the Anlo to vote for continuity under the new NDC – the civilian mutation of the PNDC.[110] It was the only way forward. Demographic statistics underscored a continuous decline in Keta's population from 16,719 in 1960 to 12,595 in 1984.[111] A growth rate of 0.5 per cent per annum made the Keta District the slowest-growing district in the country. Its unemployment rate of 38 per cent was also far above the national average of 28 per cent.[112] Economy and society in the Keta District desperately needed succour.

The Keta Basin Integrated Development Project in the elections of 1992 and 1996
Political campaigning in the 1992 and 1996 elections took on a strong ethnic tone. But ethnicity is also about political mobilization for material rewards. In Anlo, the Keta Basin Integrated Development Project took on a broad relevance because of its comprehensive economic proposals. The Anlo believed that the NDC was the only credible party that could deliver, as it had initiated this project. Considering the fact that the two Rawlings regimes had appropriated several important businesses belonging to Akans, notably Asante, it is perhaps not surprising that these aggrieved persons would gravitate to the dominant Akan party, the New Patriotic Party (NPP). Contesting an incumbent government is no easy feat, and financially constrained opposition parties relied heavily on the propaganda of a new and vibrant private press. Perhaps more than any other medium, it was the press that firmly wrote ethnicity into the elections of 1992, which ushered in the Fourth Republic, and those of 1996.[113]

[108] Cooperativa Muratori and Cementisti, 'Keta', 37–41.

[109] Ibid., 181–3.

[110] Analyses of the 1992 and 1996 elections have stressed the theme of 'continuity' and the NDC's record for promoting development in rural areas as an important factor for its electoral support. See Nugent, 'Living in the past'; and Richard Jeffries and Clare Thomas, 'The Ghanaian elections of 1992', *African Affairs* 92, 368 (1993): 331–66.

[111] Republic of Ghana, *1984 Population Census of Ghana: Special Report on Localities by Local Authorities – Volta Region* (Accra, 1989), 24.

[112] Keta District Assembly, 'Medium Term (5 Years) Development Plan (1996–2000)' (May 1996), 2, 26. The author is grateful to Obed Nutsugah for sharing this document with him.

[113] See, for example, *Ghanaian Chronicle* (7–13 September 1992).

The old CPP camp formed four competing parties: the People's Heritage Party (PHP), the National Independence Party (NIP), the People's National Convention (PNC) and the National Convention Party (NCP). Intriguingly, the last party counted among its ranks PNDC stalwarts such as Kojo Tsikata, suggesting a divide-and-rule tactic by the incumbent government. Significantly, the NCP did join the NDC in an electoral alliance in 1992, and its flag bearer, K.N. Arkaah, did become the vice-president of President Rawlings.[114]

Paul Nugent accurately described the NPP as an Akan-dominated party:

[It] represented a significant section of the Ghanaian elite, chiefly professionals and business-men, drawn from the Akan heartlands of the defunct Progress Party ... The rest of the country was not as visibly represented in the higher echelons of the party. For example, the only signifi-cant faces from the Volta Region were those of Major Courage Quarshigah ... and his lawyer Ray Kakraba.[115]

The party's presidential candidate was the author's former professor and eminent historian, Albert Adu Boahen. All the competing parties were keenly sensitive about ethnicity and sought to make their parties regionally representative in the choice of presidential and vice-presidential candidates. Rawlings chose a coastal Akan and Boahen the northerner Alhaji R.I. Alhassan. The press portrayal of the election as a straight fight between the Ewe-led NDC and the Akan-led NPP obscured the important historical fact that the Danquah–Busia tradition had been rather strong in the Volta Region.[116] The result was that the NPP's campaign in the Volta Region was rather cursory and condescending, alienating potential supporters. But the NPP seemed confident in its belief that it would sweep to victory in the presidential and parliamentary elections scheduled, respectively, for November and December 1992.

The opposition parties were dumbfounded at the resounding victory of Rawlings in the presidential elections on 3 November 1992, winning nine out of the ten regions – Ashanti being the exception – with an overall poll of 58.3 per cent of the votes cast. The NDC's electoral return from the Volta Region was an outstanding 93.3 per cent. The opposition parties cried fraud and collectively boycotted the parliamentary elections in December.[117] After a thorough review of the electoral results and the complaints of the opposition parties, Richard Jeffries, Clare Thomas and Nugent concluded that Rawlings and the NDC would have won the 1992 election. The message of continuity was a powerful one, and the tangible rewards of economic recovery – potable water, roads and electricity in villages – swept the rural vote.[118] The overwhelming electoral victories notched up by the ruling party in the Volta constituencies raised suspicion:

Where the opposition parties did have legitimate cause for suspicion was in relation to the results of the Volta Region. At first glance, what is striking is the majority for Rawlings (93.3 per cent of

[114] Nugent, *Big Men, Small Boys*, 224–5.
[115] Ibid., 223.
[116] Ibid., 249.
[117] For the opposition's case, see Oquaye, 'Ghanaian elections of 1992'; A.A. Boahen, 'A note on the Ghanaian elections', *African Affairs* 94, 375 (1995): 277–80; and New Patriotic Party, *The Stolen Verdict* (Accra, 1993).
[118] Nugent, *Big Men, Small Boys*, 247; idem, 'Living in the past'; and Jeffries and Thomas, 'Ghanaian elections of 1992'.

the votes cast) … Even the northern constituencies that had returned Progress Party Members of Parliament in 1969 appeared to have voted heavily for Rawlings: his share of the vote was cited as 88 per cent in Akan, 86 per cent in Krachi and 83.2 per cent in Nkwanta. The majorities were even more impressive the further south one moves, rising as high as 98.1 per cent in the case of Anlo constituency.[119]

Though the size of the Anlo vote for Rawlings may be suspicious in its almost total denial of the existence of the four opposition parties, it was a logical vote as this chapter has argued. Rawlings and the NDC were the Anlo ticket to physical security and economic revival. An important consequence of the Volta Region vote in 1992 was that opposition parties in the 1996 election would concede the region – especially Anlo – to the ruling NDC without any major campaigns in the region. Strangely enough, nothing happened on the Keta sea defence and development package in the interim between 1992 and the next election in 1996.

The 1996 electoral campaign opened on a sharper note of ethnic rivalry. Whereas several Ghanaians felt some discomfort at privileging ethnicity in the run-up to the 1992 elections, the electoral results of 1992, especially that of Volta Region, convinced many that indeed ethnicity had become crucial in the general elections. Images from the Ewe unification past came into play with a disturbing emphasis on the separateness of the Ewe. The *Ghanaian Voice* fired an early salvo:

> President J.J. Rawlings has been called upon to advise his tribesmen in the Volta Region to purge themselves out of tribal politics as a first step towards the realization of national unity.
>
> Major [rtd] Yeboah [Western Regional campaign manager of the NPP] said if any blame should be apportioned for tribal politics in Ghana, that blame should go to Rawlings' tribesmen.
>
> He referred to the 1992 presidential election results which showed that in the Volta Region President Rawlings scored almost 100 per cent votes cast by his tribesmen.[120]

Allegations floated in the private press that Rawlings at a rally in Ho in November 1996 had instigated the Ewe to vote massively for his party in 1996 for the NPP planned to expel the Ewe to Togo if it won the December 1996 elections.[121]

The NDC won the 1996 elections again, including all the nineteen constituencies in the Volta Region, with rather spectacular margins in the five Anlo constituencies. The Anlo-Ewe vote was more resounding in the two constituencies of Keta and Anlo, the sites of coastal erosion and economic decline. In none of the Anlo constituencies did the presidential vote fall below 95.8 per cent, and it was as high as 98.7 per cent in Keta and 99.2 per cent in Anlo.[122] Political pundits analysed the Volta Region vote in an endeavour to understand the pattern of block voting.[123] Surprisingly, even case studies of the 1996 elections in Anlo constituencies do not highlight the relevance of the Keta Basin Integrated Development Project.[124] Though reference is made to

[119] Nugent, *Big Men, Small Boys*, 239.

[120] *Ghanaian Voice* (1–3 July 1996).

[121] *Ghanaian Chronicle* (4 December 1996). NPP General Secretary, Agyenim Boateng, also blamed the total NPP loss in the Volta Region on vicious allegations by the NDC that an NPP win would, among other things, mean a return of the Volta Region to Togo. See *Weekend Statesman* (20–26 December 1996).

[122] *Daily Graphic* (11 December 1996).

[123] *Ghanaian Chronicle* (13–19 December 1996).

[124] See, for example, Joseph R.A. Ayee, 'Measuring public opinion on key political and economic issues: a survey

some of the items within this package. But the NDC was clearly aware that the environmental platform was central to winning the Anlo vote. The party became more outspoken on its environmental and economic package for Anlo in the months preceding the 1996 elections.

Keta District was agog with excitement when the government announced in 1996 that it had secured the needed funding from the Export–Import Bank of the United States for the Keta sea defence project. Coincidentally, this happened to be an election year. This comprehensive project was now named the 'Keta Basin Integrated Development Project', with sea defence as only one phase. The contract was awarded to an American firm, Great Lakes Dredge and Dock Company, with Messrs Pentrexx Limited as their Ghanaian representatives. The project certainly drew inspiration from the earlier Italian report of 1987; it encompassed sea defence, land reclamation, a shrimp industry, a salt industry and chemical industries based on the Keta Lagoon, such as the manufacture of caustic soda.[125] By October 1996, there were signs that the project was indeed taking off. A team from Messrs Pentrexx and the Land Valuation Office visited the Keta District to document and evaluate damaged properties along the shoreline in readiness for removal.[126]

Instructively, the NDC government chose the annual Anlo celebration of the *hogbetsotso* festival on 2 November 1996 to showcase its salvation plan for the Keta District. The festival was held at the durbar grounds behind the Anloga police station, and the convergence of the national state, the Anlo State and the NDC in this festival was striking. NDC colours and T-shirts were in evidence everywhere, and street pedlars sold NDC sun-visor caps alongside *hogbetsotso* caps for C200 (Photo 7.2). Justice Archer represented Rawlings, and the ailing *awoamefia* also had his representative. One of the highlights of the festival was the spectacular entrance of the Amen Fishing Company, the largest fishing company in Anlo, in a canoe painted in NDC colours (black, red, green and white), oars in NDC colours and the *akatamanso* (umbrella) party emblem and clothed in NDC T-shirts. Their boat was on the back of a Kia truck, and they mimed their paddling at sea.

The approach to the durbar ground featured two mounted exhibitions illustrating what the Keta area would look like after the sea defence project (Photo 7.3). The Anlo elder who poured the libation at the festival explicitly prayed for an NDC victory at the coming elections to enable the party to complete what it had begun. It was announced to loud cheers that Rawlings would be coming to Keta on 13 November to commission the sea defence project. NDC government officials used the day to brief Anlo chiefs on the progress of the sea defence project. At Togbui James Ocloo's house later that day, the author saw for the first time 'Akatamanso Schnapps' made by Gihoc Distilleries and with the NDC umbrella and party colours on its packaging. Togbui

124 (cont.) of the December 1996 general elections in the Keta and Anlo constituencies', in Joseph R.A. Ayee, ed., *The 1996 General Elections and the Democratic Consolidation in Ghana* (Accra, 1988), 275–301; and Ahiawordor, 'Case of Ketu South and Ketu North constituencies'.
125 Interview with Steven Selormey, Dzelukope, 17 October 1996; interview with Obed Nutsugah and Fred Akligo, Dzelukope, 18 March 1997.
126 Interview with Steven Selormey, Dzelukope, 17 October 1996.

Photo 7.2 NDC women supporters at the *hogbetsotso* festival, 2 November 1996 *(by author)*.

Photo 7.3 Sea defence project exhibit, Anloga, 2 November 1996 *(by author)*.

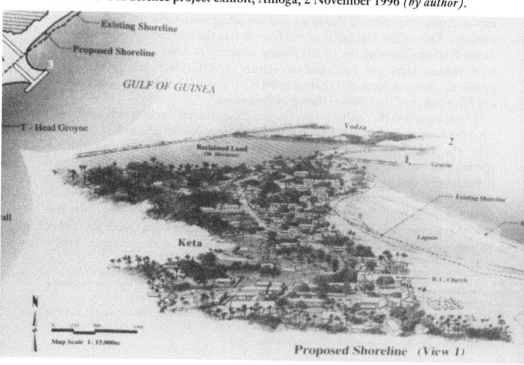

James Ocloo had received two such bottles from government officials who came to update him on the schedule for the sea defence works. For the Anlo, the day of reckoning had come, and their patience and faith in the ruling government had paid off.

On Friday, 15 November 1996, Rawlings did indeed visit Keta to commission the Keta Basin Integrated Development Project, and he cut the sod for the commencement of the first phase of shoreline protection. The *Daily Graphic* confirmed the information disseminated at *hogbetsotso*:

> Under the project, estimated at $42 million, about 8 kilometres of the coast from Keta to Kedzi will be protected against sea erosion, flood relief involving the construction of an outfall at Kedzi, access road from Havedzi/Kedzi to Keta and the reclamation of 110 hectares of land. Work will be undertaken by the Great Lake Dredge and Dock Company, Pentrexx Limited.[127]

Ebenezer Kobina Fosu, Minister for Works and Housing, reported that the Ghana Parliament had approved the Exim Bank loan and that the necessary arrangements had been made with the contractor for the work to begin immediately.[128]

By April 1997, Trafalgar House, a British construction company, had begun work on a road to connect Havedzi with Keta for the sea defence project. But there were also disturbing signs that all was not well with the sea defence project. Ghana Television news announced at the beginning of March 1997 that the dredger for the Keta project had arrived at Tema harbour on 25 February and would proceed to Keta in two weeks' time. The dredger had still not arrived at Keta when the author left Ghana in early September 1997. In June 1997, the government announced a probe into the affairs of the Keta sea defence project. In July 1997, Mawuse Dake, chief executive of Bidex International Limited and a long-time consultant on the Keta sea defence project, expressed his indignation at the way the contract award for the Keta sea defence project had been handled:

> I refer to my letter dated 20th June 1997 on the above [re probe into Keta sea defence project]. It is now more than four weeks since you announced your intention to institute a probe into the affairs of the sea defence project. I offered to assist the probe with documentary and oral evidence in support of my assertion that the process of award of contract 'was fraught with fraudulent intentions and practices'. A false start is invariably indicative of a bad process.[129]

For the Anlo of Keta district this may have seemed like *déjà vu*. The events of 1978 seemed to be repeating themselves.

There lurks a fear that the Keta defence project may be an election year issue, which subsides after an election to be resurrected in the next election. But on it hinges the future of the Keta District, and its residents are naturally reluctant to give up hope. The Anlo elder S.S. Dotse explained:

> In fact, it is very difficult to comment on this. Before the election, we had a lot of promises, but this has not materialized. First, they said January [1997], and then they said February, now they say April. The majority is saying May. But fiscal problems with the government are another matter. If the money is not there, this project may not be viable. If the proceeds from this area would be equal to the money spent, then there must be a possibility. From the look of things

[127] *Daily Graphic* (18 November 1996).
[128] Ibid.
[129] *Public Agenda* (21–27 July 1997).

this will be done by the government out of magnanimity ... So there is no cause for us to grumble.[130]

Nothing substantive had commenced on the sea defence project as of April 1998. At a meeting at the Keta District Assembly Hall on 22 April 1998, the area residents were once again assured that the Keta sea defence project would surely take off in May or June that year.[131] The date was postponed to October 1998.[132] It was becoming hard for the Anlo to shake off their disappointment. President Rawlings personally intervened to prop up hope when he declared in his January 1999 sessional address to Parliament that the Keta sea defence project will start and that he will personally supervise the work.[133]

In early 1999 the NDC government announced additional features to the Keta Basin Integrated Development Project. The original estimate of $42.78 million was raised by an extra $41.24 million to make a total of $84.02 million. The added package included the reclamation of 283 hectares of land from the lagoon side and 2.681 million cubic metres of sand nourishment on the seaside.[134] The Exim Bank reportedly approved the revised figure around February 1999, and representatives of the bank visited the Keta area on 19 February 1999.[135] Ghanaians believe that 'good things come to those who wait'. And as the millennium drew to an end, Anlo denizens of the Keta District looked forward to a renaissance of their economy and society. Incidentally, the millennium year was also an election year.

Conclusion

This chapter has reviewed the salience of landscape and environmental issues to transformations in Anlo-Ewe political identity over the twentieth century. Landscape and the environment informed the Anlo discourse on political inclusion and exclusion in the Gold Coast colony and the Ghanaian nation-state. As independent Ghanaian governments resorted to scapegoating the Ewe for Ghana's economic ills, the discourse on environmental citizenship enabled the Anlo to draw attention to their environmental crisis and to critique the political ecology of Ghanaian governments without being accused of disloyalty to the Ghanaian nation-state. The chapter examines Ewe ethnicity in the twentieth century and contextualizes this at the local Anlo level. Ethnicity is a means of mobilizing to access state resources, and in Anlo the prospect of the Keta Basin Integrated Development Project, promised by a government with a large Ewe and Anlo presence, underpins the massive support for the NDC party.

[130] Interview with S.S. Dotse, Adzido, 21 March 1997.
[131] Personal correspondence from Togbuivi Kumassah, 23 April 1998.
[132] Personal correspondence from Togbuivi Kumassah, 29 June 1998.
[133] Personal correspondence from Togbuivi Kumassah, 15 January 1999.
[134] Internet site of Radio Joy FM, 25 April 1999. Http://www.joy997fm.com.gh/news/onlinen1.htm.
[135] Personal correspondence from Togbuivi Kumassah, 27 February 1999.

8

Living with the Sea

Society & Culture in Contemporary Anlo

We have the lagoon and we have the sea. When you are born here, the only work you can do is to go fishing. There is no land here that you can farm. If you do not know how to fish, there is no way that you can live here. If your father and mother have white-collar jobs, then you can survive without fishing.

(Eugene Doe, secondary school leaver, Keta, 15 October 1996)

Between the sea and the lagoon

This book has examined the enormous impact of the sea and the lagoons in shaping economy, culture and society in Anlo. The above epigraph states a truism in twentieth-century littoral Anlo society. In this century the Anlo can be described as 'people of the sea'. However, as late as the end of the eighteenth century, the historical record noted an Anlo shyness of the sea. The absence of natural harbours, the rough surf and a parallel sand bar that rendered launching and landing boats a perilous experience partly explain the Anlo cautiousness. The Anlo preferred the safe and calm waters of the lagoon system that united the area between the Volta River and the Lagos Channel or what was referred to as the Slave Coast.[1] This book has attempted to reconstruct the historical processes by which the Anlo became people of the sea. The Anlo were originally 'land' people, who migrated from Notsie to the south-eastern Gold Coast in the mid-seventeenth century. They were neither aquatic nor maritime people, and their land-bound orientation explains the continuing salience of land in Anlo history and the fierce attachment to land. This is in sharp contrast to maritime peoples, who often held land ownership in disdain and eschewed rootedness.[2]

The influx of war refugees shortly after Anlo settlement in the Gold Coast intensified competition for scarce land in Anlo, but these strangers also brought

[1] Chapter 1.
[2] Rita Astuti, *People of the Sea: Identity and Descent among the Vezo of Madagascar* (Cambridge, 1995), is a classic representation of this phenomenon in Africa.

relevant technical knowledge in boat construction, salt-making and fishing methods. The Anlo actively entered the coasting and lagoon trade along the Slave Coast, supplying the important items of fish and salt. Anlo coastal towns, such as Keta and Woe also served as provisioning stops for European ships in the era of the Atlantic slave-trade. The Anlo entered the slave-trade and constituted the last region in what became colonial Gold Coast to give up the slave-trade, reluctantly, in the mid-nineteenth century. In their evasion of European attempts to impose abolition, the Anlo environment with its interconnected lagoons and creeks proved to be the ideal smuggler's paradise. Abolition caused an upheaval in Anlo economy and society and generated a desperate search for economic alternatives. The introduction of the beach-seine net or *yevudor* in the mid-nineteenth century was timely and under-pinned the successful Anlo transition to maritime fishing. Largely operated from the beach, this net enabled the Anlo to avoid lengthy sea-fishing expeditions or offshore fishing; they maximized marine catches without necessarily becoming seafaring.[3] An important dimension to the effective Anlo transition to maritime fishing was the transfer of relevant marine and sky deities from related peoples along the Slave Coast. Becoming people of the sea involved both technological and cognitive adaptations.[4]

Lagoons and the sea dominated the Anlo environment and loomed large in the daily lives of littoral dwellers. Anlo's littoral communities were located on a thin sand spit sandwiched between the sea and the large Keta Lagoon. But even farming communities in inland Anlo depended on the lagoon for water transport, and all came to the important coastal market of Keta, a trading emporium on the upper Slave Coast. The Keta Lagoon and the sea were, perhaps, the most important economic resources in Anlo. The narrowness of the sand spit east of Tegbi made fishing and salt making the major economic pursuits in this part of Anlo. The availability of land – albeit limited – made farming a viable option west of Tegbi, and the traditional Anlo capital of Anloga was the centre of farming along the coast. Limited land is reflected in the small sizes of farms, the current average farm size being 0.5 hectares, compared with the national average of 3.7 hectares.[5] Communities north of the Keta Lagoon also farmed, and foodstuffs were exchanged in a north–south direction. In Anlo today, almost everyone has knowledge of fishing, and the communally owned Keta Lagoon ensures a basic livelihood for men, women and children. Multiple fishing techniques, some of which required little or no real capital investment, made the lagoon a democratic economic resource. *Tekali* was particularly useful when the lagoon became shallow. This involved two people drawing a long rope across the surface of the lagoon, while others formed a line behind the rope. Fish ducked the rope and got stuck in the mud of the lagoon bed because of the shallow water. A silvery reflection indicated the location of the trapped fish, and those behind the rope picked up the fish and deposited them in baskets. Women especially favoured the use of bottles in fishing. Commonly, an empty beer bottle would be perforated in the middle, maize

---

[3] Chapter 2.

[4] Chapter 4.

[5] Keta District Assembly, 'Medium Term (5 Year) Development Plan (1996–2000) for Keta District' (May 1996), 66.

dough placed in it and the top sealed. This constitutes a fish trap, and it is set at the edges of the lagoon, while the owner keeps watch over the bottle. As soon as a fish enters to eat the maize dough, the incision is covered with the palm and the bottle quickly removed. The trap is reset. Angling, basket traps, nets and dams are also deployed in lagoon fishing.[6]

Maritime fishing was another matter and required heavy investment.[7] Sea-fishing nets were mostly made from imported European manufactured materials, and the size of these nets made them costly. But the sea also served as an important highway, which brought European missionaries and traders, who transformed Anlo society and economy. They brought the education and commerce that opened up new socio-economic opportunities and cemented Keta's emergence as a cosmopolitan centre and the economic jewel of Anlo. Behind the missionaries and the European traders came colonial rule, attracted by the revenue prospects of the booming commerce generated by the activities of the former. Keta became the colonial administrative headquarters for the Keta District, and later of the Keta-Ada District. This is how the 'white-collar' jobs in the epigraph originated.[8]

The sea could also become a means of destruction, and acute coastal erosion from the early twentieth century devastated the Keta area and initiated the long-term causes of socio-economic decline. The Anlo turned to the colonial government for a solution to their environmental hazard, but the colonial government ruled that it was not responsible for uneconomic environmental programmes. Shoreline stabilization and marine fisheries were not central to a colonial environmental policy, which focused largely on the conservation of forests and the regulation of timber felling and mineral extraction. A disappointed Anlo resorted to their knowledge of the past and a belief system that hinted at ancestral ability to manipulate the sea. The Anlo perceived a breach in their moral ecology, the equilibrium of the social, cosmological and natural worlds that facilitated a successful pursuit of life and underpinned the Anlo understanding of their landscape. The futility of a 'moral' solution provided a back-drop for an Anlo critique of colonial rule and the 'modernity' that had encouraged the dismissal of custom and the loss of valuable knowledge about the sea.[9] As Keta lost its little land and suffered urban decline, the commercial firms and the government departments that had underpinned the town's cosmopolitan status relocated and took away the 'white-collar' jobs. In the renewed search for other economic pursuits, migrant maritime fishing, intensive vegetable farming and distillation of local gin became central in the Anlo economy. Land loss and the destruction of properties also encouraged emigration and depopulation.[10] The result has been the rather large proportion of young and old people in the Keta District, those who cannot become migrant labour. Adult men are also overrepresented in the migrating group, and women headed nearly 30 per cent of all households in the Keta district in the 1990s.[11]

[6] Interview with Geoffrey James Ocloo, Keta, 19 March 1997.
[7] Chapter 5.
[8] Chapter 3.
[9] Chapter 4.
[10] Chapter 5.
[11] Keta District Assembly, 'Medium Term Development Plan', 29.

Living with the Sea

The worlds east and west of the Volta River

A major theme in this book has examined the 'separate' worlds east and west of the Volta and the political and economic amalgamation of these two zones in the colonial and postcolonial eras. The partition of Eweland by the British and the Germans created two competing magnets in Anlo economy and society: Accra and Lome. The geographical divide created by the Volta meant that the Anlo had more frequent relations with Lome than with Accra. Geographical integration between these two zones was enhanced by the construction of the Adomi Bridge on the middle Volta in the mid-1950s and the more recent Sogakope Bridge on the lower Volta. Knowledge of Anlo west of the Volta remained paltry at best in the colonial era and has persisted into the postcolonial period. Esther Kwawukume, daughter of Sri II, narrated an incident during the First World War that underscored this unfortunate phenomenon:

> In the 1914 War, when the British soldiers were proceeding from the Gold Coast to Togoland, they were instructed that when they cross the Volta, they would be in German Togoland. They crossed at Atiteti and began shooting. They said that the place was Togoland. It was Captain Kojo Tsikata's [maternal] grandfather . . . then F. & A. Swanzy's storekeeper . . . his name was Jackson Ocloo, [who] sent a message to Togbui Sri II. Togbui Sri asked one of his sons to sit on a bicycle and take the Union Jack to Atiteti. As soon as the soldiers saw the Union Jack they stood at attention. They were led to Anloga. From Anloga Togbui Sri took them to Lome.[12]

If the soldiers had crossed the Volta north of Peki Blengo, they would have been in German Togoland. Crossing south at the Volta estuary put them in the Gold Coast, but they were none the wiser.

Perhaps it is this geo-mental distance – apart from the fact that independent Ghanaian governments have inherited colonial environmental policies – that has promoted official aloofness in Keta's ongoing struggle with the sea. It etched in Anlo consciousness a sense of marginality within the Gold Coast political economy. That Anlo lagged behind in development compared with other coastal states west of the Volta strengthened Anlo suspicions of political discrimination.[13] Anlo strengthened its ties with Ewe communities to the east, and it would become the moving force in the Ewe unification movement after the First and Second World Wars.[14] The relative underdevelopment of the Trans-Volta Region and the fact that the region received little benefit from the construction of hydroelectric dams, and yet suffered massive displacement and new health risks, united the southern and northern sections of the Trans-Volta in a common cause. The vibrant nationalism of the Convention People's Party (CPP), with its promise of political and economic benefits in an independent Ghana, won Anlo hearts and secured the support and leadership talents of Anlos such as Gbedemah and the Chapmans. Post-Nkrumah governments lacked his vision of the nation-state as a building block for a pan-African state. Political constituencies shrank, and the world east of the Volta again became a casualty in political economies orchestrated from Accra. In the interim, coastal devastation, environmental

[12] Interview with Esther Kwawukume, Keta, 23 January 1997.
[13] Chapter 6.
[14] Chapter 7.

deterioration and socio-economic decline progressed sharply in Anlo. The lagoon and the sea closed in on Anlo communities.

The indignity of being displaced at home

Coastal erosion affected not only the Anlo material world, but also the cognitive world or psyche. Setriakor Nyomi emphasizes the importance of land among the Anlo as an economic asset and a spiritual base. He states that for the Anlo, 'land (*Anyigba*) is a unifying force of the people who are touched by it, both living and dead'.[15] Chapter 5 noted that even individually acquired land among the Ewe was perceived as belonging to the lineage as a whole, for it is the lineage that owns land. Similarly, the house, even when built by individual effort, belongs to more than the individual and represents the social base of the family and lineage. Those who owned land and houses were viewed as 'stewards', who held property in trust for the lineage. As Nyomi points out, building a house in Ghana is often a lifelong venture, which reaches fruition just around one's retirement. It involves careful saving over time and piecemeal building. Until recently, mortgage companies were rare in Ghana. Erosion discourages insurance companies from insuring houses in the Keta area.[16] The destruction of a house by the sea not only erases one's lifetime savings and retirement home, but also the social base of the family and lineage. Instructively, the notions of 'self' and property 'ownership' in Anlo are both expressed by the Ewe word *nuto*.[17] Nyomi emphasizes that:

> If, in the language, the notions of self and ownership are expressed in the same word, then the loss of one stands a good chance of affecting the other. In the case of Keta sea erosion victims, this may be one of the reasons why loss of property has often meant loss of self-worth.[18]

Anlo elders who had lost houses to the sea were saddened by their inability to bequeath houses – social bases – to their heirs.[19]

A visit to Kedzikope beach on 23 August 1996 brought home the pain of being displaced in one's own native land. The sea had just destroyed several houses in Adzido, and the displaced residents had been settled temporarily in tents donated by the government (Photo 8.1). Being at home, they could not be declared refugees. They are 'displaced', not 'refugees'. This therefore limited the relief services they could receive. The paradoxical situation of these displaced persons was vivid: homeless at home, destitute and yet able-bodied, they were pushed into the growing ranks of a landless and a non-propertied wage-labour force that worked in fishing companies and on shallot farms. Talking about the loss of homes was always a difficult experience. Togbui James Ocloo IV discussed several subjects, but he was never able to bring himself to discuss the erosion of the house he had built around 1963. When

---

[15] Setriakor Kobla Nyomi, 'A pastoral theological perspective on ministry to persons dealing with loss to natural disasters in Ghana' (PhD thesis, Princeton Theological Institute, 1991), 108.

[16] Ibid., 112–17.

[17] Ibid., 113.

[18] Ibid., 117.

[19] See, for example, interview with James Ocloo IV, Keta, 5 September 1996; interview with Freda Adabanu and Regina Ayayee, Keta, 20 September 1996; interview with Joseph Kingsley Abdallah, Keta, 16 October 1996; interview with Nancy Dovlo, Agbenyefia Attipoe and Christian C. Dormenu, 20 March 1997.

Photo 8.1 Displaced persons at Kedzikope, 23 August 1996 *(by author)*.

the Anlo of the Keta area appeal to Ghanaian governments to save them from the sea and refuse to relocate, it is a defence of life as they know it – and as their ancestors knew it. Perhaps, no government appreciates this fact more than the Provisional National Defence Council–National Democratic Congress (PNDC–NDC). And this is no doubt because of the prominent Anlo presence. After all, the family house of Rawlings's mother also lies beneath the sea. The Anlo's complete electoral support for the NDC reflects their revival of hope and trust that the government would save them from the sea and preserve their society.

Society and culture in contemporary Anlo

The ambivalence of power

One is struck by the centrality of ecology, history and spiritual power in the matrix of daily life in Anlo. This impression is strengthened when Anlo is compared with the northern Ewe at Ho and Hohoe. In Anlo, the constant presence of women attached to shrines – *yewesi, agbosi, trɔkosi* – underscored the pervasive influence of spirituality. Public shrines (*dulegbawo*) stood at the entrances of towns such as Anloga and Vodza, and family gods stood at the entrance of lineage houses. The latter is referred to as *agbonufia* or 'keeper of the gate' (sentinel god). During fieldwork in Anlo, the funeral ceremonies of Yewe priestesses were seen as major social events attended by all and sundry. The pervasiveness of spirituality is less distinct among the northern Ewe. The sea and lagoon and the Anlo endeavour to harness these water bodies spiritually and materially in part explain the spirituality of Anlo life.

220

Irwin remarks that: 'Hazardous environments and social powerlessness do indeed seem to coexist.'[20] The Anlo may feel particularly powerless in their relations to Ghanaian governments and the wider nation, but this handicap is not reflected in internal relations of power. Power operates within contemporary Anlo society in highly ambivalent ways and a weakened environment or material base may have accentuated the avariciousness of power in the interests of accumulation. The contraction of the Anlo economy from the late colonial period and the 'disengagement' of the state from environmental, social and economic issues central to the Anlo could have reinforced precolonial forms of accumulation, which exploited the supernatural or superstition. At the height of slavery and the slave-trade in precolonial Anlo, priests may have exploited the institution of *trɔkosi* (female religious servitude) to increase their pool of dependants. People constituted wealth and priests felt themselves in social competition with rich traders. The Introduction highlighted how the presence of different ecozones in Anlo underpinned the coexistence of various modes of production with subtle differences in social formation. Some sub-economies had either pronounced or little contact with the outside world and the transformative impact of colonial capitalism. And the overlapping modes of production may account for some of the continuities in contemporary Anlo of precolonial forms of accumulation. In Anlo it is difficult to distinguish between political power and religious or ritual power, for both are intimately meshed. There is the chief's court, but shrines and their priests also adjudicate in civil matters. And the fear of supernatural sanctions or spiritual retribution informs daily Anlo life. Two incidents in Anlo drew national and international attention to the ambiguity of power in internal relations in Anlo. The first revealed that virgin girls were being pledged in perpetual servitude to shrines as atonement for sins committed by relatives. The second dealt with the Yewe cult's claim that those killed by lightning had been eliminated by their patron, the thunder god. The cult thus exercised certain rights over the deceased corpse.

Trɔkosi *or female religious servitude*

The 1996–7 period witnessed intense debates in Ghana over *trɔkosi*, a system by which females were pledged to religious shrines in perpetuity, being replaced by their families on their death. The activities of a number of local and international non-governmental organizations (NGOs) had brought this institution to national attention and agitated for its abolition, as ritual bondage was illegal and the institution was an abuse of fundamental human rights. For many west of the Volta, it was a startling revelation that 'female slavery' existed in the Ewe states of Tongu and Anlo and among the neighbouring Adangme in contemporary Ghana.[21] That this inimical

[20] Alan Irwin, *Citizen Science: A Study of People, Expertise and Sustainable Development* (London and New York, 1995), 177.

[21] Cudjoe Azumah in his study of the institution in Tongu defined *trɔkosi* as 'slaves of the gods', and not as 'wives of the gods', as others claim. *Trɔ* means 'god', and *kosi* may be defined variously as 'slave', 'virgin' or 'wife'. Cudjoe Azumah, 'The *trokosi* practice in north Tongu: its impact on the rights of women and children' (BA thesis, Sociology Department, University of Ghana, 1996). Robert Kwame Ameh, 'trokosi (child slavery) in Ghana: a policy approach', *Ghana Studies* 1 (1998) 35–62, also refers to the *trɔkosi* institution as slavery. It is

system was featured on several news programmes, including CNN's 'World Report' on 23 February 1997 and the Columbia Broadcasting System (CBS) news documentary programme '60 Minutes', underscored the international dimensions of the issue. For Ghana, obviously, this was very embarrassing. *Trɔkosi* was debated in the Ghana Parliament, and a Bill was under preparation in 1996 to ban the practice.

How did this institution escape national attention until the 1990s? The ecological setting of Tongu and Anlo is an important aspect of the institution's invisibility. Towns and villages in which *trɔkosi* flourished such as Dorfor, Battor, Volo and Tefle in Tongu, and Anloga, Vui, Alakple, Tebgui and Anyako in Anlo are riverine, lagoon, creek or island settlements. The same environmental assets that enabled this area to persist in the slave-trade and smuggling in the precolonial and early colonial periods account for the invisibility of *trɔkosi*. Accessibility is difficult and many of these places are isolated from the outside world. The intimate links between religious and political power also meant that the institution had the knowledge and support of chiefs; indeed, in some places the chief and the priest were the same person. Secrecy and fear compelled compliance within the general community. Interestingly, the institution of *trɔkosi* among the Tongu had attracted official attention in the colonial era, and an official investigation was conducted between 1919 and 1924 into the practice at the Atigo shrine in Battor. Strangely, the colonial government ruled that the Atigo shrine was central to farming, fishing and everyday life at Battor and should not be suppressed. In the opinion of the investigating District Commissioner (DC) of Ada, W. Price Jones, '[a]part from this pernicious habit of handing girls over to the fetish I see no reason why the fetish Atigo should be interfered with'.[22] One can only conclude that it was the government's eagerness to utilize local structures of authority in the cost–effective policy of indirect rule that encouraged the government to turn a blind eye to the *trɔkosi* institution. The girls at the Atigo shrine were told in the 1920s that they had the liberty to return home to their families. The colonial government ignored a complaint from a Battor individual in 1923 that the Atigo shrine was still keeping *trɔkosis*.[23] The matter disappeared from official view until the 1990s.

As the debate over *trɔkosi* became national in the 1990s, some Anlo harnessed their knowledge of history in defence of this institution and to distinguish their practice from what existed among the Tongu-Ewe. The key issues in this debate revolved around the human rights of the individual versus the right of a community to practise its religion and culture. Anlo views on *trɔkosi* were varied. Some disapproved, others

---

[21 (cont.)] imprecise to subsume *trɔkosi* under 'slavery', with all the connotations of the latter. Recent scholarship has criticized such scholarly imprecision in studies of slavery in Africa. See Claude Meillassoux, *The Anthropology of Slavery: The Woman of Iron and Gold* (Chicago, 1991); and Joseph E. Inikori, 'Slavery in Africa and the transatlantic slave-trade', in Alusine Jalloh and Stephen E. Maizlish, eds, *The African Diaspora* (Arlington, TX, 1996), 39–72. A detailed examination of *trɔkosi* in Anlo against the wider context of slavery and slave-trade in Anlo's history is offered in Emmanuel Akyeampong, 'History, memory, slave-trade and slavery in Anlo, Ghana' (14th Annual O. Truman Driggs Distinguished Lecture, University of Minnesota at Morris, 14 September 1999). A revised version will appear in *Slavery and Abolition* (December 2001).

[22] NAG, Accra, ADM 11/1/768. Acting DC of Ada, W. Price Jones, to Commissioner for the Eastern Province (CEP), 19 March 1920.

[23] Ibid. CEP to Secretary of Native Affairs, Koforidua, 10 September 1924.

feigned ignorance and a few offered an informed defence of the institution. S.S. Dotse explained the origins of *trɔkosi*: 'If there is no offence, there is no *trɔkosi*.'[24] Apparently the vicious circle of pledging a female relative originates with a crime and the cursing of the culprit at a shrine. Misfortune and deaths result in the culprit's family, and consultation with a diviner reveals the cause and the remedy. The culprit's family pledges a female member of the family as *trɔkosi* to the shrine. The family is responsible for the material welfare of the *trɔkosi*, and they are bound to replace the *trɔkosi* on her death. The institution in its present manifestation is limited to women, and the pledged are always virgin girls. The exploitation of the sexuality and labour of the *trɔkosi* by the priests is its most blatant feature.

Spearheaded by NGOs such as the Christian International Needs and the Swiss 'Sentry Movement' – and with the strong support of the Commissioner for Human Rights and Administrative Justice – hundreds of *trɔkosi* have been liberated in Tongu. Several ceremonies were conducted in 1996–7 during which the shrine owners were compensated in money, cattle and schnapps. The *trɔkosi* are presented with 'liberation certificates' and taught skills such as sewing, baking and weaving by the NGOs in rehabilitation programmes.[25] Liberation ceremonies included those conducted at the Lomo and Me shrines in Volo in October 1996,[26] at three shrines in Dorfor in December 1996[27] and at the Atigo shrine in Battor in January 1997.[28] In contrast, no 'liberation ceremonies' were conducted at Anlo shrines, though the practice also existed there. Anlo gods or shrines that hold *trɔkosi* include Nyigbla in Anloga, Nogokpo in Some, Klikor in Some, Vodumi in Anyako, Agbaku in Anloga, Avutsu at Alakple and Hugbato at Atiavi.

Togbui Addo VIII, chief of Klikor, and Togbui Honi II, a chief at Klikor and custodian of the Yewe shrine at Dzelukope, have provided one of the most informed defences of *trɔkosi*.[29] Central to their defence was the distinction between the Anlo practice of *fiasidi* and the Tongu *trɔkosi*. Togbui Addo emphasized that Nyigbla had instituted the practice among the Anlo:

> Briefly, *fiasidi* was an institution for training women, to be marriageable to the noble in society. You know everything that involved schooling revolved around the shrine, so that there is some fear ... *Fiasidi* is actually coined from three Ewe words: *fia* means 'king'; *asi* means 'wife'; and *di* is just the verb 'to marry'. So if you say *fiasidi*, it simply means 'a woman who is fit for a king to marry'. It was an honour to marry a *fiasidi*.[30]

Greene points out that the practice of *fiasidi* in Anlo dates to the late eighteenth century, when the Amlade clan god Sui became powerful enough to demand female servants from families that sought its services. The family replaced the *fiasidi* on her

[24] Personal communication from S.S. Dotse, 19 September 1996.
[25] For profiles of some ex-*trɔkosi*, see The *Mirror* (16 November 1996).
[26] *Daily Graphic* (26 October 1996).
[27] *Public Agenda* (10–15 December 1996).
[28] *Weekly Spectator* (25 January 1997).
[29] Interview with Togbui Addo VIII, Klikor, 22 April 1997; personal communication from Togbui Honi II, 18 October 1996.
[30] Interview with Togbui Addo VIII, Klikor, 22 April 1997.

death.[31] Boys could be *fiasidi*, though girls were more common. With the ascendancy of Nyigbla as the chief Anlo deity, the Nyigbla shrine began to demand *fiasidi* at the beginning of the nineteenth century for its services. Nyigbla also instituted the ceremony of *foasi*, by which two or more women were annually recruited to serve the god. But those acquired through *foasi*, known as *zizidzelawo*, were voluntary affiliates to the shrine and not involuntary pledges like the *fiasidi*. In fact, the practice of *fiasidi* was not very common, and it was the institution of *foasi* that recruited personnel to serve the Nyigbla. The *fiasidi* were often married to members of powerful priestly families, cementing alliances between Anlo families and powerful shrines.[32]

In Klikor today the three shrines of Togbui Adzima, Ablogame, and Mama Wena continue the practice of *fiasidi*. Unlike the practice in Tongu, where the *trɔkosi* live and serve at the shrine, Klikor's *fiasidi* are brought initially for an identification ceremony as young girls and later for a final ceremony on coming of age. Like ordinary people these *fiasidi* go to school and may marry men of their choice. Togbui Honi II's father married a *fiasidi*, and he himself married one. Seduction of a *fiasidi* or *trɔkosi* brings dire consequences, and the culprit is mulcted in fines or required to replace the 'spoiled' woman with a virgin from his family. Priests cannot exploit the sexuality and labour of *fiasidi*. The only requirement of *fiasidi* is that they attend the annual ceremony of the shrine.[33] Togbui Addo VIII and Togbui Honi II argue that some priests have commercialized and abused the system, but this does not negate the utility of the system. For instance, the *fiasidi* shrines in Klikor, far from being atavistic institutions, built a three-classroom block and a kindergarten in use in Klikor today.[34] Importantly, *fiasidi* is central to Anlo religion and culture and was instituted by the gods and not the priests.

Indeed, in October 1996, the Klikor constituency submitted to the Attorney General Obed Asamoah a written memorandum in defence of the institution in Anlo.[35] This was ineffective, however, and, in December 1996, a Bill was ready for Parliament's approval to make *trɔkosi* in its variant forms a second-degree felony. Parties guilty of giving *trɔkosi* or receiving them would be liable on conviction to imprisonment for a term not less than three years. In the attached memorandum to the Bill, the Attorney General declared that: 'The customary practice which subjects a girl to virtual servitude for the atonement of an offence committed by some other person in her family cannot be justified and allowed to continue given the present constitution of this country.'[36] The Bill was duly passed in Parliament in June 1998. It remains to be seen whether legislative fiat can abrogate a practice supposedly instituted and maintained by the gods and not humans.

---

[31] Sandra E. Greene, *Gender, Ethnicity, and Social Change on the Upper Slave Coast: A History of the Anlo-Ewe* (Portsmouth, 1996), 64.

[32] Ibid., 87–90.

[33] Personal communication from Togbui Honi II, 18 October 1996.

[34] Ibid.

[35] Ibid.

[36] *Public Agenda* (10–15 December 1996).

Death by lightning: the case of David Amekudzi

Another case that brought the Anlo more unwanted national attention in April 1997 – and highlighted the competing sources of power within Anlo – was the death by lightning of David Amekudzi, a Woe junior secondary school student. This incident involved the other important water body in Anlo – the Keta Lagoon. Hevieso, god of thunder and patron deity of the Yewe cult, is credited with all deaths by lightning.[37] Such corpses can only be buried after costly fines and rituals by the Yewe cult. The *Mirror* reported the case of Amekudzi:

> According to Kudzo Woeko, a family spokesman, David left home [on 7 April 1997] on a fishing expedition on Easter Monday with a cousin on the Keta Lagoon. Soon after they left home it began to rain so the deceased and his cousin decided to take shelter near a mangrove where their canoe was until the rain subsided with David covering himself with the sail in their canoe. There was a sudden thunder followed by lightning that struck David dead.[38]

The Yewe cult, of course, claimed credit for the death and alleged that David had been insolent to a member of the cult. Items required by the shrine they contacted at Anyako comprised C600,000 (Ghanaian cedis), three bottles of schnapps, five gallons of *akpeteshie* and a goat. This was beyond the means of David's family and, as late as 21 April 1997, the corpse lay unburied at the lagoon side in Woe. Interestingly, it was an NGO based at Adidome, Fetish Slaves Liberation Movement (FESLIM), that was negotiating with the bereaved family and the shrine to bury the body.[39] The police feigned official ignorance of the matter, and the several local Christian churches did not intercede.

Togbuivi Kumassah – a chief, a Christian and a scholar – explained why Anlo who were not Yewe members preferred not to intervene in these matters. The Yewe people forbade any contact with the corpse. The Anlo believe that, when lightning kills someone, the energy force remains in the body for a while. Anyone who goes close to the corpse and enters this energy field can develop incurable rheumatism or become a hunchback.[40] Did Christians believe in this? Kumassah provided an instructive analogy. He compared the various sources of spiritual power to different fuel types – charcoal, gas, electricity, solar. They can all cook food, but some have disadvantages. If you want to use charcoal, you should be able to withstand the smoke. There are several forces in this world other than Jesus. Some will give you instantaneous gratification at an undisclosed but heavy price. Christ is supreme.[41]

Even the Evangelical Presbyterian Church (EPC), the dominant religious body in the Volta Region, has been divided over the efficacy of certain forms of spiritual intercession – speaking in tongues, corporate prayer, healing, praise during worship and the style of baptism.[42] This Church emerged in 1922 from the Bremen Mission

---

[37] See Chapter 4.

[38] *Mirror* (12 April 1997).

[39] Ibid. (19 April 1997).

[40] Personal communication from Togbuivi Kumassah, 21 April 1997.

[41] Ibid.

[42] For the different views, see interview with Rev. Dogbe, Pastor in charge of the Keta EP Church of Ghana, Keta, 18 March 1997; interview with Rev. Fred Lawluvi, Pastor in charge of the Anloga EP Church, Ghana, Anloga, 20 March 1997.

field in Eweland. From the 1970s, Pentecostal influences have penetrated the orthodox churches, and the EPC was not an exception. A significant section of the EPC demanded a more satisfying style of worship and formed prayer groups in which gifts of the Holy Spirit were encouraged. The attempt by the moderator of the church, Professor N.K. Dzobo, to seek a third term of office in 1991 – contrary to the constitution of the church – brought about a split in a church already divided over the form of worship. It did not help matters that Dzobo also sought to introduce a new 'Meleagbe theology', which incorporated aspects of Anlo religion and culture into EPC doctrine.[43] Both factions – the EP Church, Ghana and the Pentecostalist-influenced EP Church of Ghana – claimed to be the true representatives of the Bremen Mission heritage, and intense struggles and legal suits have erupted over control of EP church buildings and schools. In the Anlo littoral, it appears that most of the congregations moved into the EP Church of Ghana, though the landed properties of the church – schools, chapels – have mostly been retained by the EP Church, Ghana. In Keta, the manse and the chapel succumbed to sea erosion and the bulk of the members went to a new site as EP Church of Ghana.[44] Meyer's insightful work highlights the endeavour of Ewe Christians to resolve the continuing fear of old sources of spiritual power and how these old categories have been subsumed under the Christian label of the 'devil'.[45] How to disarm the 'devil' remains an ongoing challenge for Ewe Christians.

With all these potent, competing forms of power, why has no one spiritually solved the problem of sea erosion? Togbui Honi II shared his thoughts:

> Certainly, some of us do believe that this thing can be controlled. If we go back to our roots to find out what we do for the sea to calm down. At a time the *Awoamefia* Togbui Adeladza II, the present one [now deceased, 27 August 1997], took this decision at the Traditional Council that we have to come together to find out why our forefathers came to live here peacefully and today we are facing this havoc. We agreed to do it, and I had been assigned particularly to organize the priests to come and do this thing. At that time the amount involved was only C50,000, which we could get. But at the Traditional Council we have a split voice, the Christians said no, others said no, so we couldn't do it.[46]

Now the Anlo await the more mundane sea defence project of the NDC government to resolve its long-standing problem of coastal erosion. For over three centuries the Anlo have lived between the lagoon and the sea, but have not overcome their awe of these majestic bodies of water. This book has reviewed why and how these water bodies have shaped the economy, society and culture of Anlo since the mid-seventeenth century.

---

[43] The best discussion of the EPC split is found in Birgit Meyer, 'Translating the devil: an African appropriation of pietest Protestantism – the case of the Peki Ewe in southeastern Ghana, 1847–1992' (PhD thesis, University of Amsterdam, 1995), ch. 8.
[44] Personal correspondence from G.K. Nukunya, 28 September 1999.
[45] Meyer, 'Translating the devil'.
[46] Interview with Togbui Honi II, Dzelukope, 4 September 1996.

Conclusion

Every village, town, community and region has a history, but not all become the subject of an historical monograph. What is the import of the rich microhistory chronicled in this book? First, the book examines the development of maritime tradition among the Anlo. Much of African historical writing has been land-bound, and the Anlo offer an important contrasting study. Secondly, the literature on environmental and ecological history in Africa has stressed the issues of desiccation and deforestation. The Anlo example sheds light on different environmental concerns: coastal erosion and the epidemiological and hydrological consequences of dams. Thirdly, the eco-social history of the Anlo reveals the mutualism between people and environment, and how social history – which examines everyday life – can be enriched through close attention to the material basis of a community or society.

Theoretically, this book did not begin as a materialist interpretation of history, though this interpretative strand became strong in the course of writing. That there is a material base to most social institutions and social interaction is not in doubt. To cite Martin Klein, this book adopted the concept of mode of production 'not so much from a reading of Marx as from the study of history'.[47] As stated in the Introduction, conceptualizing this study was problematic. The chapters were written before the conceptual framework in the Introduction. Most introductory chapters begin with the theoretical framework and end with the historical context and chapter outline. The order is reversed in this book to reflect the actual intellectual process through which the book emerged. The puzzling aspects of Anlo's history – the harvesting of nature, the political economy of warfare, slavery and the slave-trade, mercantile commerce, migrant fishing, shallot farming and the accompanying social structures and social relations – made sense when subjected to the mode of production analysis. The evidence and the analysis of a materialist interpretation were embedded in the chapters, so, apart from the introductory chapter and the strengthening of concepts and linkages to ensure continuity through the chapters, the impulse to situate the book more firmly in the mode of production model was resisted. That would have been to strive for a theoretical neatness that may not be in consonance with historical experience.

Modes of production theorists have identified specific production systems in Africa: the lineage mode of production, the tributary mode of production and a slave mode of production. The relevance of commerce or long-distance trade is under-scored for the last two modes of production, and the capitalist mode of production eventually affected all during the colonial era.[48] What is intriguing in the Anlo case is not the existence of these models in pure forms in place and time, but their

[47] Martin A. Klein, 'The use of mode of production in historical analysis', *Canadian Journal of African Studies* 19, 1 (1985): 9.
[48] Ray A. Kea, *Settlements, Trade, and Polities in the Seventeenth-century Gold Coast* (Baltimore, 1982); Emmanuel Terray, 'Long-distance exchange and the formation of the state: the case of the Abron-Kingdom of Gyaman', *Economy and Society* 3 (1974): 315–45; C. Meillassoux, *Maidens, Meal and Money: Capitalism and the Domestic Community* (Cambridge, 1981); and idem, *The Anthropology of Slavery*.

coexistence across different microenvironments and sometimes within the same microenvironment. Thus, Anlo could boast of cosmopolitan Keta and the *trɔkosi* institution. Shifts in the material base, for instance from the slave-trade to the colonial market economy, also witnessed transitional phases that occasioned unique economic pursuits, such as smuggling. And much of these changes in material base, social institutions and social interaction took place in relatively small communities and not necessarily along the axis of class conflict. This does not mean that social competition did not exist. The external forces of global capital, Christianity and Western imperialism would also transform the material base and the superstructure of Anlo, especially from the late nineteenth century. Social and class dynamics in Anlo consequently changed.

But ideas, values and beliefs remained important in Anlo society. The environment or nature is not just exploited; it is also conceptualized. Hence the forging of a maritime tradition involved not only technological adaptation, but also religious or spiritual innovation. And, when environmental crisis struck, it was to the same belief system that the Anlo repaired for explanations. This book avoids both environmental and materialist determinism. Historical experience is often more complex than theories acknowledge.

Bibliography

Archives

Ghana
National Archives of Ghana (NAG)
Accra and Ho depositories
James Ocloo Family Private Papers
Keta District Assembly
Economic Reports on the District
Institute of African Studies, University of Ghana
Aduamah, E.Y. (n.d.) Ewe Traditions 1–19

England
Public Records Office (Kew) (PRO)
FO, CO 554 and CO 96 Series
London School of Hygiene and Tropical Medicine
Collection on Health and Disease in Ghana
Rhodes House Library (Oxford)
Alexander Howard Ross Private Papers
William Forbes Mclaren Private Papers
David Scot Private Papers
Charles Richard Edelsten Private Papers

Germany
North German Missionary Society
Collection on the Ewe of Ghana and Togo
Bremen State Archives
Photos and Correspondence from Keta Station

Serials

Daily Graphic
Ewe News-Letter
Free Press
Ghanaian Chronicle
Ghanaian Voice
Gold Coast Advocate
Gold Coast Chronicle
Gold Coast Leader
Public Agenda
Mirror
Weekend Statesman
Weekly Spectator
West Africa

Published primary and secondary works

Abbink, Jon. 'Ritual and environment: the *Mosit* ceremony of the Ethiopian Me'en people', *Journal of Religion in Africa* 25, 2 (1995): 163–90.
Acheson, James M. 'Anthropology of fishing', *Annual Review of Anthropology* 10 (1981): 275–316.
Ackerman, William C., Gilbert F. White and E.B. Worthington. *Man-Made Lakes: Their Problems and*

Bibliography

Environmental Effects. Geophysical Monograph 17, American Geophysical Union, Washington D.C., 1973.

Agbodeka, Francis, ed. *A Handbook of Eweland*, Vol.I: *The Ewes of Southeastern Ghana*. Accra: Woeli Press, 1997.

Ahiawordor, Stevens K.M. 'A study of the 1996 presidential and parliamentary elections in Ghana: the case of Ketu South and Ketu North constituencies'. In *The 1996 General Elections and Democratic Consolidation in Ghana*, ed. Joseph R.A. Ayee, 461–78. Accra: Gold-Type, 1998.

Akinjogbin, I.A. *Dahomey and its Neighbours 1708–1778*. Cambridge: Cambridge University Press, 1967.

Akyeampong, Emmanuel. 'The state and alcohol revenues: promoting "economic development" in Gold Coast/Ghana', *Histoire Sociale* 27, 3 (1994): 393–411.

——. *Drink, Power, and Cultural Change: A Social History of Alcohol in Ghana, c. 1800 to Recent Times*. Portsmouth: Heinemann, 1996.

——. 'What's in a drink? Class struggle, popular culture and the politics of akpeteshie (local gin) in Ghana, 1930–1967', *Journal of African History* 37, 2 (1996): 215–36.

——. 'Sexuality and prostitution among the Akan of the Gold Coast, c. 1650–1950', *Past and Present* 156 (August 1997): 144–73.

——. 'Christianity, modernity, and the weight of tradition in the life of Asantehene Agyeman Prempeh I, c. 1888–1931', *Africa* 69, 2 (1999): 279–311.

——. '*Wo pe tam won pe ba* (you like cloth but you don't want children): urbanization, individualism, and gender relations in colonial Ghana, c. 1900–1939'. In *Africa's Urban Past*, ed. David Anderson and Richard Rathbone, 222–34. Oxford: James Currey, 2000.

Akyeampong, Emmanuel and Pashington Obeng. 'Spirituality, gender, and power in Asante history', *International Journal of African Historical Studies* 28, 3 (1995): 481–508.

Allman, Jean M. 'Of "spinsters", "concubines" and "wicked women": reflections on gender and social change in colonial Asante', *Gender and History* 30, 2 (1991): 176–89.

——. 'Making mothers: missionaries, medical officers and women's work in colonial Asante, 1924–1945', *History Workshop* 38 (Autumn 1994): 23–47.

——. 'Rounding up spinsters: gender chaos and unmarried women in colonial Asante', *Journal of African History* 37, 2 (1996): 195–214.

Amanor, Kojo Sebastian. *The New Frontier. Farmers' Response to Land Degradation: A West African Study*. London: Zed Books, 1994.

Ameh, Robert Kwame. 'Trokos: (child slavery) in Ghana: a policy approach', *Ghana Studies* 1 (1998): 35–62.

Amenumey, D.E.K. 'The pre-1947 background to the Ewe unification question', *Transactions of the Historical Society of Ghana* 10 (1960): 65–85.

——. 'Geraldo de Lima: a reappraisal'. *Transactions of the Historical Society of Ghana* 9 (1968): 65–78.

——. *The Ewe in Pre-colonial Times*. Accra: Sedco Publishing, 1986.

——. *The Ewe Unification Movement: A Political History*. Accra: Ghana Universities Press, 1989.

——. 'A brief history'. In *A Handbook of Eweland* Vol. I: *The Ewes of Southeastern Ghana*, ed. Francis Agbodeka, 14–27. Accra: Woeli Press, 1997.

Anderson, Benedict. *Imagined Communities: Reflections on the Origin and Spread of Nationalism*. London: Verso Press, 1983.

Anderson, David and Richard Grove, eds. *Conservation in Africa: People, Policies and Practice*. Cambridge: Cambridge University Press, 1987.

Anlo Traditional State. *Funeral Rites for the Late Togbui Adeladza II*. Accra: Commercial Associates, 1998.

Appadurai, Arjun. *Modernity at Large: Cultural Dimensions of Globalization*. Minneapolis: University of Minnesota Press, 1996.

Arhin, Kwame. 'Rank and class among the Asante and Fante in the nineteenth century', *Africa* 53, 3 (1983): 2–22.

Arnold, David and Ramachandra Guha, eds. *Nature, Culture, Imperialism: Essays on the Environmental History of South Asia*. Delhi: Oxford University Press, 1996.

Asiwaju, A.I., ed. *Partitioned Africans: Ethnic Relations across Africa's International Boundaries, 1884–1984*. Lagos: Lagos University Press, 1984.

Asiwaju, A.I. and Robin Law. 'From the Volta to the Niger, c. 1600–1800'. In *History of West Africa*, Vol. 1, ed. J.F.A. Ajayi and Michael Crowder, 412–64. Harlow, Essex: Longman, 1985.

Astuti, Rita. *People of the Sea: Identity and Descent among the Vezo of Madagascar*. Cambridge: Cambridge University Press, 1995.

Ati, Hassan A. Abdel. 'The damming of the River Atbara and its downstream impact'. In *African River Basins and Dryland Crises*, ed. M.B.K. Darkoh, 21–43. Uppsala: Reprocentralen HSC, 1992.

Austin, Dennis. *Politics in Ghana 1946–1960*. London: Oxford University Press, 1964.

Austin, Gareth. 'Human pawning in Asante, 1800–1950'. In *Pawnship in Africa: Debt Bondage in Historical Perspective*, ed. Toyin Falola and Paul Lovejoy, 119–59. Boulder: Westview Press, 1994.

Bibliography

Awoonor, Kofi. *This Earth, My Brother*. Portsmouth: Heinemann, 1972.

Ayee, Joseph R.A. 'Measuring public opinion on key political and economic issues: a survey of the Keta and Anlo constituencies in the Volta Region'. In *The 1996 General Elections and Democratic Consolidation in Ghana*, ed. Joseph R.A. Ayee, 275–301. Accra: Gold-Type, 1998.

Barnes, Kwamina. *Economics of the Volta River Project*. Tema: State Publishing Corporation, 1966.

Beinart, William and Peter Coates. *Environment and History: The Taming of Nature in the USA and South Africa*. London and New York: Routledge, 1995.

Benneh, G. 'Land tenure and Sabala farming system in the Anlo area of Ghana: a case study', *Research Review* 7, 2 (1971): 74–93.

Berner, Lewis. *Entomological Report on Development of the River Volta Basin*. Westminster: Wightman Mountain, 1950.

Boahen, A.A. *Ghana: Evolution and Change in the Nineteenth and Twentieth Centuries*. London: Longman, 1975.

——. *African Perspectives on Colonialism*. Baltimore: Johns Hopkins University Press, 1987.

——. *The Ghanaian Sphinx: Reflections on the Contemporary History of Ghana, 1972–1987*. Accra: Ghana Academy of Arts and Sciences, 1989.

——. 'A note on the Ghanaian elections', *African Affairs* 94, 375 (1995): 277–80.

Bolster, W. Jeffrey. *Black Jacks: African American Seamen in the Age of Sail*. Cambridge, MA: Harvard University Press, 1997.

Bosman, Willem. *A New and Accurate Description of the Coast of Guinea, Divided into the Gold, the Slave, and the Ivory Coasts*, 3rd edn. London: J. Knapton, 1721.

Brooks, George. *The Kru Mariner in the Nineteenth Century: An Historical Compendium*. Newark: University of Delaware, 1972.

——. 'A historical schema for Western Africa based on seven climate periods', *Cahiers d'Etudes Africaines* 26 (1986): 43–62.

——. *Landlords and Strangers: Ecology, Society, and Trade in Western Africa, 1000–1630*. Boulder: Westview Press, 1993.

Brown, David. 'Who are the tribalists? Social pluralism and political ideology in Ghana', *African Affairs* 81, 322 (1982): 37–69.

——. 'Sieges and scapegoats: the politics of pluralism in Ghana and Togo', *Journal of Modern African Studies* 21, 3 (1983): 431–60.

Bryant, Raymond L. 'Political ecology: an emerging research agenda in Third World studies', *Political Geography* 11, 1 (1992): 12–36.

Canadian Journal of African Studies 19, 1 (1985). Special issue on modes of production in Africa.

Cardinall, A.W. *The Gold Coast, 1931*. Accra: Government Printer, 1931.

Casely Hayford, J.E. *Gold Coast Native Institutions*. London: Sweet and Maxwell, 1903.

Chanock, Martin. *Law, Custom, and Social Order: The Colonial Experience in Malawi and Zambia*. Cambridge: Cambridge University Press, 1985.

Chapman, D.A. *Our Homeland: A Regional Geography*, Book 1 – *South-east Gold Coast*. Accra: Achimota Press, 1943.

——. *The Anlo Constitution*. Accra: Achimota Press, 1944.

Christensen, James B. 'Motor power and woman power: technological and economic change among the Fanti fishermen of Ghana'. In *Those who Live from the Sea: A Study in Maritime Anthropology*, ed. M.E. Smith, 71–95. St Paul, NY: West Publishing, 1977.

Chu, K.Y., H.K. Kpo and R.K. Klumpp. 'Mixing of *Schistosoma haematobium* strains in Ghana', *Bulletin of the World Health Organization* 56, 4 (1978): 601–8.

Cohen, David William and E.S. Atieno Odhiambo. *Siaya: The Historical Anthropology of an African Landscape*. London: James Currey, 1989.

Colson, Elizabeth. 'Places of power and shrines of the land', *Paideuma* 43 (1997): 47–57.

Comaroff, Jean and Comaroff, John, eds. *Modernity and its Malcontents: Ritual and Power in Postcolonial Africa*. Chicago: University of Chicago Press, 1993.

Croll, Elisabeth and David Parkin, eds. *Bush Base: Forest Farm – Culture, Environment and Development*. London and New York: Routledge, 1992.

Cronon, William. *Changes in the Land: Indians, Colonists, and the Ecology of New England*. New York: Hill and Wang, 1983.

Crosby, Alfred W. *Germs, Seeds, and Animals: Studies in Ecological History*, London: M.E. Sharpe, 1994.

Cruickshank, Brodie. *Eighteen Years on the Gold Coast of Africa*, 2 vols. London: Hurst and Blackett, 1853.

Crummey, Donald D. and C.C. Stewart, eds, *Modes of Production in Africa: The Precolonial Era*. Beverly Hills: Sage, 1981.

Bibliography

Darkoh, M.B.K., ed. *African River Basins and Dryland Crises*. Uppsala: Reprocentralen HSC, 1992.

Debrunner, Hans. *A Church between Colonial Powers: A Study of the Church in Togo*. London: Lutterworth Press, 1965.

de Marees, Pieter. *Description and Historical Account of the Gold Kingdom of Guinea*. Trans. and ed. Albert van Dantzig and Adam Jones. Oxford: Oxford University Press, 1987.

de Surgy, Albert. *La Pêche maritime traditionnelle à l'ancienne 'Côte de Guinée': origines et développement*. Kara, Togo: Centre d'Études et de Recherches de Kara, 1969.

Dickson, Kwamina B. 'Evolution of seaports in Ghana: 1800–1928', *Annals of the Association of American Geographers* 55, 1 (1965): 98–111.

——. *A Historical Geography of Ghana*. Cambridge: Cambridge University Press, 1969.

Dike, K. O. *Trade and Politics in the Niger Delta 1830–1885*. Oxford: Clarendon Press, 1956.

Douglas, Mary and Baron Isherwood. *The World of Goods*. New York: Basic Books, 1981.

Dzobo, N.K. *African Proverbs: Guide to Conduct*, 2 vols. Accra: Waterville Publishing House, 1975.

Ellis, A.B. *The Ewe Speaking Peoples of the Slave Coast of West Africa*. London: Chapman and Hall, 1890.

Evans, S.M., C.J. Vanderpuye and A.K. Armah. *The Coastal Zone of West Africa: Problems and Management*. Cleadon: Penshaw Press, 1997.

Faculty of Architecture. *Keta Study*. University of Science and Technology, Occasional Report No. 15, *c.* 1971.

Fage, J.D. 'A commentary on Duarte Pacheco Periera's account of the Lower Guinea coastlands in his *Esmeraldo de Situ Orbis*, and on some other early accounts', *History in Africa* 7 (1980): 47–80.

Fair, Laura. 'Kickin' it: leisure, politics and football in colonial Zanzibar, 1900–1950s', *Africa* 67, 2 (1997): 224–51.

——. 'Dressing up: clothing, class and gender in post-abolition Zanzibar', *Journal of African History* 39, 1 (1998): 63–94.

Fairhead, James and Melissa Leach. *Misreading the African Landscape: Society and Ecology in a Forest–Savanna Mosaic*. Cambridge: Cambridge University Press, 1996.

——. 'Deforestation in question: dialogue and dissonance in ecological, social and historical knowledge of West Africa – cases from Liberia and Sierra Leone', *Paideuma* 43 (1997): 193–225.

Falola, Toyin and Paul Lovejoy, eds. *Pawnship in Africa: Debt Bondage in Historical Perspective*. Boulder: Westview Press, 1994.

Finley, Moses I. 'Slavery', *International Encyclopaedia of the Social Sciences* 14 (1968): 307–13.

Freeman, Richard Austin. *Travels and Life in Ashanti and Jaman*. Westminster: Archibald Constable, 1898.

Galkoswki, F. *Anloga, eine Hochburg des Heidentums*. Bremen: North German Missionary Society, 1907.

Gayibor, Nicoue L., ed. *Sources orales de la région d'Aneho*. Niamey: Centre for Linguistic and Historical Studies by Oral Tradition, 1980.

Giblin, James L. *The Politics of Environmental Control in Northeastern Tanzania, 1840–1940*. Philadelphia: University of Pennsylvania Press, 1992.

Gilroy, Paul. *The Black Atlantic: Modernity and Double Consciousness*. Cambridge, MA: Harvard University Press, 1993.

Gocking, Roger. 'Competing systems of inheritance before the British courts of the Gold Coast', *International Journal of African Historical Studies* 23, 4 (1990): 601–18.

——. 'British justice and native tribunals of the southern Gold Coast Colony', *Journal of African History* 34, 1 (1993): 93–113.

——. 'Indirect rule in the Gold Coast: competition for office and the invention of tradition', *Canadian Journal of African Studies* 28, 3 (1994): 421–45.

Goody, Jack. *Technology, Tradition, and the State in Africa*. London: Oxford University Press, 1971.

——. *Production and Reproduction: A Comparative Study of the Domestic Domain*. Cambridge: Cambridge University Press, 1976.

Greene, Sandra E. 'Land, lineage and clan in early Anlo', *Africa* 51, 1 (1981): 451–64.

——. 'The past and present of an Anlo-Ewe oral tradition', *History in Africa* 12 (1985): 73–87.

——. 'Social change in eighteenth-century Anlo: the role of technology, markets and military conflict', *Africa* 58, 1 (1988): 70–86.

——. *Gender, Ethnicity, and Social Change on the Upper Slave Coast: A History of the Anlo-Ewe*. Portsmouth: Heinemann, 1996.

——. 'Religion, history and the supreme gods of Africa: a contribution to the debate', *Journal of Religion in Africa* 26, 2 (1996): 122–38.

——. 'The individual as stranger in nineteenth-century Anlo: the politics of identity in precolonial West Africa'. In *The Cloth of Many Silk Colors*, ed. John Hunwick and Nancy Lawler, 91–127. Evanston: Northwestern University Press, 1996.

——. 'Sacred terrain: religion, politics and place in the history of Anloga (Ghana)', *International Journal of*

Bibliography

African Historical Studies 30, 1 (1997): 1–22.

Grier, Beverly. 'Pawns, porters, and petty traders: women in the transition to cash crop agriculture in colonial Ghana', *Signs* 17, 2 (1992): 304–28.

Grove, J. M. 'Some aspects of the economy of the Volta Delta (Ghana)', *Bulletin de l'Institut Fondamental d'Afrique Noire* 28, 1–2 (1966): 381–432.

Grove, J.M. and A.M. Johansen. 'The historical geography of the Volta Delta, Ghana, during the period of Danish influence', *Bulletin de l'Institut Fondamental d'Afrique Noire* 30, 4 (1968), 1374–1421.

Grove, Richard H. *Green Imperialism: Colonial Expansion, Tropical Island Edens and the Origins of Environmentalism, 1600–1800.* Cambridge: Cambridge University Press, 1995.

———. *Ecology, Climate and Empire: Colonialism and Global Environmental History, 1400–1940.* Cambridge, UK: White Horse Press, 1997.

Gutkind, Peter C.W. 'Trade and labor in early precolonial African history: the canoemen of Southern Ghana'. In *The Workers of African Trade*, ed. Catherine Coquery–Vidrovitch and Paul E. Lovejoy, 25–49. Beverly Hills: Sage, 1985.

Guyer, Jane I. and Samuel M. Eno Belinga. 'Wealth in people as wealth in knowledge: accumulation and composition in Equatorial Africa', *Journal of African History* 36, 1 (1995): 91–120.

Guyer, Jane and Paul Richards. 'The invention of biodiversity: social perspectives on the management of biological variety in Africa', *Africa* 66, 1 (1996): 1–13.

Gyekye, Kwame. *Tradition and Modernity: Philosophical Reflections on the African Experience.* New York and Oxford: Oxford University Press, 1997.

Hargreaves, J.D. 'The Atlantic Ocean in West African history'. In *Africa and the Sea*, ed. Jerry Stone, 5–13. Aberdeen: Aberdeen African Studies Group, 1985.

Harms, Robert W. *River of Wealth, River of Sorrow: The Central Zaire Basin in the Era of the Slave and Ivory Trade, 1500–1891.* New Haven and London: Yale University Press, 1981.

———. *Games against Nature: An Eco-cultural History of the Nunu of Equatorial Africa.* Cambridge: Cambridge University Press, 1987.

Harries, Patrick. *Work, Culture, and Identity: Migrant Labourers in Mozambique and South Africa, c. 1860–1910.* Portsmouth: Heinemann, 1994.

Härtter, G. 'Der Fischfang im Evheland', *Zeitschrift für Ethnologie* 38, 1–2 (1906): 51–63.

Hendrickson, Hildi, ed. *Clothing and Difference: Embodied Identities in Colonial and Post-colonial Africa.* Durham: Duke University Press, 1996.

Hendrix, Melvin K. 'Technology and maritime fisheries on the Sierra Leone Peninsula, c. 1600–1980'. In *Africa and the Sea*, ed. Jerry Stone, 64–79. Aberdeen: Aberdeen African Studies Group, 1985.

Herskovits, Melville J. *Dahomey: An Ancient West African Kingdom*, 2 vols. New York: J.J. Augustin, 1938.

Hill, Polly. *Studies in Rural Capitalism in West Africa.* Cambridge: Cambridge University Press, 1970.

———. *Talking with Ewe Seine Fishermen and Shallot Farmers.* Cambridge: African Studies Centre, 1986.

Ingold, Tim. 'Culture and the perception of the environment'. In *Bush Base: Forest Farm – Culture, Environment and Development*, ed. Elisabeth Croll and David Parkin, 39–56. London and New York: Routledge, 1992.

Inikori, Joseph, E. 'Slavery in Africa and the transatlantic slave trade'. In Alusine Jalloh and Stephen E. Maizlish, eds, *The African Diaspora*, Arlington, TX: Texas A&M University Press, 1996.

Irvine, F. R. *Fishes and Fisheries of the Gold Coast.* London: Crown Agents, 1947.

Irwin, Alan. *Citizen Science: A Study of People, Expertise and Sustainable Development.* London and New York: Routledge, 1995.

Isert, Paul Erdmann. *Letters on West Africa and the Slave Trade (1788).* Trans. and ed. Selena A. Winsnes. Oxford: Oxford University Press, 1992.

Janzen, John. *The Quest for Therapy in Lower Zaire.* Berkeley: University of California Press, 1978.

Jeffries, Richard and Clare Thomas. 'The Ghanaian elections of 1992', *African Affairs* 62, 368 (1993): 331–66.

Johnson, M. 'Ashanti East of the Volta', *Transactions of the Historical Society of Ghana* 8 (1965): 33–59.

Jones, Adam. *German Sources for West African History 1599–1669.* Wiesbaden: Franz Steiner Verlag, 1983.

Jopp, Keith. *Volta: The Story of Ghana's Volta River Project.* Accra: Volta River Authority, 1965.

Jorion, Paul. 'Going out or staying home: migration strategies among Xwla and Anlo-Ewe Fishermen', *Maritime Anthropological Studies* 1, 2 (1988): 129–55.

Jurer, N.R. and D.A. Bates, Reports on the Geology and Hydrology of the Coastal Area East of the Akwapian Range'. Accra: Government Printing Department, 1945.

Justesen, Ole. 'Aspects of eighteenth century Ghanaian history as revealed by Danish sources', *Ghana Notes and Queries* 12 (June 1972): 9–12.

Kandeh, H.B.S. and Paul Richards. 'Rural people as conservationists: querying neo-Malthusian assumptions about biodiversity in Sierra Leone', *Africa* 66, 1 (1996): 90–103.

233

Bibliography

Kea, Ray A. 'Akwamu–Anlo relations, c. 1750–1813', *Transactions of the Historical Society of Ghana* 10 (1969): 29–63.

Kimble, David. *Political History of Ghana 1850–1928*. Oxford: Clarendon Press, 1963.

——. *Settlements, Trade, and Polities in the Seventeenth-Century Gold Coast*. Baltimore: The Johns Hopkins University Press, 1982.

——. '"I am here to plunder on the general road": bandits and banditry in the pre-nineteenth-century Gold Coast'. In *Banditry, Rebellion and Social Protest in Africa*, ed. Donald Crummey, 109–32. London: James Currey, 1986.

Klein, Martin A. 'The use of mode of production in historical analysis', *Canadian Journal of African Studies* 19, 1 (1985): 9–12.

Klein, Norman A. 'Toward a new understanding of Akan origins', *Africa* 66, 2 (1996): 248–73.

Kloos, Helmut, ed. *The Ecology of Health and Disease in Ethiopia*. San Francisco: Westview Press, 1993.

Kloos, Helmut, Abdulhamid Bedri Kello and Abdulaziz Addus. 'The health impact of the 1984/85 Ethiopian resettlement programme: three case studies'. In *African River Basins and Dryland Crises*, ed. M.B.K. Darkoh, 147–65. Uppsala: Reprocentralen HSC, 1992.

Kludze, A.K.P. *Ewe Law of Property*. London: Sweet and Maxwell, 1973.

Klumpp, R.K., and K.Y. Chu. 'Ecological studies of *Bulinus rohlfsi*, the intermediate host of *Schistosoma haematobium* in the Volta Lake', *Bulletin of the World Health Organization* 55, 6 (1977): 715–30.

Klutse, W.S. Chapman. *The Keta Coast Erosion and Dredging for Development, and some Landmarks for Anlo History*. Accra: Arakan Press, 1984.

Knoll, Arthur J. *Togo under Imperial Germany 1884–1914*. Stanford: Hoover Institution Press, 1978.

Kodzo-Vordoagu, J.G. *Anlo Hogbetsotso Festival*. Accra: Domak Press, c. 1994.

Kopytoff, Igor, ed. *The African Frontier: The Reproduction of Traditional African Societies*. Bloomington: Indiana University Press, 1987.

Larkin, Brian. 'Indian films and Nigerian lovers: media and the creation of parallel modernities', *Africa* 67, 3 (1997): 406–40.

Law, Robin. 'Trade and politics behind the Slave Coast: the lagoon traffic and the rise of Lagos, 1500–1800', *Journal of African History* 24, 3 (1983): 321–48.

——. 'Between the sea and the lagoon: the interaction of maritime and inland navigation on the precolonial Slave Coast', *Cahiers d'etudes Africaines* 114, xxix–2 (1989): 209–37.

——. *The Slave Coast of West Africa 1550–1750: The Impact of the Atlantic Slave Trade on African Society*. Oxford: Clarendon Press, 1991.

Lawson, Rowena. 'The structure, migration and resettlement of Ewe fishing units', *African Studies* 17, 1 (1958): 21–7.

Lentz, Carola and Paul Nugent, eds. *Ethnicity in Ghana: The Limits of Invention*. London: Macmillan, forthcoming.

Leslie, Charles. 'Medical pluralism in world perspective'. *Social Science and Medicine* 14B (1980): 191–5.

Lovett, Margot. 'Gender relations, class formation, and the colonial state in Africa'. In *Women and the State in Africa*, ed. Jane L. Parpart and Kathleen Staudt, 23–46. Boulder: Lynne Rienner, 1989.

Luig, Ute and Achim von Oppen. 'Landscape in Africa: process and vision – an introductory essay', *Paideuma*, 43 (1997): 7–45.

McCaskie, T. C. 'Peoples and animals: constru(ct)ing the Asante experience', *Africa* 62, 2 (1992): 221–44.

McFarland, Daniel M. *Historical Dictionary of Ghana*. Metuchen: Scarecrow Press, 1985.

Macmillan, Della E. *Sahel Visions: Planned Settlement and River Blindness Control in Burkina Faso*. Tucson: University of Arizona Press, 1995.

McNeill, William H. *Plagues and Peoples*. New York: Doubleday, 1977.

Maier, Donna J.E. 'Slave labor and wage labor in German Togo'. In *Germans in the Tropics: Essays in German Colonial History*, ed. Arthur J. Knoll and Lewis H. Gann, 73–91. Westport: Greenwood Press, 1987.

Malinowski, Bronislaw. *Argonauts of the Western Pacific*. London: Routledge and Kegan Paul, 1922.

——. *Magic, Science and Religion*. New York: Doubleday, 1948.

Mamattah, Charles M.K. *The Ewes of West Africa*. Accra: Advent Press, 1979.

Manchuelle, François. *Willing Migrants: Sonike Labor Diasporas*. Athens, OH and Oxford: Ohio University Press and James Currey, 1997.

Mann, Kristin and Richard Roberts, eds. *Law in Colonial Africa*. Portsmouth: Heinemann, 1991.

Manning, Patrick. 'Merchants, porters, and canoemen in the Bight of Benin'. In *The Workers of African Trade*, ed. Catherine Coquery-Vidrovitch and Paul E. Lovejoy, 51–74. Beverly Hills: Sage, 1985.

——. 'Coastal society in the Republic of Benin: reproduction of a regional system', *Cahiers d'Etudes Africaines* 114, xxix–2 (1989): 239–57.

Bibliography

——. *Slavery and African Life: Occidental, Oriental and African Slave Trades*. Cambridge: Cambridge University Press, 1990.

Manoukian, Madeline. *The Ewe-Speaking People of Togoland and the Gold Coast*. London: International African Institute, 1952.

Martin, Phyllis. 'Contesting clothes in colonial Brazzaville', *Journal of African History* 35, 3 (1994): 401–26.

——. *Leisure and Society in Colonial Brazzaville*. Cambridge: Cambridge University Press, 1995.

Marx, K. *Capital*, vol. 1. London: Lawrence and Wishart, 1970.

Meillassoux, C. 'From reproduction to production: a Marxist approach to economic anthropology', *Economy and Society* 1 (1972): 93–108.

——. 'The social organization of the peasantry: the economic basis of kinship', *Journal of Peasant Studies* 1, 1 (1973): 81–90.

——. *Maidens, Meal and Money: Capitalism and the Domestic Community*. Cambridge: Cambridge University Press, 1981.

——. *The Anthropology of Slavery: The Woman of Iron and Gold*. Chicago: University of Chicago Press, 1991.

Metcalfe, G.E. *Great Britain and Ghana: Documents of Ghana History*, 2nd edn. Aldershot: Gregg Revivals, 1994. First edition 1964.

Miers, Suzanne and Igor Kopytoff, eds. *Slavery in Africa: Historical and Anthropological Perspectives*. Madison: University of Wisconsin Press, 1977.

Miers, Suzanne and Richard Roberts, eds. *The End of Slavery in Africa*. Madison: University of Wisconsin Press, 1988.

Moxon, James. *Volta, Man's Greatest Lake: The Story of Ghana's Akosombo Dam*. London: Andre Deutsch, 1984.

Müller, Hartmut. 'Bremen und Westafrika', *Jahrbuch der Wittheit zu Bremen* 15 (1971): 45–92.

New Patriotic Party. *The Stolen Verdict*. Accra: New Patriotic Party, 1993.

Nicholson, Sharon. 'The methodology of historical climate reconstruction and its application to Africa', *Journal of African History* 20, 1 (1979): 31–49.

Ninsin, Kwame A. *Political Struggles in Ghana 1967–1981*. Accra: Tornado Publishers, 1985.

Nkrumah, Kwame. *Ghana: The Autobiography of Kwame Nkrumah*, 3rd edn. New York: International Publishers, 1976.

Nørregård, Georg. *Danish Settlements in West Africa 1658–1850*. Trans. Sigurd Mammen. Boston: Boston University Press, 1966.

Nugent, Paul. *Big Men, Small Boys and Politics in Ghana*. Accra: Asempa Press, 1995.

——. 'Living in the past: urban, rural and ethnic themes in the 1992 and 1996 elections in Ghana', *Journal of Modern African Studies* 37, 2 (1999): 287–319.

——. 'Power versus knowledge: smugglers and the state along Ghana's eastern frontier, 1920–1992'. In *Frontiers and Borderlands: Anthropological Perspectives*, ed. Michael Rösler and Tobias Wendl, 77–99. Frankfurt am Main: Peter Lang, 1999.

——. '"A few lesser peoples": the central Togo minorities and their Ewe neighbours'. In Carola Lentz and Paul Nugent, eds, *Ethnicity in Ghana: The Limits of Invention*. London: Macmillan, forthcoming.

Nukunya, G.K. *Kinship and Marriage among the Anlo Ewe*. London: Athlone Press, 1969.

——. 'Land tenure, inheritance, and social structure among the Anlo', *Universitas* 3, 1 (1973): 64–82.

——. 'The effects of cash crops on an Ewe community'. In *Changing Social Structure in Ghana*, ed. Jack Goody. London: International African Institute, 1975.

——. *The History of the Woe Evangelical Presbyterian Church 1887–1987*. Accra: EP Church, 1987.

——. 'The Anlo-Ewe and full-time maritime fishing: another view', *Maritime Anthropological Studies* 2, 2 (1989): 154–73.

——. 'The land and the people'. In *A Handbook of Eweland*, Vol. I: *The Ewes of Southeastern Ghana*, ed. Francis Agbodeka, 8–13. Accra: Woeli Press, 1997.

——. 'Social and political organization'. In *A Handbook of Eweland*, Vol. I: *The Ewes of Southeastern Ghana*, ed. Francis Agbodeka, 47–72. Accra: Woeli Press, 1997.

Obeng, L.E., ed. *Man-made Lakes*. Accra: Ghana Universities Press, 1969.

Ocloo, Christian Yao. *The Anlo Shallot Revolution, 1930s–1992: A Study of the Local Agricultural History of Anloga in the Volta Region of Ghana*. Trondheim: Norwegian University of Science and Technology, 1996.

Odotei, Irene. 'The migration of Ghanaian women in the canoe fishing industry', *Maritime Anthropological Studies* 5, 2 (1992): 88–95.

Okali, Christine. *Cocoa and Kinship in Ghana: The Matrilineal Akan of Ghana*. London: Kegan Paul, 1983.

Oppong, Christine, ed. *Female and Male in West Africa*. London: Allen and Unwin, 1983.

Oquaye, Mike. 'The Ghanaian elections of 1992: a dissenting view', *African Affairs* 94, 375 (1995): 259–75.

Osswald, C. *Fifty Years' Mission Work at Keta*. Bremen: North German Missionary Society, 1903.

235

Bibliography

Overa, Ragnhild. 'Wives and traders: women's careers in Ghanaian canoe fisheries', *Maritime Anthropological Studies* 6, 1–2 (1993): 110–35.

Ozanne, Paul. 'Ladoku: an early town', *Ghana Notes and Queries* 7 (January 1965): 6–7.

Parpart, Jane L. '"Where is your mother?": gender, urban marriage, and colonial discourse on the Zambian copperbelt, 1925–1945', *International Journal of African Historical Studies* 27, 2 (1994): 241–71.

Parrinder, E.G. *The Story of Ketu: An Ancient Yoruba Kingdom*. Ibadan: Ibadan University Press, 1956.

——. *West African Religion*, 2nd edn. London: Epworth Press, 1969.

Patterson, Orlando. *Slavery and Social Death: A Comparative Study*. Cambridge, MA: Harvard University Press, 1982.

Poggie, John J., Jr and Carl Gersuny. 'Risk and ritual: an interpretation of fishermen's folklore in a New England community', *Journal of American Folklore* 85 (1972): 66–72.

Prins, A.H.J. *Sailing from Lamu: A Study of Maritime Culture in Islamic East Africa*. Assen: Van Gorcum and Co., 1965.

Ramseyer F. A. and J. Kühne. *Four Years in Ashantee*. London: James Nisbet and Co., 1875.

Ranger, Terrence. 'Making Zimbabwean landscapes: painters, projectors and priests', *Paideuma* 43 (1997), 59–73.

Rathbone, Richard. 'Businessmen in politics: party struggle in Ghana, 1949–1957', *Journal of Development Studies* 9, 3 (1973): 391–402.

Rattray, R.S. 'History of the Ewe people', *Etudes Togolaises* 11, 1 (1967): 92–8.

Reefe, Thomas Q. 'The biggest game of all: gambling in traditional Africa'. In *Sport in Africa: Essays in Social History*, ed. William J. Baker and James A. Mangan, 47–78. New York: Africana Publishing House, 1987.

Reindorf, C.C. *History of the Gold Coast and Asante*. Basle: Basle Mission, 1895.

Richards, Paul. 'Ecological change and the politics of African land-use', *African Studies Review* 26, 2 (1983): 1–72.

Roberts, Andrew. *The Colonial Moment in Africa*. Cambridge: Cambridge University Press, 1990.

Roberts, Penelope A. 'The state and the regulation of marriage: Sefwi Wiawso (Ghana), 1900–1940'. In *Women, State and Ideology: Studies from Africa and Asia*, ed. Haleh Afshar, 48–69. London: Macmillan, 1987.

Robertson, Claire C. *Sharing the Same Bowl: A Socioeconomic History of Women and Class in Accra, Ghana*. Madison: University of Wisconsin Press, 1984.

Robertson, Claire and Martin A. Klein, eds. *Women and Slavery in Africa*. Madison: University of Wisconsin Press, 1983.

Robertson, G.A. *Notes on Africa; Particularly those Parts which are Situated between Cape Verde and the River Congo*. London: Sherwood, Neely and Jones, 1819.

Rohns, Hedwig. *Zwanzig Jahre Missions-Diakonissenarbeit im Ewelande*. Bremen: North German Missionary Society, 1912.

Sarbah, John Mensah. *Fanti National Constitution*, 3rd edn. London: Frank Cass, 1968.

Schack, William A. and Elliot P. Skinner, eds. *Strangers in African Societies*. Berkeley: University of California Press, 1979.

Schildkrout, Enid. *People of the Zongo: The Transformation of Ethnic Identities in Ghana*. Cambridge: Cambridge University Press, 1978.

Schock-Quinteros, Eva and Dieter Lenz. *150 Years of North German Mission 1836–1986*. Bremen: North German Missionary Society, 1989.

Schoenbrun, David Lee, *A Green Place, A Good Place: Agrarian Change, Gender and Social Identity in the Great Lakes Region to the 15th Century*. Portsmouth and Oxford: Heinemann and James Currey, 1998.

Schoffeleers, J.M., ed. *Guardians of the Land: Essays on Central African Territorial Cults*. Gwelo, Mambo Press, 1979.

Seidel, H. 'Der Yewe-Dienst im Togolande', *Zeitschrift für Afrikanische und Oceanische Sprachen* 3, 2 (1897): 157–85.

Shillington, Kevin. *Ghana and the Rawlings Factor*. London: Macmillan, 1992.

Smith, Robert. 'The canoe in West African history', *Journal of African History* 11, 4 (1970): 513–33.

Smock, David R., and Audrey Smock. *The Politics of Pluralism: A Comparative Study of Lebanon and Ghana*. New York: Elsevier, 1975.

Sprigge, R.G.S. 'Eweland's Adangbe', *Transactions of the Historical Society of Ghana* 10 (1969): 87–128.

Stone, Jerry C., ed. *Africa and the Sea*. Aberdeen: Aberdeen University African Studies Group, 1985.

Taylor, Christopher. *Milk, Honey and Money: Changing Concepts in Rwandan Healing*. Washington, DC: Smithsonian Institution Press, 1992.

Tengan, Edward B. 'The Sisala universe: its composition and structure (an essay in cosmology)', *Journal of Religion in Africa* 20, 1 (1990): 2–19.

Terray, Emmanuel. 'Long-distance exchange and the formation of the state: the case of the Abron-Kingdom of Gyaman', *Economy and Society* 3 (1974): 315–45.

Bibliography

Tonkin, Elizabeth. 'Creating Kroomen: ethnic diversity, economic specialism and changing demand'. In *Africa and the Sea*, ed. Jerry Stone, 27–47. Aberdeen: Aberdeen African Studies Group, 1985.

Vail, Leroy. 'Ecology and history: the example of eastern Zambia', *Journal of Southern African Studies* 3, 2 (1977): 129–55.

———. ed. *The Creation of Tribalism in Southern African*. London: James Currey, 1991.

van Binsbergen, Wim and Peter Geschiere, eds. *Old Modes of Production and Capitalist Encroachment: Anthropological Explorations in Africa*. London: KPI, 1985.

van Dantzig, Albert. *The Dutch and the Guinea Coast 1674–1742: A Collection of Documents from the General State Archive at the Hague*. Accra: Ghana Academy of Arts and Sciences, 1978.

———. *Forts and Castles of Ghana*. Accra: Sedco, 1980.

Vaughan, Megan. *Curing their Ills: Colonial Power and African Illness*. Stanford: Stanford University Press, 1991.

Vercruijsse, Emile. *The Penetration of Capitalism: A West African Study*. London: Zed Books, 1984.

Vieta, Kojo T. *The Flagbearers of Ghana: Profiles of One Hundred Distinguished Ghanaians*, vol. I. Accra: Ena Publications, 1999.

Walker, K.J. 'The state in environmental management: the ecological dimension', *Political Studies* 37 (1989): 25–38.

Watts, Sheldon. *Disease, Power, and Imperialism*. New Haven: Yale University Press, 1997.

Webster, J.B. and A.A. Boahen, with M. Tidy. *The Revolutionary Years: West Africa since 1800*. Harlow: Essex: Longman, 1980.

Welch, Claude. *Dream of Unity: Pan-Africanism and Political Unification in West Africa*. Ithaca: Cornell University Press, 1966.

Westermann, D. 'Ein Bericht über den Yehwekultus der Ewe', *Mitteilungen des Seminars für Orientalische Sprachen* 33, 3 (1930): 1–55.

White, Luise. *The Comforts of Home: Prostitution in Colonial Nairobi*. Chicago: University of Chicago Press, 1990.

Wilbert, Johannes. *Mindful of Famine: Religious Climatology of the Warao Indians*. Cambridge, MA: Harvard University Press, 1996.

Wilks, Ivor. 'The rise of the Akwamu Empire', *Transactions of the Historical Society of Ghana* 3, 2 (1957): 99–136.

Wilson, Louis E. *The Krobo People of Ghana to 1892: A Political and Social History*. Athens: Ohio University Center for International Studies, 1991.

Worster, Donald. 'Appendix: doing environmental history'. In *The Ends of the Earth: Perspectives on Modern Environmental History*, ed. Donald Worster, 289–307. Cambridge: Cambridge University Press, 1988.

Wyllie, Robert. 'Migrant Anlo fishing companies and socio-political change: a comparative study', *Africa* 39, 4 (1969), 396–410.

Yarak, Larry. *Asante and the Dutch, 1744–1873*. Oxford: Clarendon Press, 1990.

Younger, Stephen and Jean-Baptiste Zongo. 'West Africa: the Onchocerciasis Control Program'. In *Successful Development in Africa: Case Studies of Projects, Programs, and Policies*, ed. R. Bheenick, 27–46. Washington, DC: World Bank, 1989.

Unpublished works

Adjorlolo, Theophilus W. 'The history of education in Anlo with special reference to Keta from 1850–1960'. BA thesis, University of Ghana, 1977.

Agboada, Napoleon K. 'The reign and times of Togbi sri II of Anlo (1906–1956)'. BA thesis, University of Ghana, 1984.

Agbodzi, Margaret Adzo. 'The impact of shallot farming on the socio-economic status of women in Anloga'. BA thesis, University of Ghana, 1986.

Akorli-Ayim, Felicia E. 'On the history of Keta with particular reference to its role in the Anlo struggle against European domination'. BA thesis, University of Ghana, 1972.

Akyeampong, Emmanuel. 'History, memory, slave-trade and slavery in Anlo, Ghana', 14th Annual O. Truman Driggs Distinguished Lecture, University of Minnesota at Morris, 14 September 1999.

Amable, Sophia. 'The 1953 riot in Anloga and its aftermath'. BA thesis, University of Ghana, 1977.

Amanu, Winfred N. 'Coping with ill-health in riverine communities along the Volta Lake'. BA thesis, University of Ghana, 1994.

Amegashie, Justice M.Y. 'The concept of renewal – a study in Anlo thought'. BA thesis, University of Ghana, 1976.

Amuzu, A. K. 'The economic resources and activities of the Keta Lagoon and their contribution to the life of the people of South Anlo'. BA thesis, University of Ghana, 1961.

Armah, A.K. and D.S. Amlalo. 'Coastal zone profile of Ghana'. National Workshop on Integrated Coastal Area

Bibliography

Management, Accra, 1997.

Ashong, Richard. 'A historical study of hydro electricity in Ghana'. BA thesis, University of Ghana, 1993.

Azumah, Cudjoe. 'The Trokosi practice in north Tongu: its impact on the rights of women and children'. BA thesis, University of Ghana, 1996.

Bensah, Christian R.K. 'Anlo belief in life after death'. BA thesis, University of Ghana, 1979.

Cooperativa Muratori and Cementisti. 'Keta Sea Defence – Ghana'. June 1987.

Fiagbedzi, Nissio S. 'Sogbadzi songs: a study of Yewe music'. Dip. in African Music, University of Ghana, 1966.

Fiagbedzi, Tobias N. 'Migration and early settlement of Anyako'. BA thesis, University of Ghana, 1994.

Fiawoo, F.K. 'Togbui Sri II Awoamefia of Anlo'. May 1956.

Gaba, C.R. 'Anlo traditional religion: a study of the Anlo traditional believer's conception of and communion with the "holy"'. PhD thesis, University of London, 1965.

Ghermay, Hermon. 'Contaminated waters: resettlement and schistosomiasis in Ethiopia (1956–1988)'. History 1912 seminar paper, Harvard University, 1999.

Grau, Eugene Emil. 'The Evangelical Presbyterian Church (Ghana and Togo) 1914–1916: a study in European mission relations affecting the beginning of an indigenous church'. PhD thesis, Hartford Seminary Foundation, 1964.

Guyer, Jane. 'Household budgets and women's income'. Boston University, African Studies Center Working Paper 28, 1980.

Keta District Assembly. 'Medium Term (5 Year) Development Plan (1996–2000) for Keta District'. May 1996.

Klumpp, Ralph K. 'A study of the transmission of *Schistosoma haematobium* in Volta Lake, Ghana'. PhD thesis, London School of Hygiene and Tropical Medicine, 1983.

Klutse, Evans. 'A social history of Keta – an Anlo community'. BA thesis, University of Ghana, 1976.

Kumassah, John Fred Kwaku. 'Keta: a declining Anlo urban centre'. BA thesis, University of Ghana, 1978.

Leach, Melissa and James Fairhead. 'Silence from the forest: exploring the ramifications of international environmental analysis in West Africa'. African Studies Association United Kingdom, London, 1998.

Lentz, Carola. 'Agricultural expansion in changing contexts: settlement histories in southwestern Burkina Faso'. Africa Seminar Series, Harvard University, 1998.

Meyer, Birgit. 'Translating the devil: an African appropriation of pietist Protestantism – the case of the Peki Ewe in southeastern Ghana, 1847–1992'. PhD thesis, University of Amsterdam, 1995.

Nyomi, Setriakor Kobla. 'A pastoral theological perspective on ministry to persons dealing with loss to natural disasters in Ghana'. PhD thesis, Princeton Theological Institute, 1991.

O'Laughlin, Michael, 'Out of the depths'. Paper presented at Harvard University's Seminar on Environmental Values, 28 October 1997.

Overa, Ragnhild. 'Partners and competitors: gendered entrepreneurship in Ghanaian canoe fisheries'. PhD thesis, University of Bergen, 1998.

Quarcoopome, Nii Otokunor. 'Rituals and regalia of power: art and politics among the Dangme and Ewe, 1800 to present'. PhD thesis, University of California at Los Angeles, 1993.

Sebuabe, Rudolph K. 'The life and work of T.S.A. Togobo 1900–1984'. BA thesis, University of Ghana, 1997.

Sorkpor, Gershon A. 'Geraldo de Lima and the Awunas (1862–1904)'. MA thesis, University of Ghana, 1966.

Torgby, Richard Tetteh. 'A study of the Yewe secret society among the Ewe speaking people of southern Ghana'. BA thesis, University of Ghana, 1977.

Yegbe, J.B. 'The Anlo and their neighbours 1850–1890'. MA thesis, University of Ghana, 1966.

Index

Index

241

Index

242

Index

Index

United States 165, 169
urbanization 7, 9, 76, 86-9, 133

Van Lare Commission of Enquiry into
    Representational and Electoral Reform 197
Vietor, E M. and Sons (company) 60, 74, 82
Voduda(god) 108-9
Vodza 12, 17, 48, 53, 58, 61, 108, 137, 172, 184-5,
    208, 220
Volta Lake 170, 172-5, 182
Volta River 23, 27-30, 35-7, 394-6, 49-52, 55, 59-60
    62, 79, 1 18-19, 127, 141, 161, 168-81, 185, 188-
    9 192-3, 195-8; *see also* dams
Volta River Project 164-7, 169-70, 197

Wakuti Report (1969) 204
warfare 15, 17, 27, 41-3, 45, 47-8, 50-2, 54-5, 60-1,
    111; *see also under name*
water 72, 107, 110-11; *see also* irrigation
Water, Mami 122-3
wealth 47-8, 51, 54, 66-8, 102, 108
Wenya 24-6, 28

Wesleyan Missionary Society 94
West African Aluminium Ltd 165, 167-8
Wheta 6, 28
Whuti 6, 28, 42, 58, 82, 103, 114-15
Whydah 8, 27, 29, 31, 38, 40, 44-5, 49, 52, 108-10
Williams family 61, 63, 85, 99, 102
Winneba 79, 158, 183
Woe 6, 10, 26, 28, 32, 42, 45, 51-5, 57-9, 67, 73, 82,
    103, 114, 118, 133, 145-6, 150-1, 153, 216
Woe Benevolent Shallot Farmers Association 149
women 16, 40, 46, 54, 67, 70, 77, 85-93, 95-6, 122,
    142-51, 155, 178-9, 216-17, 220; religious
    bondage 11, 68, 221-4
World War I 128, 142, 191, 218
World War II 165, 192-4, 218
Wuta Mission House 83, 85

Yewe cult 11, 72, 106-11, 114, 119, 121-3, 126, 220-
    1, 225
Yoruba 24, 26, 40

Zabrama people 184, 204

Printed and bound by CPI Group (UK) Ltd, Croydon, CR0 4YY

09/06/2025

14685713-0002